APPIAN

III

LCL 4

APPIAN

ROMAN HISTORY

VOLUME III

EDITED AND TRANSLATED BY

BRIAN McGING

HARVARD UNIVERSITY PRESS
CAMBRIDGE, MASSACHUSETTS
LONDON, ENGLAND
2019

First published 2019

LOEB CLASSICAL LIBRARY® is a registered trademark
of the President and Fellows of Harvard College

Library of Congress Control Number 2019940172
CIP data available from the Library of Congress

ISBN 978-0-674-99726-4

*Composed in ZephGreek and ZephText by
Technologies 'N Typography, Merrimac, Massachusetts.
Printed on acid-free paper and bound by
Maple Press, York, Pennsylvania*

CONTENTS

ΑΠΠΙΑΝΟΥ ΡΩΜΑΪΚΗ
ΙΣΤΟΡΙΑ

APPIAN'S ROMAN
HISTORY

XI

ΣΥΡΙΑΚΗ[1]

1. Ἀντίοχος ὁ Σελεύκου τοῦ Ἀντιόχου, Σύρων καὶ Βαβυλωνίων καὶ ἑτέρων ἐθνῶν βασιλεύς, ἕκτος δὲ ἀπὸ Σελεύκου τοῦ μετ' Ἀλέξανδρον Ἀσίας τῆς περὶ Εὐφράτην βεβασιλευκότος, ἐσβαλὼν ἐς Μηδίαν τε καὶ Παρθυηνὴν καὶ ἕτερα ἔθνη ἀφιστάμενα ἔτι πρὸ αὑτοῦ, καὶ πολλὰ καὶ μεγάλα δράσας, καὶ μέγας Ἀντίοχος ἀπὸ τοῦδε κληθείς, ἐπαιρόμενος τοῖς γεγονόσι καὶ τῇ δι' αὐτὰ προσωνυμίᾳ, Συρίαν τε τὴν κοίλην καὶ Κιλικίας ἔστιν ἃ Πτολεμαίου τοῦ Φιλοπάτορος, Αἰγύπτου βασιλέως ἔτι παιδὸς ὄντος, ἐπιδραμὼν περιέσπασε, 2 καὶ μικρὸν οὐδὲν ἐνθυμούμενος Ἑλλησποντίους ἐπῄει καὶ Αἰολέας καὶ Ἴωνας ὡς οἱ προσήκοντας ἄρχοντι τῆς Ἀσίας, ὅτι καὶ πάλαι τῶν τῆς Ἀσίας βασιλέων 3 ὑπήκουον. ἔς τε τὴν Εὐρώπην διαπλεύσας Θρᾴκην

---

[1] Ἀππιανοῦ Συριακὴ Ῥωκαϊκῶν β α ́ L; Ἀππιανοῦ ῥήτορος Ῥωμαϊκῶν Συριακή ια P

---

[1] Antiochus III the Great ruled the Seleucid kingdom from 223 to 187.

BOOK XI

THE SYRIAN BOOK

1. Antiochus, son of Seleucus, grandson of Antiochus, king of the Syrians, Babylonians, and other peoples, was, after the Seleucus who succeeded Alexander, the sixth ruler of the Euphrates region of Asia.[1] He invaded Media and Parthia, as well as other nations which had revolted before his reign, and did many great things, as a result of which he was called Antiochus "the Great." Galvanized by these successes and the title they had won for him, he invaded and annexed Coele Syria and some parts of Cilicia belonging to Ptolemy (son of?) Philopator, the king of Egypt who was still a young boy.[2] With ambitious plans in mind, he 2 attacked the Hellespont, Aeolia, and Ionia as if they belonged to him because he was king of Asia and they had once been subject to the kings of Asia. Crossing to Europe, 3 he subdued Thrace and forcibly reduced any who resisted.

[2] It is usually thought that Appian consistently confused the child-king Ptolemy V Epiphanes with his father, Ptolemy IV Philopator. But here the Greek could mean "Ptolemy son of Philopator," thus correctly referring to Ptolemy V Epiphanes, son of Philopator; and elsewhere the mistake may be more apparent than real. See *Mac.* 4.1, and below, 2.8, 4.14, with Goukowsky 2007, lxxxiv.

ὑπήγετο καὶ τὰ ἀπειθοῦντα ἐβιάζετο, Χερρόνησόν τε
ὠχύρου, καὶ Λυσιμάχειαν ἀνῴκιζεν, ἣν Λυσίμαχος
μὲν ὁ Θρᾴκης ἐπὶ Ἀλεξάνδρῳ βασιλεύσας ἔκτισεν
ἐπιτείχισμα τοῖς Θραξὶν εἶναι, οἱ Θρᾷκες δ᾽ ἀποθανόν-
4 τος τοῦ Λυσιμάχου καθῃρήκεσαν. καὶ ὁ Ἀντίοχος
συνῴκιζε, τούς τε φεύγοντας τῶν Λυσιμαχέων κατα-
καλῶν, καὶ εἴ τινες αὐτῶν αἰχμάλωτοι γεγονότες
ἐδούλευον ὠνούμενος, καὶ ἑτέρους προσκαταλέγων,
καὶ βοῦς καὶ πρόβατα καὶ σίδηρον ἐς γεωργίαν ἐπιδιδούς, καὶ οὐδὲν ἐλλείπων ἐς ταχεῖαν ἐπιτειχίσματος
οἰκοδομήν·² πάνυ γὰρ αὐτῷ τὸ χωρίον ἐφαίνετο λαμπρῶς ἔχειν ἐπὶ ὅλῃ Θρᾴκῃ, καὶ ταμιεῖον εὔκαιρον ἐς
τὰ λοιπὰ ὧν ἐπενόει πάντων ἔσεσθαι.

5   2. [Ταῦτα δ᾽ αὐτῷ διαφορᾶς φανερᾶς καὶ πρὸς
Ῥωμαίους ἦρξεν. ὡς γὰρ δὴ μετῄει τὰς τῇδε Ἑλλη-
νίδας πόλεις,]³ οἱ μὲν δὴ πλέονες αὐτῷ προσετίθεντο
καὶ φρουρὰς ἐσεδέχοντο δέει τῆς δυνάμεως,⁴ Σμυρναῖοι δὲ καὶ Λαμψακηνοὶ καὶ ἕτεροι ἔτι ἀντέχοντες
ἐπρεσβεύοντο ἐς Φλαμινῖνον τὸν Ῥωμαίων στρατηγόν, ἄρτι Φιλίππου τοῦ Μακεδόνος μεγάλῃ μάχῃ
περὶ Θετταλίαν κεκρατηκότα· ἐγίγνετο γὰρ δὴ καὶ τὰ
Μακεδόνων καὶ τὰ Ἑλλήνων ἐπίμικτα ἀλλήλοις ἀνὰ
μέρη καὶ χρόνους, ὥς μοι ἐν τῇ Ἑλληνικῇ γραφῇ
6 δεδήλωται. καὶ γίγνονταί τινες Ἀντιόχῳ καὶ Φλαμι-

----

² οἰκοδομήν Wilhelm: ὁρμήν codd.
³ Ταῦτα . . . πόλεις add. Schweig. ex Plethone
⁴ δυνάμεως LQ P Pletho: ἁλώσεως BJ

He fortified Chersonesus, and resettled Lysimachea, which Lysimachus, Alexander's successor as ruler of Thrace, had founded as a bastion against the Thracians, who destroyed it after the death of Lysimachus. Antiochus   4 resettled it by recalling the town's exiles, buying back any prisoners of war who had been sold into slavery, and enrolling new citizens, giving them cattle, sheep and iron farming equipment, and neglecting nothing that would lead to the rapid construction of a fortification. For the place seemed to him to be brilliantly suited for control of the whole of Thrace, and strategically located as a base for all the rest of the plans he had in mind for the future.

2. [But this was also the beginning of an open disagree-   5 ment with Rome. For, as he moved around the Greek cities in the area][3] most, to be sure, sided with him and accepted his garrisons out of fear of his military strength. The people of Smyrna and Lampsacus, however, and some others who continued to hold out against him, sent a mission to the Roman general Flamininus, who had recently overcome Philip of Macedon in a great battle in Thessaly[4]—an example of how Greek and Macedonian affairs overlapped geographically and chronologically, as I have demonstrated in my book of Hellenic history.[5] There now   6 takes place a number of embassies exchanged between

[3] Schweighäuser unconvincingly wanted to add the opening of this chapter from the extracts of Appian's *Syriake* made in the fifteenth century by the Byzantine scholar Gemistius Plethon.

[4] T. Quinctius Flamininus (consul in 198) defeated Philip at the battle of Cynoscephalae in 197.

[5] The tenth book of Appian's Roman history, which does not survive, seems to have been called the Hellenic and Ionian Book.

νίνῳ διαπρεσβεύσεις τε ἐς ἀλλήλους καὶ ἀπόπειραι
7 ἀτελεῖς. ἐκ πολλοῦ δὲ οἱ Ῥωμαῖοι καὶ ὁ Ἀντίοχος ὑπόπτως εἶχον ἀλλήλοις, οἱ μὲν οὐκ ἀτρεμήσειν ὑπολαμ-
βάνοντες Ἀντίοχον ἐπαιρόμενον ἀρχῆς τε μεγέθει καὶ
εὐπραξίας ἀκμῇ, ὁ δὲ Ῥωμαίους οἱ μόνους αὐξομένῳ
μάλιστα ἐμποδὼν ἔσεσθαι, καὶ κωλύσειν ἐς τὴν
8 Εὐρώπην περαιούμενον. οὐδενὸς δέ πω φανεροῦ γεγονότος αὐτοῖς ἐς ἔχθραν ἀφίκοντο πρέσβεις ἐς Ῥώμην
παρὰ Πτολεμαίου τοῦ Φιλοπάτορος, αἰτιωμένου Συ-
9 ρίαν τε καὶ Κιλικίαν Ἀντίοχον αὐτὸν ἀφελέσθαι. καὶ
οἱ Ῥωμαῖοι τῆς ἀφορμῆς ἐπέβαινον ἄσμενοι, κατὰ
καιρὸν σφίσι γενομένης, καὶ πρέσβεις ἐς τὸν Ἀντίοχον ἔστελλον, οἳ λόγῳ μὲν ἔμελλον συναλλάξειν
Πτολεμαῖον Ἀντιόχῳ, ἔργῳ δὲ κατασκέψεσθαι τὴν
ὁρμὴν Ἀντιόχου καὶ κωλύσειν ὅσα δύναιντο.
10 3. Τούτων δὴ τῶν πρέσβεων Γναῖος ἡγούμενος
ἠξίου τὸν Ἀντίοχον Πτολεμαίῳ μέν, ὄντι Ῥωμαίων
φίλῳ, συγχωρεῖν ἄρχειν ὅσων ὁ πατὴρ αὐτῷ κατέλιπε, τὰς δ' ἐν Ἀσίᾳ πόλεις, ὧν Φίλιππος ὁ Μακεδὼν
ἦρχεν, αὐτονόμους ἐᾶν· οὐ γὰρ εἶναι δίκαιον Ἀντίο-
11 χον κρατεῖν ὧν Φίλιππον ἀφείλοντο Ῥωμαῖοι. ὅλως
δ' ἀπορεῖν ἔφη τί τοσοῦτον στόλον ὁ Ἀντίοχος καὶ
τοσαύτην στρατιὰν ἄγων ἄνωθεν ἐκ Μήδων ἔλθοι τῆς
Ἀσίας ἐπὶ θάλασσαν, ἔς τε τὴν Εὐρώπην ἐσβάλοι,
καὶ πόλεις ἐν αὐτῇ κατασκευάζοιτο, καὶ Θρᾴκην ὑπά-

---

6 As above at 1.1, the Greek could mean either "from Ptolemy
Philopator" or "from Ptolemy, son of Philopator."

Antiochus and Flamininus, probing each other inconclu-
sively. Rome and Antiochus had been suspicious of one   7
another for some time. The Romans assumed that Antiochus was too buoyed up by the size of his empire and
degree of his success not to cause trouble; and Antiochus
thought that the Romans were the only ones who would
definitely stand in the way of his expansion, and try to
prevent him crossing to Europe. But there was still no   8
open hostility between them when envoys arrived in
Rome from Ptolemy (son of?) Philopator[6] accusing Antiochus of taking Syria and Cilicia from him. The Romans   9
were delighted to seize on what was for them a timely
opportunity to send ambassadors to Antiochus. Their job
was supposedly to reconcile Ptolemy and Antiochus, but
in reality it was to track Antiochus' ambition and do everything they could to keep it in check.

3. Gnaeus,[7] as leader of the Roman mission, demanded   10
that Antiochus allow Ptolemy, who was a friend of the Roman people, to rule the whole of his paternal inheritance,
and leave independent the towns in Asia which Philip king
of Macedon had governed. For it was not right that Antiochus should control territories that Rome had taken from
Philip. And, he continued, they were completely at a loss   11
to understand why Antiochus had come with such a large
fleet and brought such a large army up from Media to the
coast of Asia, and why he had invaded Europe, built towns
there and subdued Thrace, unless these actions were

[7] Polybius (18.49.2) and Livy (33.39) both call the ambassador
sent in 196 Lucius Cornelius, probably L. Cornelius Lentulus,
who had been consul in 199.

12 γοιτο, εἰ μὴ ταῦτά ἐστιν ἑτέρου πολέμου θεμέλια. ὁ δ᾽
ἀπεκρίνατο Θράκην μέν, τῶν προγόνων αὐτοῦ γενομένην τε καὶ δι᾽ ἀσχολίας ἐκπεσοῦσαν, αὐτὸς ἐπὶ
σχολῆς ὢν ἀναλαμβάνειν, καὶ Λυσιμάχειαν ἐγείρειν
οἰκητήριον Σελεύκῳ τῷ παιδὶ εἶναι, τὰς δ᾽ ἐν Ἀσίᾳ
πόλεις αὐτονόμους ἐάσειν, εἰ τὴν χάριν οὐ Ῥωμαίοις
13 ἀλλ᾽ ἑαυτῷ μέλλοιεν ἕξειν. "Πτολεμαίῳ δ᾽," ἔφη, "Καὶ
συγγενής εἰμι καὶ ὅσον οὔπω καὶ κηδεστὴς ἔσομαι,
καὶ χάριν ὑμῖν αὐτὸν ὁμολογεῖν παρασκευάσω.
ἀπορῶ δὲ κἀγὼ τίνι Ῥωμαῖοι δικαίῳ τὴν Ἀσίαν πο-
λυπραγμονοῦσιν, ἐμοῦ τὴν Ἰταλίαν οὐ πολυπραγμο-
νοῦντος."

14   4. Οὕτω μὲν ἀπ᾽ ἀλλήλων ἄπρακτοι διεκρίθησαν,
ἀπορρηγνύντες ἤδη τὰς ἀπειλὰς ἐς τὸ φανερώτερον·
λόγου δὲ καὶ δόξης ἐμπεσούσης ὅτι Πτολεμαῖος ὁ
Φιλοπάτορος[5] ἀποθάνοι, κατὰ σπουδὴν ὁ Ἀντίοχος
ἀπῄει ὡς Αἴγυπτον ἔρημον ἄρχοντος ἁρπασόμενος.
15 καὶ αὐτῷ κατὰ Ἔφεσον Ἀννίβας ὁ Καρχηδόνιος
συμβάλλει, φεύγων τὴν πατρίδα δι᾽ ἐχθρῶν διαβο-
λάς, οἳ Ῥωμαίοις αὐτὸν ἔφασκον εἶναι δύσεριν τε καὶ
φιλοπόλεμον καὶ οὔποτε εἰρηνεύειν δυνάμενον. τότε δ᾽
ἦν ὅτε Καρχηδόνιοι Ῥωμαίοις ὑπήκουον ἔνσπονδοι.
16 Ἀννίβαν μὲν δὴ διώνυμον ἐπὶ στρατηγίαις ὄντα ὁ
Ἀντίοχος ὑπεδέχετο λαμπρῶς καὶ εἶχεν ἀμφ᾽ αὐτόν·
περὶ δὲ τὴν Λυκίαν Πτολεμαῖον περιεῖναι μαθὼν Αἰγύπτου μὲν ἀπέγνω, Κύπρον δ᾽ ἐλπίσας αἱρήσειν ἀντὶ

---

[5] Φιλοπάτορος Goukowsky: Φιλοπάτωρ codd.

8

preparations for another war. Antiochus' answer was that, 12
in relation to Thrace, it had belonged to his ancestors. It
had fallen out of their control when they were distracted,
and as he himself now had the time, he was repossessing
it. As for Lysimachea, he had built it to be a residence for
his son Seleucus; and with respect to the towns of Asia
he would leave them independent, if they acknowledged
their gratitude to him, not the Romans. "I am a relative of 13
Ptolemy," he said, "and will soon also be related to him by
marriage, and I will make sure he expresses his gratitude
to you. I too am at a loss to understand something, by what
right the Romans interfere in Asia, when I do not interfere
in Italy."

4. And so they parted without achieving anything, but 14
with both sides now breaking out into more open threats.
When the rumor spread of a report that Ptolemy son of
Philopator[8] had died, Antiochus left in a hurry to seize
Egypt, now that it had no ruler. At Ephesus he met Hanni- 15
bal the Carthaginian, who had been forced into exile from
his own country by the slanders of his enemies: they kept
telling the Romans that he was quarrelsome, loved fighting wars and would never be capable of living in peace.
This was a time when Carthage was, by treaty, subject to
Rome. Hannibal was widely celebrated for his military 16
exploits, and Antiochus welcomed him splendidly and
kept him in his entourage. When he was in Lycia, Antiochus heard that Ptolemy had not died, and gave up on his
plans for Egypt. Hoping to take Cyprus instead of Egypt,

[8] The manuscripts say Ptolemy Philopator, but a small emen-
dation restores the correct Ptolemy (V Epiphanes), son of
Philopator: see note 2, above.

17 Αἰγύπτου διέπλει κατὰ τάχος ἐς αὐτήν. χειμῶνι δ᾽ ἀμφὶ τὸν Σάρον ποταμὸν συμπεσών, καὶ πολλὰς τῶν νεῶν ἀποβαλών, ἐνίας δ᾽ αὐτοῖς ἀνδράσι καὶ φίλοις, ἐς Σελεύκειαν τῆς Συρίας κατέπλευσε, καὶ τὸν στόλον κατεσκεύαζε πεπονημένον. γάμους τε τῶν παίδων ἔθυεν, Ἀντιόχου καὶ Λαοδίκης, ἀλλήλοις συναρμόζων.

18 5. Ἤδη δὲ τὸν πρὸς Ῥωμαίους πόλεμον ἐγνωκὼς ἀποκαλύπτειν, ἐπιγαμίαις τοὺς ἐγγὺς βασιλέας προκατελάμβανε, καὶ Πτολεμαίῳ μὲν ἐς Αἴγυπτον ἔστελλε Κλεοπάτραν τὴν Σύραν ἐπίκλησιν, προῖκα Συρίαν τὴν κοίλην ἐπιδιδούς, ἣν αὐτὸς ἀφῄρητο τοῦ Πτολεμαίου, θεραπεύων ἤδη τὸ μειράκιον, ἵν᾽ ἐν τῷ πολέμῳ τῷ πρὸς Ῥωμαίους ἀτρεμῇ· Ἀντιοχίδα δ᾽ ἔπεμπεν Ἀριαράθῃ τῷ Καππαδοκῶν βασιλεῖ, καὶ τὴν

19 ἔτι λοιπὴν Εὐμένει τῷ Περγάμου βασιλεῖ. ὁ δέ (ἑώρα γὰρ αὐτὸν ἤδη Ῥωμαίοις τε πολεμησείοντα καὶ πρὸς τήνδε τὴν χρείαν τὸ κῆδος αὐτῷ συναπτόμενον) ἠρνήσατο, καὶ τοῖς ἀδελφοῖς Ἀττάλῳ τε καὶ Φιλεταίρῳ, θαυμάζουσιν ὅτι κῆδος βασιλέως τοσοῦδε καὶ γείτονος, αὐτοῦ τε κατάρχοντος καὶ δεομένου, παραιτοῖτο, ἐπεδείκνυ τὸν ἐσόμενον πόλεμον ἐν μὲν ἀρχῇ τι παρ᾽ ἀμφοῖν ἕξειν ἰσοπαλές, σὺν χρόνῳ δ᾽ ὑπεροίσειν τὰ

20 Ῥωμαίων δι᾽ εὐψυχίαν καὶ ταλαιπωρίαν. "Ἐγὼ δ᾽," ἔφη, "Ῥωμαίων μὲν ἐπικρατούντων βεβαίως τῆς ἀρχῆς τῆς ἐμῆς ἄρξω, Ἀντιόχου δὲ νικῶντος ἐλπὶς μὲν

he quickly set sail for the island. But he encountered a   17
storm off the river Sarus and lost many ships, some with
all on board, men and courtiers. So he sailed to Seleucea
in Syria and repaired the damage to his fleet. Here he
celebrated the marriage he had arranged between two of
his children, Antiochus and Laodice.[9]

5. He now decided to be open about his war against   18
Rome, but first made marriage alliances with kings of the
region. To Ptolemy of Egypt he gave his daughter, Cleopatra surnamed Syra, giving Coele Syria as her dowry. He
himself had annexed this from Ptolemy, but he now set
about appeasing the young man so that he would take no
part in the war against Rome. To Ariarathes king of Cappadocia, he sent Antiochis, and to Eumenes king of Pergamum, his last remaining daughter.[10] Eumenes could see   19
that Antiochus was already stirring up war against Rome
and was trying to make the marriage alliance for that purpose. So he turned it down. When his brothers, Attalus
and Philetaerus, expressed surprise that he would refuse
a marriage connection with such a great king, who was a
neighbor of his, and was the one initiating the request,
Eumenes explained that at the beginning of the coming
war the conflict would be evenly balanced between the
two sides, but that the Romans would win in the end,
because of their courage and endurance. "With respect to   20
myself," he said, "if the Romans are victorious, I will be
secure in the government of my kingdom. But if Antiochus

[9] Brother-sister marriage in the Seleucid family is otherwise
unattested.   [10] Ariarathes IV Eusebes ("Pious") ruled Cappadocia from about 220 to about 163. Eumenes II of Pergamum
was king from 197 to 158.

ἀφαιρεθῆναι πάντα πρὸς γείτονος, ἐλπὶς δὲ καὶ
ἔχοντα βασιλεύσειν βασιλευόμενον ὑπ' ἐκείνου."

21   6. Ὁ μὲν δὴ τοιοῖσδε λογισμοῖς τοὺς γάμους ἀπεώ-
σατο, ὁ δ' Ἀντίοχος αὖθις ἐφ' Ἑλλησπόντου κατῄει,
καὶ περιπλεύσας ἐς Χερρόνησον πολλὰ καὶ τότε τῆς
22   Θρᾴκης ὑπήγετό τε καὶ κατεστρέφετο. Ἕλληνας δ',
ὅσοι τοῖς Θραξὶν ὑπήκουον, ἠλευθέρου, καὶ Βυζαν-
τίοις ἐχαρίζετο πολλὰ ὡς ἐπίκαιρον ἐπὶ τοῦ στόματος
πόλιν ἔχουσιν. Γαλάτας τε δώροις καὶ καταπλήξει
τῆς παρασκευῆς ἐς συμμαχίαν ὑπήγετο, ἀξιομάχους
ἡγούμενος ἔσεσθαί οἱ διὰ τὰ μεγέθη τῶν σωμάτων.
23   μετὰ δὲ τοῦτο ἐς Ἔφεσον κατῆρε, καὶ πρέσβεις ἐς
Ῥώμην ἔπεμπε Λυσίαν τε καὶ Ἡγησιάνακτα καὶ Μέ-
νιππον, οἳ τῷ μὲν ἔργῳ τῆς βουλῆς ἀποπειράσειν
ἔμελλον, τῷ λόγῳ δ' ὁ Μένιππος ἔφη τὸν βασιλέα
περὶ τὴν Ῥωμαίων φιλίαν ἐσπουδακότα, καὶ βουλό-
μενον αὐτοῖς εἶναι καὶ σύμμαχον ἂν ἀξιῶσι, θαυμά-
ζειν ὅτι κελεύουσι τῶν ἐν Ἰωνίᾳ πόλεων ἀφίστασθαι,
καὶ φόρους τισὶν ἀφιέναι, καὶ τῆς Ἀσίας ἔνια μὴ πο-
λυπραγμονεῖν, καὶ Θρᾴκην ἐᾶν ἀεὶ τῶν προγόνων
αὐτοῦ γενομένην· ἅπερ οὐ τοῖς φίλοις ἀλλὰ τοῖς ἡτ-
24   τημένοις τοὺς κεκρατηκότας ἐπικελεύειν. οἱ δὲ τῆς
πρεσβείας συνιέντες ἐπὶ διαπείρᾳ σφῶν ἀφιγμένης,
διὰ βραχέος ἀπεκρίναντο αὐτοῖς, ἐὰν Ἀντίοχος αὐτονόμους τοὺς Ἕλληνας ἐᾷ τοὺς ἐν Ἀσίᾳ καὶ τῆς Εὐρώπης ἀπέχηται, Ῥωμαίοις αὐτὸν ἔσεσθαι φίλον, ἂν
θέλῃ.

25   7. Τοσάδε μὲν ἀπεκρίναντο Ῥωμαῖοι, καὶ τὰς αἰτίας

12

triumphs, I expect either to be deprived of everything by my neighbor, or, if I manage to hold on to it, to rule under his rule."

6. This was his rationale for turning down the marriage. 21 Antiochus made his way to the Hellespont again, sailed across to Chersonesus, and on this occasion too either brought over to his side, or forcibly subjected much of Thrace. He freed those Greeks under Thracian control, 22 and was very generous to the people of Byzantium, as their city was strategically located at the mouth of the Euxine Sea. With gifts and fear of his armament he brought the Galatians into alliance with him, believing that they would be good fighters because they had such big bodies. After 23 this, he put in at Ephesus and sent as ambassadors to Rome Lysias, Hegesianax, and Menippus. The real purpose of their mission was to probe the senate's intentions, but what Menippus actually said was as follows. The king was eager to enjoy the friendship of the Romans and wanted to be their ally, if they agreed, but he was astonished that they were ordering him to evacuate the towns of Ionia and remit the tribute of certain places, or not to interfere in some areas of Asia and to abandon Thrace, even though it had always belonged to his ancestors. This was not how to behave to friends, but how victors issue orders to the vanquished. Realizing that the embassy had 24 come to test them, the senate answered tersely, that if Antiochus left the Greeks of Asia independent and stayed out of Europe, he could be a friend to Rome, if that is what he wanted.

7. This was all the Romans said in reply, and they added 25

ταῖς ἀποκρίσεσιν οὐκ ἐπέθεσαν· ὁ δ᾽ Ἀντίοχος ἐς πρώτην ἐπινοῶν τὴν Ἑλλάδα ἐσβαλεῖν, κἀκεῖθεν ἄρξασθαι τοῦ πρὸς Ῥωμαίους πολέμου, ὑπετίθετο τὴν
26 γνώμην τῷ Καρχηδονίῳ Ἀννίβᾳ· ὁ δ᾽ ἔφη τὴν μὲν Ἑλλάδα ἐκ πολλοῦ τετρυμένην ἔργον εὐχείρωτον εἶναι, τοὺς δὲ πολέμους ἅπασι χαλεποὺς μὲν οἴκοι διὰ λιμὸν τὸν ἐπιγιγνόμενον, ἔξω δὲ κουφοτέρους· καὶ τὰ Ῥωμαίων οὔ ποτε Ἀντίοχον ἐν τῇ Ἑλλάδι καθαιρήσειν, ἀγορᾶς τε οἰκείας καὶ παρασκευῆς ἱκανῆς εὐπο-
27 ρούντων. ἐκέλευεν οὖν τι προλαβεῖν τῆς Ἰταλίας καὶ πολεμεῖν ἐκεῖθεν ὁρμώμενον, ἵνα Ῥωμαίοις ἀσθενέ-
28 στερα ᾖ καὶ τὰ οἴκοι καὶ τὰ ἔξω. "Ἔχω δ᾽ ἐμπείρως," ἔφη, "Τῆς Ἰταλίας, καὶ μυρίοις ἀνδράσι δύναμαι καταλαβεῖν αὐτῆς τὰ ἐπίκαιρα, ἔς τε Καρχηδόνα τοῖς φίλοις ἐπιστεῖλαι τὸν δῆμον ἐς ἀπόστασιν ἐγεῖραι, δυσφοροῦντα τέως ἐφ᾽ ἑαυτοῦ καὶ πρὸς Ῥωμαίους ἀπίστως ἔχοντα, τόλμης τε καὶ ἐλπίδος ἐμπλησόμε-
29 νον, εἰ πύθοιτό με πορθοῦντα τὴν Ἰταλίαν αὖθις." ὁ δ᾽ ἄσμενος ἀκούσας τοῦ λόγου, καὶ μέγα, ὥσπερ ἦν, ἐς τὸν πόλεμον ἡγούμενος Καρχηδόνα προσλαβεῖν, αὐτίκα αὐτὸν ἐπιστέλλειν τοῖς φίλοις ἐκέλευεν.
30 8. Ὁ δὲ οὐκ ἐπέστειλε μέν (οὐ γὰρ ἀσφαλὲς ἡγεῖτό πω, Ῥωμαίων τε πάντ᾽ ἀνερευνωμένων, καὶ τοῦ πολέμου μή πω φανεροῦ γεγονότος, καὶ πολλῶν οἱ διαφερομένων ἐν Καρχηδόνι, καὶ τῆς πολιτείας οὐδὲν βέβαιον οὐδ᾽ εὐσταθὲς ἐχούσης, ἃ καὶ μετ᾽ ὀλίγον ἀνέτρεψε τὴν Καρχηδόνα), Ἀρίστωνα δ᾽ ἔμπορον Τύριον ἐπὶ προφάσει τῆς ἐμπορίας ἔπεμπε πρὸς τοὺς

no explanation for their response. Antiochus was intending to invade Greece first, and from there launch his war
against Rome. When he informed Hannibal of his plan,
Hannibal said that Greece had been in distress for a long   26
time and would prove an easy task, but the wars that everyone found difficult were those conducted at home,
because of the food shortage they caused; those conducted
abroad were easier. Antiochus would never defeat Roman
power in Greece, as they were too well supplied with their
own food and plentiful military resources. He recom-   27
mended, therefore, that Antiochus form a bridgehead in
Italy and use it as a base of operations for war, to weaken
Rome both at home and abroad. "I have some experience   28
of Italy," he said, "and with ten thousand men I can hold
the strategic points of the country and write to my supporters in Carthage, telling them to stir up the people to
revolt: they are already unhappy with their own situation,
they do not trust the Romans, and if they hear that I am
ravaging Italy again, they will be filled with courage and
hope." Antiochus was happy to hear this, and thinking,   29
correctly, that it would be a big advantage to get Carthage
on his side in the war, he instructed him to write to his
supporters immediately.

8. Hannibal did not send a letter, however, as he   30
thought it was not yet safe to do so: the Romans had spies
everywhere, the war was not yet openly declared, he had
many opponents in Carthage, and there was nothing stable
or steady about its government—which proved its ruin not
much later. But he did send Ariston, a merchant from
Tyre, to his supporters, supposedly on business, asking

φίλους, ἀξιῶν, ὅταν αὐτὸς ἐς τὴν Ἰταλίαν ἐμβάλῃ, τότε ἐκείνους τὴν Καρχηδόνα ἐς ἄμυναν ὧν ἐπεπόν-
31 θεσαν ἐγείρειν. καὶ ὁ μὲν Ἀρίστων οὕτως ἔπραξεν, οἱ δὲ τοῦ Ἀννίβου ἐχθροί, αἰσθόμενοι τῆς Ἀρίστωνος ἐπιδημίας, ἐθορύβουν ὡς ἐπὶ νεωτέροις ἔργοις, καὶ
32 τὸν Ἀρίστωνα ἐζήτουν περιιόντες. ὁ δέ, ἵνα τὴν δια-βολὴν μὴ ἐξαίρετον ἔχοιεν οἱ Ἀννίβου φίλοι, πρού-θηκε νυκτὸς λαθὼν γράμματα πρὸ τοῦ βουλευτηρίου, ὅτι πάντας ὁ Ἀννίβας τοὺς βουλευτὰς παρακαλοίη τῇ πατρίδι συνάρασθαι μετ' Ἀντιόχου. καὶ τοῦτο πράξας
33 ἀπέπλευσεν. ἅμα δ' ἡμέρᾳ τὸ μὲν δέος ἐξῄρητο τῶν Ἀννίβου φίλων ἐκ τῆς Ἀρίστωνος ἐπινοίας, ὡς πρὸς ἅπασαν τὴν γερουσίαν ἀπεσταλμένου, ἡ δὲ πόλις ἐπεπλήρωτο θορύβου ποικίλου, δυσμενῶς μὲν ἔχουσα Ῥωμαίοις, λήσεσθαι δ' οὐ προσδοκῶσα.

34 9. Καὶ τὰ μὲν Καρχηδονίων ὧδε εἶχε, Ῥωμαίων δὲ πρέσβεις, ἕτεροί τε καὶ Σκιπίων ὁ Καρχηδονίους ἀφε-λόμενος τὴν ἡγεμονίαν, ἐς ὁμοίαν πεμφθέντες Ἀντιό-χου τῆς τε γνώμης ἀπόπειραν καὶ τῆς παρασκευῆς κατάσκεψιν, ἐπεὶ τὸν βασιλέα ηὗρον οἰχόμενον ἐς
35 Πισίδας, ἐν Ἐφέσῳ περιέμενον, ἔνθα συνῄεσαν θα-μινὰ ἐς λόγους τῷ Ἀννίβᾳ, Καρχηδόνος τε σφίσιν ἔτι οὔσης ἐνσπόνδου καὶ οὔπω φανερῶς Ἀντιόχου πο-λεμίου, καταμεμφόμενοι τὸν Ἀννίβαν ὅτι τὴν πατρίδα φύγοι, Ῥωμαίων οὐδὲν οὔτε ἐς αὐτὸν οὔτε ἐς τοὺς

---

[11] It is generally believed that Scipio Africanus was not on this

them to rouse Carthage to avenge what she had suffered, as soon as he himself invaded Italy. Ariston did as he was 31 ordered, but when Hannibal's enemies heard that Ariston was visiting Carthage, they caused an uproar as if a revolution were taking place, and went round looking everywhere for him. So that Hannibal's supporters would not 32 be singled out for attack, he put up a notice outside the council house at night without being seen, in which Hannibal called on all councilors to join Antiochus in helping their country. Having done this, Ariston sailed off. The next day, Hannibal's supporters were relieved of their 33 fear by Ariston's ingenuity, which gave the impression that he had been sent to the whole council. The city was filled with all sorts of confusion, however, as it was ill-disposed to Rome, but did not think this could be kept secret.

9. This was how things stood in Carthage. At Rome, 34 ambassadors, among others the Scipio who had deprived the Carthaginians of their dominance, were sent to test out Antiochus' intentions and review the state of his military preparations—just like the Seleucid mission to Rome.[11] On learning that Antiochus had gone to Pisidia, the Roman envoys waited for him in Ephesus, where 35 they held frequent meetings with Hannibal, as Carthage was still under treaty with them, and Antiochus was not yet openly hostile. The Roman representatives criticized Hannibal for fleeing his own country, when, in conformity with the treaty, Rome had committed no offense against

mission and that his encounter with Hannibal, described below, was a fiction. Livy (35.14.5) attributes the story to Claudius Quadrigarius and before him to the second-century historian Gaius Acilius.

ἄλλους Καρχηδονίους ἐπὶ ταῖς συνθήκαις ἁμαρτόν-
36 των. ἔπρασσον δὲ ταῦθ᾽, ὕποπτον ἐργαζόμενοι γενέσθαι τῷ βασιλεῖ τὸν Ἀννίβαν ἐκ τῆς συνεχοῦς σφῶν
37 ὁμιλίας τε καὶ συνόδου. καὶ τοῦθ᾽ ὁ μὲν στρατηγικώ-
τατος Ἀννίβας οὐχ ὑπενόησεν, ὁ δὲ βασιλεὺς πυθόμενος ὑπώπτευσε, καὶ ἀμβλύτερος ἦν ἀπὸ τοῦδε πι-
στεύειν ἔτι τῷ Ἀννίβᾳ· καὶ γάρ τι καὶ ζήλου προὐπῆν
ἐς αὐτὸν ἤδη καὶ φθόνου, μὴ τῶν γιγνομένων τὸν
ἔπαινον Ἀννίβας ἀποφέροιτο.

38   10. Λέγεται δ᾽ ἐν ταῖσδε ταῖς διατριβαῖς ἐν τῷ
γυμνασίῳ λεσχηνεῦσαί ποτε πρὸς ἀλλήλους Σκιπίωνα καὶ Ἀννίβαν περὶ στρατηγίας πολλῶν ἐφεστώ-
των, καὶ τοῦ Σκιπίωνος ἐρομένου τίς δοκεῖ οἱ στρατηγὸς ἄριστος γενέσθαι, τὸν Ἀννίβαν εἰπεῖν, "Ὁ
39 Μακεδὼν Ἀλέξανδρος." Σκιπίωνα δ᾽ ἡσυχάσαι μὲν
ἐπὶ τῷδ᾽, ἐξιστάμενον ἄρα Ἀλεξάνδρῳ, ἐπανερέσθαι
δὲ τίς εἴη δεύτερος μετ᾽ Ἀλέξανδρον. καὶ τὸν φάναι,
"Πύρρος ὁ Ἠπειρώτης," τὴν ἀρετὴν ἄρα τὴν στρατη-
γικὴν ἐν τόλμῃ τιθέμενον· οὐ γὰρ ἔστιν εὑρεῖν μεγα-
40 λοτολμοτέρους τῶνδε τῶν βασιλέων. δακνόμενον δ᾽
ἤδη τὸν Σκιπίωνα ὅμως ἐπανερέσθαι ἔτι τίνι διδοίη
τὰ τρίτα, τάχα γοῦν ἐλπίζοντα ἕξειν τὰ τρίτα. τὸν
δέ, "Ἐμαυτῷ," φάναι· "Νέος γὰρ ὢν ἔτι Ἰβηρίας
τε ἐκράτησα, καὶ στρατῷ τὰ Ἄλπεια ὄρη μεθ᾽ Ἡρα-
κλέα πρῶτος ὑπερῆλθον, ἔς τε τὴν Ἰταλίαν, ὑμῶν οὐ-
δενός πω θαρροῦντος, ἐμβαλὼν τετρακόσια ἀνέστησα
ἄστη, καὶ περὶ τῇ πόλει τὸν ἀγῶνα πολλάκις ὑμῖν
ἐπέστησα, οὔτε μοι χρημάτων οὔτε στρατιᾶς ἐπιπε-

him or the other Carthaginians. They did this to create   36
suspicion of Hannibal in the king's mind as a result of the
discussions and meetings he continually had with them.
For all his military brilliance, Hannibal failed to see this,   37
and the king did indeed begin to harbor suspicions about
him when he heard of what was going on, and was thereafter more reluctant to trust him any longer. For Antiochus was already somewhat jealous of him and resentful
that Hannibal might get all the glory for his exploits.

10. There is a story that at one of these conversations   38
in the gymnasium, with a large audience present, Scipio
and Hannibal were discussing military command. When
Scipio asked Hannibal who in his opinion was the greatest
general, Hannibal answered, "Alexander of Macedon." To   39
this Scipio said nothing, no doubt accepting Alexander's
primacy, but inquired further of Hannibal who he thought
was second after Alexander. "Pyrrhus of Epirus," he said,
presumably intending to identify daring as the most important virtue in a commander: and it is indeed impossible
to find anyone more exceedingly daring than these two
kings. Although now irritated, Scipio nevertheless per-   40
sisted with his questioning: to whom would Hannibal give
the third place? He must have expected that he would at
least get third place, but Hannibal said, "To myself! For
when I was still a young man I conquered Iberia, and was
the first person since Heracles to cross the Alps with an
army. I invaded Italy, and with none of you now showing
any spirit, I destroyed four hundred towns, and threatened
Rome itself on many occasions, even though I received no
additional help from Carthage, either in the form of

41 μπομένης ἐκ Καρχηδόνος." ὡς δὲ αὐτὸν ὁ Σκιπίων
εἶδεν ἀπομηκύνοντα τὴν σεμνολογίαν, ἔφη γελάσας,
"Ποῦ δ' ἂν ἑαυτὸν ἔταττες, ὦ Ἀννίβα, μὴ νενικημένος
ὑπ' ἐμοῦ·" τὸν δέ φασιν, αἰσθανόμενον ἤδη τῆς ζηλοτυπίας, εἰπεῖν ὅτι "Ἔγωγε ἔταξα ἂν ἐμαυτὸν πρὸ
42 Ἀλεξάνδρου." οὕτω μὲν ὁ Ἀννίβας ἐπέμεινέ τε τῇ σε-
μνολογίᾳ, καὶ τὸν Σκιπίωνα λαθὼν ἐθεράπευσεν ὡς
καθελόντα τὸν ἀμείνονα Ἀλεξάνδρου· διαλυομένης δὲ
τῆς συνόδου Σκιπίωνα μὲν ὁ Ἀννίβας ἐπὶ ξενίαν
ἐκάλει, Σκιπίων δὲ ἐλθεῖν ἂν ἔφη μάλα προθύμως, "Εἰ
μὴ συνῆσθα νῦν Ἀντιόχῳ πρὸς Ῥωμαίους ὑπόπτως
ἔχοντι."

43 11. Ὧδε μὲν ἐκεῖνοι, τῆς στρατηγίας ἀξίως, τὴν
ἔχθραν ὡρίζοντο τοῖς πολέμοις, Φλαμινῖνος δ' ἀνο-
μοίως. ἡττηθέντος γὰρ ὕστερον Ἀντιόχου φεύγοντα
τὸν Ἀννίβαν καὶ ἀλώμενον περὶ Βιθυνίαν, πρεσβεύων
ἐφ' ἕτερα πρὸς Προυσίαν, οὔτε τι πρὸς τοῦ Ἀννίβου
προπαθών, οὔτε Ῥωμαίων ἐντειλαμένων, οὔτε φο-
βερὸν ἔτι αὐτοῖς γενέσθαι δυνάμενον Καρχηδόνος
κατεστραμμένης, ἔκτεινε διὰ τοῦ Προυσίου φαρμάκῳ,
44 λεγόμενον μὲν ἐσχηκέναι ποτὲ χρησμὸν ὧδε ἔχοντα,
"Λίβυσσα κρύψει βῶλος Ἀννίβου δέμας," καὶ οἰόμε-
νον ἐν Λιβύῃ τεθνήξεσθαι, ποταμὸς δ' ἔστι Λίβυσ-
σος ἐν τῇ Βιθυνίᾳ, καὶ πεδίον ἐκ τοῦ ποταμοῦ Λί-

money or reinforcements." When Scipio saw that Hanni-   41
bal was going to go on talking pompously at length, he
laughed and said: "Where would you rank yourself, Hannibal, if you had not been defeated by me?" Hannibal, now
recognizing Scipio's feelings of rivalry, so the story contin-
ues, replied, "For my own part, I would have ranked myself ahead of Alexander." In this way Hannibal both con-   42
tinued to be self-important, and at the same time discreetly
flattered Scipio by suggesting that he had defeated someone greater than Alexander. At the end of their meeting,
Hannibal offered Scipio hospitality. Scipio said he would
very gladly accept, "if you were not now associating with
Antiochus, who is an object of suspicion to Rome."

11. So it was that these men, in a manner worthy of   43
their generalship, confined their hostility to the wars they
fought. It was a different matter with Flamininus. For, at
a later date, after the defeat of Antiochus, when Hannibal
was a fugitive and traveling in Bithynia, Flamininus sent a
mission to Prusias on other business, but got him to poison
Hannibal, even though Flamininus himself had no previous grievance with him, and had received no orders from
Rome, and even though Hannibal, with Carthage destroyed, could no longer instill fear in the Romans.[12] It is   44
said that Hannibal once received an oracle that predicted
the following: "Libyssan soil will cover the corpse of
Hannibal." He thought this meant he would die in Africa,
but there is a river called the Libyssus in Bithynia, and a

[12] Prusias I was king of Bithynia from about 228 to 182.
Hannibal's death occurred in 183 or 182. Appian can be referring
at this point only to the defeat of Carthage in the Second Punic
War in 202, not to its destruction in 146.

APPIAN

βυσσα. καὶ τάδε μὲν ἐς ὑπόμνημά τε τῆς Ἀννίβου καὶ
Σκιπίωνος μεγαλονοίας καὶ Φλαμινίνου σμικρότητος
παρεθέμην.

45   12. Ὁ δ' Ἀντίοχος ἐκ Πισιδῶν ἐς τὴν Ἔφεσον
ἐπανήει, καὶ χρηματίσας τοῖς Ῥωμαίων πρέσβεσι
Ῥοδίους μὲν καὶ Βυζαντίους καὶ Κυζικηνούς, καὶ ὅσοι
ἄλλοι περὶ τὴν Ἀσίαν εἰσὶν Ἕλληνες, αὐτονόμους
ἐπηγγείλατο ἐάσειν, εἰ γίγνοιντο αὐτῷ συνθῆκαι
πρὸς Ῥωμαίους, Αἰολέας δὲ καὶ Ἴωνας οὐ συνεχώρει
ὡς ἐκ πολλοῦ καὶ τοῖς βαρβάροις βασιλεῦσι τῆς
46   Ἀσίας εἰθισμένους ὑπακούειν. οἱ μὲν δὴ Ῥωμαίων
πρέσβεις ἐς οὐδὲν αὐτῷ συμβαίνοντες (οὐ γὰρ ἐπ'
ἔργῳ συμβάσεων ἐληλύθεσαν ἀλλ' ἐς ἀπόπειραν)
ᾤχοντο ἐς Ῥώμην· Ἀντιόχῳ δ' ἧκον Αἰτωλῶν πρέσβεις, ὧν Θόας ἦρχεν, αὐτοκράτορά τε στρατηγὸν
Αἰτωλῶν Ἀντίοχον ἀποφαίνοντες, καὶ διαπλεῖν ἐς τὴν
Ἑλλάδα ἤδη παρακαλοῦντες ὡς ἐπὶ ἔργον ἕτοιμον.
47   οὐδὲ εἴων ἀναμένειν τὴν στρατιὰν ἀπὸ τῆς Ἀσίας τῆς
ἄνω κατιοῦσαν, ἀλλὰ τὰ Αἰτωλῶν ὑπερεπαίροντες,
καὶ Λακεδαιμονίους ἐπαγγελλόμενοι σφίσι καὶ Φίλιππον ἐπὶ τοῖς Λακεδαιμονίοις τὸν Μακεδόνα, Ῥωμαίοις
μηνίοντα, συμμαχήσειν, ἐπέσπερχον ἐς τὴν διάβα-
48   σιν. ὁ δ' ἠρεθίζετο μάλα κουφόνως, καὶ οὐδὲ τοῦ παιδὸς αὐτῷ προσαγγελθέντος ἐν Συρίᾳ τεθνάναι τῆς
ὁρμῆς τι ἐνδούς, διέπλει μετὰ μυρίων ὧν τότε εἶχε
49   μόνων ἐς Εὔβοιαν. καὶ τήνδε μὲν αὐτὸς παρεστήσατο
ἅπασαν, ἐνδοῦσαν ὑπὸ ἐκπλήξεως· Μικιθίων δέ, αὐτοῦ στρατηγός, τοῖς περὶ Δήλιον Ῥωμαίοις ἐπιπεσὼν

22

plain called Libyssa after the river. I have made this comparison as a testimony to the magnanimity of Hannibal and Scipio, and small-mindedness of Flamininus.

12. On his return to Ephesus from Pisidia, Antiochus 45 entered into discussions with the Roman ambassadors. He stated that he would leave Rhodes, Byzantium, Cyzicus, and all the other Greeks of Asia independent, if a treaty was concluded between himself and Rome, but he would not give up the Aeolians or Ionians, since they had long been used to obeying even the barbarian kings of Asia. The Roman envoys, of course, returned to Rome without 46 making any agreement with Antiochus. In fact they had not come for the purpose of making agreements, but to test him out. An Aetolian mission led by Thoas now arrived to appoint Antiochus supreme commander of the Aetolians, and invite him to sail for Greece at once, telling him that it would be an easy operation. They did not even want 47 to let him wait for the army that was coming down to the coast from upper Asia, but by exaggerating the resources of the Aetolians, and promising an alliance with the Spartans and, in addition, Philip of Macedon, who was angry with Rome, they pressed him into making the crossing to Greece. He became very foolishly overexcited—even the 48 announcement of his son's death in Syria did not make him any less impulsive—and he sailed across to Euboea with ten thousand men, which was all he had at the time. He 49 personally won over the whole island, which surrendered to him in a panic. Micithio, one of his generals, attacked

(ἱερὸν δ' ἐστὶ τὸ χωρίον Ἀπόλλωνος) τοὺς μὲν αὐτῶν
ἔκτεινε, τοὺς δ' ἐζώγρησεν.

50   13. Ἀμύνανδρός τε, ὁ Ἀθαμάνων βασιλεύς, ἐς συμμαχίαν Ἀντιόχῳ συνῆλθε διὰ τοιᾶσδε προφάσεως.
τῶν τις Μακεδόνων Ἀλέξανδρος, ἐν Μεγάλῃ πόλει
τραφεὶς καὶ τῆς αὐτόθι πολιτείας ἀξιωθείς, ἐτερα-
τεύετο γένος Ἀλεξάνδρῳ τῷ Φιλίππου προσήκειν, γενομένους τέ οἱ παῖδας ὠνόμασεν, ἐς πίστιν ὧν ἐλογο-
ποίει, Φίλιππόν τε καὶ Ἀλέξανδρον καὶ Ἀπάμαν, ἣν
51   Ἀμυνάνδρῳ πρὸς γάμον ἠγγύησεν. ἀγαγὼν δ' αὐτὴν
Φίλιππος ὁ ἀδελφὸς ἐς τὸν γάμον, ἐπεὶ τὸν Ἀμύναν-
δρον εἶδεν ἀσθενῆ καὶ πραγμάτων ἄπειρον, παρέμενε,
52   τὴν ἀρχὴν διὰ τὸ κῆδος διοικῶν. τοῦτον οὖν τὸν
Φίλιππον ὁ Ἀντίοχος τότε ἐπελπίζων ἐς τὴν Μακεδόνων ἀρχὴν ὡς ἐς οἰκείαν οἱ κατάξειν, προσέλαβε
τοὺς Ἀθαμάνας ἐς τὴν συμμαχίαν, ἐπὶ δ' αὐτοῖς καὶ
Θηβαίους, αὐτὸς ἐς Θήβας παρελθών τε καὶ δημη-
53   γορήσας. ὁ μὲν δὴ Θηβαίοις τε καὶ Ἀμυνάνδρῳ καὶ
Αἰτωλοῖς ἐπὶ τοσῷδε πολέμῳ μάλα ματαίως ἐθάρρει,
καὶ ἐς Θεσσαλίαν ἐσκόπει πότερον εὐθὺς ἢ μετὰ χειμῶνα δέοι στρατεύειν· Ἀννίβαν δ' ἐπὶ τῇ σκέψει τῇδε
ἡσυχάζοντα ἐκέλευε γνώμην πρῶτον ἐσενεγκεῖν.

54   14. Ὁ δ' ἔφη, "Θεσσαλοὺς μὲν οὐ δυσχερές, εἴτε
νῦν εἴτε μετὰ χειμῶνα ἐθέλοις, ὑπάγεσθαι. τὸ γὰρ
ἔθνος ἐκ πολλοῦ πεπονηκὸς ἔς τε σὲ νῦν καὶ ἐς
Ῥωμαίους αὖ, εἴ τι γίγνοιτο νεώτερον, μεταβαλεῖται.
55   ἤλθομεν δ' ἄνευ τῆς οἰκείας δυνάμεως, Αἰτωλοῖς ἐπ-
άγουσι πεισθέντες ὅτι καὶ Λακεδαιμόνιοι καὶ Φίλιππος

the Roman force at Delium (the place is a sanctuary of
Apollo), killing some, and taking the rest prisoner.

13. Amynander, king of the Athamanes, made an alli- 50
ance with Antiochus for the following reason. A certain Macedonian man named Alexander, who had been
brought up in Megalopolis and made a citizen there, in-
vented a tale that he was related to Alexander, son of
Philip. To add credibility to his story he named his children Philip, Alexander and Apamas. Apamas he betrothed
in marriage to Amynander. When her brother Philip es- 51
corted her to the wedding, he could see that Amynander
was weak and politically inexperienced, and he stayed
there, administering the kingdom by virtue of the familial
relationship. So, Antiochus, by raising the hopes of this 52
Philip that he would restore him to the kingdom of Macedon, which, Antiochus said, belonged to him anyway,
brought the Athamanes into alliance with him. In addition
to the Athamanes, Antiochus also made an alliance with
the Thebans by going there himself and making a speech
in their public assembly. It was extremely unwise of him 53
to rely on the Thebans, Amynander, and the Aetolians for
such a great war, and his only consideration was whether
he should invade Thessaly immediately, or after the winter. As Hannibal had nothing to say on this question, Antiochus asked him first what he thought.

14. His reply was as follows. "There will be no difficulty 54
in subduing the Thessalians, whether you want to do it
now or after the winter. For they are a people who have
long been exhausted, and they will go over to you now, or
to the Romans later, if anything bad should happen to you.
We have come here without our own army, brought over 55
by the Aetolians and persuaded by them that the Spartans

25

ἡμῖν συμμαχήσουσιν· ὧν Λακεδαιμονίους μὲν καὶ
πολεμεῖν ἡμῖν ἀκούω μετ᾽ Ἀχαιῶν, Φίλιππον δὲ οὐχ
ὁρῶ σοι παρόντα, δυνατὸν ἐν τῷδε τῷ πολέμῳ ῥοπήν,
56 ὁποτέρωσε προσθοῖτο, ποιῆσαι. τῆς δὲ γνώμης ἔχο-
μαι τῆς αὐτῆς, τὴν στρατιὰν ἀπὸ τῆς Ἀσίας καλεῖν
ὅτι τάχιστα, καὶ μὴ ἐν Ἀμυνάνδρῳ καὶ Αἰτωλοῖς τὰς
ἐλπίδας ἔχειν, ὅταν δ᾽ ἀφίκηται, τὴν Ἰταλίαν πορθεῖν,
ἵνα τοῖς οἰκείοις κακοῖς περισπώμενοι τὰ σὰ λυπῶσιν
ἥκιστα, καὶ περὶ τῶν σφετέρων δεδιότες μηδαμοῦ
57 προΐωσιν. ὁ δὲ τρόπος οὐκέθ᾽ ὅμοιος ᾧ προύλεγον,
ἀλλὰ χρὴ τὸ μὲν ἥμισυ τῶν νεῶν τὰ παράλια τῆς
Ἰταλίας πορθεῖν, τὸ δὲ ἥμισυ ναυλοχεῖν ἐφεδρεῦον ἐς
τὰ συμφερόμενα, αὐτὸν δὲ σὲ τῷ πεζῷ παντὶ προκα-
θήμενον τῆς Ἑλλάδος, ἀγχοῦ τῆς Ἰταλίας, δόξαν
ἐμποιεῖν ἐσβολῆς, καὶ εἰ δύναιό ποτε, καὶ ἐσβαλεῖν.
58 Φίλιππον δὲ πειρᾶσθαι μὲν προσάγεσθαι μηχανῇ
πάσῃ, πλεῖστον ἐς ἑκατέρους ἐν τῷδε τῷ πολέμῳ δυ-
νάμενον· ἢν δ᾽ ἀπειθῇ, τὸν σὸν υἱὸν αὐτῷ Σέλευκον
ἐπιπέμπειν διὰ Θρᾴκης, ἵνα καὶ ὅδε περισπώμενος
οἰκείοις κακοῖς μηδὲν ᾖ τοῖς πολεμίοις χρήσιμος.”
59 τοσάδε μὲν ὁ Ἀννίβας εἶπε, καὶ ἦν ἄριστα πάντων·
ὑπὸ δὲ φθόνου τῆς τε δόξης αὐτοῦ καὶ συνέσεως οἵ
τε ἄλλοι καὶ αὐτὸς οὐχ ἧσσον ὁ βασιλεύς, ἵνα μὴ
δοκοίη σφῶν ὁ Ἀννίβας τῇ στρατηγίᾳ προφέρειν,
μηδὲ ἡ δόξα τῶν ἐσομένων ἐκείνου γένοιτο, μεθῆκαν
ἅπαντα, πλὴν ὅτι Πολυξενίδας ἐπὶ τὴν στρατιὰν ἐς
τὴν Ἀσίαν ἐπέμφθη.
60   15. Ῥωμαῖοι δ᾽ ἐπεὶ τῆς ἐσβολῆς τῆς ἐς τὴν Ἑλ-

and Philip will join forces with us. What I hear about them is, in fact, that the Spartans have combined with the Achaeans to fight against us; and as for Philip, I don't see him here standing by you, although he has the capacity to make the decisive difference in this war, depending on which side he joins. My opinion is the same as before. You 56 should summon the army from Asia as quickly as possible and not place any hope in Amynander and the Aetolians. When the army arrives, you should devastate Italy, so that, preoccupied by their own troubles, the Romans inflict as little damage on you as possible, and are too afraid for their own welfare to take any military initiative. My rec- 57 ommendation on how to do this is different from my ear- lier advice. Now you need to raid the coast of Italy with half your fleet, and station the other half in readiness for any opportunities that arise, while you yourself protect Greece with your whole army from a position near to Italy, giving the impression you are going to attack, and in fact doing so, whenever you can. Use all means at your disposal 58 to bring Philip over to your side, since he has the greatest capacity to help either side in this war. But if he cannot be persuaded, send your son Seleucus against him through Thrace, so that he too is distracted by his domestic trou- bles, and thus of no use to the enemy." This was what 59 Hannibal said, and it was the best advice of all. But jealous of his reputation and wisdom, the other courtiers, no less than the king himself, worried that Hannibal would ap- pear to be a better general than themselves, and that he would get the credit for the forthcoming successes, com- pletely ignored the advice, except for the fact that Polyxe- nidas was sent to Asia to collect the army.

15. As soon as they heard of Antiochus' invasion of 60

λάδα Ἀντιόχου καὶ τῶν ἐπὶ Δηλίου Ῥωμαίων ἀναιρέ-
σεώς τε καὶ αἰχμαλωσίας ἐπύθοντο, πολεμεῖν ἐψηφί-
61 σαντο. οὕτω μὲν ὁ Ἀντιόχου τε καὶ Ῥωμαίων πόλεμος,
ἐκ πολλοῦ δι᾿ ὑπονοίας ἀλλήλοις γενόμενος, τότε
πρῶτον ἀπερρήγνυτο ἐς ἔργον· οἷα δ᾿ Ἀντιόχου τῆς
τε Ἀσίας τῆς ἄνω πολλῶν καὶ μεγάλων ἐθνῶν καὶ τῆς
ἐπὶ θαλάσσῃ, χωρὶς ὀλίγων, ὅλης ἐπικρατοῦντος, ἔς
τε τὴν Εὐρώπην ἐπιβεβηκότος ἤδη, καὶ δόξαν ἐπίφο-
βον καὶ παρασκευὴν ἱκανὴν ἔχοντος, πολλά τε ἄλλα
καθ᾿ ἑτέρων ἐξειργασμένου λαμπρά, δι᾿ ἃ καὶ μέγας
ἦν ἐπώνυμον αὐτῷ, τὸν πόλεμον οἱ Ῥωμαῖοι χρόνιον
62 σφίσι καὶ μέγαν ἔσεσθαι προσεδόκων. Φίλιππόν τε
τὸν Μακεδόνα δι᾿ ὑποψίας εἶχον, ἄρτι ὑπὸ σφῶν κα-
ταπεπολεμημένον, καὶ Καρχηδονίους, μὴ οὐ πιστοὶ
σφίσιν ὦσιν ἐπὶ ταῖς συνθήκαις, Ἀννίβου συνόντος
63 Ἀντιόχῳ. τούς τε ἄλλους σφῶν ὑπηκόους ὑπονοοῦν-
τες, μὴ καὶ παρὰ τούτων τι νεώτερον ἐς τὴν Ἀντιόχου δόξαν γένοιτο, στρατιὰν ἐς ἅπαντας, ἐφεδρεύειν
εἰρηνικῶς αὐτοῖς, καὶ στρατηγοὺς ἐπὶ τῇ στρατιᾷ,
περιέπεμπον, οὓς αὐτοὶ καλοῦσιν ἐξαπελέκεας, ὅτι
τῶν ὑπάτων δυώδεκα πελέκεσι καὶ δυώδεκα ῥάβδοις,
ὥσπερ οἱ πάλαι βασιλεῖς, χρωμένων, τὸ ἥμισυ τῆς
ἀξιώσεως ἔστι τοῖσδε τοῖς στρατηγοῖς καὶ τὰ ἡμίσεα
64 παράσημα. ὡς δ᾿ ἐν μεγάλῳ φόβῳ, καὶ περὶ τῆς
Ἰταλίας ἐδείμαινον, μὴ οὐδ᾿ αὐτὴ σφίσιν ᾖ πιστὴ ἢ
βέβαιος ἐπ᾿ Ἀντιόχῳ. πεζὸν δὴ πολὺν ἐς Τάραντα
διέπεμπον, ἐφεδρεύειν τοῖς ἐπιοῦσι, καὶ νεῶν στόλος

Greece, and of the murder and capture of Roman citizens at Delium, Rome voted for war. So it was then for the first 61 time that war actually broke out between Antiochus and Rome, although it had been brewing for a long time because of their mutual suspicion. Antiochus was master of many powerful peoples from upper Asia, and, apart from a few exceptions, controlled the whole coastal zone; he had now crossed into Europe, bringing a formidable reputation and substantial military resources; and his many brilliant successes against other opponents had won him the title "the Great." In view of these factors, Rome expected that this would be a major war and last a long time. They were also suspicious of Philip of Macedon, although 62 they had recently defeated him, and, due to Hannibal's presence in Antiochus' company, did not trust the Carthaginians to abide by their treaty. Equally apprehensive that 63 their other subjects too might be led by Antiochus' reputation to rebel, they sent armed forces to all their provinces, to keep peaceful watch on them, with praetors in command of the armies. The Romans call praetors "six-ax men" because while consuls have twelve bundles of rods and twelve axes, as the kings once had, the praetors I am talking about have half the standing and half the insignia of office.[13] There was such a state of anxiety that the Romans were even uneasy about Italy itself, that it would not remain solidly loyal to them against Antiochus. So they sent a large force of infantry to Tarentum to guard against

[13] Appian is explaining the *fasces*, the bundle of rods surrounding an ax, carried by lictors, that were the symbols of magisterial authority. Lictors accompanied magistrates at all times in public, walking in front of them in single file, carrying the *fasces*.

τὴν παράλιον περιέπλει. τοσόσδε φόβος ἦν Ἀντιόχου
65 τὰ πρῶτα. ὡς δὲ αὐτοῖς τὰ ἐς τὴν ἀρχὴν συνετετά-
χατο πάντα, ἐπ' αὐτὸν Ἀντίοχον ἤδη κατέλεγον ἀπὸ
μὲν σφῶν αὐτῶν ἐς δισμυρίους ἄνδρος, ἀπὸ δὲ τῶν
συμμάχων τὸ διπλάσιον, ὡς ἅμα τῷ ἦρι τὸν Ἰόνιον
διαβαλοῦντες.

66   16. Καὶ οἱ μὲν τὸν χειμῶνα ὅλον ἐν τούτῳ παρασκευῆς ἦσαν, ὁ δ' Ἀντίοχος ἤλαυνεν ἐπὶ Θετταλούς,
καὶ γενόμενος ἐν Κυνὸς κεφαλαῖς, ἔνθα τὸ πταῖσμα
τοῖς Μακεδόσιν ὑπὸ Ῥωμαίων γεγένητο, τὰ λείπανα
τῶν τότε πεσόντων ἄταφα ἔτι ὄντα μεγαλοπρεπῶς
ἔθαπτε, δημοκοπῶν ἐς Μακεδόνας, καὶ Φίλιππον αὐτοῖς διαβάλλων οὐ θάψαντα τοὺς ὑπὲρ αὐτοῦ πεσόν-
67 τας. ὧν πυθόμενος ὁ Φίλιππος, ἐνδοιάζων ἔτι καὶ
περισκοπῶν ὁποτέρωσε προσθοῖτο, αὐτίκα εἵλετο τὰ
Ῥωμαίων, Βαίβιόν τε στρατηγὸν αὐτῶν, ἄρχοντά
τινος πλησίον στρατοῦ, καλέσας ἐλθεῖν ἔς τι χωρίον,
πίστεις αὖθις ἐδίδου Ῥωμαίοις ἀδόλως συμμαχήσειν
68 κατ' Ἀντιόχου. ἐφ' οἷς αὐτὸν ὁ Βαίβιος ἐπήνει, καὶ
θαρρήσας αὐτίκα ἔπεμπε διὰ τῆς Μακεδονίας Ἄππιον
Κλαύδιον μετὰ δισχιλίων πεζῶν ἐς Θεσσαλίαν. καὶ ὁ
Ἄππιος ἀπὸ τῶν Τεμπῶν Ἀντίοχον Λαρίσσῃ παρα-
καθήμενον ἰδὼν πῦρ πολὺ ἤγειρεν, ἐπικρύπτων τὴν
69 ὀλιγότητα. καὶ ὁ Ἀντίοχος, ὡς Βαιβίου καὶ Φιλίππου

---

14 For the defeat of Philip in 197, see above, note 4.
15 M. Baebius Tamphilus was praetor in 192; he reached the
consulship in 181.

invading forces, and a naval force patrolled the coast. Such
was the level of fear raised by Antiochus in the beginning.
When all matters of imperial administration had been put   65
in order, they then enrolled an army against Antiochus
himself of twenty thousand Romans and twice that number of allies, with the intention of crossing the Ionian sea
at the beginning of spring.

16. While they spent the whole winter in these prepara-   66
tions, Antiochus for his part marched against the Thessalians and came to Cynoscephalae, where the Macedonians had been defeated by the Romans.[14] Here he
organized a magnificent funeral for the remains of those
who had fallen in the battle but were still unburied: he was
trying to win popular support among the Macedonians,
but was also discrediting Philip in their eyes for not burying those who had died on his behalf. When he heard this,   67
Philip, who had still not made up his mind about which
side to join, immediately chose Rome. He invited Baebius,
one of their generals in command of an army in the neigh-
borhood, to meet him at an appointed place, and again
gave a pledge that he would assist Rome against Antiochus
as a true ally.[15] Baebius praised him for this and immedi-   68
ately felt confident enough to send Appius Claudius across
Macedonia into Thessaly with two thousand infantry.[16]
From Tempe Appius could see Antiochus besieging La-
rissa, and he lit many camp fires to hide the small size of
his force. Antiochus was very alarmed at the thought that   69

[16] This is presumably the Appius Claudius to whom Livy
(34.50.10) refers as a legate of Flamininus, and the future consul
of 185.

παρόντων διαταραχθείς, ἐξέλιπε τὴν πολιορκίαν,
πρόφασιν τὸν χειμῶνα ποιούμενος, καὶ ἐς Χαλκίδα
παρῆλθεν, ἔνθα κόρης εὐπρεποῦς ἔρωτι ἁλούς, ὑπὲρ
ἔτη πεντήκοντα γεγονὼς καὶ τοσόνδε πόλεμον δια-
φέρων, ἔθυε γάμους καὶ πανηγύρεις ἦγε, καὶ τὴν δύναμιν ἐς πᾶσαν ἀργίαν καὶ τρυφὴν ἐπὶ τὸν χειμῶνα
70 ὅλον ἀνῆκεν. ἀρχομένου δ' ἦρος ἐμβαλὼν ἐς Ἀκαρ-
νανίαν ᾔσθετο μὲν τῆς ἀργίας τοῦ στρατοῦ δυσέργου
πρὸς ἅπαντα ὄντος, καὶ τότε τῶν γάμων αὐτῷ καὶ τῆς
πανηγύρεως μετέμελεν· ὑπαγαγόμενος δ' ὅμως τινὰ
τῆς Ἀκαρνανίας, καὶ τὰ λοιπὰ πολιορκῶν, ἐπεὶ τάχιστα Ῥωμαίους ἐπύθετο περᾶν τὸν Ἰόνιον, ἐς Χαλκίδα
ἀνεζεύγνυ.

71   17. Ῥωμαῖοι δ' ὑπὸ σπουδῆς τοῖς τότε ἑτοίμοις
ἱππεῦσι δισχιλίοις καὶ πεζοῖς δισμυρίοις καὶ ἐλέφασί
τισιν, ἡγουμένου σφῶν Ἀκιλίου Μανίου Γλαβρίωνος,
ἐς Ἀπολλωνίαν ἐκ Βρεντεσίου διαβαλόντες ἐπὶ Θεσσαλίας ἐβάδιζον καὶ τὰς πόλεις ἐξέλυον τῶν πολιορ-
κιῶν, ἐν ὅσαις δ' ἦσαν ἤδη Ἀθαμάνων φρουραί, τὰς
72 φρουρὰς ἐξέβαλλον. καὶ τὸν Μεγαλοπολίτην Φίλιππον αἰχμάλωτον ἔλαβον, ἐλπίζοντα ἔτι τὴν Μακεδόνων ἀρχήν. εἷλον δὲ καὶ τῶν Ἀντιοχείων ἐς τρισχι-
73 λίους. ἅμα δὲ ταῦτα ὁ Μάνιος εἰργάζετο, καὶ ὁ
Φίλιππος ἐς Ἀθαμανίαν ἐμβαλὼν πᾶσαν αὐτὴν
ὑπήκοον ἔλαβεν, Ἀμυνάνδρου φυγόντος ἐς Ἄμβρα-
74 κίαν. ὧν ὁ Ἀντίοχος αἰσθανόμενός τε, καὶ τὴν ὀξύτητα
τῶν γιγνομένων καταπλαγείς, ἔδεισεν ὡς ἐπὶ αἰφνιδίῳ καὶ ταχείᾳ μεταβολῇ, καὶ τῆς εὐβουλίας Ἀννίβου

Baebius and Philip had arrived, and abandoned the siege, using the winter as his excuse. He retired to Chalcis where he fell in love with a beautiful young woman. Although he was over fifty years old, and shouldering the burden of such a major war, he celebrated his wedding with her and held a public festival, abandoning his army to a life of complete idleness and luxury over the whole winter. At the 70 beginning of spring, when he invaded Acarnania, he realized that this inactivity had made his army ineffective for all operations, and he then began to regret his marriage and the festival. Nevertheless, he reduced part of Acarnania, and besieged the remaining parts, but as soon as he learned that the Romans were crossing the Ionian sea, he immediately withdrew to Chalcis.

17. Under the command of Manius Acilius Glabrio, the 71 Romans quickly crossed from Brundisium to Apollonia with the two thousand cavalry, twenty thousand infantry and few elephants they had ready at the time.[17] They marched into Thessaly to relieve the towns under siege, and where there were already Athamanian garrisons, expelled them. Philip of Megalopolis, who was still expecting 72 to be given the kingdom of Macedon, they took prisoner. They also captured about three thousand of Antiochus' men. While Manius was doing this, Philip invaded Atha- 73 mania and, with Amynander fleeing to Ambracia, subjected the whole of it to his rule. When Antiochus heard 74 this, he was shocked at how quickly things were happening, and it was then that, frightened at such a sudden and swift change of fortune, he began to appreciate how good

[17] Manius Acilius Glabrio took up this command when he was consul in 191.

τότε ἤσθετο, ἔς τε τὴν Ἀσίαν ἄλλους ἐπ᾽ ἄλλοις ἔπεμπεν ἐπισπέρχων Πολυξενίδαν ἐς τὴν διάβασιν, αὐτὸς
75 δ᾽ ὅσους εἶχε, πανταχόθεν συνεκάλει. γενομένων δ᾽
αὐτῷ τῶν μὲν οἰκείων πεζῶν μυρίων καὶ ἱππέων πεντακοσίων, ἐπὶ δὲ τούτοις <. . .>[6] διά τινων συμμάχων,
Θερμοπύλας κατέλαβεν ὡς τὴν δυσχωρίαν προβα-
λούμενος τοῖς πολεμίοις καὶ τὸν στρατὸν ἐκ τῆς
76 Ἀσίας ἀναμενῶν. δίοδος δ᾽ ἐστὶν αἱ Θερμοπύλαι
στενὴ καὶ ἐπιμήκης, καὶ αὐτὴν περιέχει τῇ μὲν
θάλασσα τραχεῖα καὶ ἀλίμενος, τῇ δὲ ἕλος ἄβατόν τε
77 καὶ βαραθρῶδες. κορυφαί τε εἰσὶν ἐν αὐτῇ δύο ὀρῶν
ἀπόκρημνοι, καὶ τούτων μὲν Τειχιοῦντα καλοῦσι τὴν
δὲ Καλλίδρομον. ἔχει δὲ ὁ τόπος θερμῶν ὑδάτων πη-
γάς, καὶ Θερμοπύλαι ἀπὸ τοῦδ᾽ ἐπικλῄζονται.
78   18. Τεῖχος οὖν ἐνταῦθα διπλοῦν ὁ Ἀντίοχος ᾠκοδο-
μήσατο, καὶ τὰς μηχανὰς ἐπὶ τὸ τεῖχος ἐπέθηκεν. ἔς
τε τὰς κορυφὰς τῶν ὀρῶν Αἰτωλοὺς ἀνέπεμψε, μή τις
λάθοι κατὰ τὴν λεγομένην ἀτραπὸν περιελθών, ᾗ
δὴ καὶ Λακεδαιμονίοις τοῖς ἀμφὶ Λεωνίδαν Ξέρξης
79 ἐπέθετο, ἀφυλάκτων τότε τῶν ὀρῶν ὄντων. Αἰτωλοὶ δὲ
χιλίους μὲν ἑκατέρῳ τῶνδε τῶν ἄκρων ἐπέστησαν,
τοῖς δὲ λοιποῖς ἐστρατοπέδευον ἐφ᾽ ἑαυτῶν περὶ πόλιν
80 Ἡράκλειαν. ὁ δὲ Μάνιος ἐπεὶ κατεῖδε τὴν τῶν πολεμίων παρασκευήν, σημεῖον ἔδωκεν ἐς ἕω μάχης· καὶ
δύο τῶν χιλιάρχων, Μᾶρκον Κάτωνα καὶ Λεύκιον
Οὐαλέριον, ἐκέλευσε νυκτός, ἐπιλεξαμένους ἑκάτερον

6 Post τούτοις indicat lacunam Goukowsky

Hannibal's advice had been. He sent repeated messages to Asia to press Polyxenidas to make the crossing to Greece, and summoned from everywhere what troops he himself had. In total his own forces amounted to ten thou- 75 sand infantry and five hundred cavalry. In addition to these ‹. . .›[18] with the help of some additional allies, he occupied Thermopylae in order to put difficult terrain between himself and the enemy, while he waited for the army to come from Asia. Thermopylae comprises a long, 76 narrow pass, bordered on one side by the sea, which is rough and harborless, on the other by an impassable and deep marsh. There are two very steep mountain peaks in 77 it, one called Teichious, the other Callidromus. The place also has hot springs, from which Thermopylae gets its name.[19]

18. Antiochus built a double wall here, and placed his 78 siege engines on the wall. He sent Aetolians to occupy the mountain tops, to prevent anyone secretly circling round along the famous path used by Xerxes to attack Leonidas and his Spartans, the mountains having been left unguarded at that time. The Aetolians stationed one thou- 79 sand men on each of the peaks, and the rest made camp by themselves near the town of Heraclea. When Manius 80 saw the enemy's preparations, he gave the signal for battle to be joined at dawn, and ordered two tribunes, Marcus Cato and Lucius Valerius, to pick as many men as they wanted and circle around the mountains during the night,

[18] There may be a short lacuna in the text, which does not make easy sense as it stands.

[19] Thermopylae means "hot gates."

ὁπόσους ἐθέλοι, τὰ ὄρη περιελθεῖν καὶ τοὺς Αἰτωλοὺς
81 ἀπὸ τῶν ἄκρων, ὅπῃ δύναιντο, βιάσασθαι. τούτων ὁ
μὲν Λεύκιος ἀπεκρούσθη τοῦ Τειχιοῦντος, ἀγαθῶν
ἐνταῦθα τῶν Αἰτωλῶν γενομένων· ὁ δὲ Κάτων τῷ
Καλλιδρόμῳ παραστρατοπεδεύσας, κοιμωμένοις ἔτι
τοῖς ἐχθροῖς ἐπέπεσε περὶ ἐσχάτην φυλακήν, καὶ πολὺς ἀμφ' αὐτὸν ἐγίγνετο ἀγών, βιαζόμενον ἐς ὑψηλὰ
82 καὶ ἀπόκρημνα κωλυόντων τῶν πολεμίων. ἤδη δὲ καὶ
Μάνιος ἐπῆγε τὴν στρατιὰν Ἀντιόχῳ κατὰ μέτωπον,
ἐς λόχους ὀρθίους διῃρημένην· ὧδε γὰρ μόνως ἐν
83 στενοῖς ἐδύνατο. καὶ ὁ βασιλεὺς τοὺς μὲν ψιλοὺς καὶ
πελταστὰς προμάχεσθαι τῆς φάλαγγος ἐκέλευσεν,
αὐτὴν δ' ἔστησε πρὸ τοῦ στρατοπέδου, ἐπὶ δεξιὰ δ'
αὐτῆς τοὺς σφενδονήτας καὶ τοξότας ἐπὶ τῶν ὑπω-
ρειῶν, τοὺς δ' ἐλέφαντας ἐν ἀριστερᾷ, καὶ τὸ στῖφος
ὃ μετ' αὐτῶν ἀεὶ συνετάσσετο, παρὰ τῇ θαλάσσῃ.

84   19. Γενομένης δ' ἐν χερσὶ τῆς μάχης, τὰ μὲν πρῶτα
τὸν Μάνιον οἱ ψιλοὶ πανταχόθεν ἐπιτρέχοντες ἐλύ-
πουν· ἐπεὶ δὲ αὐτοὺς φιλοπόνως δεχόμενός τε καὶ ἀνα-
χωρῶν καὶ αὖθις ἐπιὼν ἐτρέψατο, τοὺς μὲν ψιλοὺς ἡ
φάλαγξ ἡ τῶν Μακεδόνων διαστᾶσα ἐς αὑτὴν ἐδέξατο καὶ συνελθοῦσα ἐκάλυψε, καὶ τὰς σαρίσσας ἐν
τάξει πυκνὰς προὐβάλοντο, ᾧ δὴ μάλιστα οἱ Μακεδόνες ἐξ Ἀλεξάνδρου καὶ Φιλίππου κατεπλήσσοντο
τοὺς πολεμίους, ἀντίοις δόρασι πολλοῖς καὶ μακροῖς
85 οὐ τολμῶντας πελάζειν. αἰφνίδιον δ' ὤφθη τῶν Αἰτωλῶν ἐκ τοῦ Καλλιδρόμου φυγὴ καὶ βοή, καθαλλο-
86 μένων ἐς τὸ Ἀντιόχου στρατόπεδον. τὸ μὲν δὴ πρῶτον

and force the Aetolians from the peaks, however they could manage it.[20] Of these, Lucius was driven away from 81 Mount Teichious where the Aetolians fought bravely, but Cato, having camped near Mount Callidromus, fell on the enemy around the last watch while they were still asleep. There was a stiff fight around him as he tried to force his way up the high and steep terrain, and the enemy tried to prevent him. Manius now led his army in a frontal assault 82 on Antiochus, having divided it into columns, this being the only possibility in the narrow space. The king ordered 83 his light-armed troops and peltasts to fight in front of the phalanx, and stationed the phalanx in front of the camp, with the slingers and archers on the right at the foot of the mountain, and the elephants and the unit that was always drawn up with them on the left beside the sea.

19. When the battle started, first of all the light-armed 84 troops gave Manius a difficult time by attacking from all directions. He received them steadfastly, and by dropping back and then advancing again, beat them off. The Macedonian phalanx opened to let them in, and then closed to protect them, with sarissas to the front in a massed line. This was the precisely the formation that, since the time of Alexander and Philip, the Macedonians employed to intimidate their enemies, who would not dare to advance against the countless long spears facing them. Suddenly, 85 however, the Aetolians on Callidromus were seen to be fleeing, and their shouting was heard, as they ran down into the camp of Antiochus. At first neither side knew what 86

[20] M. Porcius Cato and L. Valerius Flaccus were the two consuls of 195. They were now serving as legates of Acilius Glabrio at the battle of Thermopylae in 191.

ἑκατέροις ἄγνοιά τε τοῦ γιγνομένου καὶ θόρυβος ἦν
ὡς ἐν ἀγνοίᾳ· ὡς δὲ ὁ Κάτων ἐπεφαίνετο διώκων
αὐτοὺς μετὰ πολλῆς βοῆς, καὶ ὑπὲρ τὸ στρατόπεδον
ἐγίγνετο ἤδη τὸ Ἀντιόχου, ἔδεισαν οἱ τοῦ βασιλέως,
περί τε τῆς Ῥωμαίων μάχης ἐπιφόβως ἐκ πολλοῦ
πυνθανόμενοι, καὶ σφᾶς εἰδότες ὑπὸ ἀργίας καὶ τρυφῆς δι' ὅλου τοῦ χειμῶνος ἐς δυσεργίαν διεφθαρμέ-
87 νους. τούς τε σὺν τῷ Κάτωνι σαφῶς μὲν οὐ καθορῶν-
τες ὁπόσοι τινὲς εἶεν ὑπὸ δὲ τοῦ φόβου πλείους
νομίζοντες εἶναι, καὶ περὶ τῷ στρατοπέδῳ δείσαντες,
ἀκόσμως ἐς αὐτὸ κατέφυγον ὡς ἀπ' αὐτοῦ τοὺς πο-
88 λεμίους ἀμυνούμενοι. Ῥωμαῖοι δ' αὐτοῖς παραθέοντες
συνεσέπεσον ἐς τὸ στρατόπεδον, καὶ ἦν ἄλλη φυγὴ
89 τῶν Ἀντιοχείων ἐκεῖθεν ἄκοσμος. ὁ δὲ Μάνιος μέχρι
μὲν ἐπὶ Σκάρφειαν ἐδίωκαν αὐτοὺς κτείνων τε καὶ ζω-
γρῶν, ἀπὸ δὲ τῆς Σκαρφείας ἐπανιὼν διήρπαζε τὸ
στρατόπεδον τοῦ βασιλέως καὶ τοὺς Αἰτωλοὺς ἐπι-
δραμόντας τῷ Ῥωμαίων χάρακι παρὰ τὴν ἀπουσίαν
αὐτῶν ἐξήλασεν ἐπιφανείς.

90   20. Ἀπέθανον δ' ἐν τῇ μάχῃ καὶ τῇ διώξει Ῥωμαίων
μὲν ἀμφὶ τοὺς διακοσίους, Ἀντιόχου δέ, σὺν τοῖς λη-
91 φθεῖσιν, ἀμφὶ τοὺς μυρίους. αὐτὸς δ' ὁ βασιλεὺς ἀπὸ
μὲν τῆς πρώτης τροπῆς μετὰ πεντακοσίων ἱππέων ἐς
Ἐλάτειαν ἀμεταστρεπτὶ διέδραμεν, ἀπὸ δ' Ἐλατείας
ἐς Χαλκίδα καὶ ἐς Ἔφεσον μετ' Εὐβοίας τῆς νεο-
γάμου (τοῦτο γὰρ αὐτὴν ὠνόμαζεν) ἐπὶ τῶν νεῶν ἔφυγεν, οὐδὲ τούτων ἁπασῶν· ἀγορὰν γάρ τινας αὐτῶν
διαφερούσας ὁ Ῥωμαίων ναύαρχος ἐπαναχθεὶς δι-

was happening, and confusion resulted from the uncertainty. But when Cato appeared pursuing the Aetolians with great shouting and was already above Antiochus' camp, the king's men were terrified, long used to hearing the frightening stories of how the Romans fought, and knowing well that they had been reduced to ineffectiveness by an entire winter spent in luxurious idleness. They 87 could not see clearly how many men Cato had with him, but fear led them to exaggerate the number, and, worried about their camp, they fled to it in disorder, with the intention of fighting off the enemy from there. But the Romans 88 kept pace with them as they ran, and they all tumbled into the camp together, from where there was another chaotic flight of Antiochus' men. Manius pursued them as far as 89 Scarphea, killing and taking prisoners, but turning back from Scarphea, he plundered the king's camp and by his mere appearance drove off the Aetolians, who had taken advantage of his absence to break into the Roman palisade.

20. About two hundred Romans were killed in the 90 battle and pursuit, while Antiochus lost about ten thousand, including prisoners. At the first sign of defeat and 91 without even looking back, the king himself escaped to Elatea with five hundred cavalry. From Elatea he made his way to Chalcis and from there fled by sea to Ephesus with his new wife, Euboea: for that is what he called her. But he did not have all his fleet, since the Roman admiral had attacked and sunk some of his ships as they were

92 ἐφθάρκει. οἱ δ᾽ ἐν ἄστει Ῥωμαῖοι τῆς νίκης πυθόμενοι, ταχείας τε οὕτω καὶ εὐχεροῦς σφίσι φανείσης,
ἔθυον, ἐκ φοβερᾶς τῆς Ἀντιόχου δόξης τὴν πρώτην
πεῖραν ἀσπασάμενοι. Φίλιππόν τε τῆς συμμαχίας
ἀμειβόμενοι, τὸν υἱὸν αὐτῷ Δημήτριον, ὁμηρεύοντα
ἔτι παρὰ σφίσιν, ἔπεμψαν.

93   21. Καὶ τάδε μὲν ἦν ἐν ἄστει, Μάνιος δὲ Φωκέας
μὲν καὶ Χαλκιδέας, καὶ ὅσοι ἄλλοι τῷ Ἀντιόχῳ συν-
επεπράχεσαν, δεομένους ἀπέλυσε τοῦ δέους, τὴν δ᾽
Αἰτωλίαν αὐτός τε καὶ Φίλιππος ἐδῄουν, καὶ τὰς πό-
94 λεις ἐπολιόρκουν. Δαμόκριτόν τε τὸν στρατηγὸν τῶν
Αἰτωλῶν ἐνταῦθα ὁ Μάνιος ἔλαβε κρυπτόμενον, ὃς
Φλαμινίνῳ παρὰ τὸν Τίβεριν ἠπείλει στρατοπεδεύειν.
95 ὁ μὲν δὴ Μάνιος ἐπὶ Καλλιπόλεως διώδευε τὸ ὄρος ὃ
καλοῦσι Κόρακα, ὑψηλότατόν τε ὀρῶν[7] καὶ δυσόδευτον καὶ ἀπόκρημνον, μετὰ στρατοῦ βαρυτάτου τε καὶ
λαφύρων καταγόμου· πολλοὶ δ᾽ ἐξέπιπτον ὑπὸ τῆς
δυσοδίας ἐς τὰ ἀπόκρημνα, καὶ σκεύεσιν αὐτοῖς καὶ
96 ὅπλοις κατεφέροντο. καὶ αὐτοὺς δυνηθέντες ἂν οἱ
Αἰτωλοὶ συνταράξαι οὐδὲ ὤφθησαν, ἀλλ᾽ ἐς Ῥώμην
97 περὶ εἰρήνης ἐπρέσβευον. Ἀντίοχος δὲ τὴν στρατιὰν
ἀπὸ τῶν ἄνω σατραπειῶν κατὰ σπουδὴν ἐπὶ θάλασσαν ἐκάλει, καὶ τὰς ναῦς ἐπεσκεύαζε, ναυαρχοῦντος
98 αὐτῷ Πολυξενίδου Ῥοδίου φυγάδος. ἔς τε Χερρόνησον διαπλεύσας πάλιν αὐτὴν ὠχύρου, καὶ Σηστὸν καὶ
Ἄβυδον ἐκρατύνετο, δι᾽ ὧν ἔδει τὴν φάλαγγα τὴν

---

[7] ὀρῶν Goukowsky: ὁρῶν codd.

transporting supplies. When news of such a quick and ap- 92
parently easy victory reached Rome, the people offered
sacrifice, well pleased with their first encounter with Antiochus' formidable reputation. They rewarded Philip for
his assistance by returning his son Demetrius, who was
still a hostage at Rome.

21. Such was the situation in the city. As for Manius, 93
when petitioned by Phocis, Chalcis, and any others who
had made common cause with Antiochus, he relieved them
of their fears, and he and Philip ravaged Aetolia and laid
siege to its towns. It was here that Manius captured in his 94
hiding place the Aetolian general, Damocritus, who had
threatened Flamininus that he would make camp beside
the Tiber.[21] Manius then made his way toward Callipo- 95
lis, with an army heavily equipped and laden with spoils,
across what they call Mount Corax, although he could see
that it was extremely high, difficult to traverse, and very
precipitous. The road was so bad that many of the men fell
over the cliffs, and were carried down along with their
equipment and arms. Although the Aetolians could have 96
thrown them into confusion, they were not even to be
seen, as they were in the process of sending a mission to
Rome to seek peace. Antiochus called for his army to come 97
with all speed from the upper satrapies to the coast, and
fitted out the fleet, with Polyxenidas, a Rhodian exile, as
his admiral. He then sailed over to Chersonesus and forti- 98
fied it again, reinforcing Sestus and Abydus too, through

[21] The story is reported in Livy 36.24.12.

99 Ῥωμαίων ἐς τὴν Ἀσίαν ὁδεῦσαί τε καὶ περᾶσαι. Λυσιμάχειαν δὲ ταμιεῖον τῷδε τῷ πολέμῳ ποιούμενος,
ὅπλα καὶ σῖτον πολὺν ἐς αὐτὴν συνέφερεν, ἡγούμενος
αὐτίκα οἱ Ῥωμαίους πεζῷ τε πολλῷ καὶ ναυσὶν ἐπι-
100 θήσεσθαι. οἱ δὲ Μανίῳ μὲν αἱροῦνται διάδοχον ἐπὶ
τὴν στρατηγίαν Λεύκιον Σκιπίωνα, ὃς τότε αὐτοῖς
ὕπατος ἦν, ἀπράκτῳ δ᾽ ὄντι καὶ ἀπειροπολέμῳ σύμβουλον αἱροῦνται τὸν ἀδελφὸν Πούπλιον Σκιπίωνα
τὸν Καρχηδονίους ἀφελόμενον τὴν ἡγεμονίαν καὶ
πρῶτον ὀνομασθέντα Ἀφρικανόν.

101   22. Καὶ οἱ μὲν Σκιπίωνες ἔτι ἦσαν ἐν παρασκευῇ,
Λίουιος δ᾽ ὁ φύλαξ τῆς Ἰταλίας, ἐπὶ τὴν ναυαρχίαν
αἱρεθεὶς Ἀτιλίῳ διάδοχος, αὐτίκα ταῖς τε ἰδίαις ναυ-
σίν, αἷς τὴν Ἰταλίαν περιέπλει, καὶ παρὰ Καρχηδονίων αὐτῷ τισὶ δοθείσαις καὶ συμμαχίσιν ἄλλαις ἐς
Πειραιᾶ κατήχθη, καὶ τὸν ὑπ᾽ Ἀτιλίῳ στόλον παραλαβὼν ἔπλει καταφράκτοις ὀγδοήκοντα καὶ μιᾷ, ἑπο-
μένου καὶ Εὐμένους πεντήκοντα ἰδίαις· καὶ ἦν κατά-
102 φρακτον καὶ τῶνδε τὸ ἥμισυ. ἔς τε Φώκαιαν ὑπήκοον
μὲν Ἀντιόχου, ὑπὸ δ᾽ ἐκπλήξεως αὐτοὺς δεχομένην
κατήγοντο, καὶ τῆς ἐπιούσης ἐς ναυμαχίαν ἀνέπλεον.
103 ἀντανήγετο δ᾽ αὐτοῖς ὁ ναύαρχος ὁ Ἀντιόχου Πολυξενίδας διακοσίαις ναυσί, κουφοτέραις τῶν πολεμίων
παρὰ πολύ· ᾧ δὴ καὶ μάλιστα προύλαβε τοῦ πελά-

---

22 P. Cornelius Scipio Africanus (consul 205, 194), victor in
the war against Hannibal, served as legate to his brother, L. Cor-

which the Roman legions would have to march on their way to Asia. He made Lysimachea his supply base for this 99 war, stockpiling arms and a large amount of grain in the belief that Rome would soon launch an attack against him with a large army and navy. The Romans choose Lucius 100 Scipio to succeed Manius in the command. He was consul at the time, but as he was not a man of action and had little experience of war, they appoint his brother Publius Scipio, who had destroyed Carthaginian dominance and was the first to receive the title "Africanus," as his legate.[22]

22. While the Scipios were still making their prepara- 101 tions, Livius was in charge of the coastal defense of Italy, having been appointed to succeed Atilius as commander of the fleet.[23] He immediately took his own ships, with which he patrolled the coasts of Italy, along with some given to him by the Carthaginians and other allied ships, and set sail for the Piraeus. Here he took over Atilius' fleet and put to sea with eighty-one decked ships, accompanied by Eumenes with fifty of his own, half of them decked. They landed at Phocaea, which, although it was one of 102 Antiochus' subjects, was frightened into receiving them, and sailed out next day for battle. Antiochus' admiral, 103 Polyxenidas, came out to oppose them with two hundred ships. These were much lighter than the enemy's vessels, which was a distinct advantage to Polyxenidas, as the Ro-

nelius Scipio Asiagenes (consul 190; his *cognomen* was later Latinized to "Asiaticus"), in the war against Antiochus.

[23] A. Atilius Serranus (praetor 192, 173, consul 170) commanded the fleet from 192 until he was succeeded by C. Livius Salinator (praetor 202, 191, consul 188) in 191.

104 γους ἔτι Ῥωμαίων ἀναπειρωμένων. καὶ δύο τῶν Καρχηδονίων ναῦς ἰδὼν προπλεούσας, τρεῖς τῶν ἰδίων
ἐπιπέμψας εἷλε τὰς δύο κενάς, ἐξαλομένων τῶν Λι-
105 βύων ἐς τὸ πέλαγος. Λίουιος δ' ἐπὶ τὰς τρεῖς ἐφέρετο
πρῶτος ὑπ' ὀργῆς τῇ στρατηγίδι νηί, πολὺ προύχων
τοῦ στόλου. αἱ δ', ὡς μιᾷ, σὺν καταφρονήσει <. . .>
χεῖράς τε σιδηρᾶς ἐπέβαλον, καὶ συνεστηκότων τῶν
106 σκαφῶν ὁ ἀγὼν ἦν ὥσπερ ἐν γῇ. πολὺ δὲ κρείσσους
ὄντες οἱ Ῥωμαῖοι ταῖς εὐτολμίαις, ἐπιβάντες ἐς τὰς
ἀλλοτρίας ἐκράτουν, καὶ μιᾷ νηὶ δύο ὁμοῦ φέροντες
107 ἐπανῆεσαν. καὶ τόδε μὲν τῆς ναυμαχίας προαγώ-
νισμα ἦν· ἐπεὶ δὲ οἱ στόλοι συνέπεσον ἀλλήλοις,
ἰσχύι μὲν καὶ προθυμίᾳ τὰ Ῥωμαίων ἐπεκράτει, διὰ
δὲ βαρύτητα τῶν σκαφῶν τοὺς ἐχθροὺς οὐκ ἐδύναντο
καταλαμβάνειν κούφαις ναυσὶν ὑποφεύγοντας, ἕως οἳ
μὲν ἐς τὴν Ἔφεσον ὀξέως κατέφυγον, οἳ δ' ἐς Χίον
ἀπῆραν, ἔνθα αὐτοῖς Ῥοδίων νῆες συμμαχίδες ἦλθον
108 ἑπτὰ καὶ εἴκοσιν. Ἀντίοχος δὲ περὶ τῆσδε τῆς ναυμαχίας πυθόμενος, Ἀννίβαν ἔστελλεν ἐπὶ Συρίας ἐς
νεῶν ἄλλων ἔκ τε Φοινίκης καὶ Κιλικίας παρασκευήν.
109 23. Καὶ τόνδε μὲν ἐπανιόντα Ῥόδιοι κατέκλεισαν
ἐς Παμφυλίαν, καί τινας αὐτοῦ τῶν νεῶν εἷλον, καὶ
τὰς λοιπὰς ἐφεδρεύοντες ἐφύλασσον· Πόπλιος δὲ Σκιπίων ἀφικόμενος ἐς Αἰτωλίαν μετὰ τοῦ ὑπάτου, καὶ
τὸν Μανίου στρατὸν παραλαβών, τὰς μὲν ἐν Αἰτωλίᾳ
πολιορκίας ὑπερεῖδεν ὡς μικρὸν ἔργον, καὶ τοῖς Αἰτωλοῖς δεομένοις ἐπέτρεψεν αὖθις ἐς Ῥώμην πρεσβεῦ-

mans were still inexperienced sailors. When he noticed   104
that two Carthaginian ships were sailing ahead of the others, he sent three of his own against them and captured
them, but without their crews, as the Africans jumped
overboard into the sea. Sailing far ahead of the rest of the   105
fleet, Livius in his anger was the first to bear down with
his flagship on Polyxenidas' three ships. Enjoying an advantage of three to one, these overconfidently ‹sailed to
the attack?›[24] and engaged Livius' ship with iron hooks.
But with the vessels now locked together, the fighting
turned into a sort of land battle. As the Romans were far   106
superior in courage, they boarded the enemy's ships and
took possession of them, returning with one ship towing
two behind it. This was a prelude to the main battle. When   107
the fleets engaged, Roman power and determination won
the day, but, because of the weight of their own galleys,
they were unable to capture the enemy, who escaped in
their lighter vessels. They eventually took refuge after a
swift passage in Ephesus, while the Romans sailed to
Chios, where they were joined by twenty-seven allied
ships from Rhodes. On learning of this battle, Antiochus   108
sent Hannibal to Syria to fit out new ships from Phoenicia
and Cilicia.

23. But on his return journey, the Rhodians cut him off   109
in Pamphylia, capturing some of his ships, and taking up
station to blockade the rest. Publius Scipio now arrived in
Aetolia with the consul and took over the army of Manius.
He did not bother to besiege the towns in Aetolia, regarding it as an inconsequential task, but granted their request
to send another mission to Rome concerning their situa-

[24] There is a probably short lacuna in the text at this point.

σαι περὶ σφῶν, ἐπὶ δὲ τὸν Ἀντίοχον ἠπείγετο πρὶν
110 ἐκβῆναι τῷ ἀδελφῷ τὴν στρατηγίαν. διὰ δὲ Μακεδόνων ᾤδευε καὶ Θρᾳκῶν ἐπὶ τὸν Ἑλλήσποντον, δυσχερῆ καὶ χαλεπὴν ὁδὸν αὐτῷ γενομένην ἄν, εἰ μὴ
Φίλιππος ὁ Μακεδὼν ὡδοποίει καὶ ὑπεδέχετο καὶ
παρέπεμπεν ἐζευγμένοις τε ποταμοῖς ἐκ πολλοῦ καὶ
ἀγοραῖς ἑτοίμοις· ἐφ' οἷς αὐτὸν οἱ Σκιπίωνες αὐτίκα
τῶν ὑπολοίπων χρημάτων ἀπέλυσαν, ἐπιτετραμμένοι
111 τοῦθ' ὑπὸ τῆς βουλῆς, εἰ πρόθυμον εὕροιεν. ἐπέστελλον δὲ καὶ ἐς Προυσίαν τὸν Βιθυνῶν βασιλέα, κα-
ταλέγοντες ὅσοις βασιλεῦσι Ῥωμαῖοι συμμαχήσασι
τὰς ἀρχὰς ἐπηύξησαν· Φίλιππον δέ, φασί, τὸν Μακεδόνα καὶ πολέμῳ κρατήσαντες ἄρχειν ἐῶσι, "Καὶ τὸν
παῖδα αὐτῷ τῆς ὁμηρείας ἀπελύσαμεν, καὶ τὸ ἔτι
ὄφλημα τῶν χρημάτων ⟨ἐξαλείφομεν⟩."[8] οἷς ὁ Προυσίας ἡσθεὶς συνέθετο συμμαχήσειν ἐπ' Ἀντίοχον.
112 Λίουιος δ' ὁ ναύαρχος ἐπεὶ τῆς ὁδοιπορίας τῶν Σκι-
πιώνων ἐπύθετο, Παυσίμαχον μὲν τὸν Ῥόδιον μετὰ
τῶν Ῥοδίων νεῶν ἐν τῇ Αἰολίδι κατέλιπε, καὶ μέρος
τι τοῦ ἰδίου στόλου, ταῖς δὲ πλείοσιν ἐς τὸν Ἑλλή-
113 σποντον ἔπλει τὸν στρατὸν ὑποδεξόμενος. καὶ Ση-
στὸς μὲν αὐτῷ καὶ Ῥοίτειον καὶ ὁ Ἀχαιῶν λιμὴν καὶ
τινα ἄλλα προσέθετο, Ἄβυδον δὲ ἀπειθοῦσαν ἐπολιόρκει.
114   24. Παυσίμαχος δ' οἰχομένου Λιουίου πείρας τε
πυκνὰς καὶ μελέτας τῶν ἰδίων ἐποιεῖτο, καὶ μηχανὰς
ποικίλας συνεπήγνυτο, πυρφόρα τε ἀγγεῖα σιδηρᾶ
ἐξῆπτε κοντῶν μακρῶν, αἰωρεῖσθαι τὸ πῦρ ἐς τὸ

tion, and then hurried against Antiochus before the period
of his brother's command expired. His journey took him   110
through Macedonia and Thrace to the Hellespont, on
what would have been a demanding and difficult route, if
Philip of Macedon had not repaired the roads, offered him
hospitality and given him an escort, having some time
before bridged the rivers and made provisions available.
In return for this the Scipios immediately canceled the
monies he still owed, the senate having given permission
for this, if they found Philip to be enthusiastic in the Roman cause. They also wrote to Prusias the king of Bithynia,   111
listing all the monarchs in alliance with Rome whose kingdoms Rome had enlarged. They pointed out, for example,
that although they had defeated Philip of Macedon in a
war, they still allow him to rule, "and we returned his son
to him from his detention as a hostage, and canceled his
outstanding debt." Prusias was impressed with this and
agreed to assist them as an ally against Antiochus. Livius,   112
the admiral, when he learned that the Scipios were on
their way, left Pausimachus of Rhodes in Aeolis with the
Rhodian ships and a part of his own force, and sailed with
most of his fleet to the Hellespont to be there for the army
when it arrived. Sestus, Rhoetium, the Harbor of the   113
Achaeans, and a few other places submitted to him, but
Abydus resisted and he besieged it.

24. On Livius' departure, Pausimachus set constant   114
challenges and exercises for his own men, and constructed
all sorts of war machines. For instance, he attached iron
vessels containing fire to long poles, so that the fire hung

---

8 ἐξαλείφομεν add. Goukowsky

APPIAN

πέλαγος, ἵνα τῶν μὲν ἰδίων σκαφῶν πολὺ προύχῃ,
115 τοῖς δὲ πολεμίοις προσιοῦσιν ἐμπίπτῃ. καὶ αὐτὸν
τάδε φιλοπονούμενον Πολυξενίδας ὁ Ἀντιόχου ναύαρχος, Ῥόδιός τε ὢν καὶ ὅδε καί τισιν αἰτίαις ἐκπεσὼν
τῆς πατρίδος, ἐνήδρευεν, ὑπισχνούμενος τὸν Ἀντιόχου στόλον ἐγχειριεῖν, εἰ συνθοῖτο συμπράξειν ἐς
116 κάθοδον αὐτῷ. ὁ δὲ ὑπώπτευε μὲν ἐπίκλοπον ἄνδρα
καὶ πανοῦργον, καὶ ἐς πολὺ καλῶς ἐφυλάσσετο· γρά-
ψαντος δ᾽ αὐτῷ τοῦ Πολυξενίδου περὶ τῆς προδοσίας
ἐπιστολὴν αὐτόγραφον, καὶ ἐπ᾽ αὐτῇ καὶ ἀναζεύξαντος ἀπὸ τῆς Ἐφέσου, καὶ τὴν στρατιὰν ὑποκριθέντος
ἐς χορτολογίαν περιπέμπειν, ὁ Παυσίμαχος τήν τε
ἀνάζευξιν ὁρῶν, καὶ οὐκ ἐλπίσας ἄν τινα περὶ προδοσίας ἐπιστολὴν αὐτόγραφον οὐκ ἀληθεύοντα πέμψαι,
πάγχυ πιστεύσας ἐξέλυσε τὰς φυλακὰς καὶ ἐς σιτο-
117 λογίαν καὶ αὐτὸς περιέπεμπεν. ὁ δὲ Πολυξενίδας ἐπεὶ
κατεῖδεν αὐτὸν ἐνηδρευμένον, αὐτίκα τὴν παρασκευὴν
συνῆγε, καὶ Νίκανδρον τὸν πειρατὴν σὺν ὀλίγοις ἐς
τὴν Σάμον περιέπεμπε, κατὰ τὴν γῆν ὄπισθεν τοῦ
118 Παυσιμάχου θορυβοποιεῖν. ἐκ δὲ μέσων νυκτῶν αὐτὸς
ἐπέπλει, καὶ περὶ τὴν ἑωθινὴν φυλακὴν ἐπέπιπτεν ἔτι
κοιμωμένῳ. ὁ δὲ ἐν αἰφνιδίῳ κακῷ καὶ ἀδοκήτῳ τοὺς
στρατιώτας ἐκέλευε, τὰς ναῦς ἐκλιπόντας, ἀπὸ τῆς
119 γῆς ἀμύνεσθαι τοὺς πολεμίους. προσπεσόντος δ᾽ ὄπισθεν αὐτῷ τοῦ Νικάνδρου, νομίσας καὶ τὴν γῆν προ-
ειλῆφθαι οὐχ ὑπὸ τῶν ἑωραμένων μόνων ἀλλ᾽, ὡς ἐν
νυκτί, πολὺ πλειόνων, πάλιν ἐς τὰς ναῦς ἐνέβαινε
θορυβούμενος, πρῶτός τε ἐς μάχην ἀνήγετο, καὶ

48

over the water well away from his own ships and ready to
be dropped on the enemy ships as they approached. While   115
Pausimachus was working hard on these things, Antiochus' admiral, Polyxenidas, developed a plan to trick him.
Like Pausimachus, Polyxenidas was also from Rhodes, but
as a result of certain charges against him was an exile from
the city. He promised to hand over Antiochus' fleet to him,
if Pausimachus agreed to help him to win recall to Rhodes.
Pausimachus distrusted such a devious and cunning man,   116
and for a long time was sensibly wary of him. But when
Polyxenidas wrote him a signed letter concerning the betrayal, and in addition withdrew from Ephesus, and pretended to send his army off on a foraging expedition,
Pausimachus noted the withdrawal, and, in the belief that
no one would actually sign a letter about an act of betrayal
unless he was telling the truth, he gave him his complete
trust, dropped his guard and sent his own troops off
to forage for supplies. Polyxenidas realized that he had   117
caught him in his trap, and immediately collected his army
and dispatched the pirate Nicander to Samos with a small
force to cause a disturbance on land in Pausimachus' rear.
He himself sailed in the middle of the night, and around   118
the dawn watch attacked Pausimachus while his army still
slept. In response to this sudden and unexpected crisis,
the latter ordered his soldiers to leave their ships and defend themselves against the enemy on land. But when   119
Nicander fell on them from the rear, Pausimachus believed, as happens in the dark, that the land position had
been occupied not just by the forces he could see, but by
a far larger contingent. So, in a state of confusion, he embarked on the ships again, and was both the first into

49

120 πρῶτος ἔπιπτε λαμπρῶς ἀγωνιζόμενος. τῶν δ᾽ ἄλλων
οἱ μὲν ἐλήφθησαν οἱ δ᾽ ἀπώλοντο. καὶ τῶν νεῶν ἑπτὰ
μέν αἳ τὸ πῦρ ἔφερον, οὐδενὸς αὐταῖς διὰ τὴν φλόγα
προσιόντος ἔφυγον, τὰς δὲ λοιπὰς εἴκοσιν ὁ Πολυξενίδας ἀναδησάμενος ἐς τὴν Ἔφεσον κατήχθη.

121 25. Καὶ ἐπὶ τῇδε τῇ νίκῃ Φώκαια αὖθις καὶ Σάμος
καὶ Κύμη πρὸς Ἀντίοχον μετετίθεντο. δείσας δ᾽ ὁ
Λίουιος περὶ τῶν σφετέρων νεῶν, ἃς ἐν τῇ Αἰολίδι
κατελελοίπει, κατὰ σπουδὴν ἐς αὐτὰς ἐπανῄει. καὶ
Εὐμένης πρὸς αὐτὸν ἠπείγετο, Ῥόδιοί τε Ῥωμαίοις
122 ναῦς ἑτέρας εἴκοσιν ἔπεμπον. μικρὸν δὲ διαλιπόντες
ἅπαντες ἀνεθάρρησαν, καὶ ἐπὶ τὴν Ἔφεσον ἔπλεον ἐς
ναυμαχίαν ἐσκευασμένοι. οὐδενὸς δ᾽ αὐτοῖς ἀντεπι-
πλέοντος, τὸ μὲν ἥμισυ τῶν νεῶν ἐς ἐπίδειξιν ἔστη-
σαν ἐν μέσῃ τῇ θαλάσσῃ μέχρι πολλοῦ, ταῖς δ᾽
ὑπολοίποις ἐς γῆν πολεμίαν καταχθέντες <. . .>[9] ἐπολιόρκουν,[10] μέχρι Νίκανδρος αὐτοῖς ἐκ τῆς μεσογείας
ἐπιπεσὼν τήν τε λείαν ἀφείλετο καὶ ἐς τὰς ναῦς
κατεδίωξεν.

123 26. Οἱ μὲν δὴ πάλιν ἐς Σάμον ἀνήγοντο, καὶ ὁ
χρόνος ἔληγε Λιουίῳ τῆς ναυαρχίας· τοῦ δ᾽ αὐτοῦ
χρόνου Σέλευκος ὁ Ἀντιόχου τὴν Εὐμένους γῆν ἐδῄου
καὶ Περγάμῳ παρεκάθητο, τοὺς ἄνδρας ἐς τὴν πόλιν
124 κατακλείσας. ὅθεν ὁ Εὐμένης ἐς Ἐλαίαν, τὸ τῆς ἀρχῆς ἐπίνειον, διέπλει κατὰ σπουδήν, καὶ σὺν αὐτῷ

[9] Post καταχθέντες lacunam indicat Goukowsky
[10] ἐπολιόρκουν codd: ἐπόρθουν prop. Schweig.

50

battle and the first to fall, fighting heroically. The rest were   120
either captured or killed. Of his fleet, the seven ships that
carried the fire mechanism escaped, since no one would
approach them for fear of the flames, and Polyxenidas
roped together the remaining twenty and towed them to
Ephesus.

25. After this victory, Phocaea again changed alle-   121
giance back to Antiochus' side, along with Samos and
Cyme too. Livius was afraid for his own ships that he had
left in Aeolis, and rushed back to them. Eumenes hurried
to join him and Rhodes sent another twenty-five ships to
the Romans. In no time at all they had all regained their   122
confidence, and sailed to Ephesus ready for battle. But
since no one came out to face them, they stationed half
their fleet in a long line on the open sea for show, and with
the remainder made descents on enemy territory ⟨. . .⟩
and besieged it.[25] Eventually, Nicander attacked from inland, robbed them of their plunder and chased them back
to their ships.[26]

26. They set sail again to Samos, and Livius' term as   123
commander of the fleet came to an end. Around the same
time, Seleucus, Antiochus' son, ravaged Eumenes' territory and took up position outside Pergamum, shutting its
troops up in the city. Because of this, Eumenes sailed   124
quickly to Elaea, the main naval base of his kingdom, ac-

[25] The text is uncertain at this point, and there may be a lacuna.

[26] Livy (37.13.9–10) talks of the garrison commander of Ephesus, Andronicus, at this point, not Nicander. Appian has just (*Syr.*
24.117) mentioned a pirate called Nicander and may have confused the names.

Λεύκιος Αἰμίλιος Ῥηγίλλος ὁ Λιουίου τὴν ναυαρχίαν
125 παραδεδεγμένος. ἧκον δὲ καὶ παρὰ τῶν Ἀχαιῶν Εὐμένει σύμμαχοι χίλιοι πεζοὶ καὶ ἱππεῖς ἑκατὸν ἐπί-
λεκτοι, ὧν Διοφάνης ὁ στρατηγὸς ἀπὸ τοῦ τείχους
ἰδὼν τοὺς Σελευκείους παίζοντάς τε καὶ μεθύοντας
ἐκ καταφρονήσεως, ἔπειθε τοὺς Περγαμηνοὺς ἑαυτῷ
126 συνεκδραμεῖν ἐπὶ τοὺς πολεμίους. οὐχ ὑφισταμένων
δ' ἐκείνων, ὥπλισε τοὺς ἰδίους χιλίους καὶ τοὺς ἑκατὸν ἱππέας. καὶ προαγαγὼν ὑπὸ τὸ τεῖχος ἔστησεν
ἀτρεμεῖν, ὑπερορώντων αὐτοὺς ἐς πολὺ τῶν πολεμίων
127 ὡς ὀλίγους τε καὶ οὐ τολμῶντας ἐς χεῖρας ἐλθεῖν. ὁ
δ' ἀριστοποιουμένοις ἐπιδραμὼν ἐθορύβησέ τε καὶ
ἐτρέψατο τοὺς προφύλακας, τῶν δ' ἄλλων ἐπὶ τὰ
ὅπλα ἀναπηδώντων, καὶ τοὺς ἵππους περιχαλινούν-
των ἢ φεύγοντας διωκόντων ἢ δυσχερῶς ἀναβαινόν-
των οὐκ εὐσταθοῦντας, ἐκράτει πάνυ λαμπρῶς, ἐπι-
βοώντων ἄνωθεν ἀπὸ τοῦ τείχους τῶν Περγαμηνῶν,
128 καὶ οὐδὲ τότε προελθεῖν ὑφισταμένων. κτείνας δ'
ὅσους ἐδύνατο ὡς ἐν ἐπιδείξει ταχείᾳ, καί τινας αἰχμαλώτους ἑλὼν ἄνδρας τε καὶ ἵππους, ἐπανῄει κατὰ
129 σπουδήν. καὶ τῆς ἐπιούσης αὖθις ἵστη τοὺς Ἀχαιοὺς
ὑπὸ τὸ τεῖχος, οὐδὲ τότε τῶν Περγαμηνῶν αὐτῷ συν-
εξιόντων. Σέλευκος δ' ἱππεῦσι πολλοῖς αὐτῷ προσ-
130 επέλαζε προκαλούμενος. ὁ δὲ τότε μὲν οὐκ ἐπεξῄει,
παρ' αὐτὸ τὸ τεῖχος ἑστώς, ἀλλ' ἐφυλάσσετο· ἐπεὶ δ'
ὁ Σέλευκος παραμείνας ἐς μεσημβρίαν, καμνόντων οἱ

companied by Lucius Aemilius Regillus, Livius' successor
as commander of the fleet.[27] One thousand allied infantry   125
and one hundred select cavalrymen also arrived from the
Achaeans in support of Eumenes. Looking out from the
walls of Pergamum, their commander, Diophanes, saw
that Seleucus' men were showing their contempt by drinking and having fun, and he tried to persuade the Pergamenes to join him in making a sortie against the enemy.
As they refused, he armed his own thousand men and   126
hundred cavalry, and led them out under the city walls,
where he made them hold position. The enemy ignored
them for a long time, as being such a small force and one
that was not showing the confidence to join battle. But   127
Diophanes attacked while they were eating their meal,
caused consternation in their pickets and put them to
flight, and won a most brilliant victory over the others as
they ran for their weapons, tried to bridle their horses or
catch those that had bolted, and had difficulty in mounting
them when they would not stand still. The Pergamenes
cheered them on from high up on the walls, but still refused to venture forth from the city. Having killed as many   128
as he could in such a short exhibition of fighting, Diophanes hurried back with some prisoners he had taken and
their horses. Next day he again stationed the Achaeans   129
under the walls, but the Pergamenes would still not leave
the city with him. When Seleucus challenged him to battle
by approaching with a large force of cavalry, he did not   130
advance at that stage, but stood right by the walls and
waited for his opportunity. Seleucus stayed until midday

[27] L. Aemilius Regillus was praetor and commander of the
fleet in 190.

ἤδη τῶν ἱππέων ἐπέστρεφε καὶ ἐπανῄει, τοῖς τελευ-
ταίοις αὐτοῦ ὁ Διοφάνης ἐπιθέμενος καὶ θορυβοποιή-
σας, καὶ βλάψας ὅσα καὶ τότε δυνατὸς ἦν, εὐθὺς
131 ἐπανῄει πάλιν ὑπὸ τὸ τεῖχος. καὶ τόνδε τὸν τρόπον
συνεχῶς ἔν τε χορτολογίαις καὶ ξυλείαις ἐνεδρεύων
καὶ ἀεί τι καὶ ἐνοχλῶν ἀπό τε Περγάμου τὸν Σέλευκον
ἀνέστησε καὶ ἀπὸ τῆς ἄλλης Εὐμένους χώρας ἐξήλασεν.

132   27. Πολυξενίδᾳ δὲ καὶ Ῥωμαίοις μετ᾽ οὐ πολὺ γίγνεται ναυμαχία περὶ Μυόννησον, ἐς ἣν συνῄεσαν
Πολυξενίδας μὲν ναυσὶν ἐνενήκοντα καταφράκτοις,
Λεύκιος δ᾽ ὁ Ῥωμαίων ναύαρχος ὀγδοήκοντα τρισί·
133 καὶ τούτων ἦσαν ἐκ Ῥόδου πέντε καὶ εἴκοσιν. ὧν ὁ
στρατηγὸς Εὔδωρος ἐτέτακτο μὲν ἐπὶ τοῦ λαιοῦ
κέρως, ἰδὼν δὲ ἐπὶ θάτερα Πολυξενίδαν πολὺ πρού-
χοντα Ῥωμαίων, ἔδεισέ τε μὴ κυκλωθεῖεν, καὶ περιπλεύσας ὀξέως ἅτε κούφαις ναυσὶ καὶ ἐρέταις ἐμ-
πείροις θαλάσσης, τὰς ναῦς τὰς πυρφόρους τῷ
Πολυξενίδᾳ πρώτας ἐπῆγε, λαμπομένας τῷ πυρὶ πάν-
134 τοθεν. οἱ δ᾽ ἐμβαλεῖν μὲν αὐταῖς οὐκ ἐτόλμων διὰ τὸ
πῦρ, κύκλῳ δ᾽ αὐτὰς περιπλέοντες ἐνέκλινόν τε καὶ
θαλάσσης ἐπίμπλαντο καὶ ἐς τὰς ἐπωτίδας ἐτύπτοντο,
μέχρι Ῥοδίας νεὼς ἐς Σιδονίαν ἐμβαλούσης, καὶ τῆς
πληγῆς εὐτόνου γενομένης, ἄγκυρα ἐκπίπτουσα τῆς
Σιδονίας ἐς τὴν Ῥοδίαν ἐπάγη τε καὶ συνέδησεν
ἄμφω πρὸς ἀλλήλας, ὅθεν ἦν ὁ ἀγὼν ἀτρεμούντων
135 τῶν σκαφῶν τοῖς ἐπιβάταις ὥσπερ ἐν γῇ. καὶ προσ-
ιουσῶν ἄλλων ἐς ἐπικουρίαν ἑκατέρᾳ πολλῶν, φιλο-

before turning round and leading his now tired cavalrymen back. It was then that Diophanes attacked his rear
and threw it into confusion, inflicting as much damage as
he could at the time, and immediately retreating under
the walls. By continually obstructing foraging and wood-   131
collecting expeditions in this way, and constantly causing
them some trouble, Diophanes forced Seleucus to move
away from Pergamum, and indeed drove him out from the
rest of Eumenes' territory altogether.

27. A little later, Polyxenidas and the Romans fought a   132
sea battle near Myonessus, Polyxenidas bringing a fleet of
ninety decked ships, and Lucius, the Roman commander,
eighty-three, of which twenty-five came from Rhodes. Al-   133
though Eudorus, the Rhodian commander, was drawn up
on the left wing, he saw Polyxenidas on the other wing
extend his line far beyond the Roman ships, and, fearing
that they would be surrounded, he quickly sailed around,
taking advantage of his fast ships and rowers, who were
experienced seamen. He first sent in the fireships against
Polyxenidas, shooting flames from all parts. The enemy   134
did not dare to attack because of the flames, but sailing
around them in circles, began to list and take on water, and
waves kept crashing against the catheads. Eventually a
Rhodian ship rammed a Sidonian and the impact was so
severe that the anchor of the Sidonian fell onto the Rhodian ship, lodging there and locking the ships together. As
neither of them could move, the contest turned into a sort
of land battle for the crews. Many other ships came to   135

νεικία τε παρ' ἀμφοῖν ἐγίγνετο λαμπρά, καὶ τὸ μέσον
τῶν Ἀντιόχου νεῶν ἔρημον ἐκ τούτου γενόμενον αἱ
Ῥωμαίων νῆες διέπλεον, καὶ τοὺς πολεμίους ἔτι ἀγνο-
136 *οῦντας ἐκύκλουν. ὡς δ' ἔμαθόν ποτε, ἐγίγνετο φυγὴ*
καὶ τροπή, καὶ διεφθάρησαν Ἀντιόχου νῆες μιᾶς δέ-
ουσαι τριάκοντα, ὧν τρισκαίδεκα αὐτοῖς ἀνδράσιν
ἐλήφθησαν. Ῥωμαίων δ' ἀπώλοντο μόναι δύο. καὶ ὁ
Πολυξενίδας τὴν Ῥοδίαν ναῦν ἐπαγόμενος ἐς τὴν
Ἔφεσον κατήχθη.

137 28. Τοῦτο μὲν δὴ τῇ ναυμαχίᾳ τῇ περὶ τὴν Μυόννησον ἦν τέλος· οὔπω δ' αὐτῆς ὁ Ἀντίοχος αἰσθόμενος Χερρόνησόν τε καὶ Λυσιμάχειαν ἐπιμελῶς
ὠχύρου, μέγα, ὥσπερ ἦν, τὸ ἔργον ἡγούμενος ἐπὶ
Ῥωμαίοις, ὅπου γε καὶ τὴν ἄλλην Θρᾴκην διελθεῖν
στρατοπέδῳ δυσόδευτον αὐτοῖς ἂν ἐγένετο καὶ δύσ-
138 βατον, εἰ μὴ Φίλιππος διέφερεν. ἀλλ' ὁ Ἀντίοχος ὢν
καὶ τὰ ἄλλα κουφόνους ἀεὶ καὶ ταχὺς ἐς μεταβολήν,
ἐπεὶ τῆς ἥσσης ἐπύθετο τῆς περὶ τὴν Μυόννησον,
πάμπαν ἐξεπλάγη, νομίσας αὑτῷ τι δαιμόνιον ἐπι-
βουλεύειν· παρὰ γὰρ λόγον ἕκαστα χωρεῖν, Ῥωμαίων
μὲν ἐν τῇ θαλάσσῃ κρατούντων, ἐν ᾗ πολὺ προύχειν
αὐτὸς ἐνόμιζε, Ῥοδίων δ' Ἀννίβαν ἐς Παμφυλίαν
κατακεκλεικότων, Φιλίππου δὲ Ῥωμαίους παραπέμ-
ποντος ἀβάτους ὁδούς, ὃν μάλιστα μνησικακήσειν
139 αὐτοῖς ὢν ἔπαθεν ὑπελάμβανεν. ὑπὸ δὴ τῶνδε πάντων
ἐκταρασσόμενός τε, καὶ θεοῦ βλάπτοντος ἤδη τοὺς
λογισμούς, ὅπερ ἅπασι προσιόντων ἀτυχημάτων ἐπιγίγνεται, Χερρόνησον ἐξέλιπεν ἀλογίστως, πρὶν καὶ

assist each of them, and the rivalry on both sides was magnificent. This engagement left a gap in the middle of Antiochus' line, through which the Roman ships sailed and surrounded the enemy before they knew it. Once they 136 realized what had happened, they turned and fled. Antiochus lost twenty-nine of his ships, thirteen of them captured, crews and all. The Romans lost only two. Polyxenidas took possession of the Rhodian ship and put in at Ephesus.

28. Such was the result of the sea battle at Myonessus. 137 Before he became aware of it, Antiochus was busily engaged in fortifying Chersonesus and Lysimachea, rightly regarding the task as an important action in his defense against the Romans, seeing that even the road across the rest of Thrace was hardly passable for an army, and they would not have managed to get through, if Philip had not guided them. As a general rule, Antiochus was flighty and 138 quick to change his mind, but at the news of his defeat at Myonessus, he went into a state of complete shock, and thought that there was some divinity plotting against him. Everything was going against plan: the Romans had won a victory at sea, where he believed he had considerable superiority; the Rhodians had confined Hannibal in Pamphylia; Philip was escorting the Romans over impassable roads, when Antiochus assumed he would be particularly ill-disposed to them for what he had suffered at their hands. He was deeply distressed by all this, and with a god 139 now impairing his judgment, as happens to everyone when adversity affects them, he abandoned Chersonesus for no

APPIAN

ἐς ὄψιν ἐλθεῖν τοῖς πολεμίοις, οὔτε μετενεγκὼν ὅσος
ἦν ἐν αὐτῇ σῖτος σεσωρευμένος πολὺς ἢ ὅπλα ἢ
χρήματα ἢ μηχανή, οὔτε ἐμπρήσας, ἀλλ' ὑγιεῖς
140 ἀφορμὰς τοσάσδε τοῖς πολεμίοις καταλιπών. Λυσιμαχέας τε αὐτῷ καθάπερ ἐκ πολιορκίας συμφεύγον-
τας μετ' οἰμωγῆς, ἅμα γυναιξὶ καὶ παιδίοις, ὑπε-
ρεώρα, μόνου τοῦ διάπλου τοῦ περὶ Ἄβυδον εἶρξαι
τοὺς πολεμίους ἐπινοῶν, καὶ τὴν λοιπὴν ἔτι ἐλπίδα
141 τοῦ πολέμου πᾶσαν ἐν τούτῳ τιθέμενος. οὐ μὴν οὔτε
τὸν διάπλουν ἐφύλαξεν ὑπὸ θεοβλαβείας, ἀλλ' ἐς τὸ
μεσόγειον ἠπείχθη ἐπανελθεῖν, φθάνων τοὺς πολεμίους, οὔτε τινα φυλακὴν ἐν τῷ διάπλῳ κατέλιπεν.
142   29. Οἱ δὲ Σκιπίωνες ἐπεὶ τῆς ἀναχωρήσεως αὐτοῦ
ἐπύθοντο, Λυσιμάχειάν τε δρόμῳ κατέλαβον, καὶ τῶν
ἐν Χερρονήσῳ θησαυρῶν τε καὶ ὅπλων κρατήσαντες
τὸν Ἑλλήσποντον ἔρημον ὄντα φυλακῆς εὐθὺς ἐπέρων
μετὰ σπουδῆς, ἔφθασάν τε Ἀντίοχον ἔτι ἀγνοοῦντα
143 ἐν Σάρδεσι γενόμενοι. ὁ δ' ἐκπλαγεὶς ἐβαρυθύμει, καὶ
τὰ ἴδια αὐτοῦ ἁμαρτήματα ἐς τὸ δαιμόνιον ἀνατιθεὶς
Ἡρακλείδην τὸν Βυζάντιον ἔπεμπεν ἐς τοὺς Σκιπίωνας ἐπὶ διαλύσεσι τοῦ πολέμου, Σμύρναν τε καὶ
Ἀλεξάνδρειαν αὐτοῖς διδοὺς τὴν ἐπὶ Γρανίκῳ καὶ
Λάμψακον, δι' ἃς ἦρξεν αὐτοῖς ὁ πόλεμος, καὶ τὸ
144 ἥμισυ τῆς δαπάνης τοῦδε τοῦ πολέμου. ἐνετέλλετο δέ,
εἰ δέοι, καὶ τῶν Ἰάδων πόλεων δοῦναι καὶ τῶν Αἰολίδων ὅσαι τὰ Ῥωμαίων ἐν τῷδε τῷ ἀγῶνι εἵλοντο, καὶ
145 εἴ τι ἄλλο αἰτοῖεν οἱ Σκιπίωνες. ταῦτα μὲν εἶχεν ἐς τὸ
φανερὸν λέγειν ὁ Ἡρακλείδης, ἰδίᾳ δὲ πρὸς Πόπλιον

58

reason, even before the enemy came into sight, and failed
to take with him or burn the large supply of grain he had
stockpiled there, or the arms, money, and artillery, but left
all these substantial resources there in perfect condition
for the enemy. He ignored the people of Lysimachea, who   140
followed him in his flight with their wives and children,
weeping as if their city had been captured after a siege,
and concentrated solely on preventing the enemy from
crossing at Abydus, placing all his remaining hopes for
winning the war on this. But he was so deranged that he   141
did not defend the crossing, failing even to leave a guard
there, but hurried to reach the interior before the enemy.

29. When the Scipios heard of his retreat, they cap-   142
tured Lysimachea at a sprint, took possession of the gra-
naries and weapons in Chersonesus and immediately
made a swift crossing of the Hellespont, unguarded as it
was, arriving in Sardis before Antiochus and while he was
still unaware of them. Shocked and despondent, and   143
blaming his own faults on the gods, Antiochus now sent
Heracleides of Byzantium to the Scipios to bring about a
cessation of hostilities. He agreed to surrender Smyrna,
Alexandria on the Granicus, and Lampsacus, the cities
which had caused the war in the first place, and to pay half
the costs of the war. Heracleides was also instructed to   144
give up, if necessary, the Ionian and Aeolian towns that
had sided with Rome during this conflict, and agree to
anything else the Scipios demanded. This was what he was   145
to say publicly. In private, he was to promise Publius

Σκιπίωνα ἔφερε παρ' Ἀντιόχου χρημάτων τε πολλῶν
146 ὑποσχέσεις καὶ τοῦ παιδὸς ἀφέσεις. ἡρήκει γὰρ
αὐτὸν ἐν τῇ Ἑλλάδι ὁ Ἀντίοχος, ἐς Δηματριάδα ἐκ
Χαλκίδος διαπλέοντα· καὶ ἦν ὁ παῖς Σκιπίων ὁ Καρχηδόνα ὕστερον ἑλών τε καὶ κατασκάψας, καὶ δεύτερος ἐπὶ τῷδε τῷ Σκιπίωνι Ἀφρικανὸς ὀνομασθείς,
Παύλου μὲν υἱὸς ἦν τοῦ Περσέα τὸν Μακεδόνα ἑλόντος, Σκιπίωνος δὲ τῷ γένει θυγατριδοῦς καὶ θέσει
147 παῖς. κοινῇ μὲν οὖν οἱ Σκιπίωνες τῷ Ἡρακλείδῃ τήνδε
ἔδοσαν τὴν ἀπόκρισιν, ἐὰν ὁ Ἀντίοχος εἰρήνης δέη-
ται, μὴ τῶν Ἰάδων μηδὲ τῶν Αἰολίδων αὐτὸν ἐκστῆναι πόλεων, ἀλλὰ πάσης τῆς ἐπὶ τάδε Ταύρου, καὶ
τὴν δαπάνην τοῦ πολέμου πᾶσαν ἐσενεγκεῖν, δι' αὐ-
148 τὸν γενομένου. ἰδίᾳ δὲ ὁ Πόπλιος ἔφη τῷ Ἡρακλείδῃ
Ῥωμαίους, εἰ μὲν ἔτι Χερρονήσου καὶ Λυσιμαχείας
κρατῶν ὁ Ἀντίοχος ταῦτα προύτεινεν, ἀσμένως ἂν
λαβεῖν· τάχα δ' εἰ καὶ μόνον ἔτι τοῦ Ἑλλησπόντου
τὸν διάπλουν ἐφύλασσε· νῦν δ' αὐτοὺς ἤδη περάσαν-
τάς τε καὶ ἐν ἀσφαλεῖ γενομένους, καὶ τὸν χαλινόν,
φασίν, ἐνθέντας, καὶ ἐπὶ τῷ χαλινῷ τὸν ἵππον ἀνα-
149 βάντας, οὐκ ἀνέξεσθαι διαλύσεων ἐπ' ὀλίγοις. αὐτὸς
δὲ χάριν εἰδέναι τῷ βασιλεῖ τῆς προαιρέσεως, καὶ
μᾶλλον εἴσεσθαι λαβὼν τὸν υἱόν· ἀμείβεσθαι δ' αὐ-

---

28 Appian is wrong here: the son of Scipio Africanus (Hannibal's conqueror) captured by Antiochus was not the famous P.
Cornelius Scipio Aemilianus, who destroyed Carthage in 146, but

Scipio a large sum of money from Antiochus and the re-
turn of his son. For Antiochus had taken him prisoner in   146
Greece while the young man was sailing from Demetrias
to Chalcis. This son was the Scipio who later captured and
destroyed Carthage, and was the second after the present
Scipio to have the title "Africanus." He was the son of the
Paullus who defeated Perseus of Macedon, and was grandson of Scipio by birth and his son by adoption.[28] The   147
Scipios issued a joint reply to Heracleides as follows. If
Antiochus wanted peace, he would have to evacuate not
just the towns of Ionia and Aeolia, but all territory this side
of the Taurus, and pay the whole cost of the war, which
came about because of him.[29] In private, Publius told   148
Heracleides that if Antiochus had made this offer while
still master of Chersonesus and Lysimachea, or perhaps
even if he was still only guarding the Hellespont crossing,
the Romans would happily have accepted. But now that
they were safely across and had, so to speak, not just bri-
dled the horse but mounted him too, they would not agree
to peace on lenient terms. Personally, he was grateful to   149
the king for his offer, and would be even more so when he
got his son back. But by way of repayment, his advice was

L. Scipio Africanus—the younger son of Scipio Africanus. Scipio
Aemilianus was not a blood relative of Africanus, but he was his
grandson by adoption: Aemilianus was, as Appian says, the son of
L. Aemilius Paullus, but he was adopted by Africanus' eldest son,
P. Cornelius Scipio.

[29] The Taurus mountains stretch from southwest Turkey to
the headwaters of the Euphrates. This condition meant effec-
tively that Antiochus was excluded from the whole of Turkey.

APPIAN

τὸν ἤδη, καὶ συμβουλεύειν δέχεσθαι τὰ προτεινόμενα
πρὶν ἐς πεῖραν ἐλθεῖν μειζόνων ἐπιταγμάτων.

150   30. Ὁ μὲν δὴ Πόπλιος ταῦτα εἰπὼν ἐς Ἐλαίαν
νοσηλευόμενος ὑπεχώρει, σύμβουλον τῷ ἀδελφῷ
Γναῖον Δομίτιον καταλιπών· ὁ δ' Ἀντίοχος, οἷόν τι καὶ
Φίλιππος ὁ Μακέδων, οἰηθεὶς τῶνδε τῶν ἐπιταγμάτων
πλέον οὐδὲν αὑτοῦ τὸν πόλεμον ἀφαιρήσεσθαι, συν-
έτασσε τὴν στρατίαν περὶ τὸν πεδίον τὸ Θυατείρων,
οὐ μακρὰν ἀπὸ τῶν πολεμίων, καὶ Σκιπίωνι τὸν υἱὸν
151   ἀπέπεμπεν ἐς Ἐλαίαν. ὁ δὲ τοῖς ἄγουσι συνεβούλευε
μὴ μάχεσθαι τὸν Ἀντίοχον ἕως αὐτὸς ἐπανέλθοι. καὶ
τῷδε πεισθεὶς ὁ Ἀντίοχος μετεστρατοπέδευεν ἀμφὶ τὸ
ὄρος τὸ Σίπυλον, τεῖχός τε καρτερὸν τῷ στρατοπέδῳ
περιετείχιζε, καὶ τὸν Φρύγιον ποταμὸν ἐν προβολῇ
τοῖς πολεμίοις ἐτίθετο, ἵνα μηδ' ἄκων ἀναγκάζοιτο
152   πολεμεῖν. Δομίτιος δὲ φιλοτιμούμενος τὸν πόλεμον
ἐφ' ἑαυτοῦ κριθῆναι, τὸν ποταμὸν ἐπέρα μάλα θρα-
σέως, καὶ σταδίους εἴκοσιν ἀπ' Ἀντιόχου διασχὼν
153   ἐστρατοπέδευσεν. τέσσαρσί τε ἡμέραις ἐφεξῆς ἐξ-
έτασσον ἑκάτεροι παρὰ τὸν χάρακα τὸν ἑαυτῶν, καὶ
154   μάχης οὐ κατῆρχον. τῇ πέμπτῃ δὲ ὁ Δομίτιος ἐξέτασ-
155   σεν αὖθις καὶ ἐπέβαινε σοβαρῶς. οὐκ ἀντεπιόντος δὲ
τοῦ Ἀντιόχου, τότε μὲν ἐγγυτέρω μετεστρατοπέδευσε,
μίαν δὲ ἄλλην διαλιπὼν ἐκήρυσσεν ἐς ἐπήκοον τῶν
πολεμίων ἐς αὔριον Ἀντιόχῳ καὶ ἄκοντι πολεμήσειν.
156   ὁ δὲ συνταραχθεὶς αὖθις μεθίει τὰ δόξαντα, καὶ δυνηθεὶς ἂν ἑστάναι μόνον ὑπὸ τὸ τεῖχος ἢ καλῶς αὐτὸν
ἀπὸ τοῦ τείχους ἀπομάχεσθαι μέχρι ῥαΐσειεν ὁ Πό-

to accept what was on offer before having to face more severe demands.

30. That is what Publius said. Afterward, he fell sick 150 and withdrew to Elaea, leaving Gnaeus Domitius as his brother's advisor.[30] Antiochus, like Philip of Macedon, thinking that he would lose nothing more by fighting than these demands already imposed, drew up his army in the plain of Thyateira not far from the enemy, and delivered Scipio's son to him at Elaea. To the escort that had brought 151 his son, Scipio proposed that Antiochus would not join battle until he himself had returned from Elaea. Antiochus agreed to this and moved his camp to Mount Sipylus. He built a strong wall around it as protection, positioning the river Phrygius between himself and the enemy, so that he would not be forced into battle against his will. But 152 Domitius, who was ambitious to decide the war all on his own, crossed the river with great self-assurance, and camped twenty stades from Antiochus. For four consecu- 153 tive days both sides took up battle formation beside their own palisade, but did not initiate combat. On the fifth day, 154 Domitius again arrayed for battle and advanced aggres- sively, but Antiochus failed to come out to meet him, and 155 Domitius moved his camp closer. After a day's interval, he made a proclamation within hearing distance of the enemy that he would fight Antiochus next day, even if the king did not want to. Confused by this, Antiochus again changed 156 his mind: although fully capable of simply taking up posi- tion by the wall and comfortably defending it against the enemy until Publius recovered from his illness, he now

[30] C. Domitius Ahenobarbus (consul 192).

πλιος, αἰσχρὸν ἡγεῖτο μετὰ πλειόνων φυγομαχεῖν·
ὅθεν ἐς μάχην παρέτασσεν.

157   31. Καὶ ἐξῆγον ἔτι νυκτὸς ἄμφω περὶ ἐσχάτην
φυλακήν, διεκόσμει δ' αὐτῶν ἑκάτερος ὧδε. τὸ μὲν
λαιὸν εἶχον ὁπλῖται Ῥωμαίων μύριοι, παρὰ τὸν ποταμὸν αὐτόν· καὶ μετ' ἐκείνους ἦσαν Ἰταλῶν ἕτεροι
μύριοι, τρεῖς ἑκατέρων <τάξεις>[11] ἐπὶ βάθος. ἐπὶ δὲ
τοῖς Ἰταλοῖς ὁ Εὐμένους στρατὸς ἐτάσσετο, καὶ
158   Ἀχαιῶν πελτασταὶ περὶ τρισχιλίους. ὧδε μὲν εἶχε τὸ
λαιόν, τὸ δεξιὸν δ' ἦν ἱππεῖς, οἵ τε Ῥωμαίων καὶ
Ἰταλῶν καὶ Εὐμένους, οὐ πλείους οὐδ' οὗτοι τρισχι-
λίων. ἀνεμεμίχατο δ' ἅπασι ψιλοί τε καὶ τοξόται πολλοί, καὶ ἀμφὶ τὸν Δομίτιον αὐτὸν ἦσαν ἱππέων ἶλαι
159   τέσσαρες. οὕτω μὲν ἐγίγνοντο πάντες ἐς τρισμυρίους,
ἐπεστάτει δὲ τοῦ μὲν δεξιοῦ Δομίτιος αὐτός, καὶ ἐς τὸ
μέσον αὐτὸν ἵστη τὸν ὕπατον, τὸ δὲ λαιὸν ἔδωκεν
160   Εὐμένει. τῶν δ' ἐλεφάντων, οὓς εἶχεν ἐκ Λιβύης, οὐδένα νομίζων ἔσεσθαι χρήσιμον ὀλιγωτέρων τε ὄντων
καὶ βραχυτέρων οἷα Λιβύων (δεδίασι δ' οἱ σμικρότε-
ροι τοὺς μείζονας), ἔστησεν ὀπίσω πάντας.
161   32. Ὧδε μὲν δὴ διετετάχατο Ῥωμαῖοι, Ἀντιόχῳ δ'
ἦν μὲν ὁ στρατὸς ἅπας ἑπτακισμύριοι, καὶ τούτων τὸ
κράτιστον ἦν ἡ φάλαγξ ἡ Μακεδόνων, ἄνδρες ἑξακι-

11 τάξεις add. Schweig.

31 This is a somewhat confusing description of the Roman
battle order, which does not seem to have a center. Livy (37.9.7–

regarded it as a disgrace to refuse battle when he had more men. So he drew up his troops in battle order.

31. Both armies left camp at about the last watch while 157 it was still dark and adopted the following battle formations. Ten thousand Roman legionaries held the left wing by the river itself, and beside them another ten thousand Italian troops, in both cases the lines being three ranks deep. Eumenes' force was stationed beside the Italians with approximately three thousand Achaean peltasts. This 158 was the Roman left wing. The Roman and Italian cavalry and those of Eumenes were on the right wing, in total not more than three thousand. Mixed in with all the cavalry was a large number of light armed soldiers and archers, and Domitius himself had an escort of four troops of cavalry. The Roman army was about thirty thousand strong in 159 total. Domitius commanded the right wing himself, and put the consul in command of the center and gave the left wing to Eumenes.[31] He did not think his elephants—they 160 were African elephants—would be effective, because they were rather few in number and, being African, too small. (Smaller elephants are afraid of bigger ones.) So he stationed them all in the rear.

32. Such was the Roman line of battle. In total Antio- 161 chus had an army of seventy thousand men. The most powerful element was the Macedonian phalanx of sixteen

13) is more coherent. The source of Appian's confusion is perhaps the fact that, according to Livy, there was not really a left wing, apart from a small group of cavalry, as the left of the Roman line was protected by the river. The two Roman and two Italian legions formed the center, with Eumenes to the right of them, and the cavalry on the far right.

σχίλιοι καὶ μύριοι, ἐς τὸν Ἀλεξάνδρου καὶ Φιλίππου
162 τρόπον ἔτι κοσμούμενοι· ἴστη δ' αὐτοὺς ἐν μέσῳ, δι-
ελὼν ἀνὰ χιλίους καὶ ἑξακοσίους ἐς δέκα μέρη, καὶ
τούτων ἑκάστου μέρους ἦσαν ἐπὶ μὲν τοῦ μετώπου
πεντήκοντα ἄνδρες, ἐς δὲ τὸ βάθος δύο καὶ τριάκοντα,
ἐς δὲ τὰ πλευρὰ ἑκάστου μέρους ἐλέφαντες δύο καὶ
εἴκοσιν. ἡ δ' ὄψις ἦν τῆς μὲν φάλαγγος οἷα τείχους,
163 τῶν δ' ἐλεφάντων οἷον πύργων. τοιοῦτον μὲν ἦν τὸ
πεζὸν Ἀντιόχῳ, ἱππεῖς δ' ἑκατέρωθεν αὐτοῦ παρετετάχατο Γαλάται τε κατάφρακτοι καὶ τὸ λεγόμενον
ἄγημα τῶν Μακεδόνων. εἰσὶ δὲ καὶ οἵδε ἱππεῖς ἐπί-
164 λεκτοι, καὶ παρ' αὐτὸ ἄγημα λέγεται. τάδε μὲν ἔξ
ἴσου τῆς φάλαγγος ἦν ἑκατέρωθεν· ἐπὶ δ' αὐτοῖς τὰ
κέρατα κατεῖχον ἐν μὲν δεξιᾷ ψιλοί τέ τινες καὶ ἕτεροι
ἱππεῖς ἀργυράσπιδες καὶ ἱπποτοξόται ⟨χίλιοι καὶ⟩[12]
διακόσιοι, τὸ δὲ λαιὸν Γαλατῶν τ' ἔθνη, Τεκτοσάγαι
τε καὶ Τρόκμοι καὶ Τολιστόβοιοι, καὶ Καππαδόκαι
τινὲς οὓς ἔπεμψεν Ἀριαράθης, καὶ μιγάδες ἄλλοι ξέ-
νοι, κατάφρακτός τε ἵππος ἐπὶ τοῖσδε ἑτέρα, καὶ ἦν
165 ἐκάλουν ἵππον ἑταιρικήν, ὡπλισμένη κούφως. ὧδε μὲν
καὶ ὁ Ἀντίοχος ἐξέτασσεν. καὶ δοκεῖ τὴν ἐλπίδα λαβεῖν ἐν τοῖς ἱππεῦσιν, οὓς πολλοὺς ἔστησεν ἐπὶ τοῦ
μετώπου, τὴν δὲ φάλαγγα πυκνὴν ἐς ὀλίγον συναγα-

---

[12] χίλιοι καὶ add. Schweig.

thousand troops, still equipped in the manner of Alexander and Philip. These he placed in the center, divided into 162 ten companies of one thousand six hundred men each, thirty-two deep, fifty men on the front line and twenty-two elephants on the flanks of each company. The phalanx looked like a wall, with towers formed by the elephants. This was how Antiochus drew up his infantry. The cavalry, 163 mail-wearing Galatians and what was known as the Macedonian *agema*, were stationed on both wings. These Macedonian cavalrymen were specially selected, which was the reason they got the name *agema*.[32] An equal number of 164 them were positioned on either side of the phalanx. Next to the cavalry on the wings, were, to the right, some light-armed troops and additional horsemen, armed with silver shields, and twelve hundred mounted archers; and on the left, Galatian peoples (the Tectosagai, Trocmi, and Toilistoboii), some Cappadocians sent by Ariarathes, a mixture of other mercenaries and another unit of mailed cavalry, along with what were called the companion cavalry, a lightly armed body of horse. This was Antiochus' battle 165 formation. It appears that he placed his main hope on the cavalry, as he stationed a large part of it in the front. In fact, he should have had most confidence in his highly trained phalanx, but showed his military inexperience by

[32] The root of the word *agema* is presumably the Greek verb *agō*, "to lead": i.e., it was something led, or brought together, a unit or corps. If its members were specially chosen from other sections of the army, they could be thought of as "the unit." It seems less likely that Appian is thinking of a derivation from the verb *agaomai*, "to admire": i.e., it was something that attracted admiration, and must, therefore, have been specially selected.

APPIAN

166 γεῖν ἀπειροπολέμως, ᾗ δὴ καὶ μάλιστα ἔδει θαρρεῖν
πάνυ ἠσκημένῃ. πολὺ δὲ καὶ ἄλλο πλῆθος ἦν λι-
θοβόλων τε καὶ τοξοτῶν καὶ ἀκοντιστῶν καὶ πελ-
ταστῶν, Φρυγῶν τε καὶ Λυκίων καὶ Παμφύλων καὶ
Πισιδῶν Κρητῶν τε καὶ Τραλλιανῶν καὶ Κιλίκων ἐς
167 τὸν Κρητῶν τρόπον ἐσκευασμένων. ἱπποτοξόται τε
ἐπὶ τοῖσδε ἕτεροι, Δάαι καὶ Μυσοὶ καὶ Ἐλυμαῖοι καὶ
Ἄραβες, οἳ καμήλους ὀξυτάτας ἐπικαθήμενοι τοξεύ-
ουσί τε εὐμαρῶς ἀφ᾽ ὑψηλοῦ, καὶ μαχαίραις, ὅτε πλη-
168 σιάζοιεν, ἐπιμήκεσι καὶ στεναῖς χρῶνται. δρεπανηφόρα τε ἅρματα ἐν τῷ μεταιχμίῳ, προπολεμεῖν τοῦ
μετώπου, ἐτετάχατο· καὶ εἴρητο αὐτοῖς μετὰ τὴν πρώτην πεῖραν ὑποχωρεῖν.

169 33. Ὄψις τε ἦν ὥσπερ δύο στρατῶν, τοῦ μὲν ἀρχομένου πολεμεῖν, τοῦ δ᾽ ἐφεδρεύοντος· ἑκάτερος δ᾽
αὐτῶν ἐς κατάπληξιν ἐσκεύαστο δεινῶς ⟨ἔχων⟩[13]
170 πλήθει τε καὶ κόσμῳ. ἐφειστήκει δὲ τοῖς μὲν δεξιοῖς
ἱππεῦσιν Ἀντίοχος αὐτός, τοῖς δ᾽ ἐπὶ θάτερα Σέλευκος
ὁ υἱὸς Ἀντιόχου, τῇ δὲ φάλαγγι Φίλιππος ὁ ἐλεφαν-
τάρχης καὶ τοῖς προμάχοις Μύνδις τε καὶ Ζεῦξις.
171 ἀχλυώδους δὲ καὶ ζοφερᾶς τῆς ἡμέρας γενομένης, ἥ
τε ὄψις ἔσβεστο τῆς ἐπιδείξεως, καὶ τὰ τοξεύματα
πάντα ἀμβλύτερα ἦν ὡς ἐν ἀέρι ὑγρῷ καὶ σκοτεινῷ.
172 ὅπερ ἐπεὶ κατεῖδεν Εὐμένης, τῶν μὲν ἄλλων κατεφρόνησε, τὴν δὲ ῥύμην τῶν ἁρμάτων τεταγμένων ἐφ᾽ ἑαυτὸν μάλιστα δείσας, ὅσοι ἦσαν αὐτῷ σφενδονῆται
καὶ ἀκοντισταὶ καὶ ἕτεροι κοῦφοι, συναγαγὼν προσέταξε, τὰ ἅρματα περιθέοντας, ἐς τοὺς ἵππους ἀκοντί-

68

deploying it crowded together in a small space. From   166
Phrygia and Lycia and Pamphylia and Pisidia and Crete
and Tralles and Cilicia came large numbers of stone
throwers, archers, javelin throwers, and peltasts, all
equipped in the Cretan manner. In addition to these, An-   167
tiochus had other mounted archers, Dahae and Mysians
and Elymians and Arabs. The Arabs ride very fast camels,
shooting accurately from their high position and using
very long, thin knives when they close with the enemy.
Chariots armed with scythes were deployed between the   168
two battle lines to engage before the lines met. They had
instructions to withdraw after the first engagement.

33. It looked like he had two armies, one to begin the   169
battle, the other lying in reserve. Both were arrayed to
alarm the enemy, striking terror with their number and
equipment. Antiochus himself took command of the cav-   170
alry on the right, his son Seleucus of those on the left wing,
Philip, the officer in charge of the elephants, led the phalanx, and Myndis and Zeuxis the skirmishers at the front.
It was a misty, gloomy day, which obscured the view of the   171
display, and the dark, damp air made the accuracy of all
missiles unreliable. When he saw this, Eumenes did not   172
worry about the rest of Antiochus' army, but was afraid
only of the attack of the chariots which were arrayed
mostly against him. So he collected all his slingers, javelin
throwers and other light-armed troops, and ordered them
to run around the chariots firing their weapons at the

---

13 ἔχων add. Goukowsky

ζειν ἀντὶ τῶν ἐπιβατῶν· ἵππου γὰρ ἐν ἅρματι ζυγο-
μαχοῦντος ἀχρεῖον τὸ λοιπὸν ἅρμα γίγνεται, καὶ
πολλὰ καὶ τῆς ἄλλης εὐταξίας παραλύεται, τὰ δρέ-
173 πανα τῶν φιλίων δεδιότων. ὃ καὶ τότε συνηνέχθη
γενέσθαι· πληγέντων γὰρ τῶν ἵππων ἀθρόως καὶ τὰ
ἅρματα ἐς τοὺς φίλους περιφερόντων, αἵ τε κάμηλοι
πρῶται τῆς ἀταξίας ἠσθάνοντο, πλησίον τοῖς ἅρμασι
παρατεταγμέναι, καὶ μετὰ ταύτας ἡ κατάφρακτος ἵππος, οὐ ῥᾳδίως ὑπὸ τοῦ βάρους τὰ δρέπανα ἐκφεύγειν
174 δυναμένη. θόρυβός τε ἦν ἤδη πολὺς καὶ τάραχος ποι-
κίλος, ἀρξάμενος μὲν ἀπὸ τῶνδε μάλιστα, χωρῶν δὲ
ἐπὶ ὅλον τὸ μεταίχμιον, καὶ μείζων ὑπόνοια τοῦ ἀκρι-
βοῦς· ὡς γὰρ ἐν διαστήματι μακρῷ καὶ πλήθει πυκνῷ
καὶ βοῇ ποικίλῃ καὶ φόβῳ πολλῷ, τὸ μὲν ἀκριβὲς
οὐδὲ τοῖς ἀγχοῦ τῶν πασχόντων καταληπτὸν ἦν, τὴν
δὲ ὑπόνοιαν μειζόνως ἐς τοὺς ἑξῆς ἕκαστοι μετέφερον.
175   34. Ὁ δ᾽ Εὐμένης, ἐπεὶ τὰ πρῶτα καλῶς ἐπέπρακτο
αὐτῷ, καὶ τὸ μεταίχμιον, ὅσον αἵ τε κάμηλοι καὶ τὰ
ἅρματα ἐπεῖχεν, ἐγεγύμνωτο, τοὺς ἰδίους ἱππέας, καὶ
ὅσοι Ῥωμαίων αὐτῷ καὶ Ἰταλῶν παρετετάχατο, ἐπῆγεν ἐπὶ τοὺς ἀντικρὺ Γαλάτας τε καὶ Καππαδόκας καὶ
τὴν ἄλλην σύνοδον τῶν ξένων, μέγα κεκραγὼς καὶ
παρακαλῶν ἐπὶ ἄνδρας ἀπείρους τε μάχης καὶ γε-
176 γυμνωμένους τῶν προπολεμούντων. οἱ δ᾽ ἐπείθοντο,
καὶ βαρείας σφῶν τῆς ἐμβολῆς γενομένης τρέπονται
τούτους τε καὶ τοὺς παρεζευγμένους αὐτοῖς ἱππέας τε
καὶ καταφράκτους, ἐκ πολλοῦ ταρασσομένους διὰ τὰ
ἅρματα· οὓς δὴ καὶ μάλιστα, διὰ τὸ βάρος ὑποφεύ-

horses, not the drivers. For when a horse harnessed to a chariot fights against the yoke, the chariot has no further use, and indeed seriously undermines general discipline by instilling fear of the scythes in its own army. And that is the way it turned out on this occasion. When the horses were wounded they turned their chariots en masse against the men of their own side. The camels, in their position next to the chariots, were the first to lose their discipline, and after them the mailed cavalry, who found it difficult to get out of the way of the scythes because of the weight of their armor. There was now general confusion and widespread disorder, which began here, but then made its way into the whole battle zone, the anxiety proving worse than the real situation justified. For in such a big space, packed with crowds of men, with shouting of all sorts and fear everywhere, even those who were near the action could not understand exactly what was happening, but each person exaggerated their own unease and passed it on to those beside them.

34. After his success at the beginning, Eumenes cleared the space on the battlefield where the camels and chariots had been, and then led his own cavalry and the Roman and Italian horse in his division against the Galatians, Cappadocians, and general company of mercenaries facing him, roaring his encouragement against men with little experience of battle and now deprived of their champions. His own men followed their orders, and made such a heavy attack that they routed both these and the units lined up beside them, particularly the mailed cavalry, who had long been in disarray because of the chariots. Their

173

174

175

176

γειν ἢ ἀναστρέφειν εὐμαρῶς οὐ δυναμένους, κατελάμ-
177 βανόν τε καὶ συνέκοπτον. καὶ τάδε μὲν ἦν περὶ τὸ
λαιὸν τῆς φάλαγγος τῶν Μακεδόνων· ἐν δεξιᾷ δέ,
ᾗπερ αὐτὸς ὁ Ἀντίοχος ἐτέτακτο, διακόψας τὸ σύν-
ταγμα τῆς Ῥωμαίων φάλαγγος ἀπέσπασεν ἐπὶ πολὺ
διώκων.

178   35. Καὶ ἡ φάλαγξ ἡ τῶν Μακεδόνων, τεταγμένη
μέν, ὡς μεθ᾽ ἱππέων, ἐπὶ στενοῦ τε καὶ τετραγώνου,
γεγυμνωμένη δὲ τῶν ἱππέων ἑκατέρωθεν, τοὺς μὲν ψιλοὺς τοὺς ἐπὶ τοῦ μετώπου σφῶν ἔτι προπολεμοῦντας
διαστᾶσα ἐς αὑτὴν ἐδέξατο καὶ πάλιν συνῄει, Δομι-
τίου δ᾽ αὑτὴν ἱππεῦσι πολλοῖς καὶ ψιλοῖς εὐμαρῶς,
οἷα πλινθίον πυκνόν, κυκλώσαντος, οὔτ᾽ ἐκδραμεῖν ἔτι
ἔχουσα οὔτ᾽ ἐξελίξαι βάθος οὕτω πολύ, μάλα καρ-
179 τερῶς ἐκακοπάθει. καὶ ἠγανάκτουν αὐτοὶ μὲν ταῖς
ἐμπειρίαις οὐδὲν ἔχοντες ἔτι χρῆσθαι, τοῖς δὲ πολεμίοις εὔβλητοι καὶ ἐπιτυχεῖς πανταχόθεν ὄντες.
180 ὅμως δὲ τὰς σαρίσσας ἐκ τετραγώνου προβαλλόμε-
νοι πυκνὰς προὐκαλοῦντο Ῥωμαίους ἐς χεῖρας ἐλθεῖν,
181 καὶ δόξαν ἐπιβαινόντων ἀεὶ παρεῖχον. οὐ μήν τι προ-
επήδων, πεζοί τε καὶ βαρεῖς ὄντες ὑπὸ τῶν ὅπλων, καὶ
τοὺς πολεμίους ἐπὶ ἵππων ὁρῶντες, μάλιστα δὲ ἵνα μὴ
τὸ τῆς τάξεως πυκνὸν ἐκλύσειαν· μετατάξασθαι γὰρ
182 ἑτέρως οὐκ ἔφθανον. Ῥωμαῖοι δ᾽ αὐτοῖς οὐ προσεπέ-
λαζον μέν, οὐδ᾽ ἐς χεῖρας ᾖσαν, δεδιότες ἀνδρῶν
ἠσκημένων ἐμπειρίαν τε καὶ πυκνότητα καὶ ἀπόγνω-
σιν, περιθέοντες δὲ ἐσηκόντιζόν τε καὶ ἐσετόξευον.
καὶ οὐδὲν ἦν ἀχρεῖον ὡς ἐν ὀλίγῳ πολλῶν συνεστώ-

weight made it difficult for them to flee or wheel round, and they in particular were overwhelmed and killed. This 177 was the situation on the left of the Macedonian phalanx. On the right, where he himself was stationed, Antiochus cut his way through the Roman phalanx and pushed on for a long way through the breach in their line.

35. The Macedonian phalanx, flanked as it was by cav- 178 alry, had been formed into a constricted square, but when given room on both sides by the absence of cavalry, it opened to receive the light-armed troops still skirmishing to the front, and then closed ranks again. Domitius easily surrounded such a tight square with his numerous cavalry and light-armed troops. The phalanx began to suffer badly, as they were no longer able to break out or deploy the depth of their ranks on a wider front. They were also frus- 179 trated at being unable to make use of their experience, but were proving an easy target for the enemy, difficult to miss. Nevertheless, they held their spears in a solid mass 180 extending from the square, challenging the Romans to hand-to-hand combat, and constantly giving the impression of going on the attack. Not that they did charge: they 181 were heavily armed foot soldiers and could see that the enemy were mounted. Their greatest care was to avoid opening their tight formation, as they did not have the time to redeploy in a different way. The Romans did not 182 move in close or engage with them, as they were apprehensive of the experience, massed ranks, and desperation of well trained troops. Instead, they moved quickly around them, throwing their javelins and firing their arrows, none of which missed such a large body of men standing in an

APPIAN

των. οὐ γὰρ εἶχον οὔτε ἐκκλῖναι τὰ βαλλόμενα οὔτε
183 φερομένοις διαστῆναι. ὅθεν ἤδη πολλὰ κάμνοντες
ἐνεδίδοσαν ὑπὸ τῆς ἀπορίας, καὶ βάδην ὑπεχώρουν
σὺν ἀπειλῇ, πάνυ εὐσταθῶς καὶ Ῥωμαίοις ἐπιφόβως·
οὐδὲ γὰρ τότε προσπελάζειν αὐτοῖς ἐτόλμων, ἀλλὰ
περιθέοντες ἔβλαπτον, μέχρι, τῶν ἐλεφάντων ἐν τῇ
Μακεδόνων φάλαγγι συνταραχθέντων τε καὶ οὐχ
ὑπακουόντων ἔτι τοῖς ἐπιβάταις, ὁ κόσμος ὁ τῆς φυγῆς συνεχεῖτο.

184 36. Καὶ ταύτῃ μὲν ὁ Δομίτιος ἐκράτει, καὶ ἐπὶ τὸ
στρατόπεδον τοῦ Ἀντιόχου φθάσας ἐβιάζετο τοὺς ἐν
αὐτῷ φυλάσσοντας· ὁ δὲ Ἀντίοχος ἐς πολὺ διώκων
παρ' οὓς ἐκ τῆς Ῥωμαϊκῆς φάλαγγος ἐτέτακτο, οὐδενὸς οὐδ' ἐκείνοις ἱππέων ἢ ψιλοῦ παρόντος ἐς ἐπικουρίαν (οὐ γὰρ παρετετάχει Δομίτιος, ἡγούμενος οὐ
δεήσεσθαι διὰ τὸν ποταμόν), μέχρι τοῦ Ῥωμαίων
185 χάρακος ἦλθεν. ἐπεὶ δὲ αὐτὸν ὅ τε χιλίαρχος ὁ τοῦ
χάρακος φύλαξ, ἀκμῆσι τοῖς φύλαξιν ὑπαντιάσας,
ἐπέσχε τῆς ὁρμῆς καὶ οἱ φεύγοντες τοῖς ἀναμιχθεῖσι
θαρροῦντες ἐπεστρέφοντο, ἐπανῄει σοβαρὸς ὁ Ἀντίοχος ὡς ἐπὶ νίκῃ, οὐδενὸς τῶν ἐπὶ θάτερα πεπυσμένος.
186 Ἄτταλος δ' αὐτόν, ὁ Εὐμένους ἀδελφός, ἱππεῦσι πολλοῖς ὑπαντιάζει. καὶ τούσδε μὲν εὐμαρῶς ὁ Ἀντίοχος
διακόψας διέδραμε, καὶ παρατρεχόντων ἔτι καὶ μικρὰ
λυπούντων οὐκ ἐφρόντιζεν· ὡς δὲ κατεῖδε τὴν ἧτταν
καὶ τὸ πεδίον ἅπαν νεκρῶν ἰδίων πλῆρες, ἀνδρῶν τε
καὶ ἵππων καὶ ἐλεφάντων, τό τε στρατόπεδον εἰλημμένον ἤδη κατὰ κράτος, τότε δὴ καὶ ὁ Ἀντίοχος ἔφυ-

enclosed space, who were unable to knock the missiles aside, or move aside to avoid them. They were now strug- 183
gling badly from this, and in their plight gave way: they retreated in excellent order step by step, issuing threats and still an object of fear to the Romans, who even at this point did not dare to close with them. Instead they continued to run around them, inflicting wounds, until the elephants in the Macedonian phalanx became disorderly and no longer obeyed their mahouts. Then good order disintegrated into flight.

36. After his victory in this sector, Domitius got to An- 184
tiochus' camp before the king and overwhelmed those guarding it. Antiochus himself, who was chasing over a long distance the section of the Roman phalanx engaged against him—it had no cavalry or light-armed troops in support, since Domitius had not deployed any, believing that the river made it unnecessary—now came up to the Roman palisade. Here the Roman tribune in charge of 185
guarding the camp confronted him with fresh troops and halted his advance; even those fleeing were encouraged to rally by the new troops mixed in with them. Antiochus returned proud at what he thought was his victory, knowing nothing of events on the other side of the battlefield. Eumenes' brother, Attalus, tried to block him with a large 186
force of cavalry, but Antiochus easily cut his way through, and paid little attention to them as they continued to keep up with him and inflict minor damage. But when he saw the scene of his defeat, the whole plain filled with the corpses of his army—men, horses and elephants—and his camp already taken by force, that was when Antiochus fled

γεν ἀμεταστρεπτί, καὶ μέχρι μέσων νυκτῶν ἐς Σάρ-
187 δεις παρῆλθεν. παρῆλθε δὲ καὶ ἀπὸ Σάρδεων ἐς
Κελαινάς, ἣν Ἀπάμειαν καλοῦσιν, οἷ τὸν υἱὸν ἐπυν-
θάνετο συμφυγεῖν. τῆς δ᾽ ἐπιούσης ἐς Συρίαν ἐκ Κε-
λαινῶν ἀνεζεύγνυ, τοὺς στρατηγοὺς ἐν Κελαιναῖς
καταλιπὼν ὑποδέχεσθαί τε καὶ ἀθροίζειν τοὺς διαφυ-
188 γόντας. περί τε καταλύσεως τοῦ πολέμου πρέσβεις
ἔπεμπε πρὸς τὸν ὕπατον. ὁ δὲ τὰ οἰκεῖα ἔθαπτε, καὶ
ἐσκύλευε τοὺς πολεμίους, καὶ τὰ αἰχμάλωτα συνῆγεν.
ἐφάνησαν δὲ νεκροὶ Ῥωμαίων μὲν τῶν ἐξ ἄστεος ἱππεῖς εἴκοσι καὶ τέσσαρες καὶ πεζοὶ τριακόσιοι μάλιστα, οὓς ὁ Ἀντίοχος ἔκτεινεν, Εὐμένους δὲ πεντεκαί-
189 δεκα ἱππεῖς μόνοι. Ἀντιόχου δέ, σὺν τοῖς αἰχμαλώτοις
εἰκάζοντο ἀπολέσθαι περὶ πεντακισμυρίους· οὐ γὰρ
εὐμαρὲς ἦν ἀριθμῆσαι διὰ τὸ πλῆθος. καὶ τῶν ἐλεφάντων οἱ μὲν ἀνῄρηντο, πεντεκαίδεκα δ᾽ αἰχμάλωτοι
ἐγεγένητο.

190 37. Ὡς δ᾽ ἐπὶ νίκῃ λαμπροτάτῃ καὶ παραλόγως τισὶ
δοκούσῃ γενέσθαι (οὐ γὰρ εἰκὸς ἐνόμιζον ὀλιγω-
τέρους πολὺ πλειόνων ἐν ἀλλοτρίᾳ γῇ παρὰ τοσόνδε
κρατῆσαι, καὶ μάλιστα φάλαγγος Μακεδόνων, εὖ γε-
γυμνασμένης καὶ εὐανδρούσης τότε μάλιστα, καὶ δόξαν ἄμαχόν τε καὶ φοβερὰν ἐχούσης), οἱ μὲν Ἀντιόχου φίλοι τὴν προπέτειαν αὐτοῦ τῆς ἐς Ῥωμαίους
διαφορᾶς καὶ τὴν ἐξ ἀρχῆς ἀπειρίαν τε καὶ ἀβουλίαν
ἐπεμέμφοντο, Χερρόνησόν τε καὶ Λυσιμάχειαν αὐτοῖς
ὅπλοις καὶ τοσῇδε παρασκευῇ μεθέντος ἐκ χειρῶν
πρὶν καὶ ἐς πεῖραν ἐλθεῖν τοῖς πολεμίοις, καὶ τὴν τοῦ

without turning back, arriving in Sardis about midnight. From Sardis he went to Celaenae, which is called Apamea, 187 where he learned that his son had taken refuge. The next day he retreated to Syria from Celaenae and left his generals there to receive and gather the survivors. To negotiate 188 an end to the war, he sent envoys to the consul, who was burying his own dead, despoiling the enemy, and collecting prisoners. On the Roman side, and from the city itself, were found the bodies of twenty-four horsemen and about three hundred infantrymen, killed by Antiochus. Eumenes lost only fifteen of his cavalry. It is estimated that Antio- 189 chus lost about fifty thousand men, including prisoners, but it was not easy to count them, as there were so many of them. Of his elephants, some were killed and fifteen captured.

37. After this very brilliant victory, one that seemed 190 improbable to some people (for they thought it unlikely that a small army operating abroad should so thoroughly get the better of a much larger one, especially the Macedonian phalanx, which was at that time extremely well trained and dynamic, and had a formidable reputation for invincibility), Antiochus' courtiers began to blame him for his haste in falling out with Rome, and for his inexperience and bad judgment, displayed right from the beginning. He had given up Chersonesus and Lysimachea and their extensive store of weapons and war supplies without even getting to grips with the enemy, and had left the Helles-

APPIAN

Ἑλλησπόντου φυλακὴν ἐκλιπόντος, Ῥωμαίων οὐκ
ἂν εὐμαρῶς ἐλπισάντων βιάσασθαι τὴν διάβασιν.
191 κατεμέμφοντο δ' αὐτοῦ καὶ τὴν τελευταίαν ἀφροσύνην, ἀχρεῖον ἐν στενῷ τὸ κράτιστον τοῦ στρατοῦ
πεποιηκότος, καὶ τὴν ἐλπίδα θεμένου ἐν πλήθει συγ-
κλύδων ἀνδρῶν ἀρτιπολέμων μᾶλλον ἢ ἐν ἀνδράσι
διὰ μελέτην καὶ χρόνον ἐργάταις τε οὖσι πολέμου καὶ
ἐκ τοσῶνδε πολέμων τὸ φρόνημα ἐς εὐτολμίαν καὶ
192 θάρσος ηὐξημένοις. τοιαῦτα μὲν ἦν τὰ περὶ Ἀντιόχου
λογοποιούμενα, Ῥωμαίοις δ' ἐπῆρτο τὰ φρονήματα,
καὶ οὐδὲν ἔτι σφίσιν ἡγοῦντο εἶναι δυσεργὲς ὑπό τε
ἀρετῆς καὶ θεῶν ἐπικουρίας· καὶ γὰρ δὴ καὶ ἐς δόξαν
εὐτυχίας ἔφερεν ὅτι οὕτω γε ὀλίγοι ἀντὶ πολλῶν καὶ
ἐξ ἐφόδου καὶ ἐν πρώτῃ μάχῃ καὶ ἐν ἀλλοτρίᾳ γῇ
τοσῶνδε ἐθνῶν καὶ παρασκευῆς βασιλικῆς, καὶ
μισθοφόρων ἀρετῆς, καὶ δόξης Μακεδόνων, καὶ βασιλέως αὐτοῦ μεγίστην τε ἀρχὴν κεκτημένου καὶ
ἐπίκλησιν μεγάλου, κεκρατηκότες ἦσαν ἡμέρᾳ μιᾷ.
πολύ τε σφίσιν ἦν τὸ ἔπος ἐν τοῖς λόγοις, "Ἦν βασιλεὺς Ἀντίοχος ὁ μέγας."

193   38. Τοιάδε μὲν δὴ καὶ Ῥωμαῖοι περὶ σφῶν ἐμεγα-
λαύχουν· ὁ δὲ ὕπατος, ἐπεὶ αὐτῷ ῥαΐσας ὁ ἀδελφὸς
Πούπλιος ἦλθεν ἀπὸ τῆς Ἐλαίας, ἐχρημάτιζε τοῖς
Ἀντιόχου πρέσβεσιν. οἱ μὲν δὴ μαθεῖν ἠξίουν ὅ τι
ποιῶν ὁ βασιλεὺς Ἀντίοχος ἔσται Ῥωμαίοις φίλος· ὁ
194 δὲ Πόπλιος αὐτοῖς ὧδε ἀπεκρίνατο· "Αἴτιος μὲν αὐτῷ
διὰ πλεονεξίαν Ἀντίοχος καὶ τῶν νῦν καὶ τῶν πρότερον γεγονότων, ὃς ἀρχὴν μεγίστην ἔχων τε, καὶ Ῥω-

pont unguarded, when the Romans could not have expected to force a crossing with ease. They also blamed him   191
for his foolishness at the end in shutting up the most powerful part of his army in a narrow space and rendering it
useless, while placing his hopes on a large rabble of recruits, rather than on men hardened into effective war-
riors by long training, and with their spirit honed, by so
many campaigns, for deeds of daring bravery. Such was   192
the talk in Antiochus' court. At Rome, on the other hand,
confidence was high. They thought that with the help of
the gods and by virtue of their own courage, nothing was
difficult for them anymore. For, understandably, their
reputation for good fortune was bolstered by the triumph
on a single day of their small army against a large one, in
the first battle of their first offensive, won on foreign soil
against so many peoples, against the king's armament, with
his brave mercenaries and renowned Macedonians, and
against the king himself, possessed of a huge kingdom and
the title "the Great." In their conversations it was often
said, "there used to be a king called Antiochus the Great."

38. While the Romans were boasting about themselves   193
like this, and when his brother Publius had recovered and
arrived from Elaea, the consul entered into negotiations
with Antiochus' ambassadors. They asked what Antiochus
had to do to be a friend of Rome. Publius' answer was as
follows. "Greed has made Antiochus the cause of his own   194
problems, present and past. Although he possessed a huge

μαίων αὐτὸν ἐώντων ἔχειν, Πτολεμαίου συγγενοῦς
ἰδίου καὶ Ῥωμαίοις φίλου Συρίαν τὴν κοίλην ἀφείλετο,
καὶ ἐς τὴν Εὐρώπην οὐδὲν αὐτῷ προσήκουσαν ἐμβαλὼν Θρᾴκην κατεστρέφετο καὶ Χερρόνησον ὠχύρου καὶ Λυσιμάχειαν ἤγειρεν, ἔς τε τὴν Ἑλλάδα διελθὼν ἐδουλοῦτο τοὺς Ἕλληνας ὑπὸ Ῥωμαίων ἄρτι
αὐτονόμους ἀφειμένους, μέχρι περὶ Θερμοπύλας ἡτ-
195 τήθη μάχῃ. καὶ φυγὼν οὐδ᾽ ὣς ἔληξε τῆς πλεονεξίας,
ἀλλὰ κἀν τῇ θαλάττῃ πολλάκις ἐλαττωθεὶς σπονδῶν
μέν, ἄρτι τὸν Ἑλλήσποντον ἡμῶν πεπερακότων,
ἐδεήθη, διὰ δὲ ὑπεροψίαν τὰ προτεινόμενα ὑπερεῖδε,
καὶ στράτευμα αὖθις πολὺ καὶ παρασκευὴν ἄπειρον
ἐφ᾽ ἡμᾶς συναγαγὼν ἐπολέμει, βιαζόμενος ἐς πεῖραν
ἐλθεῖν τοῖς ἀμείνοσι, μέχρι συνηνέχθη μεγάλῳ κακῷ.
196 ἡμᾶς δὲ εἰκὸς μὲν ἦν αὐτῷ μείζονα τὴν ζημίαν ἐπι-
θεῖναι, βιασαμένῳ πολλάκις Ῥωμαίοις ἐς χεῖρας ἐλ-
θεῖν· ἀλλ᾽ οὐχ ὑβρίζομεν ταῖς εὐπραξίαις, οὐδ᾽ ἐπιβα-
197 ροῦμεν τοῖς ἑτέρων ἀτυχήμασιν. δίδομεν δὲ ὅσα καὶ
πρότερον αὐτῷ προὐτείνομεν, μικρὰ ἄττα προσθέντες,
ὅσα καὶ ἡμῖν ἔσται χρήσιμα καὶ αὐτῷ λυσιτελῆ πρὸς
τὸ μέλλον ἐς ἀσφάλειαν, ἀπέχεσθαι μὲν αὐτὸν τῆς
Εὐρώπης ὅλης καὶ Ἀσίας τῶν ἐπὶ τάδε τοῦ Ταύρου
198 (καὶ τούτοις ὅροι τεθήσονται), παραδοῦναι δ᾽ ἐλέφαντας ὅσους ἔχει καὶ ναῦς ὅσας ἂν ἐπιτάξωμεν, ἔς τε
λοιπὸν ἐλέφαντας μὲν οὐκ ἔχειν, ναῦς δὲ ὅσας ἂν
ὁρίσωμεν, δοῦναι δὲ καὶ εἴκοσιν ὅμηρα, ἃ ἂν ὁ στρατηγὸς ἐπιγράψῃ, καὶ χρήματα ἐς τὴν τοῦδε τοῦ πολέμου δαπάνην, δι᾽ αὐτὸν γενομένου, τάλαντα Εὐβο-

empire, which Rome allowed him to have, he took Coele
Syria from Ptolemy, his own relative and a friend of the
Romans, and then invaded Europe, which was no concern
of his, where he subdued Thrace, fortified Chersonesus,
and rebuilt Lysimachea. Crossing to Greece, he set about
enslaving the Greeks, who had recently been made independent by Rome, until he was defeated in battle at Thermopylae. Even as a fugitive he persisted in his greed. De-   195
feated at sea on a number of occasions, he only asked for
a truce after we had crossed the Hellespont, and then,
scornfully rejecting the offer made to him, he again collected a large army and limitless resources, and waged war
against us. In the end he was determined to come to trial
with his betters, and met with heavy defeat. It would be   196
quite fitting for us to impose a heavier penalty on him,
given his persistent determination to contend with Rome,
but success does not make us arrogant, nor do we add
further burdens to the misfortunes of others. So we grant   197
the same terms as we offered him before, with some small
additions intended to be useful to us and of benefit to him
in terms of his future security. Antiochus must relinquish
Europe entirely and all of Asia this side of the Taurus, the
boundaries to be specified later; he must hand over all his   198
elephants and as many ships as we prescribe, and he may
not keep elephants at all in future and only the number of
ships we allow; he must surrender twenty hostages, to be
registered by the general in command; to cover the cost
of the war, which he caused, he must pay five hundred

ἴκὰ αὐτίκα μὲν ἤδη πεντακόσια, καὶ ὅταν τάσδε
τὰς σπονδὰς ἡ σύγκλητος ἐπιψηφίσῃ, δισχίλια καὶ
πεντακόσια, δώδεκα δ' ἔτεσιν ἄλλοις ἕτερα μύρια καὶ
δισχίλια, τὸ μέρος ἑκάστου ἔτους ἀναφέροντα ἐς
199 Ῥώμην· ἀποδοῦναι δ' ἡμῖν αἰχμάλωτα καὶ αὐτόμολα
πάντα, καὶ Εὐμένει ὅσα λοιπὰ τῆς πρὸς Ἄτταλον τὸν
Εὐμένους πατέρα συνθήκης ἔχει. ταῦτα δ' Ἀντιόχῳ
πράττοντι ἀδόλως δίδομεν εἰρήνην τε καὶ φιλίαν,
ὅταν ἡ σύγκλητος ἐπιψηφίσῃ."

200 39. Τοσάδε προύτεινεν ὁ Σκιπίων, καὶ πάντα ἐδέχοντο οἱ πρέσβεις. τό τε μέρος αὐτίκα τῶν χρημάτων
καὶ τὰ εἴκοσιν ὅμηρα ἐκομίζετο, καὶ ἦν αὐτῶν Ἀντίοχος ὁ νεώτερος υἱὸς Ἀντιόχου. ἐς δὲ τὴν Ῥώμην οἵ τε
Σκιπίωνες καὶ ὁ Ἀντίοχος πρέσβεις ἔπεμπον, καὶ ἡ
201 βουλὴ τοῖς ἐγνωσμένοις συνετίθεντο. καὶ ἐγράφοντο
συνθῆκαι τοὺς Σκιπίωνος λόγους βεβαιοῦσαί τε καὶ
περὶ τῶν ἀορίστων ἐπιλέγουσαι, καὶ βραχέα ἄττα
προσεπιλαμβάνουσαι, ὅρον μὲν Ἀντιόχῳ τῆς ἀρχῆς
εἶναι δύο ἄκρας, Καλύκαδνόν τε καὶ Σαρπηδόνιον, καὶ
τάσδε μὴ παραπλεῖν Ἀντίοχον ἐπὶ πολέμῳ, ναῦς δὲ
καταφράκτους ἔχειν δυώδεκα μόνας, αἷς ἐς τοὺς
ὑπηκόους πολέμου κατάρχειν· πολεμούμενον δὲ καὶ
202 πλέοσι χρῆσθαι· μηδένα δ' ἐκ τῆς Ῥωμαίων ξενολο-
γεῖν, μηδὲ φυγάδας ἐξ αὐτῆς ὑποδέχεσθαι, καὶ τὰ
ὅμηρα διὰ τριετίας ἐναλλάσσειν, χωρίς γε τοῦ παιδὸς
203 Ἀντιόχου. ταῦτα συγγραψάμενοί τε καὶ ἐς τὸ Καπιτώλιον ἐς δέλτους χαλκᾶς ἀναθέντες, οὗ καὶ τὰς ἄλλας συνθήκας ἀνατιθέασιν, ἔπεμπον ἀντίγραφα Μαλ-

Euboic talents now on the spot, and two thousand five hundred more when the senate ratifies the treaty, along with an additional twelve thousand over a twelve year period, the installment for each year to be delivered to Rome; he must return to us all our prisoners and deserters, and to Eumenes all he still holds as a result of the treaty he made with Attalus, Eumenes' father. If Antiochus meets these conditions without deceit, we grant him peace and friendship, subject to the senate's ratification." 199

39. Antiochus' ambassadors accepted all the terms Scipio offered. The sum of money owed immediately was paid and the twenty hostages delivered, among them Antiochus, the younger son of the king. The Scipios and Antiochus both sent envoys to Rome, where the senate agreed to what had been decided. The treaty was drawn up confirming what Scipio had said, addressing some undecided issues, and adding a few brief points. The boundary of Antiochus' empire was to be the two headlands, Calycadnus and Sarpedonium: he was not permitted to sail beyond these points for the purpose of waging war. He was only allowed to have twelve decked ships for undertaking military operations against his subjects, but if attacked first, he could use more. He was banned from recruiting mercenaries in Roman territory and from taking in exiles from Rome, and the hostages had to be changed every three years, apart from Antiochus' son. They inscribed these terms on bronze tablets and set them up in the Capitol, where they set up all other treaties too, and 200 201 202 203

λίῳ Οὐούλσωνι τῷ διαδεδεγμένῳ τὴν Σκιπίωνος
204 στρατηγίαν. ὁ δ' ὤμνυ τοῖς Ἀντιόχου πρέσβεσι περὶ
Ἀπάμειαν τῆς Φρυγίας, καὶ ὁ Ἀντίοχος τῷ ἐπὶ τοῦτο
205 πεμφθέντι Θέρμῳ χιλιάρχῳ. τοῦτο μὲν δὴ Ἀντιόχῳ
μεγάλῳ τοῦ πρὸς Ῥωμαίους πολέμου τέλος ἦν. καὶ
ἐδόκει μέχρι τοῦδε προελθεῖν μόνου διὰ χάριν τὴν ἐς
τὸν παῖδα τὸν Σκιπίωνος Ἀντιόχῳ γενομένην, καί τινες τὸν Σκιπίωνα ἐπανελθόντα διέβαλλον ἐπὶ τῷδε,
καὶ δήμαρχοι δύο δωροδοκίας αὐτὸν ἐγράψαντο καὶ
προδοσίας.

206   40. Ὁ δὲ ἀδοξῶν καὶ ὑπερορῶν τοῦ ἐγκλήματος,
ἐπεὶ συνῆλθε τὸ δικαστήριον ἧς ἡμέρας ποτὲ Καρχηδόνα παρεστήσατο, θυσίαν προύπεμψεν ἐς τὸ Καπιτώλιον, καὶ ἐς τὸ δικαστήριον αὐτὸς παρῆλθεν ἐπὶ
λαμπροῦ σχήματος ἀντὶ οἰκτροῦ καὶ ταπεινοῦ τῶν
ὑπευθύνων, ὡς εὐθὺς ἐπὶ τῷδε πάντας ἐκπλῆξαί τε καὶ
ἐς εὔνοιαν, ὡς ἐπὶ χρηστῷ δὴ συνειδότι μεγαλοφρο-
207 νούμενον, προσαγαγέσθαι. λέγειν δὲ ἀρξάμενος τῆς
μὲν κατηγορίας οὐδ' ἐπεμνήσθη, τὸν δὲ βίον ἑαυτοῦ
καὶ ἐπιτηδεύματα καὶ ἔργα πάντα ἐπεξῄει, καὶ πολέμους ὅσους ἐπολέμησεν ὑπὲρ τῆς πατρίδος, καὶ
ἕκαστον αὐτῶν ὡς ἐπολέμησεν, ὁσάκις τε ἐνίκησεν,
ὡς ἐγγενέσθαι τοῖς ἀκροωμένοις τι καὶ ἡδονῆς διὰ
208 τὴν ἱστορίαν τῆς σεμνολογίας. ἐπεὶ δέ ποτε προῆλθεν
ἐπὶ Καρχηδόνα, ἐξάρας ἐς φαντασίαν τάδε μάλιστα,

they sent a copy to Manlius Vulso, Scipio's successor in the command. He administered the oath to Antiochus' ambassadors at Apamea in Phrygia, while Antiochus did the same for the tribune Thermus, who had been sent for the purpose.[33] And so the war between Antiochus the Great and Rome came to an end. There was a view expressed that it did not go any further because of the kindness shown by Antiochus to Scipio's son. When Scipio returned to Rome, some people accused him of this, and two tribunes of the people brought a charge of bribery and treason against him.

40. He showed his disdain for the charge by ignoring it, and when the day of the trial came around, as it was the anniversary of his victory over Carthage, he sent an offering to the Capitol before arriving in court dressed splendidly, instead of in the pitiful and humble garments of a defendant. This immediately made a striking impression on everyone, and engendered goodwill toward what they believed to be a good man, aware of his clear conscience. When he began to speak he did not even mention the charge against him, but talked about his life, character, all his achievements, all the wars he had fought on behalf of his fatherland, how he had conducted the campaigns of each of them, and how often he had been victorious. The result was that the audience listened with pleasure to his proud account. Once he got around to the subject of Carthage, he exalted this story in particular, to excite the

204

205

206

207

208

[33] Cn. Manlius Vulso was consul in 189, when he succeeded Scipio in Asia. Q. Minucius Thermus had been consul in 193 and was not a military tribune, but he was part of the senior senatorial commission sent to settle Asia after the war (see Livy 37.55.7).

καὶ ὁρμῆς αὐτός τε ἐμπλησθεὶς καὶ τὸ πλῆθος ἐμπλή-
σας, εἶπεν ὅτι, "Τῆσδε τῆς ἡμέρας ἐγὼ τάδε ἐνίκων
καὶ Καρχηδόνα ὑμῖν, ὦ πολῖται, περιεποίουν, τὴν
209 τέως ἡμῖν ἐπιφοβωτάτην. ἄπειμι δὴ θύσων τῆς
ἡμέρας ἐς τὸ Καπιτώλιον· καὶ ὑμῶν ὅσοι φιλοπό-
λιδες, τῆς θυσίας μοι, γιγνομένης ὑπὲρ ὑμῶν συν-
άψασθε." ταῦτα ἔφη, καὶ ἐς τὸ Καπιτώλιον ἔθει, μη-
210 δὲν τῆς δίκης φροντίσας. εἵπετο δ᾽ αὐτῷ τὸ πλῆθος
καὶ οἱ πλέονες τῶν δικαστῶν σὺν εὐφήμῳ βοῇ, καὶ
211 θύοντι ὅμοια ἐπεφώνουν. οἱ κατήγοροι δὲ ἠποροῦντο,
καὶ οὔτε αὐτῷ τὴν δίκην αὖθις ὡς ἀτέλεστον ἐτόλμη-
σαν ἐπιγράψαι, οὔτε μέμψασθαι δημοκοπίας, δυνατώτερον αὐτοῦ τὸν βίον εἰδότες ὑπονοίας τε καὶ δια-
βολῆς.

212 41. Ὁ μὲν δὴ Σκιπίων ὧδε ἐγκλήματος ἀναξίου τῶν
βεβιωμένων οἱ κατεφρόνησε, σοφώτερον, ἐμοὶ δοκεῖν,
Ἀριστείδου περὶ κλοπῆς καὶ Σωκράτους περὶ ὧν ἐνε-
καλεῖτο οὐδὲν εἰπόντων ὑπ᾽ ἀδοξίας ὁμοίας, ἢ Σωκράτους εἰπόντος ἃ δοκεῖ Πλάτωνι, μεγαλοφρονέστε-
ρον δὲ ἄρα καὶ Ἐπαμεινώνδου, ὃς ἐβοιωτάρχει μὲν
213 ἅμα Πελοπίδα καὶ ἑτέρῳ, ἐξέπεμψαν δὲ αὐτοὺς οἱ
Θηβαῖοι, στρατὸν ἑκάστῳ δόντες, ἐπικουρεῖν Ἀρκάσι
καὶ Μεσσηνίοις πολεμουμένοις ὑπὸ Λακώνων, οὔπω
δ᾽ ὅσα ἐπενόουν ἐργασαμένους ἐπὶ διαβολῇ μετ-

---

34 Aristides was the fifth-century Athenian statesman known
as "the Just," for his upright character and disdain of money.
Plutarch (*Arist.* 4.3–5) has the story of his indictment for theft.

imagination, inspiring both himself and the crowd with the following words: "On this very day, fellow citizens, I won this victory and subjected to your power Carthage, so long the most frightening menace we faced. I am now 209 leaving for the Capitol to offer sacrifice in celebration of the day. All you who love Rome, join with me in this sacrifice, which I make on your behalf." Having finished his speech, he hurried off to the Capitol, without a thought for the charge against him. The crowd went with him, so 210 too most of the jurors, shouting auspiciously, as they did while he offered sacrifice. Those who had brought the 211 charge did not know what to do, not daring to reissue the indictment on the grounds that the case was incomplete, nor to criticize him for pandering to the mob, as they were well aware that he lived his life above suspicion or slander.

41. In this way Scipio treated with contempt an accusa- 212 tion that was unworthy of the life he had lived, and acted more wisely, it seems to me, than Aristides did when accused of theft, or Socrates when facing the charges made against him.[34] Both maintained a similarly scornful silence, unless Socrates spoke the words Plato gave him. Scipio was also more high-minded than Epaminondas, when he held the office of Boeotarch, along with Pelopidas and another person.[35] The Thebans gave each of them 213 an army and sent them off to assist the Arcadians and Messenians, against whom the Laconians were conducting a war, but recalled them to face charges before they

[35] Pelopidas and Epaminondas were the two Theban generals most associated with the decade of Theban dominance, from 371 to 362. There were seven, not three, Boeotarchs, the chief federal officials of the Boeotian League.

214 ἐκάλουν. οἱ δὲ τοῖς διαδόχοις σφῶν τὴν ἀρχὴν ἐπὶ
μῆνας ἓξ οὐ μεθῆκαν, ἕως τὰ Λακεδαιμονίων φρούρια
καθεῖλον καὶ ἐπέστησαν αὖθις ἕτερα τῶν Ἀρκάδων,
Ἐπαμεινώνδου τοὺς συστρατήγους ἐς τοῦτο ἀναγκά-
ζοντός τε, καὶ ὑποδεχομένου τὸ ἔργον αὐτοῖς ἀζήμιον
215 ἔσεσθαι. ἐπεὶ δὲ αὐτοῖς ἐπανελθοῦσιν οἱ κατήγοροι,
καθ᾽ ἕνα διώκοντες, ἐτιμῶντο θανάτου (θανάτῳ γὰρ ὁ
νόμος ἐζημίου γε τὸν ἐκ βίας ἀρχὴν ἄρξαντα ἀλλοτρίαν), οἱ μὲν ἕτεροι διέφυγον οἴκτῳ τε χρώμενοι καὶ
λόγοις πλείοσι, καὶ τὴν αἰτίαν ἐς τὸν Ἐπαμεινώνδαν
ἀναφέροντες, αὐτὸν οὕτω λέγειν ὑποθέμενον αὐτοῖς
216 καὶ λέγουσιν ἐπιμαρτυροῦντα· ὁ δὲ κρινόμενος τελευ-
ταῖος "Ὁμολογῶ," ἔφη, "Παρανόμως ἄρξαι τόνδε τὸν
χρόνον, καὶ οὓς ἀπελύσατε νῦν, ἐγὼ συναναγκάσαι.
217 καὶ οὐ παραιτοῦμαι τὸν θάνατον παρανομήσας. αἰτῶ
δ᾽ ὑμᾶς ἀντὶ τῶν προβεβιωμένων μοι κατὰ τὸν τάφον
ἐπιγράψαι· οὗτός ἐστιν ὁ περὶ Λεῦκτρα νικήσας καὶ
τὴν πατρίδα, τοὺς ἐχθροὺς οὐχ ὑπομένουσαν, οὐδ᾽ εἴ
τις ξένος ἔχοι Λακωνικὸν πῖλον, ἐπὶ τὴν Σπάρτην
αὐτὴν προαγαγών. οὗτος ὑπὸ τῆς πατρίδος ἀνῄρηται,
218 παρανομήσας ἐπὶ συμφέροντι τῆς πατρίδος.'" ταῦτ᾽
εἰπὼν κατέβη τε τοῦ βήματος, καὶ παρεδίδου τὸ
σῶμα τοῖς ἐθέλουσιν ἀπαγαγεῖν. οἱ δικασταὶ δὲ τῷ τε
ὀνείδει τοῦ λόγου καὶ θαύματι τῆς ἀπολογίας καὶ αἰ-
δοῖ τοῦ ἀνδρὸς ἀπολογουμένου, τὰς ψήφους οὐχ ὑπο-
στάντες λαβεῖν, ἐξέδραμον ἐκ τοῦ δικαστηρίου.

219 42. Τάδε μὲν δή τις, ὡς ἐθέλοι, συγκρίνειν ἔχει·
Μάλλιος δὲ ὁ τοῦ Σκιπίωνος διάδοχος τὴν ἀφαιρεθεῖ-

had executed their plans. The three of them refused 214
to hand over their command to their successors for six
months, until they had driven out the Lacedaemonian garrisons and replaced them with different ones, from Arca-
dia. Epaminondas had induced his fellow generals to do
this, but promised that they would not be punished for
their action. When they returned, their accusers prose- 215
cuted them separately and demanded the death penalty,
for it was a capital offense to conduct a military command
assigned to someone else. The two others were acquitted
by arousing pity with long speeches and laying the blame
on Epaminondas, who had in fact told them to say this,
and testified to the truth of their statement. He was put 216
on trial last. "I admit," he said, "that I illegally held command for this period, and that I forced the men you have
just acquitted to do so. As I have broken the law, I make
no appeal against the death penalty. But I do ask that in 217
return for my former services, you put the following inscription on my tomb: 'Here lies the victor of Leuctra. He
led his countrymen right up to Sparta itself, when they
refused to face their enemy, or even a stranger wearing a
Laconian cap. He was put to death by his country for
breaking the law in his country's best interests.'" With 218
these words, he stepped down from the podium and surrendered his person to anyone willing to lead him off to
punishment. But the judges, out of shame at his speech,
admiration for his defense, and respect for the man who
conducted it, did not stay to take a vote, but quickly left
the courtroom.

42. I provide this material so that anyone who wants to 219
can compare the cases. Scipio's successor, Manlius, went

σαν Ἀντιόχου γῆν ἐπιὼν καθίστατο, καὶ Γαλατῶν
τῶν Ἀντιόχῳ συμμαχησάντων Τολιστοβοίους, ἀνα-
φυγόντας ἐς τὸν Μύσιον Ὄλυμπον, ἐπιμόχθως τοῦ
ὄρους ἐπιβὰς ἐτρέπετο φεύγοντας, ἕως ἔκτεινε καὶ
κατεκρήμνισεν ὅσους ἀριθμήσασθαι διὰ τὸ πλῆθος
220 οὐκ ἐγένετο, αἰχμαλώτους δ᾽ ἔλαβεν ἐς τετρακισμυ-
ρίους, ὧν τὰ μὲν ὅπλα κατέκαυσε, τὰ δὲ σώματα, οὐ
δυνάμενος τοσόνδε πλῆθος ἐν πολέμοις περιάγεσθαι,
221 τοῖς ἐγγὺς βαρβάροις ἀπέδοτο. ἐν δὲ Τεκτοσάγαις τε
καὶ Τρόκμοις ἐκινδύνευσε μὲν ἐξ ἐνέδρας, καὶ ἔφυγεν·
ἐπανελθὼν δὲ ἐς αὐλιζομένους τε καὶ βεβυσμένους
ὑπὸ πλήθους περιέστησε τοὺς ψιλοὺς αὐτοῖς, καὶ
περιτρέχων ἐκέλευσεν ἐσακοντίζειν μήτε προσπλεκο-
222 μένους μήτε πλησιάζοντας. οὐδενὸς δὲ βέλους ἀτυ-
χοῦντος διὰ τὴν πυκνότητα τῶν πολεμίων, ἔκτεινεν ἐς
ὀκτακισχιλίους, καὶ ἐδίωξε τοὺς λοιποὺς ὑπὲρ Ἅλυν
223 ποταμόν. Ἀριαράθου δὲ τοῦ Καππαδοκῶν βασιλέως,
καὶ τοῦδε συμμάχους πέμψαντος Ἀντιόχῳ, δεδιότος τε
καὶ δεομένου καὶ διακόσια τάλαντα πέμψαντος ἐπὶ τῇ
δεήσει τὴν χώραν οὐκ ἐπέδραμεν, ἀλλ᾽ ἐς τὸν Ἑλλήσποντον ἐπανῆλθε σὺν γάζῃ τε πολλῇ καὶ χρήμασιν
ἀπείροις καὶ λείᾳ βαρυτάτῃ καὶ στρατῷ καταγόμῳ.
224 43. Τάδε μὲν καλῶς ἐπέπρακτο τῷ Μαλλίῳ· τὸ δ᾽
ἐντεῦθεν ἀλόγως πάμπαν ὥρᾳ θέρους πλεῦσαι μὲν
ὑπερεῖδεν, οὔτε τὸ βάρος ὧν ἐπήγετο ποιησάμενος
ἐνθύμιον, οὔτ᾽ ἐπειγόμενος διαπονεῖν ἢ γυμνάζειν
ὁδοιπορίαις ἔτι στρατὸν οὐκ ἐς πόλεμον ὁρμῶντα
225 ἀλλ᾽ ἐς οἰκείαν μετὰ λαφύρων ἐπανιόντα, διὰ δὲ

around the territory taken from Antiochus and put it in order. Of the Galatians who fought on Antiochus' side, the Tolistoboii had fled to Mount Olympus in Mysia. Here, Manlius climbed the mountain with difficulty and routed them as they fled. He killed and threw over the cliffs so many that it was impossible to count them, but he cap- 220
tured about forty thousand, burned their weapons and, as for the captives themselves, sold them to the neighboring barbarians, as he could not take such a large number around with him when he was at war. He faced danger 221
from the Tectosagi and Trocmi as a result of an ambush, but escaped, and returned to find them packed together, because of their great number, while making camp, which he surrounded with light-armed troops. Hurrying around, he ordered his men to discharge their missiles, but not to approach or join battle. None of the missiles missed such 222
a tightly bunched enemy force: he killed about eight thousand of them and chased the remainder beyond the river Halys. When king Ariarathes of Cappadocia, who had also 223
sent military assistance to Antiochus, became alarmed and made an appeal to Manlius, sending two hundred talents in addition to his entreaty, Manlius did not overrun his territory, but returned to the Hellespont with an army groaning under the weight of great treasures, huge amounts of money and heavy plunder.

43. This much had been well done by Manlius, but he 224
then very foolishly, as it was summer, neglected to return by sea. Taking no account of the weight of what he was transporting, and under no pressure to keep exercising or training his army with forced marches, since it was not going to war, but was on its way home with plunder, he 225

91

Θράκης ὥδευε, στενὴν καὶ μακρὰν καὶ δύσβατον
ὁδόν, πνίγους ὥρᾳ, οὔτ' ἐς Μακεδονίαν Φιλίππῳ προ-
επιστείλας ἀπαντᾶν, ἵνα παραπέμψειεν αὐτόν, οὔτε
τὸν στρατὸν ἐς μέρη πολλὰ διελών, ἵνα κουφότερον
βαδίζῃ καὶ τὰ χρήσιμα εὐμαρέστερα ἔχῃ, οὔτε τὰ
σκευοφόρα συντάξας ἐς λόχους ὀρθίους, ἵν' εὐφυ-
226   λακτότερα ᾖ. ἀλλ' ἀθρόως ἦγεν ἅπαντας ἐπὶ μῆκος
πολύ, καὶ τὰ σκευοφόρα εἶχεν ἐν μέσῳ, μήτε τῶν πρό-
σθεν αὐτοῖς δυναμένων ἐπικουρεῖν μήτε τῶν ὄπισθεν
227   ὀξέως διὰ μῆκος ὁμοῦ καὶ στενότητα τῆς ὁδοῦ. ὅθεν
αὐτῷ πανταχόθεν ἐς τὰ πλάγια τῶν Θρᾳκῶν ἐπικειμένων, πολὺ μέρος ἀπώλεσε τῆς τε λείας καὶ τῶν δη-
μοσίων χρημάτων καὶ αὐτοῦ δὴ τοῦ στρατοῦ. μετὰ δὲ
τῶν ὑπολοίπων ἐς Μακεδονίαν διεσώθη. ᾧ δὴ καὶ
μάλιστα ἐγένετο καταφανὲς ὅσον ὤνησε παραπέμπων
τοὺς Σκιπίωνας ὁ Φίλιππος, καὶ ὅσον ἥμαρτεν Ἀντίο-
228   χος ἐκλιπὼν τὴν Χερρόνησον. ὁ δὲ Μάλλιος ἔκ τε
Μακεδονίας ἐς Θεσσαλίαν διελθὼν καὶ ἐκ Θεσσαλίας
ἐς Ἤπειρον, ἐς Βρεντέσιον ἐπέρα, καὶ τὴν λοιπὴν
στρατιὰν ἐς τὰ οἰκεῖα διαφεὶς ἐπανῆλθεν ἐς Ῥώμην.

229   44. Ῥόδιοι δὲ καὶ Εὐμένης ὁ Περγάμου βασιλεὺς
μέγα φρονοῦντες ἐπὶ τῇ κατ' Ἀντιόχου συμμαχίᾳ,
Εὐμένης μὲν αὐτὸς ἐς Ῥώμην ἐστέλλετο, Ῥόδιοι δὲ
230   πρέσβεις ἔπεμπον. ἡ βουλὴ δὲ Ῥοδίοις μὲν ἔδωκε Λυκίους τε καὶ Κᾶρας, οὓς οὐ πολὺ ὕστερον ἀπέστησεν
αὐτῶν ὡς Περσεῖ τῷ Μακεδόνι μᾶλλον ἢ σφίσι πολεμοῦσι τῷ Περσεῖ προθυμοτέρων γενομένων, Εὐμένει δὲ παρέσχον ὅσα λοιπὰ ἀφῄρηντο Ἀντίοχον, χω-

marched through Thrace in stifling heat on a narrow, long, and difficult road. He did not send ahead to Macedonia to get Philip to meet him and act as guide; he did not divide his army into different sections so that it could move more quickly and have easier access to what it needed; he did not incorporate his baggage train into columns for ease of protection. Instead, he led the whole army in one long line, with the baggage train in the middle, where neither the vanguard nor the rearguard could come to their assistance quickly because of the distance involved and at the same time the narrowness of the road. For this reason, when the Thracians attacked his flanks from all directions, he lost much of the booty and public monies, and indeed much of the army too. He escaped with the remainder into Macedonia. These events made it very clear how valuable Philip had been to the Scipios as an escort, and what a mistake Antiochus had made in abandoning the Chersonesus. Manlius crossed from Macedonia into Thessaly, from Thessaly to Epirus and from there to Brundisium, where he disbanded and sent what was left of his army to their homes, and returned to Rome.

44. The Rhodians and king Eumenes of Pergamum were very proud of the assistance they had given against Antiochus. Eumenes set out for Rome in person, while the Rhodians sent ambassadors. The senate gave Lycia and Caria to Rhodes, although they took them away again not long after, on the grounds that when Rome was at war with Perseus of Macedon, the Rhodians had been more well disposed toward Perseus than Rome. The rest of the lands taken from Antiochus were given to Eumenes, apart from

231 ρὶς Ἑλλήνων τῶν ἐν αὑτοῖς. τούτων δὲ ὅσοι μὲν
Ἀττάλῳ τῷ πατρὶ Εὐμένους ἐτέλουν φόρους, ἐκέλευσαν Εὐμένει συμφέρειν, ὅσοι δ' Ἀντιόχῳ πρῶτον ἐτέλουν, ἀπέλυσαν τῶν φόρων καὶ αὐτονόμους ἀφῆκαν.

232   45. Ὧδε μὲν Ῥωμαῖοι διέθεντο τὰ δορίκτητα, Ἀντιόχου δ' ὕστερον τοῦ μεγάλου βασιλέως τελευτήσαντος
γίγνεται Σέλευκος ὁ υἱὸς διάδοχος· καὶ τὸν ἀδελφὸν
ὅδε Ἀντίοχον ἐξέλυσε τῆς ὑπὸ Ῥωμαίοις ὁμηρείας,

233 ἀντιδοὺς τὸν ἑαυτοῦ παῖδα Δημήτριον. Ἀντιόχου δ'
ἐπανιόντος ἐκ τῆς ὁμηρείας καὶ ὄντος ἔτι περὶ Ἀθήνας, ὁ μὲν Σέλευκος ἐξ ἐπιβουλῆς Ἡλιοδώρου τινὸς
τῶν περὶ τὴν αὐλὴν ἀποθνήσκει, τὸν δ' Ἡλιόδωρον
Εὐμένης καὶ Ἄτταλος ἐς τὴν ἀρχὴν βιαζόμενον ἐκ-
βάλλουσι, καὶ τὸν Ἀντίοχον ἐς αὐτὴν κατάγουσιν,
ἑταιριζόμενοι τὸν ἄνδρα· ἀπὸ γὰρ τινῶν προσκρου-

234 σμάτων ἤδη καὶ οἵδε Ῥωμαίους ὑπεβλέποντο. οὕτω
μὲν Ἀντίοχος ὁ Ἀντιόχου τοῦ μεγάλου Συρίας ἐπε-
κράτησεν· ὅτῳ παρὰ τῶν Σύρων ἐπώνυμον ἦν ἐπι-
φανής, ὅτι τῆς ἀρχῆς ἁρπαζομένης ὑπὸ ἀλλοτρίων

235 βασιλεὺς οἰκεῖος ὤφθη. συνθέμενος δὲ φιλίαν καὶ
συμμαχίαν Εὐμένει, Συρίας καὶ τῶν περὶ αὐτὴν ἐθνῶν
ἐγκρατῶς ἦρχε, σατράπην μὲν ἔχων ἐν Βαβυλῶνι
Τίμαρχον, ἐπὶ δὲ ταῖς προσόδοις Ἡρακλείδην,
ἀδελφὼ μὲν ἀλλήλοιν, ἄμφω δὲ αὐτοῦ γενομένω παι-
δικά.

---

[36] Seleucus IV Philopator ("Father-loving") ruled Syria from
187 to 175.   [37] Antiochus IV Epiphanes ("Made Manifest"),
king of Syria from 175 to 164.

the Greek states in those territories. Of these, the cities   231
that had paid tribute to Attalus, Eumenes' father, Rome
now ordered to pay their contribution to Eumenes, and
those that originally paid their taxes to Antiochus, were
freed of tribute altogether and made independent.

45. This is how the Romans disposed of what they had   232
acquired in the war. Later on, when Antiochus the Great
died, his son Seleucus succeeds to the throne.[36] Seleucus
had his brother Antiochus released as a hostage in Rome,
and replaced him with his own son, Demetrius. When   233
Antiochus was still in Athens on his way home from captivity, Seleucus dies as a result of a plot led by a certain
Heliodorus, one of his courtiers. When he tried to force
his way into power, however, Eumenes and Attalus expelled him, and restored Antiochus to the throne, in order
to win his favor. For, as a result of certain disagreements,
they too now had their suspicions of Rome. In this way   234
Antiochus, son of Antiochus the Great, took power in
Syria.[37] He was given the title Epiphanes by the Syrians,
because when an attempt was made by outsiders to seize
the throne, he made an epiphany as a real king. Having   235
struck a treaty of friendship and alliance with Eumenes,
he ruled Syria and its neighboring peoples with a firm
hand. He had Timarchus as satrap in Babylon, and put
Heracleides in charge of finances, two brothers, both of
them who had been favorites of his.[38]

[38] It seems likely that Appian has confused Timarchus and
Heracleides with another set of brothers, Aristos and Themison,
whom the third-century BC historian Phylarchus identified as
lovers of Antiochus II—according to Athenaeus (10.438C). See
Goukowsky 2007, 139n551.

236   46. Ἐστράτευσε δὲ καὶ ἐπὶ Ἀρταξίαν τὸν Ἀρμενίων
βασιλέα. καὶ αὐτὸν ἑλὼν ἐτελεύτησεν, ἐνναετὲς παιδίον ἀπολιπών, Ἀντίοχον, ᾧ προσέθηκαν ὄνομα Εὐπάτωρ οἱ Σύροι διὰ τὴν τοῦ πατρὸς ἀρετήν. καὶ τὸ
237   παιδίον ἔτρεφε Λυσίας. ἡ δὲ σύγκλητος ἤσθη φανέν-
τος ἐν ὀλίγῳ τοῦ Ἀντιόχου γεννικοῦ καὶ ταχέως ἀπο-
238   θανόντος. Δημήτριόν τε τὸν Σελεύκου μὲν υἱὸν Ἀντιόχου δὲ τοῦ Ἐπιφανοῦς ἀδελφιδοῦν, υἱωνὸν δὲ τοῦ
μεγάλου Ἀντιόχου, ἀνεψιὸν ὄντα τῷδε τῷ παιδίῳ,
ὁμηρεύοντα ἔτι ἐν τῇ Ῥώμῃ καὶ ἔτος ἄγοντα τρίτον
ἐπὶ τοῖς εἴκοσιν, ἐς τὴν βασιλείαν καταχθῆναι παρα-
καλοῦντα ὡς αὑτῷ μᾶλλον προσήκουσαν, οὐ κατήγαγον, οὐ συμφέρειν σφίσιν ἡγούμενοι τελειότερον ἄρ-
239   χειν Σύρων ἀντὶ παιδὸς ἀτελοῦς. πυνθανόμενοι δ' ἐν
Συρίᾳ στρατόν τ' ἐλεφάντων εἶναι καὶ ναῦς πλείονας
τῶν ὡρισμένων Ἀντιόχῳ, πρέσβεις ἔπεμπον, οἳ τοὺς
ἐλέφαντας συγκόψειν ἔμελλον καὶ τὰς ναῦς διαπρή-
240   σειν. οἰκτρὰ δὲ ἡ ὄψις ἦν ἀναιρουμένων θηρίων
ἡμέρων τε καὶ σπανίων, καὶ νεῶν κατεμπιπραμένων·
καί τις ἐν Λαοδικείᾳ Λεπτίνης τὴν ὄψιν οὐκ ἐνεγκών,
Γναῖον Ὀκτάουιον τὸν τῶνδε τῶν πρέσβεων ἡγεμόνα,
ἀλειφόμενον ἐν τῷ γυμνασίῳ, διεχρήσατο.

241   47. Καὶ τὸν μὲν Ὀκτάουιον ἔθαπτεν ὁ Λυσίας, Δημήτριος δὲ αὖθις ἐς τὴν σύγκλητον ἐσελθὼν ἐδεῖτο
τῆς γοῦν ὁμηρείας μόνης ἀπολυθῆναι, ὡς Ἀντιόχου
242   μὲν ἀντιδοθείς, Ἀντιόχου δ' ἀποθανόντος. ἐπεὶ δ' οὐκ

46. He also conducted a campaign against Artaxias, 236
king of Armenia, whom he killed, and then died himself.
He left a nine-year-old son, Antiochus, to whom the Syrians gave the title Eupator on account of his father's excellence.[39] Lysias acted as tutor for the boy. The senate were 237
pleased that Antiochus Epiphanes died prematurely, as he
had shown signs of nobility in his short reign. Demetrius, 238
the son of Seleucus, nephew of Antiochus Epiphanes,
grandson of Antiochus the Great and first cousin of the
young boy, was still a hostage in Rome, and now in his
twenty-third year, when he asked to be installed on the
throne, to which he maintained he had a better claim; the
Romans refused. They thought it would be more advantageous to them if an immature boy ruled Syria rather than
a grown man. When they learned that there was an army 239
of elephants in Syria and more ships than had been allowed in the treaty with Antiochus, they sent a mission
with instructions to hamstring the elephants and burn the
ships. It was a sad sight to see the destruction of these 240
gentle and rare animals, and the burning of the ships, and
in Laodicea, a man called Leptines, unable to bear what
he was seeing, killed Gnaeus Octavius, the leader of the
Roman mission, as he was oiling himself in the gymnasium.[40]

47. Lysias had Octavius buried. Demetrius approached 241
the senate a second time, asking that at least he be released as a hostage, since he had been handed over as a
replacement for Antiochus, who was now dead. When 242

[39] The boy-king, Antiochus V Eupator ("Of Good Father"),
ruled from 164 to162.   [40] Cn. Octavius (consul 165) was
sent on this mission in 163 and killed by Leptines in 162.

ἐτύγχανεν οὐδὲ τοῦδε, λαθὼν ἐξέπλευσε, καὶ δεξα-
μένων αὐτὸν ἀσμένως τῶν Σύρων ἦρχε, τόν τε Λυσίαν
καὶ τὸ παιδίον ἐπ' αὐτῷ διαφθείρας, καὶ Ἡρακλείδην
ἐκβαλών, καὶ Τίμαρχον ἐπανιστάμενον ἀνελών, καὶ
τἆλλα πονηρῶς τῆς Βαβυλῶνος ἡγούμενον· ἐφ' ᾧ καὶ
243 Σωτήρ, ἀρξαμένων τῶν Βαβυλωνίων, ὠνομάσθη. κρα-
τυνάμενος δὲ τὴν ἀρχὴν ὁ Δημήτριος στέφανόν τε
Ῥωμαίοις ἀπὸ χρυσῶν μυρίων, χαριστήριον τῆς ποτὲ
παρ' αὐτοῖς ὁμηρείας, καὶ Λεπτίνην τὸν ἀνδροφόνον
Ὀκταουίου. οἱ δὲ τὸν μὲν στέφανον ἐδέχοντο, Λεπτίνην δὲ οὐκ ἔλαβον, ὡς δή τι τοῦτ' ἔγκλημα τοῖς
244 Σύροις ταμιευόμενοι. Δημήτριος δὲ καὶ ἐκ τῆς Καππαδοκῶν ἀρχῆς Ἀριαράθην ἐκβαλών, Ὀλοφέρνην ἐπὶ
χιλίοις ταλάντοις ἀντ' αὐτοῦ κατήγαγεν, ἀδελφὸν εἶναι δοκοῦντα Ἀριαράθου.

245   48. Καὶ Ῥωμαίοις ἐδόκει μέν, ὡς ἀδελφούς, Ἀριαράθην καὶ Ὀλοφέρνην βασιλεύειν ὁμοῦ, ἐκπεσόντων
δὲ καὶ τῶνδε καὶ Ἀριοβαρζάνου μετ' αὐτοὺς οὐ πολὺ
ὕστερον ὑπὸ Μιθριδάτου τοῦ Ποντικοῦ βασιλέως, ὁ
Μιθριδάτειος πόλεμος ἐπὶ τῷδε καὶ ἐφ' ἑτέροις ἤρξατο συνίστασθαι, μέγιστός τε καὶ πολυτροπώτατος
ἔθνεσι πολλοῖς γενόμενος, καὶ παρατείνας ἐς ἔτη
μάλιστα τεσσαράκοντα, ἐν οἷς πολλαὶ μὲν ἀρχαὶ

---

41 Demetrius I Soter ("Savior") ruled from 162 to 150.

42 Ariarathes V Eusebes Philopator ("Pious, Father-loving")
ruled from about 163 to about 130. The senate divided the king-

even this argument failed, he escaped secretly by ship, and, on receiving a warm welcome from the Syrians, took over the throne, having killed Lysias and the boy as well. Heraclides he expelled and executed Timarchus, who had risen in revolt and had governed Babylon in a generally corrupt manner. It was for this reason that, on the proposal of the Babylonians, Demetrius received the title Soter.[41] When he had consolidated his rule, he sent a crown worth 243 ten thousand pieces of gold to Rome, in thanks for the conditions he had formerly enjoyed as a hostage there, along with Leptines, the murderer of Octavius. The Romans accepted the crown, but would not take Leptines, as they wanted to store this up as a charge to make against the Syrians. Demetrius drove Ariarathes out of the king- 244 dom of Cappadocia, and installed Olophernes in his place, in return for one thousand talents. Olophernes was sup- posed to be a brother of Ariarathes.

48. The Romans decided that, if they were brothers, 245 they should rule jointly.[42] The brothers and, not long after, their successor Ariobarzanes were driven out by Mithri- dates, the Pontic king.[43] This and other incidents resulted in the Mithridatic War, a major conflict that extended over nearly forty years and had greatly varying effects on many

dom between him and his brother Orophernes, but Ariarathes expelled him.

[43] A misleadingly compressed chronology, which skips half a century, taking the reader to the reign of Mithridates VI Eupator ("Of Good Father"), who ruled Pontus from about 120 until his death in 63. The first of three wars he fought against Rome began in 89. Ariobarzanes I of Cappadocia spent much of his reign (ca. 95–63/2) being repeatedly expelled and restored.

Σύροις ἐκ τοῦ βασιλείου γένους ὀλιγοχρόνιοι πάμπαν
ἐγένοντο, πολλαὶ δὲ τροπαὶ καὶ ἐπαναστάσεις ἐπὶ τὰ
246 βασίλεια. Παρθυαῖοί τε προαποστάντες ἀπὸ τῆς τῶν
Σελευκιδῶν ἀρχῆς Μεσοποταμίαν ἐς ἑαυτοὺς περι-
247 έσπασαν, ἢ τοῖς Σελευκίδαις ὑπήκουεν. καὶ βασιλεὺς
Ἀρμενίας Τιγράνης ὁ Τιγράνους ἔθνη πολλὰ τῶν πε-
ριοίκων ἰδίοις δυνάσταις χρώμενα ἑλών, βασιλεὺς
ἀπὸ τοῦδε βασιλέων ἡγεῖτο εἶναι, καὶ τοῖς Σελευκί-
248 δαις ἐπεστράτευεν οὐκ ἐθέλουσιν ὑπακούειν. οὐχ ὑπο-
στάντος δ᾽ αὐτὸν Ἀντιόχου τοῦ εὐσεβοῦς, ὁ Τιγράνης
ἦρχε Συρίας τῆς μετ᾽ Εὐφράτην, ὅσα γένη Σύρων
μέχρι Αἰγύπτου. ἦρχε δὲ ὁμοῦ καὶ Κιλικίας (καὶ γὰρ
ἥδε τοῖς Σελευκίδαις ὑπήκουε), Βαγαδάτην στρατηγὸν ἐπιτάξας ἅπασιν, ἐπὶ ἔτη τεσσαρεσκαίδεκα.

249 49. Λευκόλλου δὲ τοῦ Ῥωμαίων στρατηγοῦ Μιθριδάτην διώκοντος ἐς τὸν Τιγράνην ὑποφεύγοντα, ὁ
Βαγαδάτης ᾔει μετὰ τοῦ στρατοῦ Τιγράνῃ βοηθή-
σων, καὶ ἐν τῷδε παραδὺς ἐς τὴν Συρίαν Ἀντίοχος ὁ
250 Ἀντιόχου τοῦ εὐσεβοῦς ἦρχε τῶν Σύρων ἑκόντων. καὶ
αὐτῷ Λεύκολλος μέν, ὁ Τιγράνῃ πρῶτός τε πολεμήσας καὶ τῆς ἐπικτήτου γῆς αὐτὸν ἐξελάσας, οὐκ
ἐφθόνησεν ἀρχῆς πατρῴας· Πομπήιος δέ, ὁ ἐπὶ Λευ-
κόλλῳ Μιθριδάτην ἐξελών, Τιγράνῃ μὲν Ἀρμενίας

---

44 Tigranes II the Great ruled Armenia from about 100 to his
death in the mid-fifties. Antiochus X Eusebes Philopator ("Pious,
Father-loving") became king of Syria in 95, but it is not clear when
his reign ended.

peoples. In this period there were many kings of Syria
from the royal family who had very short reigns, and the
crown faced many crises and revolts. The Parthians, who   246
themselves had earlier seceded from Seleucid rule, annexed Mesopotamia, which was subject to the Seleucids.
The king of Armenia, Tigranes, son of Tigranes, subjected   247
many neighboring peoples with their own princes, and as
a result had himself styled "king of kings." He campaigned
against the Seleucids when they refused to submit. When   248
Antiochus Eusebes offered no resistance, Tigranes became king of all the Syrian peoples this side of the Euphrates as far as Egypt. At the same time he ruled Cilicia as
well for a period of fourteen years—it too had been subject to the Seleucids—and put Bagadates in command of
all these regions.[44]

49. When the Roman general Lucullus was pursuing   249
Mithridates, who had taken refuge with Tigranes, Bagadates went with his army to help Tigranes. In the meantime, Antiochus, son of Antiochus Eusebes, slipped into
Syria and took over the throne, with the approval of the
Syrian people.[45] Lucullus, who had been the first to cam-   250
paign against Tigranes and had driven him out of the territories he had annexed, did not begrudge Antiochus
his ancestral kingdom. But Lucullus' successor, Pompey,
when he had defeated Mithridates, allowed Tigranes to

[45] L. Licinius Lucullus (consul 74) fought against Mithridates
from 74 until 67. His command was split among different Roman
commanders, until Pompey took over in 66. The son of Antiochus
Eusebes, Antiochus XIII Asiaticus, was approved as king by Lucullus in 69, but was deposed by Pompey in 64, thus bringing the
Seleucid kingdom to an end.

συνεχώρησεν ἄρχειν, Ἀντίοχον δὲ ἐξέβαλε τῆς Σύρων
ἀρχῆς, οὐδὲν ἐς Ῥωμαίους ἁμαρτόντα, ἔργῳ μὲν ὅτι
ἦν εὔκολον αὐτῷ, στρατιὰν ἔχοντι, πολλὴν ἀρχὴν
ἄνοπλον ἀφελέσθαι, λόγῳ δὲ ὅτι τοὺς Σελευκίδας,
ὑπὸ Τιγράνους ἐκπεσόντας, οὐκ εἰκὸς ἦν ἔτι Συρίας
ἄρχειν μᾶλλον ἢ Ῥωμαίους Τιγράνην νενικηκότας.

251   50. Οὕτω μὲν δὴ Κιλικίας τε καὶ Συρίας τῆς τε
μεσογείου καὶ κοίλης καὶ Φοινίκης καὶ Παλαιστίνης,
καὶ ὅσα ἄλλα Συρίας ἀπὸ Εὐφράτου μέχρι Αἰγύπτου
καὶ μέχρι θαλάσσης ὀνόματα, ἀμαχὶ Ῥωμαῖοι κατ-
252 έσχον. ἐν δὲ γένος ἔτι τὸ Ἰουδαίων ἐνιστάμενον ὁ
Πομπήιος ἐξεῖλε κατὰ κράτος, καὶ τὸν βασιλέα Ἀρι-
στόβουλον ἔπεμψεν ἐς Ῥώμην, καὶ τὴν μεγίστην
πόλιν Ἱεροσόλυμα καὶ ἁγιωτάτην αὐτοῖς κατέσκαψεν,
ἣν δὴ καὶ Πτολεμαῖος ὁ πρῶτος Αἰγύπτου βασιλεὺς
καθῃρήκει, καὶ Οὐεσπασιανὸς αὖθις οἰκισθεῖσαν κατ-
253 έσκαψε, καὶ Ἀδριανὸς αὖθις ἐπ᾽ ἐμοῦ. καὶ διὰ ταῦτ᾽
ἐστὶν Ἰουδαίοις ἅπασιν ὁ φόρος τῶν σωμάτων βαρύ-
τερος ⟨τοῦ⟩[14] τῆς ἄλλης περιουσίας. ἔστι δὲ καὶ Σύροις καὶ Κίλιξιν ἐτήσιος, ἑκατοστὴ τοῦ τιμήματος
254 ἑκάστῳ. Πομπήιος μὲν οὖν τῶνδε τῶν ὑπὸ τοῖς Σελευκίδαις γενομένων ἐθνῶν τοῖς μὲν[15] ἐπέστησεν οἰκείους
βασιλέας ἢ δυνάστας, καθὰ καὶ Γαλατῶν τῶν ἐν
Ἀσίᾳ, τοῖς δὲ δυνάσταις ἐβεβαίωσε τὰς τετραδαρ-
χίας, συμμαχήσασίν οἱ κατὰ Μιθριδάτου. καὶ οὐ

14 τοῦ add. Goukowsky
15 post μὲν lac. indic. Schweig.

rule Armenia, and deposed Antiochus from the Syrian throne, even though he had committed no offense against Rome. The fact is, it was easy for Pompey, with an army under his command, to take over a large, defenseless kingdom. The argument used, however, was that, as the Seleucids had been driven out by Tigranes, it was not fitting that they should continue to rule Syria rather than the Romans, who had defeated Tigranes.

50. In this way, and without fighting, the Romans came 251 to possess Cilicia and inland Syria and Coele Syria and Palestine and all the regions of Syria bearing other names between the Euphrates, Egypt, and the Mediterranean. The Jewish people were the only ones still resisting, but 252 Pompey reduced them by force, sent their king, Aristobulus, to Rome, and destroyed their most important and holiest city, Jerusalem, just as Ptolemy, the first king of Egypt, had done before. It was rebuilt, but Vespasian destroyed it again, and once again, in my lifetime, Hadrian did the same.[46] For this reason the poll tax paid by all Jews 253 is higher than the tax on the rest of their property. The Syrians and Cilicians also pay an annual tax, assessed at one percent of their ratable valuation. Of the peoples pre- 254 viously under Seleucid rule, for some of them Pompey set up their own kings or princes, as in the case of the Galatians of Asia, while the existing princes, who had assisted him in the war against Mithridates, he confirmed in their tetrarchies.[47] Not long after, these too gradually came

[46] Neither Ptolemy I nor Pompey destroyed Jerusalem. Both of them captured the city. The city and the Temple were destroyed in AD 70, during Vespasian's principate, but by his son Titus. [47] The text of this sentence is uncertain. Schweighäuser thought there was a lacuna in it.

πολὺ ὕστερον καὶ τάδε περιῆλθεν ἐς Ῥωμαίους, ἐπὶ
Καίσαρος μάλιστα τοῦ Σεβαστοῦ, κατὰ μέρη.

255   51. Συρίας δ' εὐθὺς ὁ Πομπήιος Σκαῦρον τὸν ἐν
τοῖς πολέμοις ἑαυτῷ γενόμενον ταμίαν ἔταξεν ἡγεῖσθαι, καὶ ἡ βουλὴ Φίλιππον ἐπὶ Σκαύρῳ τὸν Μάρ-
κιον, καὶ Μαρκελλῖνον Λέντλον ἐπὶ τῷ Φιλίππῳ,
256   ἄμφω στρατηγικοὺς κατ' ἀξίωσιν. ἀλλὰ τῶνδε μὲν
ἑκατέρῳ διετὴς ἐτρίφθη χρόνος, τοὺς γείτονας ἐν-
οχλοῦντας Ἄραβας ἀμυνομένῳ. καὶ τοῦδε χάριν ἐς τὸ
ἔπειτα ἐγένοντο Συρίας στρατηγοὶ τῶν τὰ ἐπώνυμα
ἀρξάντων ἐν ἄστει, ἵνα δὴ ἔχοιεν ἐξουσίαν καταλό-
257   γου τε στρατιᾶς καὶ πολέμου οἷα ὕπατοι. καὶ πρῶτος
ἐκ τῶνδε ἐπέμφθη Γαβίνιος μετὰ στρατιᾶς. καὶ πολεμεῖν αὐτὸν ὁρμῶντα Μιθριδάτης μὲν ὁ Παρθυαίων
βασιλεύς, ἐξελαυνόμενος τῆς ἀρχῆς ὑπ' Ὑρώδου τοῦ
ἀδελφοῦ, μετῆγεν ἐξ Ἀράβων ἐπὶ Παρθυαίους, Πτολεμαῖος δὲ αὐτόν, ὁ ἑνδέκατος Αἰγύπτου βασιλεύς,
ἐκπεσὼν καὶ ὅδε τῆς ἀρχῆς, μετέπεισε χρήμασι πολ-
258   λοῖς ἀντὶ Παρθυαίων ἐπὶ Ἀλεξανδρέας ὁρμῆσαι. καὶ
κατήγαγε μὲν τὸν Πτολεμαῖον ἐπὶ τὴν ἀρχὴν ὁ Γαβίνιος, Ἀλεξανδρεῦσι πολεμήσας, ὑπὸ δὲ τῆς Ῥωμαίων βουλῆς ἔφυγεν ἐπὶ τῷ ἄνευ ψηφίσματος ἐς
Αἴγυπτον ἐμβαλεῖν, ἐπὶ πολέμῳ Ῥωμαίοις ἀπαισίῳ

---

48 M. Aemilius Scaurus was quaestor in 66 and served with
Pompey in Syria, until he was replaced by L. Marcius Philippus,
probably in 61, who in turn was replaced by Cn. Cornelius Lentulus Marcellinus (consul 56) in 59.

under Roman control, especially in the time of Caesar Augustus.

51. Pompey immediately appointed Scaurus, who had   255
been his quaestor during his campaigns, to the Syrian command. After Scaurus, the senate put two men of praetorian rank in charge of Syria, Marcius Philippus first, and Lentulus Marcellinus after Philippus.[48] But both of them   256
spent their two years of command in defending Syria against harassment by the neighboring Arabs. Because of this, governors of Syria were thereafter chosen from those who had previously held the consulship in Rome, no doubt to ensure that they had the same power as consuls to enlist armies and fight wars. The first of these to be sent out with   257
an army was Gabinius. Mithridates, king of Parthia, who had been driven from the kingdom by his brother, Hyrodes, managed to get Gabinius, as he was setting off to war, to change his objective from the Arabs to the Parthians. Then Ptolemy, the eleventh king of Egypt, another exile from his own kingdom, paid a great deal of money for Gabinius to change his mind again and attack Alexandria rather than Parthia. Gabinius waged war on the Alex-   258
andrians and restored Ptolemy to the throne, but was exiled by the senate for invading Egypt without their authorization.[49] This was considered an ill-omened war at

[49] Aulus Gabinius (consul 58) governed Syria from 57 to 55, when M. Licinius Crassus took over, after his consulship in 55. Mithridates III of Parthia was ousted by his brother, Orodes, restored by Gabinius, but eventually defeated and executed by Orodes in 54. Gabinius restored Ptolemy XII Auletes ("the flute player") to the throne of Egypt in 55.

νομιζομένῳ· ἦν γάρ τι Σιβύλλειον αὐτοῖς ἀπαγο-
259 ρεῦον. ἐπὶ δὲ Γαβινίῳ μοι δοκεῖ Κράσσος ἄρξαι
Σύρων, ὅτῳ πολεμοῦντι Παρθυαίοις ἡ μεγάλη συμ-
φορὰ γίγνεται. καὶ ἐπὶ Λευκίου Βύβλου μετὰ Κράσ-
σον στρατηγοῦντος Συρίας ἐς τὴν Συρίαν ἐσέβαλον
οἱ Παρθυαῖοι. Σάξα δὲ μετὰ Βύβλον ἡγουμένου καὶ
τὰ μέχρι Ἰωνίας ἐπέδραμον, ἀσχολουμένων Ῥωμαίων
ἐς τὰ ἐπ' ἀλλήλους ἐμφύλια.

260   52. Ἀλλὰ τάδε μὲν ἐντελῶς ἐν τῇ Παρθικῇ συγ-
γραφῇ λέξω· τῆς δὲ βίβλου τῆσδε οὔσης Συριακῆς,
ὅπως μὲν ἔσχον Συρίαν Ῥωμαῖοι καὶ συνέστησαν ἐς
τὰ νῦν ὄντα, εἴρηται, οὐκ ἀπεικὸς δὲ τὰ Μακεδόνων
ἐπιδραμεῖν, οἳ πρὸ Ῥωμαίων Συρίας ἐβασίλευον.
261 Ἀλέξανδρος μὲν δὴ βασιλεὺς ἦν ἐπὶ Πέρσαις Σύρων,
ὁ καὶ πάντων βασιλεὺς ὅσων εἶδεν· Ἀλεξάνδρου δ'
ἀποθανόντος ἐπὶ παισὶ τῷ μὲν βραχεῖ πάνυ τῷ δὲ ἔτι
κυϊσκομένῳ, οἱ μὲν Μακεδόνες, πόθῳ τοῦ Φιλιππείου
γένους, εἴλοντο σφῶν βασιλεύειν Ἀριδαῖον τὸν ἀδελφὸν Ἀλεξάνδρου, καίπερ οὐκ ἔμφρονα νομιζόμενον
εἶναι, μετονομάσαντες δὴ Φίλιππον ἀντὶ Ἀριδαίου,
τρεφομένων ἔτι τῶν παίδων Ἀλεξάνδρου (ἐφύλαξαν
262 γὰρ δὴ καὶ τὴν κύουσαν), οἱ φίλοι δ' ἐς σατραπείας
ἐνείμαντο τὰ ἔθνη, Περδίκκου διανέμοντος αὐτοῖς ὑπὸ
τῷ βασιλεῖ Φιλίππῳ. καὶ οὐ πολὺ ὕστερον τῶν βασιλέων ἀποθανόντων βασιλεῖς ἐγένοντο οἱ σατράπαι.
263 Σύρων δὴ πρῶτος γίγνεται σατράπης Λαομέδων ὁ

Rome, because there was something in the Sibylline books
that prohibited it. After Gabinius, I believe Crassus was   259
governor of Syria, the Crassus who suffers such a disastrous defeat when fighting against the Parthians. In the
governorship of Lucius Bibulus, Crassus' successor, the
Parthians invaded Syria, and when Saxa was governor after
Bibulus, they even advanced as far as Ionia, the Romans
being preoccupied at the time with their civil wars.[50]

52. I will discuss these matters in detail in my Parthian   260
book. But as this is my Syrian book, and I have described
how Rome got possession of Syria and established it in its
present form, it is not out of place to run through its history in the time of the Macedonians, who ruled it before
Rome. Alexander, of course, became king of Syria after the   261
Persians; indeed he became king of all he surveyed. Alexander died leaving one very small child and one still in the
womb, and out of love for the family of Philip, the Macedonians chose Alexander's brother Arrhidaeus as their
king, although he was not thought to be of sound mind,
and they changed his name from Arrhidaeus to Philip.
While the children were still being brought up (they even
guarded Alexander's pregnant wife), the courtiers divided   262
the peoples into satrapies, and Perdiccas, acting in the
name of king Philip, assigned the satrapies to the courtiers. Not long after, when the kings themselves died, the
satraps became kings. The first satrap of Syria is Laome-   263

[50] Crassus was defeated and killed by the Parthians at the
battle of Carrhae in 53. C. Cassius Longinus took over command
in Syria, before he was replaced by Marcus (not Lucius) Calpur-
nius Bibulus (consul 59) in 51. L. Decidius Saxa, a legate of Marc
Antony in Syria, was captured and killed by the Parthians in 40.

Μιτυληναῖος ἔκ τε Περδίκκου καὶ ἐξ Ἀντιπάτρου τοῦ
μετὰ τὸν Περδίκκαν προστατεύσαντος τῶν βασιλέων.
264 Λαομέδοντα δ᾽ ἐπιπλεύσας Πτολεμαῖος ὁ τῆς Αἰγύπτου σατράπης ἔπειθε πολλοῖς χρήμασιν ἐγχειρίσαι
οἱ τὴν Συρίαν, προβολήν τε οὖσαν Αἰγύπτου καὶ ἐπι-
265 χείρημα κατὰ Κύπρου. καὶ οὐ πειθόμενον συλλαμ-
βάνει· ὁ δὲ τοὺς φύλακας διαφθείρας πρὸς Ἀλκέταν
ἔφυγεν ἐς Καρίαν. καί τινα χρόνον ὁ Πτολεμαῖος
ἦρχε Συρίας, καὶ φρουρὰς ἐν ταῖς πόλεσι καταλιπὼν
ἐς Αἴγυπτον ἀπέπλει.
266   53. Ἀντίγονος δ᾽ ἦν Φρυγίας μὲν καὶ Λυκίας καὶ
Παμφυλίας σατράπης, ἐπίσκοπος δ᾽ εἶναι τῆς ὅλης
Ἀσίας ἐξ Ἀντιπάτρου περῶντος ἐς τὴν Εὐρώπην ἀπο-
λελειμμένος, Εὐμένη τὸν Καππαδοκίας σατράπην,
ψηφισαμένων εἶναι πολέμιον τῶν Μακεδόνων, ἐπολι-
267 όρκει. ὁ δὲ αὐτὸν ἐκφεύγει, καὶ τὴν Μηδικὴν ἐκρατύνετο ἑαυτῷ. ἀλλ᾽ Εὐμένη μὲν κτείνει καταλαβὼν ὁ
Ἀντίγονος, καὶ ἐπανιὼν ὑπεδέχθη λαμπρῶς ὑπὸ Σε-
268 λεύκου σατραπεύοντος ἐν Βαβυλῶνι. ὑβρίσαντος δέ
τινα τῶν ἡγεμόνων τοῦ Σελεύκου, καὶ οὐ κοινώσαντος
Ἀντιγόνῳ παρόντι, χαλεπήνας ὁ Ἀντίγονος ᾔτει λο-
γισμοὺς χρημάτων τε καὶ κτημάτων. ὁ δὲ ἀσθενέστε-
ρος ὢν Ἀντιγόνου πρὸς Πτολεμαῖον ἐς Αἴγυπτον ὑπ-
269 εχώρει. καὶ ὁ Ἀντίγονος εὐθὺς ἐπὶ τῇ φυγῇ τοῦ
Σελεύκου Βλίτορά τε, Μεσοποταμίας ἡγούμενον, παρ-
έλυσε τῆς ἀρχῆς, ὅτι Σέλευκον μεθῆκεν ἀπιόντα, καὶ
τὴν Βαβυλωνίαν καὶ τὴν Μεσοποταμίαν καὶ ὅσα
ἄλλα ἐκ Μήδων ἐπὶ τὸν Ἑλλήσποντον ἔθνη, καθ-

don of Mytilene, appointed on the authority of Perdiccas, and Antipater, who followed Perdiccas as regent for the royal princes. Ptolemy, satrap of Egypt, sailed against 264 Laomedon and tried to persuade him, with the offer of a large sum of money, to hand over Syria, as it offered a good defense for Egypt and a good base of operations against Cyprus. When he refused, Ptolemy arrests him, but 265 Laomedon bribed his guards and escaped to Alcetas in Caria. Ptolemy ruled Syria for a time, and then sailed back to Egypt, leaving garrisons in the towns.

53. Antigonus, satrap of Phrygia, Lycia, and Pamphylia, 266 was also left by Antipater, when he crossed over to Europe, as superintendent of the whole of Asia. When the Macedonians declared Eumenes, satrap of Cappadocia, a public enemy, Antigonus laid siege to him. Although he 267 escapes and became master of Media, Antigonus later captures and executes Eumenes. On his way home, Antigonus was entertained splendidly by Seleucus, satrap in Babylon. But Seleucus insulted one of his officers without consult- 268 ing Antigonus, although he was in his very presence. Antigonus was angered by this and demanded to see accounts of Seleucus' finances and possessions. Being less powerful than Antigonus, Seleucus withdrew to Ptolemy in Egypt. Immediately after Seleucus' flight, Antigonus relieved Bli- 269 tor of his office as governor of Mesopotamia for letting Seleucus escape, and then took control himself of Babylonia, Mesopotamia, and all the peoples between Media and

ἵστατο ἑαυτῷ, ἤδη καὶ Ἀντιπάτρου τεθνεῶτος. ἐπί-
φθονός τε εὐθὺς ἐκ τῶνδε τοῖς ἄλλοις σατράπαις ἐγί-
270 γνετο, γῆς ἄρχων τοσῆσδε. διὸ καὶ μάλιστα τῷ
Σελεύκῳ παρακαλοῦντι συνέθεντο Πτολεμαῖός τε καὶ
Λυσίμαχος ὁ Θρᾴκης σατράπης καὶ Κάσσανδρος ὁ
Ἀντιπάτρου, Μακεδόνων ἐπὶ τῷ πατρὶ ἡγούμενος· καὶ
ὁμοῦ πρεσβευσάμενοι τὸν Ἀντίγονον ἠξίουν τὴν
ἐπίκτητον αὐτῷ γενομένην γῆν τε καὶ χρήματα πρός
τε σφᾶς νείμασθαι καὶ πρὸς ἑτέρους Μακεδόνας, οἳ
271 τῶν σατραπειῶν ἐκπεπτώκεσαν. ἐπιχλευάσαντος δὲ
αὐτοὺς τοῦ Ἀντιγόνου οἱ μὲν ἐς πόλεμον καθίσταντο
κοινόν, ὁ δὲ ἀντιπαρεσκευάζετο, καὶ ἐξέβαλλε τὰς
φρουρὰς ὅσαι ἔτι ἦσαν ἐν τῇ Συρίᾳ Πτολεμαίου, καὶ
Φοινίκης τε καὶ τῆς λεγομένης κοίλης τὰ ἔτι ὑπήκοα
τοῦ Πτολεμαίου πρὸς ἑαυτὸν ἀθρόως περιέσπα.
272 54. Χωρῶν δ' ὑπὲρ τὰς Κιλικίους πύλας, Δημήτριον
τὸν υἱόν, ἀμφὶ δύο καὶ εἴκοσιν ἔτη γεγονότα, ἐν Γάζῃ
μετὰ τοῦ στρατοῦ καταλείπει πρὸς τὰς ὁρμὰς Πτολεμαίου τὰς ἀπ' Αἰγύπτου. καὶ τοῦτον ὁ Πτολεμαῖος
ἐνίκα περὶ τὴν Γάζαν μάχῃ λαμπρῶς, καὶ τὸ μει-
273 ράκιον ἐς τὸν πατέρα ἐχώρει. Πτολεμαῖος δ' αὐτίκα
τὸν Σέλευκον ἐς τὴν Βαβυλῶνα πέμπει, τὴν ἀρχὴν
ἀναληψόμενον· καὶ πεζοὺς ἐς τοῦτο ἔδωκεν αὐτῷ χι-
274 λίους, καὶ τριακοσίους ἱππέας. καὶ σὺν οὕτως ὀλίγοις
ὁ Σέλευκος τήν τε Βαβυλωνίαν, προθύμως αὐτὸν ἅμα
τῶν ἀνδρῶν ἐκδεχομένων, ἀνέλαβε, καὶ τὴν ἀρχὴν
275 μετ' οὐ πολὺ ἐς μέγα προήγαγεν. ὁ δ' Ἀντίγονος Πτολεμαῖον ἠμύνετο, καὶ ναυμαχίᾳ περὶ Κύπρον ἐνίκα

110

the Hellespont, Antipater now having died. Ruling so much territory, Antigonus quickly became an object of envy to the other satraps. It was for this reason particularly that, when Seleucus made the proposal, Ptolemy, Lysimachus (satrap of Thrace), and Cassander son of Antipater, who was leader of the Macedonians after his father, entered into an agreement with him. They sent a joint mission to Antigonus demanding that he share the additional territory and money he had acquired with themselves and the other Macedonians, who had been expelled from their satrapies. Antigonus treated them with derision. So, while they organized themselves for a joint war, Antigonus made counterpreparations, expelling all Ptolemy's remaining garrisons in Syria, and simultaneously annexing all areas still under his control in Phoenicia and what is called Coele Syria. 270 271

54. Advancing beyond the Cilician Gates, Antigonus leaves his son Demetrius, who was about twenty-two years old, with an army at Gaza to face the offensives of Ptolemy from Egypt. But Ptolemy won a brilliant victory over Demetrius near Gaza, and the young man went to join his father. Ptolemy immediately sends Seleucus to Babylon to take back power, and gave him one thousand infantry and three hundred cavalry for the task. With this small army and at the same time the enthusiastic reception of the population, Seleucus recovered Babylon, and in a short time greatly extended the kingdom. Meanwhile Antigonus took defensive measures against Ptolemy, defeating him in a notable battle at sea near Cyprus, in which his son 272 273 274 275

περιφανεῖ, Δημητρίου τοῦ παιδὸς στρατηγοῦντος· ἐφ᾽
ὅτῳ λαμπροτάτῳ γενομένῳ ὁ στρατὸς ἀνεῖπεν ἄμφω
βασιλέας, Ἀντίγονόν τε καὶ Δημήτριον, ἤδη καὶ τῶν
βασιλέων τεθνεώτων, Ἀριδαίου τε τοῦ Φιλίππου καὶ
276   Ὀλυμπιάδος καὶ τῶν υἱῶν Ἀλεξάνδρου. ἀνεῖπε δὲ καὶ
Πτολεμαῖον ὁ οἰκεῖος αὐτοῦ στρατὸς βασιλέα, ὡς μή
277   τι διὰ τὴν ἧσσαν μειονεκτοίη τῶν νενικηκότων. τοῖσδε
μὲν δὴ τυχεῖν ὁμοίων συνηνέχθη κατ᾽ ἐναντίας αἰτίας,
ἕποντο δ᾽ εὐθὺς αὐτοῖς οἱ λοιποί, καὶ βασιλεῖς ἅπαντες ἐκ σατραπῶν ἐγίγνοντο.

278   55. Οὕτω δὴ καὶ ὁ Σέλευκος ἐβασίλευσε τῆς Βαβυλωνίας. ἐβασίλευσε δὲ καὶ Μηδίας, Νικάνορα κτείνας
αὐτὸς ἐν τῇ μάχῃ, τὸν ὑπ᾽ Ἀντιγόνου Μηδίας σατρα-
279   πεύειν ἀπολελειμμένον. πολέμους δ᾽ ἐπολέμησε πολλοὺς Μακεδόσι καὶ βαρβάροις, καὶ τούτων Μακεδόσι
μὲν δύο μεγίστους, τὸν μὲν ὕστερον Λυσιμάχῳ βασιλεύοντι Θρᾴκης, τὸν δὲ πρότερον Ἀντιγόνῳ περὶ
Ἴψον τῆς Φρυγίας, αὐτῷ στρατηγοῦντι καὶ αὐτῷ μα-
χομένῳ, καίπερ ὑπὲρ ὀγδοήκοντα ἔτη γεγονότι.
280   πεσόντος δ᾽ Ἀντιγόνου κατὰ τὴν μάχην, ὅσοι βασιλεῖς τὸν Ἀντίγονον ἅμα τῷ Σελεύκῳ καθῃρήκεσαν,
τὴν Ἀντιγόνου γῆν διενέμοντο. καὶ ὁ Σέλευκος τότε
τῆς μετ᾽ Εὐφράτην Συρίας ἐπὶ θαλάσσῃ καὶ Φρυγίας
281   τῆς ἀνὰ τὸ μεσόγειον ἄρχειν διέλαχεν. ἐφεδρεύων δὲ
ἀεὶ τοῖς ἐγγὺς ἔθνεσι, καὶ δυνατὸς ὢν βιάσασθαι καὶ

---

[51] After the battle of Cyprus in 306, Demetrius I Poliorcetes

Demetrius was in command. For such a dazzling achievement the army proclaimed both Antigonus and Demetrius kings, their own kings, Arrhidaeus son of Philip and Olympias, and the sons of Alexander, having died by this stage. Ptolemy's army also declared him king so that his defeat would not make him seem less important than the victors.[51] So, for these men the outcome was the same, but for opposite reasons. Everyone else immediately followed suit, and all turned from satraps into kings.

55. This was how Seleucus became king of Babylonia. He also ruled over Media after personally killing in battle Nicanor, who had been left by Antigonus as satrap of Media. He fought many wars with Macedonians and barbarians, of which two of the most important were against the Macedonians, latterly against Lysimachus, king of Thrace, and earlier against Antigonus at Ipsus in Phrygia, where Antigonus commanded and fought in person, although he was more than eighty years old.[52] Antigonus fell in the battle, and those kings who had combined with Seleucus to destroy him divided his territory among themselves. It was then that Seleucus acquired as his share the government of all Syria between the Euphrates and the Mediterranean, and inland Phrygia. Constantly on watch for opportunities against neighboring peoples, and both pow-

276

277

278

279

280

281

("Besieger of Cities") and Antigonus I Monophthalmos ("the One-eyed") had themselves declared kings. Ptolemy I Soter ("Savior") took the royal title in 305.

[52] The victory of Seleucus I Nicator ("Victor") and Ptolemy over Antigonus at the battle of Ipsus was in 301. Seleucus defeated Lysimachus at the battle of Corupedium in 281, the year he was killed.

πιθανὸς προσαγαγέσθαι, ἦρξε Μεσοποταμίας καὶ
Ἀρμενίας καὶ Καππαδοκίας τῆς Σελευκίδος λεγομένης καὶ Περσῶν καὶ Παρθυαίων καὶ Βακτρίων καὶ
Ἀράβων καὶ Ταπύρων καὶ τῆς Σογδιανῆς καὶ Ἀραχω-
σίας καὶ Ὑρκανίας, καὶ ὅσα ἄλλα ὅμορα ἔθνη μέχρι
Ἰνδοῦ ποταμοῦ Ἀλεξάνδρῳ ἐγεγένητο δορίληπτα, ὡς
ὡρίσθαι τῷδε μάλιστα μετ' Ἀλέξανδρον τῆς Ἀσίας τὸ
πλέον· ἀπὸ γὰρ Φρυγίας ἐπὶ ποταμὸν Ἰνδὸν ἄνω
282   πάντα Σελεύκῳ κατήκουεν. καὶ τὸν Ἰνδὸν περάσας
ἐπολέμησεν Ἀνδροκόττῳ βασιλεῖ τῶν περὶ αὐτὸν Ἰνδῶν, μέχρι φιλίαν αὐτῷ καὶ κῆδος συνέθετο. καὶ
τῶνδε τὰ μὲν πρὸ τῆς Ἀντιγόνου τελευτῆς, τὰ δὲ μετ'
Ἀντίγονον ἐποίησεν.

283   56. Λέγεται δ' αὐτῷ, στρατιώτῃ βασιλέως ἔτι ὄντι
καὶ ἐπὶ Πέρσας ἑπομένῳ, χρησμὸν ἐν Διδυμέως γενέσθαι πυνθανομένῳ περὶ τῆς ἐς Μακεδονίαν ἐπανόδου,
284   "Μὴ σπεῦδ' Εὐρώπην· Ἀσίη τοι πολλὸν ἀμείνων." καὶ
ἐν Μακεδονίᾳ τὴν ἑστίαν αὐτῷ τὴν πατρῴαν, οὐδενὸς
ἅψαντος, ἐκλάμψαι πῦρ μέγα. καὶ ὄναρ αὐτοῦ τὴν
μητέρα ἰδεῖν, ὃν ἂν εὕρῃ δακτύλιον, δοῦναι φόρημα
Σελεύκῳ, τὸν δὲ βασιλεύσειν ἔνθα ἂν ὁ δακτύλιος ἐκ-
285   πέσῃ. καὶ ἡ μὲν ηὗρεν ἄγκυραν ἐν σιδήρῳ κεχα-
ραγμένην, ὁ δὲ τὴν σφραγῖδα τήνδε ἀπώλεσε κατὰ
286   τὸν Εὐφράτην. λέγεται καὶ ἐς τὴν Βαβυλωνίαν ἀπιόντα ὕστερον προσκόψαι λίθῳ, καὶ τοῦ λίθου ἀνα-
σκαφέντος ἄγκυραν ὀφθῆναι. θορυβουμένων δὲ τῶν
μάντεων ὡς ἐπὶ συμβόλῳ κατοχῆς, Πτολεμαῖον τὸν
Λάγου παραπέμποντα εἰπεῖν ἀσφαλείας τὴν ἄγκυραν,

erful in the use of force and persuasive in winning friends, Seleucus ruled over Mesopotamia and Armenia and what is known as Seleucid Cappadocia; and over Persians and Parthians and Bactrians and Arabs and Tapyri; and over Sogdiana and Arachosia and Hyrcania, and all the other adjacent peoples who had been conquered by Alexander as far as the river Indus. The result was that more of Asia fell within this man's frontiers than anyone since Alexander. For the whole world from Phrygia up as far as the river Indus answered to Seleucus. He even crossed the 282 Indus to wage war on Andracotta, king of the Indians living on the river, until they concluded a treaty of friendship and a marriage alliance. Some of this activity he carried out before the death of Antigonus, some after him.

56. There is a story that when Seleucus was still serving 283 as a soldier of King Alexander and following him in the campaign against Persia, he consulted the oracle at Didyma to ask about his return to Macedon. "Do not be in a hurry to get to Europe," was the reply, "Asia is much better for you." Another story was that his ancestral hearth in 284 Macedonia burst into a blazing fire without anyone lighting it. Yet another concerned a vision his mother had in a dream, that she was giving a ring she found to Seleucus to wear, and that he would become king on the spot where he dropped the ring. And, in fact, she did find an iron ring, 285 with an anchor engraved on it, and Seleucus did lose this signet ring beside the Euphrates. Another report recorded 286 that on a later occasion when Seleucus was setting out for Babylonia, he tripped on a stone, which when it was dug up, was found to be an anchor. The soothsayers were disturbed by this, believing it was a sign of delay, but Ptolemy son of Lagus, who was accompanying Seleucus, said that

115

287 οὐ κατοχῆς εἶναι σύμβολον. καὶ Σελεύκῳ μὲν διὰ
τοῦτο ἄρα καὶ βασιλεύσαντι ἡ σφραγὶς ἄγκυρα ἦν,
δοκεῖ δέ τισι καὶ περιόντος ἔτι Ἀλεξάνδρου καὶ
ἐφορῶντος ἕτερον τῷ Σελεύκῳ σημεῖον περὶ τῆς ἀρ-
288 χῆς τοιόνδε γενέσθαι. Ἀλεξάνδρῳ γὰρ ἐξ Ἰνδῶν ἐς
Βαβυλῶνα ἐπανελθόντι, καὶ τὰς ἐν αὐτῇ τῇ Βαβυ-
λωνίᾳ λίμνας ἐπὶ χρείᾳ τοῦ τὸν Εὐφράτην τὴν Ἀσ-
συρίδα γῆν ἀρδεύειν περιπλέοντι, ἄνεμος ἐμπεσὼν
ἥρπασε τὸ διάδημα, καὶ φερόμενον ἐκρεμάσθη δόνα-
289 κος ἐν τάφῳ τινὸς ἀρχαίου βασιλέως. καὶ ἐσήμαινε
μὲν ἐς τὴν τελευτὴν τοῦ βασιλέως καὶ τόδε, ναύτην
δέ φασιν ἐκκολυμβήσαντα περιθέσθαι τῇ κεφαλῇ τὸ
διάδημα καὶ ἐνεγκεῖν ἄβρυχον Ἀλεξάνδρῳ, καὶ λαβεῖν τῆς προθυμίας αὐτίκα δωρεὰν παρὰ τοῦ βασι-
290 λέως τάλαντον ἀργυρίου· τῶν δὲ μάντεων αὐτὸν ἀναι-
ρεῖν κελευόντων οἱ μὲν πεισθῆναι τὸν Ἀλέξανδρον
αὐτοῖς, οἱ δὲ ἀντειπεῖν. εἰσὶ δὲ οἳ τάδε πάντα ὑπερελ-
θόντες, οὐ ναύτην ὅλως φασὶν ἀλλὰ Σέλευκον ἐπὶ τὸ
διάδημα τοῦ βασιλέως ἐκκολυμβῆσαι, καὶ περιθέ-
291 σθαι Σέλευκον αὐτὸ τῇ κεφαλῇ, ἵν' ἄβροχον εἴη. καὶ
τὰ σημεῖα ἐς τέλος ἀμφοῖν ἀπαντῆσαι. Ἀλέξανδρόν
τε γὰρ ἐν Βαβυλῶνι μεταστῆναι τοῦ βίου, καὶ Σέλευκον τῆς Ἀλεξάνδρου γῆς, ὅτι πλείστης μάλιστα τόνδε
τῶν Ἀλεξάνδρου διαδόχων, βασιλεῦσαι.

292   57. Τοσαῦτα μὲν δὴ περὶ τῶν Σελεύκῳ προμαν-
τευθέντων ἐπυθόμην· γίγνεται δ' εὐθὺς Ἀλεξάνδρου
μεταστάντος ἡγεμὼν τῆς ἵππου τῆς ἑταιρικῆς ἧς δὴ
καὶ Ἡφαιστίων ἡγήσατο Ἀλεξάνδρῳ καὶ ἐπὶ Ἡφαι-

an anchor was a sign of safety, not delay. It was for this   287
reason, I suppose, that, when he was king, Seleucus' seal
was an anchor, although some believe that a different fore-
shadowing of Seleucus' future rule occurred when Alexander was still alive and watching what happened. It was
as follows. After he had returned to Babylon from India,   288
Alexander was sailing around the marshes in Babylonia
itself, to see how he could use the Euphrates to irrigate
the land of Assyria, when a gust of wind hit him and blew
his diadem off, carrying it to the tomb of some ancient
king, where it got caught in a bunch of reeds. This too was   289
an omen of the king's death, but there is a story that a sailor
dived into the water and put the diadem around his own
head and brought it back to Alexander without getting it
wet; and he immediately received a silver talent from the
king as a reward for his loyalty. The soothsayers, however,   290
advised him to have the man killed, and some say he went
along with them, others that he refused. But there are
some who pass over all these stories and say that it was not
a sailor at all who dived in after the king's diadem, but
Seleucus. So it was Seleucus who put it on his head to keep
it dry. And the omens turned out right in both cases. For   291
Alexander departed this life in Babylon, and Seleucus
came to rule over more of Alexander's empire than all the
other successors.

57. These are the prophecies I have heard about Seleu-   292
cus. As soon as Alexander died, Seleucus becomes head of
the companion cavalry, which Hephaestion, of course, had
led for Alexander and then Perdiccas. After the cavalry

στίωνι Περδίκκας, μετὰ δὲ τὴν ἵππον σατράπης τε
τῆς Βαβυλωνίας καὶ βασιλεὺς ἐπὶ τῇ σατραπείᾳ.
293 γενομένῳ δὲ αὐτῷ τὰ ἐς πολέμους ἐπιτυχεστάτῳ Νι-
κάνωρ ἐπώνυμον γίγνεται· τῷδε γὰρ ἀρέσκομαι μᾶλ-
294 λον τοῦ Νικάνορα κτεῖναι. καὶ τὸ σῶμα ὄντι εὐρώστῳ
τε καὶ μεγάλῳ, καὶ ταῦρον ἄγριον ἐν Ἀλεξάνδρου
θυσίᾳ ποτὲ ἐκθορόντα τῶν δεσμῶν ὑποστάντι μόνῳ
καὶ ταῖς χερσὶ μόναις κατειργασμένῳ, προστιθέασιν
295 ἐς τοὺς ἀνδριάντας ἐπὶ τῷδε κέρατα. πόλεις δὲ ᾤκισεν
ἐπὶ τὸ μῆκος τῆς ἀρχῆς ὅλης ἑκκαίδεκα μὲν Ἀντιο-
χείας ἐπὶ τῷ πατρί, πέντε δὲ ἐπὶ τῇ μητρὶ Λαοδικείας,
ἐννέα δ' ἐπωνύμους ἑαυτοῦ, τέσσαρας δ' ἐπὶ ταῖς γυ-
296 ναιξί, τρεῖς Ἀπαμείας καὶ Στρατονίκειαν μίαν. καὶ
εἰσὶν αὐτῶν ἐπιφανέσταται καὶ νῦν Σελεύκειαι μὲν ἥ
τε ἐπὶ τῇ θαλάσσῃ καὶ ἡ ἐπὶ τοῦ Τίγρητος ποταμοῦ,
Λαοδίκεια δὲ ἡ ἐν τῇ Φοινίκῃ καὶ Ἀντιόχεια ἡ ὑπὸ τῷ
297 Λιβάνῳ ὄρει καὶ ἡ τῆς Συρίας Ἀπάμεια. τὰς δὲ ἄλλας
ἐκ τῆς Ἑλλάδος ἢ Μακεδονίας ὠνόμαζεν, ἢ ἐπὶ ἔργοις
ἑαυτοῦ τισιν, ἢ ἐς τιμὴν Ἀλεξάνδρου τοῦ βασιλέως·
ὅθεν ἔστιν ἐν τῇ Συρίᾳ καὶ τοῖς ὑπὲρ αὐτὴν ἄνω βαρβάροις πολλὰ μὲν Ἑλληνικῶν πολλὰ δὲ Μακεδονικῶν
298 πολισμάτων ὀνόματα, Βέρροια, Ἔδεσσα, Πέρινθος,
Μαρώνεια, Καλλίπολις, Ἀχαΐα, Πέλλα, Ὠρωπός, Ἀμ-
φίπολις, Ἀρέθουσα, Ἀστακός, Τεγέα, Χαλκίς, Λάρισα,
Ἥραια, Ἀπολλωνία, ἐν δὲ τῇ Παρθυηνῇ Σώτειρα,
Καλλιόπη, Χάρις, Ἑκατόμπυλος, Ἀχαΐα, ἐν δ' Ἰνδοῖς
Ἀλεξανδρόπολις, ἐν δὲ Σκύθαις Ἀλεξανδρέσχατα. καὶ
ἐπὶ ταῖς αὐτοῦ Σελεύκου νίκαις ἔστι Νικηφόριόν τε ἐν

command, he became satrap of Babylon, and then king.
He wins the title Nicator for being so exceptionally suc-   293
cessful in the wars he fought. At least, I find this more
convincing than that he got it for killing Nicanor. He was   294
physically such a big, strong man that on one occasion
when a wild bull intended for sacrifice by Alexander escaped from his ropes, Seleucus restrained him on his own,
holding him just with his hands. For this reason, a pair of
bull's horns are added to the depiction of Seleucus on
statues of him. He founded towns throughout the whole   295
extent of his empire, naming eleven of them Antioch after
his father, five of them Laodicea after his mother, nine
of them Seleucea after himself, and four after his wives,
three called Apamea, and one Stratonicea. In the present   296
age, the most famous of them are the Seleucea by the sea,
the Seleucea on the river Tigris, the Laodicea in Phoenicia, the Antioch beside mount Libanon, and Apamea in
Syria. To the other towns he gave Greek and Macedonian   297
names, or names that recorded his own exploits, or honored King Alexander. That is why there are many towns
with Greek or Macedonian names in Syria and the barbarian regions to the east. For example, Berrhoea, Edessa,   298
Perinthus, Maronea, Callipolis, Achaea, Pella, Oropus,
Amphipolis, Arethusa, Astacus, Tegea, Chalcis, Larisa,
Heraea, Apollonia. In Parthia there is Soteira, Calliope,
Charis, Hecatompylus, Achaea; in India, Alexandropolis;
in Scythia, Alexandreschata. And in honor of Seleucus'
own victories, there is Nicephorium in Mesopotamia, and

τῇ Μεσοποταμίᾳ καὶ Νικόπολις ἐν Ἀρμενίᾳ τῇ ἀγχοτάτω μάλιστα Καππαδοκίας.

299   58. Φασὶ δὲ αὐτῷ τὰς Σελευκείας οἰκίζοντι, τὴν μὲν
ἐπὶ τῇ θαλάσσῃ, διοσημίαν ἡγήσασθαι κεραυνοῦ,
καὶ διὰ τοῦτο θεὸν αὐτοῖς κεραυνὸν ἔθετο, καὶ θρη-
300 σκεύουσι καὶ ὑμνοῦσι καὶ νῦν κεραυνόν· ἐς δὲ τὴν ἐπὶ
τοῦ Τίγρητος ἡμέραν ἐπιλέξασθαι τοὺς μάγους κε-
λευομένους, καὶ τῆς ἡμέρας ὥραν, ᾗ τῶν θεμελίων
ἄρξασθαι τῆς ὀρυχῆς ἔδει, ψεύσασθαι τὴν ὥραν τοὺς
μάγους, οὐκ ἐθέλοντας ἐπιτείχισμα τοιόνδε σφίσι
301 γενέσθαι. καὶ Σέλευκος μὲν ἐν τῇ σκηνῇ τὴν δεδο-
μένην ὥραν ἀνέμενεν, ὁ δὲ στρατὸς ἐς τὸ ἔργον ἕτοιμος, ἀτρεμῶν ἔστε σημήνειεν ὁ Σέλευκος, ἄφνω κατὰ
τὴν αἰσιωτέραν ὥραν δόξαντές τινα κελεύειν ἐπὶ τὸ
ἔργον ἀνεπήδησαν, ὡς μηδὲ τῶν κηρύκων ἐρυκόντων
302 ἔτι ἀνασχέσθαι. τὸ μὲν δὴ ἔργον ἐξετετέλεστο, Σελεύκῳ δὲ ἀθύμως ἔχοντι, καὶ τοὺς μάγους αὖθις ἀνα-
κρίνοντι περὶ τῆς πόλεως, ἄδειαν αἰτήσαντες ἔλεγον
οἱ μάγοι· "Τὴν πεπρωμένην, ὦ βασιλεῦ, μοῖραν,
χείρονά τε καὶ κρείσσονα, οὐκ ἔστιν οὔτε ἀνδρὸς οὔτε
πόλεως ἐναλλάξαι. μοῖρα δέ τις καὶ πόλεών ἐστιν
303 ὥσπερ ἀνδρῶν. καὶ τήνδε χρονιωτάτην μὲν ἐδόκει τοῖς
θεοῖς γενέσθαι, ἀρχομένην ἐκ τῆσδε τῆς ὥρας ἧς ἐγέ-
νετο· δειμαίνοντες δ' ἡμεῖς ὡς ἐπιτείχισμα ἡμῖν ἐσο-
304 μένην, παρεφέρομεν τὸ πεπρωμένον. τὸ δὲ κρεῖσσον
ἦν καὶ μάγων πανουργούντων καὶ βασιλέως ἀγνοοῦν-
τος αὐτό. τοιγάρτοι τὸ δαιμόνιον τὰ αἰσιώτερα τῷ
305 στρατῷ προσέταξεν. καὶ τοῦτο ἔνι σοι καταμαθεῖν

Nicopolis in Armenia very close to the border with Cappadocia.

58. When Seleucus was founding the two Seleuceas, they say that an omen of thunder guided him in the case of Seleucea by the sea. For this reason he established thunder as a god for the inhabitants, and to this day they worship thunder and sing hymns to it. As for Seleucea on the Tigris, it is said that when he ordered the magi to choose a day and a time when he should begin to dig the foundations, the magi lied about the time, as they did not want there to be such a stronghold against their own influence. While Seleucus was waiting in his tent for the appointed hour, and the army were in a state of readiness for the task, but standing by at ease for his signal, suddenly, at the more auspicious time, they thought they heard someone giving them the order, and sprang into action so vigorously that they could no longer be stopped even when the heralds tried to hold them back. When the work was finished, Seleucus, feeling uneasy, asked the magi again about the city. They asked for immunity and spoke as follows: "Neither a person nor a town, your majesty, can avoid what fate has assigned, for better or worse. Just like men, cities too have their destiny, and the gods decided that this city would be very long-lived, if the work began at the time it did actually begin. For our part, we were afraid that the city would prove a stronghold against our influence, and tried to prevent what was fated. But destiny proved stronger than manipulative magi or a king who was unaware of what they were doing. And so it was that the divinity issued a more auspiciously timed order to the army. In case you suspect that we are still making

299

300

301

302

303

304

305

ὧδε, ἵνα μή τι καὶ νῦν ἡμᾶς ἔτι τεχνάζειν ὑπονοῇς.
αὐτός τε γὰρ ὁ βασιλεὺς σὺ τῷ στρατῷ παρεκάθησο,
καὶ τὸ κέλευσμα αὐτὸς ἐδεδώκεις ἀναμένειν· καὶ ὁ εὐ-
πειθέστατος ὢν σοι πρὸς κινδύνους καὶ πόνους οὐκ
ἠνέσχετο νῦν οὐδὲ ἀναπαύσεως ἐπιτάγματος, ἀλλ᾽
ἀνέθορεν, οὐδὲ ἀνὰ μέρος ἀλλ᾽ ἀθρόως, ἐπιστάταις
αὐτοῖς, καὶ ἐνόμιζε κεκελεῦσθαι. καὶ ἐκεκέλευστο δή·
διόπερ οὐδὲ σοῦ κατερύκοντος αὐτοὺς ἔτι ἐπείθοντο.

306 τί ἂν οὖν βασιλέως ἐν ἀνθρώποις εἴη καρτερώτερον
ἄλλο ἢ θεός; ὃς τῆς σῆς γνώμης ἐπεκράτησε, καὶ
ἡγεμόνευσέ σοι τῆς πόλεως ἀντὶ ἡμῶν, δυσμεναίνων

307 ἡμῖν τε καὶ γένει παντὶ τῷ περιοίκῳ. ποῦ γὰρ ἔτι τὰ
ἡμέτερα ἰσχύσει, δυνατωτέρου γένους παρῳκισμένου;
ἡ μὲν δὴ πόλις σοι γέγονε σὺν τύχῃ καὶ μεγιστεύσει
καὶ χρόνιος ἔσται· σὺ δὲ ἡμῖν, ἐξαμαρτοῦσιν ὑπὸ
δέους οἰκείων ἀγαθῶν ἀφαιρέσεως, τὴν συγγνώμην
βεβαίου.” ταῦτα τῶν μάγων εἰπόντων ὁ βασιλεὺς
ἥσθη καὶ συνέγνω.

308 59. Τοιάδε μὲν ἐπυθόμην περὶ Σελευκείας· ὁ δὲ
Σέλευκος τὸν υἱὸν Ἀντίοχον, περιὼν ἔτι, τῆς ἄνω γῆς
βασιλεύειν ἀπέφηνεν ἀνθ᾽ ἑαυτοῦ. καὶ εἴ τῳ μεγαλό-
φρον εἶναι τόδε φαίνεται καὶ βασιλικόν, μεγαλοφρο-
νέστερον ἔτι καὶ σοφώτερον ἤνεγκε τὸν ἔρωτα τοῦ

309 παιδὸς καὶ τὴν ἐς τὸ πάθος αὐτοῦ σωφροσύνην. ἤρα
μὲν γὰρ ὁ Ἀντίοχος Στρατονίκης τῆς αὐτοῦ Σελεύκου
γυναικός, μητρυιᾶς οἱ γενομένης καὶ παῖδα ἤδη τῷ
Σελεύκῳ πεποιημένης, συγγιγνώσκων δὲ τὴν ἀθε-
μιστίαν τοῦ πάθους οὔτε ἐπεχείρει τῷ κακῷ οὔτε

things up, you can be sure of the truth of this from the fact that you yourself, the king, were presiding over the army, and had personally given the order to wait. Totally obedient to you in the face of danger or hard work, the soldiers could not be held back at that moment, not even when ordered to stop, but sprang to the task, not in groups, but all of them together, including officers, believing that they had been given the order. And in fact, they had been given the order. That is the reason why, even when you tried to hold them back, they no longer obeyed. For what could 306 be more powerful among men than a king, except a god? It was a god who overruled your decision, and who took control of the city on your behalf, instead of us, angry as he was at us and at all the people who live in the vicinity. For where will our interests still prevail, when there is a 307 more powerful people settled beside us? It was fated for your city to come into existence, and it will be great and long-lived. Out of fear of losing our own prosperity, we did wrong. Please confirm your pardon for us." The king was pleased with what the magi said, and he forgave them.

59. Such is the extent of what I have learned about 308 Seleucea. While he was still alive, Seleucus appointed his son Antiochus to rule the upper territories in his place. If this appears to anyone as noble and kingly behavior, his treatment of his son's passion, and of the young man's restraint with regard to his feelings, is even more noble and wise. For Antiochus was in love with his stepmother, Stra- 309 tonice, Seleucus' wife, who had already borne Seleucus a son. Recognizing the unlawful nature of his feelings, Antiochus made no attempt to act on his evil impulse, and

προύφερεν, ἀλλ' ἐνόσει καὶ παρεῖτο καὶ ἑκὼν ἐς τὸν
310 θάνατον συνήργει. οὐδ' ὁ περιώνυμος ἰατρὸς Ἐρασίστρατος, ἐπὶ μεγίσταις συντάξεσι Σελεύκῳ συνών,
εἶχε τεκμήρασθαι τοῦ πάθους, μέχρι φυλάξας καθ-
αρὸν ἐκ πάντων τὸ σῶμα, εἴκασεν εἶναι τῆς ψυχῆς
τὴν νόσον, ᾗ δὴ καὶ ἐρρωμένη καὶ νοσούσῃ τὸ σῶμα
συναίσθεται. λύπας μὲν οὖν καὶ ὀργὰς καὶ ἐπιθυμίας
ἄλλας ὁμολογεῖσθαι, ἔρωτα δ' ἐπικρύπτεσθαι πρὸς
311 τῶν σωφρόνων. οὐδὲν δὲ οὐδ' ὡς τοῦ Ἀντιόχου φρά-
ζοντος αὐτῷ λιπαροῦντι μαθεῖν ἐν ἀπορρήτῳ, παρ-
εκαθέζετο καὶ ἐφύλασσε τὰς τοῦ σώματος μεταβολάς,
312 ὅπως ἔχοι πρὸς ἕκαστον τῶν ἐσιόντων. ὡς δὲ ηὗρεν
ἐπὶ μὲν τῶν ἄλλων σβεννύμενον ἀεὶ τὸ σῶμα καὶ μα-
ραινόμενον ὁμαλῶς, ὅτε δὲ ἡ Στρατονίκη παρίοι πρὸς
αὐτὸν ἐπισκεψομένη, τὴν μὲν γνώμην ὑπ' αἰδοῦς καὶ
συνειδότος τότε μάλιστα αὐτὸν ἐνοχλούμενον καὶ σι-
ωπῶντα, τὸ δὲ σῶμα καὶ ἄκοντος αὐτοῦ θαλερώτερόν
τε γιγνόμενον αὐτῷ καὶ ζωτικώτερον, καὶ αὖθις ἀπιού-
σης ἀσθενέστερον, ἔφη τῷ Σελεύκῳ τὸν υἱὸν ἀνιάτως
313 ἔχειν αὐτῷ. ὑπεραλγήσαντος δὲ τοῦ βασιλέως καὶ
ἐκβοήσαντος εἶπεν· "Ἔρως ἔστι τὸ πάθος, καὶ ἔρως
γυναικός, ἀλλ' ἀδύνατος."

314   60. Σελεύκου δὲ θαυμάσαντος εἴ τινα μὴ δύναιτο
πεῖσαι Σέλευκος ὁ τῆς Ἀσίας βασιλεύς, ἐπὶ γάμῳ
τοιοῦδε παιδός, ἱκεσίᾳ τε καὶ χρήμασι καὶ δωρεαῖς

did not make it public, but fell ill and languished and willingly cooperated with death. Even the famous doctor, 310 Erasistratus, who attended Seleucus at a very high salary, was unable to diagnose the problem, until, having confirmed that physically Antiochus was completely healthy, he deduced that the illness was psychological.[53] He knew that when the mind is healthy or sick, it affects the body too, and that while grief, anger, and other emotions are admitted, love is kept hidden by people with self-discipline. When Antiochus said nothing, even when Erasistratus 311 begged to be told in confidence, the latter sat beside him, and watched for changes in body language and how he reacted to each person coming into his presence. He observed that in the case of everyone else, Antiochus' physical reaction was at all times equally subdued and listless, but that whenever Stratonice came to visit him, it was then that he was particularly troubled in spirit by shame and a guilty conscience and said nothing, while in spite of himself, he became physically more energetic and animated, and correspondingly more debilitated when she left. So Erasistratus reported to Seleucus that he was unable to cure his son. The king was extremely upset and cried out 313 loud, to which Erasistratus said, "His illness is love, love for a woman, but an impossible love."

60. Seleucus was amazed there would be anyone that 314 he, Seleucus, king of Asia, would be unable to persuade into marrying such a fine son, by begging or with money

[53] Pliny, *HN* 29.3.5, among others, also records the story, but he seems to know another version (see *HN* 7.37.123), in which it was Cleombrotus (the father of Erasistratus) whom Seleucus rewarded for saving Antiochus.

καὶ ὅλῃ τῇ τοσῇδε βασιλείᾳ, περιούσῃ μὲν ἐς τόνδε
τὸν κάμνοντα βασιλέα, δοθησομένῃ δὲ καὶ νῦν ἀντὶ
τῆς σωτηρίας εἰ ἤδη τις ἐθέλοι, καὶ μόνον ἀξιοῦντος
μαθεῖν τίς ἔστι τὸ γύναιον, ὁ Ἐρασίστρατος ἔφη·
315 "Τῆς ἐμῆς γυναικὸς ἐρᾷ." καὶ ὁ Σέλευκος, "Εἶτ᾽ ὦ
'γαθέ," ἔφη, "Φιλίας μὲν οὕτω καὶ χαρίτων ἔχων ἐφ᾽
ἡμῖν, ἀρετῆς δὲ καὶ σοφίας ἐν ὀλίγοις, οὐ σώσεις μοι
νέον ἄνδρα καὶ βασιλικόν, φίλου καὶ βασιλέως υἱόν,
ἀτυχοῦντα καὶ σωφρονοῦντα καὶ τὸ κακὸν ἐπικρύ-
πτοντα καὶ προτιμώμενον αὑτῷ θανάτου, ἀλλ᾽ ὑπερόψει μὲν οὕτως Ἀντίοχον, ὑπερόψει δ᾽ ἐπ᾽ αὐτῷ καὶ
316 Σέλευκον;" ὁ δ᾽ ἀπομαχόμενος εἶπε λόγον ὡς ἄφυκ-
τον, ὅτι "Μηδ᾽ ἂν σύ, καίπερ ὢν πατήρ, τῆς σῆς
Ἀντίοχος εἰ ἤρα γυναικός, μεθῆκας ἂν αὐτῷ τὴν γυ-
317 ναῖκα." ἔνθα δὴ πάντας ὤμνυ τοὺς βασιλείους θεοὺς
ὁ Σέλευκος, ἦ μὴν ἑκὼν ἂν καὶ χαίρων μεθεῖναι καὶ
διήγημα γενέσθαι καλὸν εὐνοίας ἀγαθοῦ πατρὸς ἐς
παῖδα σώφρονα καὶ ἐγκρατῆ τοῦ κακοῦ καὶ ἀνάξιον
318 τῆς συμφορᾶς. πολλά τε ὅμοια ἐπενεγκών, ἤρξατο
ἄχθεσθαι ὅτι μὴ αὐτὸς αὑτῷ γίγνοιτο ἰατρὸς ἀτυ-
χοῦντι, ἀλλὰ καὶ ἐς ταῦτα δέοιτο Ἐρασιστράτου.

319   61. Ὁ δ᾽ ἐπεὶ κατεῖδε τὴν γνώμην τοῦ βασιλέως
ἔργον ὑποφαίνουσαν, οὐχ ὑπόκρισιν, ἀνεκάλυπτε τὸ
πάθος, καὶ ὅπως αὐτὸ εὕροι κρυπτόμενον διηγεῖτο.
320 Σελεύκῳ δὲ ἡσθέντι ἔργον μὲν ἐγένετο πεῖσαι τὸν
υἱόν, ἔργον δ᾽ ἐπ᾽ ἐκείνῳ τὴν γυναῖκα· ὡς δ᾽ ἔπεισε,
τὴν στρατιὰν συναγαγών, αἰσθομένην ἴσως ἤδη τι
τούτων, κατελογίζετο μὲν αὐτοῖς τὰ ἔργα τὰ ἑαυτοῦ

and gifts, indeed with promise of the whole kingdom which would devolve by inheritance on the ailing prince, and which Seleucus would willingly hand over right now, if someone wanted it, in return for Antiochus' well-being. When he asked only to learn who the woman was, Erasistratus replied, "He is in love with my wife." "Well, good 315 sir," replied Seleucus, "as a man so possessed of our friendship and favors, and of a virtue and wisdom found only in few men, will you not save this young man and royal prince for me, the son of your king and friend, who has been unlucky, but self-controlled, hiding his misfortune and preferring to die rather than admit it? Or will you disregard Antiochus, and not just Antiochus, but Seleucus too?" Erasistratus countered with an apparently unanswerable 316 argument. "If Antiochus were in love with your wife, not even you, although you are his father, would hand her over to him." Seleucus then swore by all the gods of his king- 317 dom that he would willingly and happily hand her over, and become the subject of a fine story about the kindness of a good father for his innocent son, a son who controlled his evil impulse and did not deserve such misfortune. Adding many other statements of this sort, he began to 318 become frustrated that he could not himself treat the unhappy boy, but needed Erasistratus for this too.

61. When he saw that the king's intention was obviously 319 real, and that he was not putting on an act, Erasistratus revealed what was wrong and explained how he had discovered the secret. Seleucus was delighted, but found it 320 difficult to win over his son, and after him to win over his wife. When he did persuade them, he summoned the army, who perhaps already had some inkling of these matters, and recounted for them his achievements, how he

127

καὶ τὴν ἀρχήν, ὅτι δὴ μάλιστα τῶν Ἀλεξάνδρου διαδόχων ἐπὶ μήκιστον προαγάγοι· διὸ καὶ γηρῶντι ἤδη
321 δυσκράτητον εἶναι διὰ τὸ μέγεθος. "Ἐθέλω δέ," ἔφη,
"Διελεῖν τὸ μέγεθος ἐς τὴν ὑμετέραν τοῦ μέλλοντος
ἀμεριμνίαν, καὶ τὸ μέρος ἤδη δοῦναι τοῖς ἐμοῖς φιλ-
322 τάτοις. δίκαιοι δ᾽ ἐστέ μοι πάντες ἐς πάντα συνεργεῖν,
οἳ ἐς τοσοῦτον ἀρχῆς καὶ δυνάμεως ηὐξήθητε ὑπ᾽
323 ἐμοῦ μετ᾽ Ἀλέξανδρον. φίλτατοι δ᾽ εἰσί μοι καὶ ἀρχῆς
ἄξιοι τῶν τε παίδων ὁ τέλειος ἤδη καὶ ἡ γυνή. ἤδη δ᾽
αὐτοῖς καὶ παῖδες, ὡς νέοις, γένοιντο ταχέως, καὶ
324 πλέονες φύλακες ὑμῖν τῆς ἡγεμονίας εἶεν. ἁρμόζω
σφίσιν ἀλλήλους ἐφ᾽ ὑμῶν, καὶ πέμπω βασιλέας εἶ-
325 ναι τῶν ἐθνῶν ἤδη τῶν ἄνω. καὶ οὐ Περσῶν ὑμῖν ἔθη
καὶ ἑτέρων ἐθνῶν μᾶλλον ἢ τόνδε τὸν κοινὸν ἅπασιν
ἐπιθήσω νόμον, ἀεὶ δίκαιον εἶναι τὸ πρὸς βασιλέως
326 ὁριζόμενον." ὁ μὲν δὴ οὕτως εἶπεν, ἡ στρατιὰ δὲ ὡς
βασιλέα τε τῶν ἐπὶ Ἀλεξάνδρῳ μέγιστον καὶ πατέρα
327 ἄριστον ηὐφήμει. καὶ ὁ Σέλευκος Στρατονίκῃ καὶ τῷ
παιδὶ τὰ αὐτὰ προστάξας ἐζεύγνυ τὸν γάμον καὶ ἐπὶ
τὴν βασιλείαν ἐξέπεμψεν, ἔργον ἀοίδιμον τόδε καὶ
δυνατώτερον τῶν ἐν πολέμοις αὐτῷ γενομένων ἐργασάμενος.

328   62. Σατραπεῖαι δὲ ἦσαν ὑπ᾽ αὐτῷ δύο καὶ ἑβδο-
μήκοντα· τοσαύτης ἐβασίλευε γῆς. καὶ τὴν πλείονα
τῷ παιδὶ παραδούς, ἦρχε τῶν ἀπὸ θαλάσσης ἐπὶ Εὐ-
329 φράτην μόνον. καὶ πόλεμον τελευταῖον Λυσιμάχῳ
περὶ Φρυγίαν τὴν ἐφ᾽ Ἑλλησπόντῳ πολεμῶν, Λυσιμάχου μὲν ἐκράτει πεσόντος ἐν τῇ μάχῃ, αὐτὸς δὲ τὸν

had enlarged his kingdom to a greater extent than any of the other successors of Alexander. For this reason it was difficult for him, now an old man, to govern, because of its size. "It is my wish," he said, "to divide its great expanse, 321 so that you do not have to worry about the future, and to give a part of it now to those most dear to me. It is right 322 that you all cooperate with me in all matters, since it was by me that you were raised to such an extent of imperial power after Alexander. Those dearest to me, and worthy 323 to rule, are my now adult son and my wife. They are still young, and may they soon have children, to be new guardians of your dominance. I join them in marriage before 324 you, and now send them to rule the peoples of the upper territories. The law I prescribe for you is not the custom 325 of the Persians or any other peoples, but is common to all men—that what is decreed by the king is always right." This was what he said, and the army shouted their praise 326 of him as the greatest king after Alexander and the best of fathers. After Seleucus gave the same instructions to Stra- 327 tonice and his son, he joined them in marriage, and sent them off to their kingdom. This was a famous deed and one more effective even than anything he achieved in the wars he conducted.

62. Seleucus had seventy-two satrapies under his com- 328 mand: such was the extent of his territory. He handed over most of it to his son, and only ruled from the Mediterranean to the Euphrates himself. He fought his last war 329 against Lysimachus for possession of Hellespontine Phrygia. Having defeated Lysimachus, who died in the battle, he himself crossed the Hellespont and went up to Lysi-

Ἑλλήσποντον ἐπέρα. καὶ ἐς Λυσιμάχειαν ἀναβαίνων
330 κτείνεται. Πτολεμαῖος δ' αὐτὸν ἑπόμενος ἔκτεινεν, ὅτῳ
Κεραυνὸς ἐπίκλησις. υἱὸς δ' ἦν ὁ Κεραυνὸς ὅδε Πτολεμαίου τοῦ σωτῆρος καὶ Εὐρυδίκης τῆς Ἀντιπάτρου·
καὶ αὐτὸν ἐκπεσόντα Αἰγύπτου διὰ δέος, ὅτι νεωτάτῳ
παιδὶ ὁ Πτολεμαῖος τὴν ἀρχὴν ἐπενόει δοῦναι, ὁ
Σέλευκος οἷα φίλου παῖδα ἀτυχοῦντα ὑπεδέξατο, καὶ
ἔφερβε καὶ περιήγετο πάντῃ φονέα ἑαυτοῦ.
331   63. Καὶ Σέλευκος μὲν οὕτω τελευτᾷ, τρία καὶ ἑβδομήκοντα ἔτη βιώσας, καὶ βασιλεύσας αὐτῶν δύο καὶ
τεσσαράκοντα. καί μοι δοκεῖ καὶ ἐς τοῦτο αὐτῷ συν-
ενεχθῆναι τὸ αὐτὸ λόγιον, "Μὴ σπεῦδ' Εὐρώπην·
Ἀσίη τοι πολλὸν ἀμείνων." ἡ γὰρ Λυσιμάχεια τῆς
Εὐρώπης ἐστί, καὶ τότε πρῶτον ἀπὸ τῆς Ἀλεξάνδρου
332 στρατείας ἐς τὴν Εὐρώπην διεπέρα. λέγεται δὲ καὶ
περὶ αὐτοῦ τοῦ θανάτου ποτὲ αὐτῷ χρωμένῳ λόγιον
προαγορευθῆναι· "Ἄργος ἀλευόμενος τὸ πεπρωμένον
εἰς ἔτος ἥξεις· εἰ δ' Ἄργει πελάσαις, τότε κεν παρὰ
333 μοῖραν ὄλοιο." ὁ μὲν δὴ Ἄργος τὸ Πελοποννήσιον καὶ
Ἄργος τὸ Ἀμφιλοχικὸν καὶ Ἄργος τὸ ἐν Ὀρεστείᾳ
(ὅθεν οἱ Ἀργεάδαι Μακεδόνες) καὶ τὸ ἐν τῷ Ἰονίῳ
λεγόμενον οἰκίσαι Διομήδην ἀλώμενον, καὶ εἴ τί που
γῆς ἄλλο Ἄργος ἐκαλεῖτο, πάντα ἀνεζήτει καὶ ἐφυ-
334 λάσσετο· ἀναβαίνοντι δ' ἐς τὴν Λυσιμάχειαν αὐτῷ
ἀπὸ τοῦ Ἑλλησπόντου βωμὸς ἦν ἐν ὄψει μέγας τε καὶ
περιφανής, καὶ πυθόμενος αὐτὸν ἢ τοὺς Ἀργοναύτας
εἴσασθαι παραπλέοντας ἐς Κόλχους ἢ τοὺς Ἀχαιοὺς
ἐπὶ Ἴλιον στρατεύοντας, καὶ διὰ τοῦτο ἔτι τὸν βωμὸν

machea where he is killed. The man who killed him was   330
Ptolemy, surnamed Ceraunus, a member of his entourage.
This Ceraunus was the son of Ptolemy Soter and Euryd-
ice, daughter of Antipater. He had gone into exile from
Egypt out of fear, because Ptolemy was intending to leave
the kingdom to his youngest son. Seleucus received him
as the unfortunate son of a friend, and thus supported and
took around with him everywhere he went his own murderer.

63. So died Seleucus, having lived for seventy-three   331
years, and ruled for forty-two of them. It seems to me that
the same oracle I mentioned earlier got it right in this case
too, when it said, "Do not be in a hurry to get to Europe;
Asia is much better for you." For Lysimachea is in Europe,
and this was the first time that Seleucus had crossed over
to Europe since joining Alexander's expedition to Asia. It   332
is also said that when he was once consulting an oracle
about his death, the following prophecy was made to him:
"If you stay away from Argos, you will reach the age fate
has allotted you. But if you go near Argos, you will die
before your time." There is an Argos in the Peloponnese,   333
an Argos in Amphilochia, an Argos in Orestea (the Macedonian Argeads come from here), and another on the Ionian sea, which Diomedes is said to have founded on his
travels. Seleucus investigated these and all other places in
the world called Argos, and took care to avoid them. But   334
on his way up to Lysimachea from the Hellespont he noticed a large and conspicuous altar, which he was told had
been set up either by the Argonauts as they sailed past on
their way to Colchis, or by the Achaeans while campaign-
ing against Troy. For this reason the people who live
nearby still call the altar Argos, which is either a corrup-

τοὺς περιχώρους Ἄργος καλεῖν, ἢ διὰ τὴν ναῦν
διαφθείροντας τὸ ὄνομα ἢ διὰ τὴν πατρίδα τῶν
Ἀτρειδῶν, κτείνεται, ταῦτα ἔτι μανθάνων, ὑπὸ τοῦ
335 Πτολεμαίου προσπεσόντος ὄπισθεν. καὶ Σέλευκον μὲν
ἔκαιε Φιλέταιρος ὁ Περγάμου δυναστεύσας, πολλῶν
χρημάτων τὸ σῶμα τὸν Κεραυνὸν αἰτήσας, καὶ τὰ
336 λείψανα ἔπεμπεν Ἀντιόχῳ τῷ παιδὶ αὐτοῦ. ὁ δ' ἐν
Σελευκείᾳ τῇ πρὸς θαλάσσῃ ἀπέθετο, καὶ νεὼν αὐτῷ
ἐπέστησε καὶ τέμενος περιέθηκε· καὶ τὸ τέμενος Νι-
κατόρειον ἐπικλῄζεται.

337   64. Λυσίμαχον δὲ πυνθάνομαι, τῶν ὑπασπιστῶν
ὄντα τῶν Ἀλεξάνδρου, παρατροχάσαι ποτὲ ἐπὶ πλεῖστον αὐτῷ, καὶ καμόντα, τῆς οὐρᾶς τοῦ βασιλέως
ἵππου λαβόμενον, ἔτι συντρέχειν, πληγέντα δὲ ἐς τὸ
μέτωπον ἐπὶ τὴν φλέβα τῷ τέλει τοῦ βασιλείου δόρα-
338 τος αἱμορροεῖν· τὸν δὲ Ἀλέξανδρον, ἀπορίᾳ τελα-
μῶνος, τῷ διαδήματι αὐτοῦ τὸ τραῦμα περιδῆσαι,
καὶ ἐμπλησθῆναι μὲν αἵματος τὸ διάδημα, τὸν δὲ
Ἀλεξάνδρου μάντιν Ἀρίστανδρον φερομένῳ τῷ Λυσιμάχῳ καὶ ὧδε ἔχοντι ἐπειπεῖν ὅτι "Βασιλεύσει μὲν
339 οὗτος ὁ ἀνήρ, βασιλεύσει δ' ἐπιπόνως." ὁ μὲν δὴ καὶ
ἐβασίλευσε τεσσαράκοντα ἔτη μάλιστα σὺν οἷς ἐσα-
τράπευσε, καὶ ἐπιπόνως ἐβασίλευσε, καὶ ἑβδομηκον-
τούτης ὢν στρατευόμενος καὶ μαχόμενος ἔπεσεν.
340 εὐθὺς δ' ἐπαναιρεθέντος αὐτῷ τοῦ Σελεύκου, κείμενον
τὸ σῶμα τοῦ Λυσιμάχου κύων οἰκεῖος, ἐς πολὺ ὑπερ-
μαχῶν, ἀλύμαντον ἐξ ὀρνέων καὶ θηρίων διεφύλασσε,
341 μέχρι Θώραξ ὁ Φαρσάλιος εὑρὼν ἔθαψεν. οἱ δὲ

tion by them of the name of the ship, or because it is the native city of the sons of Atreus. Seleucus was still listening to this story when Ptolemy attacked him from behind and kills him. Philetaerus, ruler of Pergamum, paid Ceraunus   335 a great deal of money for the body of Seleucus, which he had cremated and sent the ashes to Antiochus, Seleucus' son.[54] Antiochus buried them at Seleucea on the sea, and   336 built a temple for Seleucus with a sacred precinct around it. The precinct is called Nicatoreum.

64. I have heard that Lysimachus, while he was one of   337 Alexander's shield bearers, was once running beside him for a long distance, and, growing tired, grabbed hold of the tail of his horse. He continued running, but was hit on the forehead by the end of the king's spear, on a vein which bled profusely. Alexander did not have a bandage with   338 him, and so tied up the wound with his diadem, which became soaked in blood. When Aristandrus, Alexander's seer, saw Lysimachus being carried off in this condition, he proclaimed, "This man will be king, but his reign will be a troubled one." He did indeed become king and ruled   339 for nearly forty years, including the time he was satrap, and it was a troubled reign. He died in combat while in command of an army at the age of seventy. Seleucus was   340 killed shortly after him. As Lysimachus' body lay on the ground, his dog protected it for a long time, keeping the birds and animals from defiling it, until Thorax of Pharsalia found it and buried it. Others say that Lysimachus was   341

[54] Philetaerus founded the Attalid dynasty of Pergamum. He died in 263.

Ἀλέξανδρόν φασι θάψαι, τὸν αὐτοῦ Λυσιμάχου
παῖδα, φυγόντα μὲν ὑπὸ δέους πρὸς Σέλευκον ὅτε Λυσίμαχος Ἀγαθοκλέα τὸν ἕτερον αὐτοῦ παῖδα ἀνεῖλεν,
ἐρευνησάμενον δὲ ἐν τῷ τότε τὸ σῶμα, καὶ ἐκ τοῦ
κυνὸς μάλιστα ἀνευρόντα ἤδη διεφθαρμένον. τὰ δὲ
ὀστᾶ τοὺς Λυσιμαχέας ἐνθέσθαι τῷ σφετέρῳ ἱερῷ,
342   καὶ τὸ ἱερὸν Λυσιμάχειον προσαγορεῦσαι. τοιόνδε
μὲν δὴ τέλος ἑκατέρῳ τῶνδε τῶν βασιλέων συνηνέχθη, ἀνδρειοτάτων τε καὶ τὰ σώματα μεγίστων
γενομένων, τοῦ μὲν ἐς ἑβδομήκοντα ἔτη, τοῦ δὲ ἐς
πλέονα τούτων ἔτι ἄλλα τρία, μεμαχημένων ἐκ χειρὸς
οἰκείας ἀεὶ μέχρι τοῦ θανάτου.

343   65. Σελεύκου δ' ἀποθανόντος διάδοχοι, παῖς παρὰ
πατρὸς ἐκδεχόμενοι τὴν Σύρων ἀρχήν, ἐγένοντο οἵδε,
Ἀντίοχος μὲν πρῶτος ὅδε ὁ τῆς μητρυιᾶς ἐρασθείς,
ὃς καὶ Σωτὴρ ἐπεκλήθη Γαλάτας ἐκ τῆς Εὐρώπης ἐς
344   τὴν Ἀσίαν ἐσβαλόντας, ἐξελάσας, δεύτερος δὲ Ἀντίοχος ἕτερος, ἐκ τῶνδε τῶν γάμων γενόμενος, ὅτῳ Θεὸς
ἐπώνυμον ὑπὸ Μιλησίων γίγνεται πρῶτον, ὅτι αὐτοῖς
Τίμαρχον τύραννον καθεῖλεν. ἀλλὰ τόνδε μὲν τὸν
345   Θεὸν ἔκτεινεν ἡ γυνὴ φαρμάκῳ. δύο δὲ εἶχε, Λαοδίκην
καὶ Βερενίκην, ἐξ ἔρωτός τε καὶ ἐγγύης, <. . .> Πτολεμαίου τοῦ Φιλαδέλφου θυγατέρα· καὶ αὐτὸν ἔκτεινε
Λαοδίκη, καὶ ἐπ' ἐκείνῳ Βερενίκην τε καὶ τὸ Βερενίκης

---

55 Antiochus I Soter ("Savior"), ruled 281 to 261.
56 Antiochus II Theos ("The Divine One"), ruled 261 to 246.

buried by his son, Alexander, who had fled to Seleucus out of fear, when Lysimachus killed his other son, Agathocles. On this occasion, Alexander looked for the body and, largely with the help of the dog, found it, already decomposing. The people of Lysimachea deposited the bones in their own temple, which they named the Lysimacheum. Such was the end experienced by each of these kings. 342 They were very brave and of huge physical stature, Lysimachus living to the age of seventy, Seleucus another three years, and both had continued to fight in hand-to-hand combat right up until death.

65. On the death of Seleucus, the following came after 343 him, the kingdom of Syria being passed from father to son in regular succession. The first was the Antiochus who fell in love with his stepmother. He was called "Soter" as a result of driving off the Galatians, who had invaded Asia from Europe.[55] The second was another Antiochus, a 344 product of the marriage I have just mentioned.[56] He first receives the title "Theos" from the Milesians, as he killed their tyrant, Timarchus, for them. But his wife killed this "Theos" with poison. He was married twice, first to La- 345 odice, a love match, then by betrothal, to Berenice, <. . .> a daughter of Ptolemy Philadelphus.[57] Laodice was the one who murdered him, and in addition to him, Berenice

[57] There is a short lacuna in the text, which should probably be filled as follows: "He was married twice, first to Laodice, a love match, then by betrothal, to Berenice, <the former a daughter of Achaeus, the latter> a daughter of Ptolemy Philadelphus." Ptolemy II Philadelphus ("Brother-loving") ruled Egypt from 282 to 246.

346 βρέφος. καὶ Πτολεμαῖος ὁ τοῦ Φιλαδέλφου, ταῦτα τι-
νύμενος, Λαοδίκην τε ἔκτεινε καὶ ἐς Συρίαν ἐνέβαλε
καὶ ἐς Βαβυλῶνα ἤλασεν. καὶ Παρθυαῖοι τῆς ἀποστάσεως τότε ἦρξαν ὡς τεταραγμένης τῆς τῶν Σελευκιδῶν ἀρχῆς.

347 66. Ἐπὶ δὲ τῷ Θεῷ βασιλεὺς γίγνεται Συρίας
Σέλευκος, υἱὸς τοῦ Θεοῦ τε καὶ Λαοδίκης, ᾧ Καλλίνι-
κος ἐπώνυμον. ἐπὶ δὲ Σελεύκῳ δύο παῖδες αὐτοῦ Σελεύκου, καθ᾽ ἡλικίαν ἑκάτερος αὐτῶν, Σέλευκός τε καὶ
348 Ἀντίοχος. Σελεύκῳ μὲν δὴ ἀσθενεῖ τε ὄντι καὶ πενο-
μένῳ καὶ δυσπειθῆ τὸν στρατὸν ἔχοντι ἐπεβούλευσαν
οἱ φίλοι διὰ φαρμάκων, καὶ ἐς ἔτη δύο μόνα ἐβα-
σίλευσεν· ὁ δὲ Ἀντίοχος ὅδε ἐστὶν ὁ Μέγας ἐπίκλην,
περὶ οὗ μοι πάλαι εἴρηται, Ῥωμαίοις πεπολεμηκότος.
349 ἐβασίλευσε δὲ ἔτη ἑπτὰ καὶ τριάκοντα. καὶ αὐτοῦ
περὶ τοῖν παίδοιν προεῖπον ἀμφοῖν βεβασιλευκότοιν,
Σελεύκου τε καὶ Ἀντιόχου, Σελεύκου μὲν ἔτεσι δώδεκα, ἀπράκτως ἅμα καὶ ἀσθενῶς διὰ τὴν τοῦ πατρὸς
συμφοράν, Ἀντιόχου δὲ δώδεκα οὐ πλήρεσιν, ἐν οἷς
Ἀρταξίαν τὸν Ἀρμένιον εἷλε, καὶ ἐς Αἴγυπτον ἐστρά-
τευσεν ἐπὶ ἕκτον Πτολεμαῖον, ὀρφανευόμενον μετ᾽
350 ἀδελφοῦ. καὶ αὐτῷ στρατοπεδεύοντι περὶ τὴν Ἀλεξάνδρειαν Ποπίλιος παρὰ Ῥωμαίων πρεσβευτὴς ἧκε,
φέρων δέλτον ἐν ᾗ τάδε ἐγέγραπτο, μὴ πολεμεῖν Πτο-
351 λεμαίοις Ἀντίοχον. ἀναγνόντι δὲ αὐτῷ, καὶ λέγοντι

---

58 Ptolemy III Euergetes ("Benefactor"), king of Egypt (246–221), invaded Syria as part of the Third Syrian War (246–241).

and her child. Ptolemy, the son of Philadelphus, avenged 346
this crime, however: he killed Laodice and invaded Syria,
pushing as far as Babylon.[58] It was at this point that, taking
advantage of the disturbed circumstances in the Seleucid
kingdom, the Parthians began their insurrection.

66. After Theos, Seleucus surnamed Callinicus, son of 347
Theos and Laodice, becomes king of Syria; he was followed by his two sons, Seleucus and Antiochus, in order
of age.[59] Seleucus only reigned for two years: he was weak 348
and had no money, and when he proved unable to command the obedience of the army, his courtiers plotted
against him and poisoned him. This Antiochus was the one
called "the Great," who fought a war against Rome; I have
written about him earlier in this book.[60] He was king for
thirty-seven years. Both of his sons, Seleucus and Antio- 349
chus, also ruled Syria—I have written about them too[61]—
Seleucus for twelve years, but because of his father's defeat his reign was weak and ineffective, Antiochus for just
under twelve years, a period in which he captured Artaxias
the Armenian, and launched an invasion of Egypt against
Ptolemy VI, who had been left an orphan along with one
brother. While he was encamped near Alexandria, the Ro- 350
man ambassador Popillius arrived with an order written
on a tablet instructing Antiochus not to wage war on the
Ptolemies. When he had read it, he said he would think 351

[59] Seleucus II Callinicus ("Gloriously Victorious"), ruled 246
to 225; Seleucus III Ceraunus ("Thunderbolt"), ruled 225 to 223;
Antiochus III Megas ("the Great"), ruled 223 to 187.

[60] See above, 1.1–44.231.

[61] See above, 45.232–35.

βουλεύσεσθαι, κύκλον τῇ ῥάβδῳ περιέγραψεν ὁ Πο-
352 πίλιος, καὶ εἶπεν· "Ἐνταῦθα βουλεύου." ὁ μὲν δὴ καταπλαγεὶς ἀνέζευξε, καὶ τὸ τῆς Ἐλυμαίας Ἀφροδίτης
ἱερὸν ἐσύλησε, καὶ φθίνων ἐτελεύτησε, παιδίον ἐνναετὲς ἀπολιπών, Ἀντίοχον τὸν Εὐπάτορα, ὥς μοι καὶ
περὶ τοῦδε εἴρηται.

353   67. Εἴρηται δὲ καὶ περὶ Δημητρίου τοῦ μετ' αὐτόν,
ὃς ὡμήρευεν ἐν Ῥώμῃ καὶ τῆς ὁμηρείας ἐκφυγὼν ἐβασίλευσε, Σωτὴρ καὶ ὅδε πρὸς τῶν Σύρων, δεύτερος ἐπὶ
354 τῷ Σελεύκου τοῦ Νικάτορος παιδὶ ὀνομασθείς. ἐπανί-
σταται δὲ αὐτῷ τις Ἀλέξανδρος, ψευδόμενος εἶναι τοῦ
Σελευκείου γένους· καὶ Πτολεμαῖος ὁ τῆς Αἰγύπτου
βασιλεὺς κατὰ μῖσος Δημητρίου συνελάμβανεν Ἀλε-
355 ξάνδρῳ. καὶ Δημήτριος μὲν διὰ Πτολεμαῖον ἐξέπεσε
τῆς ἀρχῆς καὶ ἐτελεύτησε· τὸν δὲ Ἀλέξανδρον ἐξέβαλε Δημήτριος ὁ Δημητρίου τοῦδε τοῦ Σωτῆρος
υἱός, καὶ ἐπὶ τῷδε, ὡς νόθον τοῦ γένους ἄνδρα νικήσας, Νικάτωρ ὑπὸ τῶν Σύρων ὠνομάσθη, δεύτερος
356 καὶ ὅδε μετὰ Σέλευκον. ἐπί τε Παρθυαίους καὶ ὅδε
μετὰ Σέλευκον ἐστράτευσε, καὶ γενόμενος αἰχμάλω-
τος δίαιταν εἶχεν ἐν Φραάτου βασιλέως, καὶ Ῥοδο-
γούνην ἔζευξεν αὐτῷ τὴν ἀδελφὴν ὁ βασιλεύς.

357   68. Παρὰ δὲ τὴν ἀναρχίαν τήνδε δοῦλος τῶν βασιλέων Διόδοτος παιδίον Ἀλέξανδρον, ἐξ Ἀλεξάνδρου
τοῦ νόθου καὶ τῆς Πτολεμαίου θυγατρός, ἐπὶ τὴν βα-

62 See above, 46.236. C. Popillius Laenas (consul 172, 158)
made his famous demand of Antiochus IV in 168.

about it, but Popillius drew a circle around him with his staff and said, "Think about it here." Antiochus was 352 shocked and withdrew. He robbed the temple of Aphrodite at Elymais and died of consumption, leaving a nine-year-old son, Antiochus Eupator, as I have already explained when dealing with him too.[62]

67. I have also dealt with his successor, Demetrius, who 353 was a hostage in Rome, but escaped his captivity and became king.[63] He too was called "Soter" by the Syrians, the second to bear the title after the son of Seleucus Nicator. A certain Alexander rose up in revolt against Demetrius, 354 pretending to be a member of the Seleucid family.[64] Ptolemy king of Egypt gave assistance to Alexander out of hatred for Demetrius. And Demetrius was driven out of 355 his kingdom by Ptolemy and died. Demetrius, however, the son of this Demetrius Soter, expelled Alexander, and for defeating an illegitimate member of the family, he was given the title "Nicator" by the Syrians, the second to be so called after Seleucus Nicator. Like Seleucus before, 356 Demetrius also invaded Parthia, but was captured and lived in the court of king Phraates, who married his sister, Rhodogune, to him.[65]

68. In the course of this power vacuum, one of the royal 357 slaves, Diodotus, installed on the throne a young boy called Alexander, a son of Alexander the bastard and Ptol-

[63] See above, 46.238–47.244.

[64] Alexander Balas ruled from 153/2 to 145.

[65] Demetrius II Nicator ruled from about 147 to 125 (including the time spent as a hostage in Parthia). The Parthian king was Arsaces V Mithridates I, not Phraates II.

σιλείαν ἤγαγεν. καὶ τὸ παιδίον κτείνας αὐτὸς ἐπετόλ-
μησε τῇ ἀρχῇ, Τρύφων ἀφ᾽ ἑαυτοῦ μετονομασθείς.

358 ἀλλ᾽ αὐτὸν Ἀντίοχος ὁ ἀδελφὸς Δημητρίου τοῦ
αἰχμαλώτου, πυθόμενος ἐν Ῥόδῳ περὶ τῆς αἰχμαλωσίας, κτείνει κατιὼν ἐς τὰ πατρῷα σὺν πόνῳ πολλῷ.

359 καὶ στρατεύει καὶ ὅδε ἐπὶ τὸν Φραάτην, τὸν ἀδελφὸν
αἰτῶν. ὁ μὲν δὴ Φραάτης αὐτὸν ἔδεισε καὶ τὸν Δημήτριον ἐξέπεμψεν· ὁ δ᾽ Ἀντίοχος καὶ ὡς συνέβαλέ τε
τοῖς Παρθυαίοις, καὶ ἡσσώμενος ἑαυτὸν ἔκτεινεν.

360 ἔκτεινε δὲ καὶ Δημήτριον ἐς τὴν βασιλείαν ἐπανελθόντα ἡ γυνὴ Κλεοπάτρα, δολοφονήσασα διὰ ζῆλον
τοῦ γάμου Ῥοδογούνης, δι᾽ ὃν δὴ καὶ Ἀντιόχῳ τῷ

361 ἀδελφῷ τοῦ Δημητρίου προὐγεγάμητο. καὶ παῖδες
ἦσαν αὐτῇ δύο μὲν ἐκ Δημητρίου, Σέλευκός τε καὶ
Ἀντίοχος, ὅτῳ γρυπὸς ἐπίκλησις, ἐκ δὲ Ἀντιόχου
Ἀντίοχος, ὅτῳ Κυζικηνὸς ἐπώνυμον. τούτων τὸν μὲν
γρυπὸν ἐς Ἀθήνας, τὸν δὲ Κυζικηνὸν ἐς Κύζικον ἐπεπόμφει τρέφεσθαι.

362 69. Σέλευκον δ᾽ εὐθὺς ἐπὶ τῷ πατρὶ Δημητρίῳ τὸ
διάδημα ἐπιθέμενον ἐπιτοξεύσασα ἔκτεινεν, εἴτε δεί-
σασα περὶ τῆς τοῦ πατρὸς δολοφονήσεως, εἴτε καὶ

363 μανιώδει πρὸς πάντας μίσει. μετὰ δὲ Σέλευκον ὁ Γρυπὸς ἐγένετο βασιλεύς, καὶ τὴν μητέρα οἱ φάρμακον

364 κεράσασαν πιεῖν ἠνάγκασεν. ἡ μὲν δὴ δίκην ποτὲ
ἔδωκεν, ἄξιος δὲ ἄρα τῆς μητρὸς ἦν καὶ ὁ Γρυπός·
ἐπεβούλευε γὰρ τῷ Κυζικηνῷ καίπερ ὄντι ὁμομητρίῳ.

emy's daughter. He then murdered the boy and ventured
to take the throne himself, changing his name to Trypho.
But Antiochus, brother of the Demetrius captured by the   358
Persians, having learned of his brother's capture while at
Rhodes, returning to his ancestral home with great difficulty, kills Trypho. He too then marches against Phraates   359
to demand the return of his brother. Phraates was afraid
of him and sent Demetrius back, but Antiochus still fought
a battle with the Parthians, was defeated, and took his own
life.[66] On Demetrius' restoration to the throne, his wife   360
Cleopatra killed him, murdering him out of indignation at
his marriage to Rhodogune, the same reason she had earlier married his brother, Antiochus. She had two sons with   361
Demetrius, Seleucus and Antiochus surnamed Grypus,
and one, Antiochus surnamed Cyzicenus, with Antiochus.
Of these sons, she had sent Grypus to Athens for his edu-
cation and Cyzicenus to Cyzicus.[67]

69. Seleucus had only just assumed the diadem after   362
his father, when Cleopatra shot and killed him with an
arrow, either because she was afraid for having murdered
his father, or because she had a manic loathing for all
people. After Seleucus, Grypus became king, and forced   363
his mother to drink the poison she had mixed for him.
So she finally received her due punishment, but Grypus   364
proved himself worthy of his mother. For he conspired
against Cyzicenus, even though he was his half brother.

---

[66] Antiochus VII Sidetes (from the town of Side) was defeated
by the Parthians in 129.   [67] Seleucus V Philometor ("Mother-
loving") was killed by his mother in 125. Antiochus VIII Grypus
("Hook-nose") was killed in 96. Antiochus IX Cyzicenus was
killed by the son of Grypus, Seleucus VI Epiphanes, in 96.

ὁ δὲ μαθὼν ἐπολέμησέ τε αὐτῷ καὶ τῆς ἀρχῆς αὐτόν
ἐξήλασε, καὶ βασιλεὺς ἀντ᾽ ἐκείνου τοῖς Σύροις ἐγέ-
365 νετο. ἀλλὰ καὶ τόνδε Σέλευκος ὁ Ἀντιόχου τοῦ Γρυ-
ποῦ παῖς, ἐπιστρατεύσας ὄντι περ θείῳ, παρείλετο
τὴν ἀρχήν. βίαιος δὲ καὶ τυραννικώτατος ὢν ἐν
Ἑστίᾳ Μόψου τῆς Κιλικίας κατεμπρήσθη κατὰ τὸ
366 γυμνάσιον. καὶ αὐτὸν διεδέξατο Ἀντίοχος ὁ υἱὸς τοῦ
Κυζικηνοῦ· ὃν ἐπιβουλευόμενον ὑπὸ Σελεύκου τοῦ
ἀνεψιοῦ οἱ μὲν Σύροι νομίζουσι περισωθῆναι δι᾽ εὐ-
σέβειαν, καὶ διὰ τοῦτο εὐσεβῆ παρωνόμασαν· ἑταίρα
δ᾽ αὐτὸν ἔσωσεν, ἐρασθεῖσα τοῦ κάλλους, ἐμοὶ δὲ δο-
κοῦσιν ἐπὶ γέλωτι αὐτῷ ποιήσασθαι τὸ ὄνομα οἱ
Σύροι· ἔγημε γὰρ οὗτος ὁ Εὐσεβὴς Σελήνην, ἣ καὶ τῷ
πατρὶ αὐτοῦ ἐγεγάμητο τῷ Κυζικηνῷ καὶ τῷ Γρυπῷ
θείῳ γενομένῳ. τοιγάρτοι αὐτὸν θεοῦ μετιόντος ἐξήλασε τῆς ἀρχῆς Τιγράνης.

367 70. Καὶ τὸν υἱὸν ἐκείνου τὸν ἐκ τῆς Σελήνης αὐτῷ
γενόμενον, ἐν Ἀσίᾳ τε τραφέντα καὶ ἀπὸ τοῦδε Ἀσια-
τικὸν ἐπίκλην, Πομπήιος ἀφείλετο τὴν Σύρων ἀρχήν,
ὥς μοι λέλεκται, ὄντα μὲν ἑπτακαιδέκατον ἐκ Σελεύκου Σύρων βασιλέα (ἐξαίρω γὰρ Ἀλέξανδρόν τε
καὶ τὸν Ἀλεξάνδρου παῖδα ὡς νόθους, καὶ τὸν δοῦλον
αὐτῶν Διόδοτον), βασιλεύσαντα δ᾽ ἐν ταῖς ἀσχολίαις
368 ταῖς Πομπηίου ἐπὶ ἓν μόνον ἔτος. ἡ δὲ ἀρχὴ τῶν Σελευκιδῶν ἐς τριάκοντα[16] ἐπὶ διακοσίοις ἐνιαυτοὺς δι-

---

[16] ἑβδομήκοντα codd: τριάκοντα prop. Scaliger

Cyzicenus found out, however, attacked and expelled him from the kingdom, and took the throne of Syria in his place. But Seleucus, the son of Antiochus Grypus, made 365 war on Cyzicenus, even though this was his uncle, and dispossessed him of the kingdom. Seleucus was violent and extremely tyrannical, and he was burned to death in the gymnasium at Mopsuestia in Cilicia. Antiochus, the 366 son of Cyzicenus, succeeded him. He was the target of a plot by his cousin Seleucus, but survived it, in the opinion of the Syrians, because of his piety, and for this reason was given the title "Eusebes."[68] Actually, it was a courtesan who saved him: she had fallen in love with him because he was so handsome, and I believe the Syrians were being ironical when they gave him this name. For this "pious" man married Selene, who had already been married to his father, Cyzicenus, and his uncle, Grypus. For this reason he was hounded by a god, and driven from his kingdom by Tigranes.

70. His son by Selene, having been brought up in Asia 367 and therefore called Asiaticus, was removed from the government of Syria by Pompey, as I have already said.[69] He was the seventeenth king of Syria after Seleucus (I exclude Alexander and his son as being illegitimate, and their slave Diodotus), and only ruled for one year while Pompey was occupied with other business. The Seleucid kingdom 368 lasted two hundred and thirty years, although if one looks

[68] For Antiochus X Eusebes Philopator, see above, note 44.
[69] See above, 49.249–50.

ίκετο· καὶ εἴ τις ἐπισκοποίη τὸν ἐς Ῥωμαίους χρόνον
ἀπ᾽ Ἀλεξάνδρου, προσθετέον ἐπὶ τοῖς διακοσίοις τριάκοντα ἔτεσι τὰ Τιγράνους τεσσαρεσκαίδεκα.

369   Τοσάδε μὲν δὴ καὶ περὶ Μακεδόνων τῶν Συρίας
βεβασιλευκότων εἶχον εἰπεῖν ὡς ἐν ἀλλοτρίᾳ συγ-
γραφῇ.

at the whole period between Alexander and the Romans, there must be added the fourteen years of Tigranes to the two hundred and thirty.

That is all I have to say about the Macedonian kings who ruled Syria, as it is not the subject of this book. 369

XII

ΜΙΘΡΙΔΑΤΕΙΟΣ[1]

1. Θρᾷκας Ἕλληνες ἡγοῦνται, τοὺς ἐς Ἴλιον μετὰ
Ῥήσου στρατεύσαντας, Ῥήσου νυκτὸς ὑπὸ Διομή-
δους ἀναιρεθέντος ὃν τρόπον Ὅμηρος ἐν τοῖς ἔπεσι
φράζει, φεύγοντας ἐπὶ τοῦ Πόντου τὸ στόμα, ᾗ στε-
νώτατός ἐστιν ἐς Θρᾴκην ὁ διάπλους, οἱ μὲν οὐκ ἐπι-
τυχόντας πλοίων τῇδε καταμεῖναι καὶ τῆς γῆς κρατῆ-
2 σαι Βεβρυκίας λεγομένης, οἱ δὲ περάσαντας ὑπὲρ τὸ
Βυζάντιον ἐς τὴν Θρᾳκῶν τῶν Βιθυνῶν λεγομένων
παρὰ Βιθύαν ποταμὸν οἰκῆσαι, καὶ λιμῷ πιεσθέντας
ἐς Βεβρυκίαν αὖθις ἐπανελθεῖν, καὶ Βιθυνίαν ἀντὶ Βεβρυκίας, ἀπὸ τοῦ ποταμοῦ παρ' ὃν ᾤκουν, ὀνομάσαι,
ἢ καὶ τὸ ὄνομα αὐτοῖς ἀλόγως σὺν χρόνῳ παρατρα-
πῆναι, οὐκ ἐς πολὺ τῆς Βιθυνίας παρὰ τὴν Βεβρυκίαν
διαφερούσης. ὧδε μὲν ἔνιοι νομίζουσιν, ἕτεροι δὲ

---

[1] τοῦ αὐτοῦ Ἀππιανοῦ Ῥωμαϊκῶν Μιθριδάτειος ιγ BJ:
Ἀππιανοῦ Ῥωμαϊκῶν Μιθριδάτειος LP

[1] For the great Byzantine scholar, Photius, the Mithridatic
Book was the twelfth of Appian's *Roman History*. The manu-

146

BOOK XII

THE MITHRIDATIC WAR[1]

1. The Greeks think that when Rhesus was killed at night by Diomedes, as Homer describes in his epic poem,[2] the Thracians who campaigned with him against Troy fled to the mouth of the Pontus, where the crossing to Thrace is shortest. Some say they were unable to find ships, remained there, and made themselves master of the country called Bebrycia; others maintain that, after pushing on beyond Byzantium to the territory of the Thracian people known as Bithynians, they settled beside the river Bithyas, but were forced by famine to return to Bebrycia, which they named Bithynia instead of Bebrycia, after the river beside which they had been living—or perhaps the name was changed by them unthinkingly over time, as there is not much difference between the words Bithynia and Bebrycia. This is what some people think. Others say that

2

scripts insert the Parthian Book as the twelfth, making the Mithridatic the thirteenth.

The manuscripts all place at the beginning of the work two chapters that Schweighäuser repositioned, for good reason, as chapters 118 and 119 (579–89, below). Later editors have nearly all followed Schweighäuser, although not, most recently, Goukowsky 2001.   [2] Hom. *Il.* 10.471–97.

Βίθυν ἄρξαι πρῶτον αὐτῶν, παῖδα Διός τε καὶ Θράκης,
οὓς ἐπωνύμους ἑκατέρᾳ γῇ γενέσθαι.

3 2. Τάδε μὲν οὖν μοι προλελέχθω περὶ Βιθυνίας· τῶν
δὲ πρὸ Ῥωμαίων αὐτῆς βασιλέων, ἐννέα καὶ τεσσαράκοντα ἐφεξῆς γενομένων, ὅτου μοι μάλιστα μνημο-
νεῦσαι προήκει τὰ Ῥωμαίων συγγράφοντι, Προυσίας
ἦν ὁ Κυνηγὸς ἐπίκλησιν, ᾧ Περσεὺς ὁ Μακεδόνων
4 βασιλεὺς τὴν ἀδελφὴν ἠγγύησεν. καὶ οὐ πολὺ ὕστερον Περσέως καὶ Ῥωμαίων ἐς χεῖρας ἐπ᾽ ἀλλήλους
ἰόντων, ὁ Προυσίας οὐδετέροις συνεμάχει. Περσέως
δ᾽ ἁλόντος ἀπήντησε τοῖς Ῥωμαίων στρατηγοῖς εἱμά
τε Ῥωμαϊκὸν ἀμπεχόμενος, ὃ καλοῦσι τήβεννον, καὶ
ὑποδήματα ἔχων Ἰταλικά, τὴν κεφαλὴν ἐξυρημένος
καὶ πῖλον ἐπικείμενος, ᾧ τρόπῳ τινὲς προΐασι τῶν ἐν
διαθήκαις ἐλευθερωθέντων, αἰσχρὸς ὢν καὶ τἆλλα
5 ὀφθῆναι καὶ βραχύς. ἐντυχὼν δ᾽ αὐτοῖς ἔφη ῥωμαϊστὶ
τῷ ῥήματι Ῥωμαίων εἰμὶ λίβερτος, ὅπερ ἐστὶν ἀπ-
ελεύθερος. γέλωτα δὲ παρασχὼν ἐς Ῥώμην ἐπέμφθη,
καὶ φανεὶς κἀνταῦθα γελοῖος ἔτυχε συγγνώμης.

6 3. Χρόνῳ δ᾽ ὕστερον Ἀττάλῳ τι χαλεπήνας, τῷ
βασιλεῖ τῆς Ἀσίας τῆς περὶ τὸ Πέργαμον, τὴν γῆν
ἐδῄου τὴν Ἀσιάδα. μαθοῦσα δ᾽ ἡ Ῥωμαίων βουλὴ
προσέπεμπε τῷ Προυσίᾳ μὴ πολεμεῖν Ἀττάλῳ, φίλῳ
Ῥωμαίων ὄντι καὶ συμμάχῳ. καὶ δυσπειθῶς ἔτι
ἔχοντι οἱ πρέσβεις μετ᾽ ἀνατάσεως προσέτασσον

---

3 Prusias II Cynegus ("The Hunter") ruled Bithynia from 182
to 149; Perseus was king of Macedon from 179 to 168.

their first ruler was Bithys, son of Zeus and Thrace, and that the two countries took their name from them.

2. So much, then, by way of preface concerning Bithynia. Of its kings before the time of the Romans—forty-nine ruled in succession—since I am writing Roman history, the one I should particularly mention is Prusias surnamed Cynegus, to whom Perseus king of Macedon betrothed his sister.[3] Not long after, when Perseus and the Romans were at war with each other, Prusias allied himself to neither side.[4] But on the capture of Perseus, he went to meet the Roman generals dressed in a Roman garment they call a "tebennus,"[5] wearing Italian shoes, with head shaved and sporting a cap—this is how some who have gained their freedom by testamentary manumission present themselves in public—and he was, besides, ugly to look at and short. When he met them, he said, using a Latin term, "I am the *libertus* of the Romans" (*libertus* means freedman). This made them laugh and he was sent to Rome; as he appeared there too an object of ridicule, Prusias gained his pardon.

3. Some time later, he became angry with Attalus, king of that part of Asia around Pergamum, and ravaged his Asiatic territory.[6] On learning of this, the Roman senate sent instructions to Prusias not to wage war against Attalus, as he was a friend and ally of Rome. When he continued to disobey, the ambassadors ordered him with threats

3

4

5

6

---

[4] The Third Macedonian War (171–168).

[5] The Greek word for the Roman toga.

[6] This war of Prusias II against Attalus II of Pergamum (159/8–139/8) lasted from 156 to 154.

πείθεσθαι τοῖς ὑπὸ τῆς συγκλήτου λεγομένοις, καὶ
ἥκειν μετὰ χιλίων ἱππέων ἔς τι μεθόριον ἐπὶ συνθήκαις, ἔνθα καὶ τὸν Ἄτταλον ἔφασαν περιμένειν
7 μετὰ τοσῶνδε ἑτέρων. ὁ δ᾽ ὡς ὀλίγων τῶν σὺν Ἀττάλῳ καταφρονήσας, καὶ ἐλπίσας αὐτὸν ἐνεδρεύσειν,
προύπεμπε τοὺς πρέσβεις ὡς μετὰ χιλίων ἑπόμενος,
πάντα δ᾽ ἀναστήσας τὸν στρατὸν ἦγεν ὡς ἐς μάχην.
Ἀττάλου δὲ καὶ τῶν πρέσβεων αἰσθομένων τε καὶ
διαφυγόντων ᾗ δυνατὸς αὐτῶν ἐγίγνετο ἕκαστος, ὁ δὲ
καὶ τῶν σκευοφόρων τῶν Ῥωμαϊκῶν ὑπολειφθέντων
ἥπτετο, καὶ χωρίον τι Νικηφόριον ἐξελὼν κατέ-
σκαπτε, καὶ τοὺς ἐν αὐτῷ νεὼς ἐνεπίμπρη, Ἄτταλόν
8 τε ἐς τὸ Πέργαμον συμφυγόντα ἐπολιόρκει, μέχρι καὶ
τῶνδε οἱ Ῥωμαῖοι πυθόμενοι πρέσβεις ἑτέρους ἔπεμπον, οἳ τὸν Προυσίαν ἐκέλευον Ἀττάλῳ τὰς βλάβας
ἀποτῖσαι. τότε οὖν καταπλαγεὶς ὁ Προυσίας ὑπήκουσε
καὶ ἀνεχώρει. ποινὴν δὲ τῶν πρέσβεων ὁρισάντων
αὐτὸν ἐσενεγκεῖν Ἀττάλῳ ναῦς καταφράκτους εἴκοσιν
αὐτίκα καὶ ἀργυρίου σὺν χρόνῳ τάλαντα πεντακόσια,
τάς τε ναῦς ἔδωκε καὶ τὰ χρήματα ἐν τῷ χρόνῳ συνέφερεν.

9   4. Ὄντι δ᾽ αὐτῷ διὰ μίσους τοῖς ὑπηκόοις ἐπὶ
ὠμότητι χαλεπῇ, Νικομήδης υἱὸς ἦν, πάνυ τοῖς Βιθυνοῖς ἀρέσκων· ὅπερ ὁ Προυσίας ὑφορώμενος ἐς
Ῥώμην αὐτὸν βιοῦν μετεστήσατο. καὶ μαθὼν εὐδοκι-
μοῦντα κἀκεῖ, προσέταξε τῆς βουλῆς δεηθῆναι τῶν
ἔτι ὀφειλομένων Ἀττάλῳ χρημάτων αὐτὸν ἀπολῦσαι.
10 Μηνᾶν τε αὐτῷ συμπρεσβεύσοντα ἔπεμπε· καὶ εἴρητο

to comply with the senate's orders, and to come with a thousand cavalry to a frontier post for treaty negotiations, where they said Attalus too was waiting with a similar number of men. Despising the small number of Attalus' escort and hoping to ambush him, he sent the ambassadors ahead to say that he was following with a thousand men, but mobilized his whole army and led them off as if he was going into battle. When Attalus and the ambassadors realized this, they escaped individually wherever they could. Prusias took possession of the Roman pack animals left behind, captured and razed to the ground a stronghold called Nicephorium, burned the temples in it, and besieged Attalus in Pergamum where he had taken refuge. Hearing of these events too, the Romans eventually sent other ambassadors who ordered Prusias to recompense Attalus for his losses. It was at this point that Prusias was struck with fear, complied, and withdrew. When the ambassadors fixed as damages the immediate transfer to Attalus of twenty decked warships and payment of five hundred silver talents over a fixed period, he handed over the ships and paid the money in the time specified.

4. Prusias himself was hated by his subjects because he was extremely cruel, but he had a son, Nicomedes, who was very popular with the Bithynians.[7] Suspicious of this, Prusias sent him off to live in Rome. Learning that he was well thought of there too, he instructed him to petition the senate to release him from the debt still owing to Attalus, and he sent Menas to join him as an ambassador. He told

[7] The future Nicomedes II Epiphanes ("Made Manifest") of Bithynia (r. 149–ca. 127).

τῷ Μηνᾷ, εἰ μὲν ἐπιτύχοι τῆς ἀφέσεως τῶν χρημάτων, ἔτι φείδεσθαι τοῦ Νικομήδους, εἰ δὲ ἀποτύχοι,
κτείνειν αὐτὸν ἐν Ῥώμῃ. κερκούρους τέ τινας ἐς τοῦτο
11 συνέπεμψεν αὐτῷ, καὶ δισχιλίους στρατιώτας. ὁ δὲ
τῆς μὲν ζημίας οὐκ ἀφεθείσης τῷ Προυσίᾳ (Ἀνδρόνικος γὰρ ἐπιπεμφθεὶς ἐς ἀντιλογίαν ὑπὸ Ἀττάλου τὴν
ζημίαν ἀπέφαινεν ἐλάσσονα τῆς ἁρπαγῆς), τὸν δὲ
Νικομήδη λόγου καὶ σπουδῆς ἄξιον ὁρῶν, ἠπόρητο,
καὶ οὔτε κτείνειν αὐτὸν ὑφίστατο οὔτε αὐτὸς ἐς Βιθυνίαν ἐπανιέναι διὰ δέος. ὅμως δ᾽ αὐτῷ βραδύνοντι
συνεὶς ὁ νεανίσκος ἐς λόγους ἦλθεν, ἐθέλοντι κἀκείνῳ.
12 συνθέμενοι δ᾽ ἐπιβουλεῦσαι τῷ Προυσίᾳ, τὸν Ἀττάλου πρεσβευτὴν Ἀνδρόνικον ἐς τὸ ἔργον προσέλαβον,
ἵνα τὸν Ἄτταλον πείσειε τὸν Νικομήδη καταγαγεῖν ἐς
Βιθυνίαν. ἀναμείναντες δ᾽ ἀλλήλους ἐν τῇ Βερνίκῃ,
πολισματίῳ τινὶ τῆς Ἠπείρου, νυκτὸς ἐσβάντες ἐς
ναῦν ἅ τε δέοι ποιεῖν συνετίθεντο, καὶ διελύθησαν ἔτι
νυκτός.
13 5. Ἅμα δ᾽ ἡμέρᾳ Νικομήδης μὲν ἐξέβαινε τῆς νεὼς
πορφύραν τε βασιλικὴν ἠμφιεσμένος καὶ διάδημα
ἐπικείμενος, Ἀνδρόνικος δ᾽ αὐτὸν ὑπαντιάσας τε καὶ
βασιλέα προσειπὼν παρέπεμπε μετὰ στρατιωτῶν ὧν
εἶχε πεντακοσίων. Μηνᾶς δὲ ὑποκρινόμενος τότε
πρῶτον ᾐσθῆσθαι Νικομήδους παρόντος, ἐς τοὺς δισ-
14 χιλίους διαδραμὼν ἐδυσφόρει. προϊὼν δὲ τῷ λόγῳ,
"Δύο," ἔφη, "Βασιλέοιν, τοῦ μὲν ὄντος ἐν τῇ χώρᾳ τοῦ
δ᾽ ἐπιόντος, ἀναγκαῖον ἡμῖν τὸ σφέτερον εὖ διατίθε-
σθαι καὶ τὸ γενησόμενον καλῶς τεκμαίρεσθαι, ὡς ἐν

Menas to spare Nicomedes if he should secure a remission
of the debt, but if not, to kill him there in Rome; and for
this purpose he sent him some boats and two thousand
soldiers. Prusias' indemnity was not remitted (for Andron- 11
icus, who had been dispatched by Attalus to argue against
the Bithynian position, showed that the indemnity was less
than the amount plundered), but Menas, realizing that
Nicomedes was a man who merited consideration and es-
teem, did not know what to do: he could not bring himself
to kill him, and he was afraid to go back himself to Bithynia. Nevertheless the young Nicomedes understood
the situation, and entered discussions with him while he
hesitated, which is what Menas also wanted. They agreed 12
to form a conspiracy against Prusias and engaged Adroni-
cus, Attalus' ambassador, in the enterprise, in order to
persuade Attalus to recall Nicomedes to Bithynia. Having
arranged a rendezvous at Bernice, a small town in Epirus,
they boarded a ship by night, agreed on the necessary action and parted while it was still dark.

5. In the morning, Nicomedes disembarked from the 13
ship wearing the royal purple and with a diadem on his
head. Andronicus went to meet him, saluted him as king
and escorted him with the five hundred troops he had at
his disposal. Menas, pretending it was only then that he
had first discovered the presence of Nicomedes, hurried
straight to his two thousand men and expressed his dismay. Continuing with his speech, he said, "Since we have 14
two kings, one already in the country, the other approaching, we must arrange things to our best advantage by cor-

τῷδε τῆς ἡμετέρας σωτηρίας βεβαιουμένης, ἣν καλῶς
15 προϊδώμεθα πότερος αὐτῶν ἐπικρατήσει. ὁ μὲν δὴ
γέρων ἐστίν, ὁ δὲ νέος· καὶ Βιθυνοὶ τὸν μὲν ἀποστρέ-
φονται, τὸν δὲ αἱροῦνται. Ῥωμαίων τε οἱ δυνατοὶ τὸν
νεανίαν ἀγαπῶσι· καὶ Ἀνδρόνικος αὐτὸν ἤδη δορυ-
φορῶν ὑποδείκνυσι τὴν Ἀττάλου συμμαχίαν, ἀρχήν
τε μεγάλην ἔχοντος καὶ Βιθυνοῖς γειτονεύοντος καὶ ἐκ
16 πολλοῦ τῷ Προυσίᾳ πεπολεμωμένου." λέγων δὲ ταῦθ᾽
ἅμα καὶ τὴν ὠμότητα τοῦ Προυσίου παρεγύμνου, καὶ
ὅσα πονηρὰ πράξειεν ἐς ἅπαντας, καὶ τὸ κοινὸν ἐπὶ
τοῖσδε Βιθυνῶν ἐς αὐτὸν ἔχθος. ὡς δὲ κἀκείνους εἶδε
τὴν Προυσίου μοχθηρίαν ἀποστρεφομένους, ἦγεν αὐτοὺς ἐς τὸν Νικομήδην αὐτίκα, καὶ προσειπὼν καὶ ὅδε
βασιλέα δεύτερος ἐπὶ Ἀνδρονίκῳ μετὰ τῶν δισχιλίων
ἐδορυφόρει.

17   6. Ἄτταλός τε τὸν νεανίαν προθύμως ὑπεδέχετο, καὶ
τὸν Προυσίαν ἐκέλευσε τῷ παιδὶ πόλεις τέ τινας ἐς
ἐνοίκησιν καὶ χώραν ἐς ἐφόδια δοῦναι. ὁ δ᾽ αὐτίκα
δώσειν ἔφη τὴν Ἀττάλου βασιλείαν ἅπασαν, ἣν δὴ
καὶ πρότερον Νικομήδει περιποιῶν ἐς Ἀσίαν ἐσβαλεῖν. ταῦτα δ᾽ εἰπὼν ἔπεμπεν ἐς Ῥώμην τοὺς Νικομήδους καὶ Ἀττάλου κατηγορήσοντάς τε καὶ προκαλε-
18 σομένους ἐς κρίσιν. οἱ δ᾽ ἀμφὶ τὸν Ἄτταλον εὐθὺς
ἐχώρουν ἐς τὴν Βιθυνίαν, καὶ προσιοῦσιν αὐτοῖς οἱ
Βιθυνοὶ κατ᾽ ὀλίγους προσετίθεντο. Προυσίας δ᾽ ἅπασιν ἀπιστῶν, καὶ Ῥωμαίους ἐλπίζων αὐτὸν ἐξαιρήσε-
σθαι τῆς ἐπιβουλῆς, Διήγυλιν τὸν Θρᾷκα, κηδεστὴν
ὄντα οἱ, πεντακοσίους Θρᾷκας αἰτήσας καὶ λαβὼν

rectly forecasting future events, as our safety will be assured by accurately predicting which one of them is going to prevail. One is an old man, the other young; the Bithynians are against one, and support the other. The leading Romans are fond of the young Nicomedes, and the fact that Andronicus is already providing a bodyguard for him, suggests the military support of Attalus, who has a powerful kingdom, is a neighbor of Bithynia and has long been treated as an enemy by Prusias." In his speech Menas also laid bare Prusias' cruelty and wicked behavior toward everyone, and the resulting general hatred of the Bithynians for him. When he saw that they too rejected the wickedness of Prusias, he immediately led them to Nicomedes and he too saluted him as king—he was the second person after Andronicus to do so—and provided a guard with his two thousand men.

6. Attalus received the young man warmly, and ordered Prusias to give his son some towns for him to settle, and territory for supplies. Prusias said that he would immediately give him Attalus' whole kingdom; indeed, in his desire to get it for Nicomedes, he had already invaded Asia on a previous occasion. After delivering his reply, he sent agents to Rome to indict Nicomedes and Attalus, and summon them to trial. The forces of Attalus immediately invaded Bithynia, and as they advanced, the Bithynians joined them in small groups. Prusias distrusted everyone, and was hoping that the Romans would rescue him from the conspiracy. He asked Diegylis the Thracian, who was his son-in-law, for five hundred Thracians and when he got

15

16

17

18

τοῖσδε μόνοις τὸ σῶμα ἐπέτρεψεν, ἐς τὴν ἀκρόπολιν
19 τὴν ἐν Νικαίᾳ καταφυγών· ὁ δὲ Ῥωμαίων στρατηγὸς
ἐν ἄστει οὔτε αὐτίκα ἐπῆγεν ἐπὶ τὴν βουλὴν τοὺς τοῦ
Προυσίου πρέσβεις, χαριζόμενος Ἀττάλῳ· ἐπαγαγών
τέ ποτε, ψηφισαμένης τῆς βουλῆς τὸν στρατηγὸν
αὐτὸν ἑλέσθαι τε καὶ πέμψαι πρέσβεις οἳ διαλύσουσι
20 τὸν πόλεμον, εἵλετο τρεῖς ἄνδρας, ὧν ὁ μὲν τὴν κεφαλήν ποτε λίθῳ πληγεὶς ἀσχήμονας ἐπέκειτο ὠτει-
λάς, ὁ δὲ τοὺς πόδας διέφθαρτο ὑπὸ ῥεύματος, ὁ δ᾽
ἠλιθιώτατος ἐνομίζετο εἶναι, ὥστε Κάτωνα τὴν πρεσβείαν ἐπισκώπτοντα εἰπεῖν τὴν πρεσβείαν ταύτην
μήτε νοῦν ἔχειν μήτε πόδας μήτε κεφαλήν.
21   7. Οἱ μὲν δὴ πρέσβεις ἐς Βιθυνίαν ἀφίκοντο, καὶ
προσέτασσον αὐτοῖς τὸν πόλεμον ἐκλῦσαι, Νικομήδους δὲ καὶ Ἀττάλου συγχωρεῖν ὑποκρινομένων οἱ
Βιθυνοὶ διδαχθέντες ἔλεγον οὐκ εἶναι δυνατοὶ φέρειν
ἔτι τὴν ὠμότητα τοῦ Προυσίου, φανεροὶ μάλιστα
22 αὐτῷ γενόμενοι δυσχεραίνοντες. οἱ μὲν δὴ πρέσβεις,
ὡς οὔπω Ῥωμαίων τάδε πυθομένων, ἐπανῆεσαν ἄπρα-
κτοι· Προυσίας δ᾽ ἐπεὶ καὶ τὰ Ῥωμαίων ἀπέγνω, οἷς
μάλιστα πιστεύων οὐδενὸς ἐς ἄμυναν ἐπεφρόντικε,
μετῆλθεν ἐς Νικομήδειαν ὡς κρατυνούμενος τὴν πόλιν καὶ τοῖς ἐπιοῦσι πολεμήσων. οἱ δὲ προδιδόντες
αὐτὸν τὰς πύλας ἀνέῳξαν, καὶ ὁ μὲν Νικομήδης ἐσῄει
μετὰ τοῦ στρατοῦ, τὸν δὲ Προυσίαν ἐς ἱερὸν Διὸς
καταφυγόντα συνεκέντησάν τινες ἐπιπεμφθέντες ἐκ
23 τοῦ Νικομήδους. οὕτω Νικομήδης ἀντὶ Προυσίου Βιθυνῶν ἐβασίλευε, καὶ αὐτὸν χρόνῳ τελευτήσαντα Νι-

them, entrusting his person to them alone, he took refuge in the citadel in Nicaea. At Rome, the urban praetor, to 19 oblige Attalus, did not immediately introduce Prusias' ambassadors into the senate. When he finally did so, the senate decreed that the praetor himself should choose ambassadors and send them to bring about an end to the war. He 20 selected three men. One of them had once been hit on the head with a stone and bore ugly scars; another was crippled from gout in his feet; and the third was considered very stupid—with the result that Cato mocked the embassy by saying that it had neither sense, nor feet, nor head.[8]

7. The ambassadors duly arrived in Bithynia and or- 21 dered them to stop the war. Nicomedes and Attalus pretended to comply, but the Bithynians said, as prompted, that they could no longer endure Prusias' cruelty, especially now that their discontent with him was in the open. As this information was not yet known at Rome, the am- 22 bassadors returned without accomplishing their mission. Because of his particular trust in the Romans, Prusias had considered no one else as a source of assistance, but he now despaired even of them, and moved to Nicomedea to fortify the city and fight the invaders; but the inhabitants betrayed him and opened the gates. While Nicomedes entered with his army, Prusias took refuge in the temple of Zeus where some men sent after him by Nicomedes stabbed him to death. This is how Nicomedes came to be 23 king of the Bithynians instead of Prusias. In time, when he

[8] A famous story, recorded in Polybius (36.14.1–5), Livy (*Per.* 50), Diodorus (32.20), Plutarch (*Cat.* 9.1).

κομήδης ὁ υἱός, ᾧ Φιλοπάτωρ ἐπίκλησις ἦν, διεδέξατο, Ῥωμαίων αὐτῷ τὴν ἀρχὴν ὡς πατρῴαν ψηφισαμένων. τὰ μὲν δὴ Βιθυνῶν ὧδε εἶχε· καὶ εἴ τῳ
σπουδὴ πάντα προμαθεῖν, υἱωνὸς τοῦδε ἕτερος Νικομήδης Ῥωμαίοις τὴν ἀρχὴν ἐν διαθήκαις ἀπέλιπεν.

24   8. Καππαδοκίας δὲ πρὸ μὲν Μακεδόνων οἵτινες
ἦρχον, οὐκ ἔχω σαφῶς εἰπεῖν, εἴτε ἰδίαν ἀρχήν, εἴτε
Δαρείου κατήκουον· Ἀλέξανδρος δέ μοι δοκεῖ τοὺς ἄρ-
χοντας τῶνδε τῶν ἐθνῶν ἐπὶ φόρῳ καταλιπεῖν, ἐπειγόμενος ἐπὶ Δαρεῖον. φαίνεται γὰρ καὶ Ἀμισόν, ἐν
Πόντῳ πόλιν Ἀττικοῦ γένους, ἐπὶ δημοκρατίαν ὡς
25   πάτριόν σφισι πολιτείαν ἀναγαγών. Ἱερώνυμος δὲ
οὐδ' ἐπιψαῦσαι τῶν ἐθνῶν ὅλως, ἀλλ' ἀνὰ τὴν παράλιον τῆς Παμφυλίας καὶ Κιλικίας ἑτέραν ὁδὸν ἐπὶ τὸν
Δαρεῖον τραπέσθαι. Περδίκκας δέ, ὃς ἐπὶ Ἀλεξάνδρῳ
τῆς Μακεδόνων ἦρχεν, Ἀριαράθην Καππαδοκίας
ἡγούμενον, εἴτε ἀφιστάμενον εἴτε τὴν ἀρχὴν αὐτοῦ
περιποιούμενος Μακεδόσιν, εἷλε καὶ ἐκρέμασε, καὶ
26   ἐπέστησε τοῖς ἔθνεσιν Εὐμένη τὸν Καρδιανόν. Εὐμένους δὲ ἀναιρεθέντος ὅτε αὐτὸν οἱ Μακεδόνες εἵλοντο
εἶναι πολέμιον, Ἀντίπατρος ἐπὶ τῷ Περδίκκᾳ τῆς ὑπὸ
Ἀλεξάνδρῳ γενομένης γῆς ἐπιτροπεύων, Νικάνορα
ἔπεμψε Καππαδοκῶν σατραπεύειν.

27   9. Μακεδόνων δὲ οὐ πολὺ ὕστερον ἐς ἀλλήλους
στασιασάντων, Ἀντίγονος μὲν ἦρχε Συρίας Λαομέ-

---

9 Nicomedes II Epiphanes was in fact succeeded by his son
Nicomedes III Euergetes ("Benefactor," ca. 127–ca. 94) and, in

died, a son of his, Nicomedes, surnamed Philopator, succeeded him, the Romans confirming by decree his rule as ancestral. This was the situation in Bithynia. If anyone wants to know the whole story in advance, another Nicomedes, this man's grandson, left the kingdom to the Romans in his will.[9]

8. I cannot say for sure who ruled Cappadocia before 24 the Macedonians, whether it had its own government or was subject to Darius, but it is my opinion that, in return for tribute, Alexander left the rulers of these peoples in place, as he was anxious to press on against Darius.[10] For even at Amisus, a town in Pontus of Attic origin, he appears to have restored democracy, on the grounds that it was their ancestral form of constitution. Hieronymus says 25 that Alexander had absolutely no contact with these peoples, but took another road against Darius along the coast of Pamphylia and Cilicia. Perdiccas, who ruled the Macedonian empire after Alexander, captured and hanged Ariarathes, governor of Cappadocia, either because he had revolted or because Perdiccas wanted his kingdom for the Macedonians; and he put Eumenes of Cardia in charge of these peoples. Eumenes was killed when the Macedonians 26 declared him a public enemy, and Antipatrus, who administered Alexander's territory after Perdiccas, sent Nicanor to be satrap of Cappadocia.

9. When internal disagreement broke out among the 27 Macedonians not long after, Antigonus expelled Laome-

due course, by his grandson, Nicomedes IV Philopator ("Father-loving," ca. 94–74), who bequeathed the kingdom to Rome.

[10] Darius III, defeated by Alexander at the battles of Issus and Gaugamela, and in 330 murdered by Bessus, satrap of Bactria.

δοντα ἐκβαλών, Μιθριδάτης δ᾽ αὐτῷ συνῆν, ἀνὴρ γένους βασιλείου Περσικοῦ. καὶ ὁ Ἀντίγονος ἐνύπνιον
ἔδοξε πεδίον σπεῖραι χρυσίῳ, καὶ τὸ χρυσίον ἐκθερί-
28 σαντα τὸν Μιθριδάτην ἐς τὸν Πόντον οἴχεσθαι. καὶ ὁ
μὲν αὐτὸν ἐπὶ τῷδε συλλαβὼν ἐβούλευεν ἀποκτεῖναι,
ὁ δ᾽ ἐξέφυγε σὺν ἱππεῦσιν ἕξ, καὶ φραξάμενός τι χωρίον τῆς Καππαδοκίας, πολλῶν οἱ προσιόντων ἐν
τῇδε τῇ Μακεδόνων ἀσχολίᾳ, Καππαδοκίας τε αὐτῆς
καὶ τῶν ὁμόρων περὶ τὸν Πόντον ἐθνῶν κατέσχεν, ἐπί
29 τε μέγα τὴν ἀρχὴν προαγαγὼν παισὶ παρέδωκεν. οἱ
δ᾽ ἦρχον, ἕτερος μεθ᾽ ἕτερον, ἕως ἐπὶ τὸν ἕκτον ἀπὸ
τοῦ πρώτου Μιθριδάτην, ὃς Ῥωμαίοις ἐπολέμησεν.
τούτου δὲ τοῦ γένους ὄντες οἱ Καππαδυκίας τε καὶ
Πόντου βασιλεῖς ἔσθ᾽ ὅτε μοι δοκοῦσι διελεῖν τὴν
ἀρχήν, καί οἱ μὲν τοῦ Πόντου κατασχεῖν οἱ δὲ Καππαδοκίας.

30   10. Ὅ γέ τοι Ῥωμαίοις πρῶτος ἐν φιλίᾳ γενόμενος
καὶ ναῦς τινὰς ἐπὶ Καρχηδονίους καὶ συμμαχίαν ὀλίγην παρασχών, βασιλεὺς Πόντου, Μιθριδάτης ὁ Εὐ-
εργέτης ἐπίκλησιν, ὡς ἀλλοτρίαν τὴν Καππαδοκίαν
ἐπέδραμεν. καὶ διαδέχεται Μιθριδάτης υἱός, ᾧ Διόνυ-
31 σος καὶ Εὐπάτωρ ἐπώνυμα ἦν. Ῥωμαῖοι δ᾽ αὐτὸν ἐκστῆναι Καππαδοκίας ἐκέλευσαν Ἀριοβαρζάνῃ, κατα-
φυγόντι τε ἐς αὐτοὺς καὶ δόξαντι ἄρα γνησιωτέρῳ

---

11 Mithridates V Euergetes ("The Benefactor") was not the
first to become a "friend and ally" of the Romans, but rather his

don and ruled Syria, having in his company Mithridates, a man of royal Persian lineage. Antigonus had a dream that he sowed a field with gold, but that Mithridates reaped the gold and went off to the Pontus. He arrested him for this 28 and planned to execute him, but Mithridates escaped with six knights, and, after fortifying a stronghold in Cappadocia where many joined him while the Macedonians were preoccupied elsewhere, he took possession of Cappadocia itself and of the neighboring peoples on the Pontus. Having greatly expanded his kingdom, he passed it on to his sons. They ruled one after the other until the sixth Mith- 29 ridates counting from the founder, and it was he who went to war with the Romans. Since the kings of both Cappadocia and Pontus were from this family, I suppose at some stage they divided their rule, some taking control of Pontus, the others of Cappadocia.

10. At any rate, a king of Pontus, Mithridates surnamed 30 Euergetes, the first to enter into friendship with the Romans (he provided some ships and a small auxiliary force against Carthage),[11] invaded Cappadocia as if it were a foreign country. He was succeeded by his son Mithridates, who had the titles Dionysus and Eupator.[12] The Romans 31 ordered him to abandon Cappadocia in favor of Ariobarzanes,[13] who had fled to them for protection and who

immediate predecessor Mithridates IV Philopator Philadelphus (ca. 155/4–152/1)—or possibly even Pharnaces I before that.

[12] Mithridates VI Eupator ("Of Good Father") Dionysus, king of Pontus (120–63).

[13] Ariobarzanes I of Cappadocia (ca. 95–63/2) spent a large part of his reign being expelled from, and restored to, his kingdom.

τοῦ Μιθριδάτου πρὸς τὴν Καππαδοκῶν ἀρχήν, ἢ καὶ
τὸ μέγεθος τῆς ἀρχῆς τοῦ Μιθριδάτου πολλῆς οὔσης
32 ὑφορώμενοί τε καὶ ἐς πλέονα διαιροῦντες ἀφανῶς. ὁ
δὲ τοῦτο μὲν ἤνεγκε, Νικομήδει δὲ τῷ Νικομήδους τοῦ
Προυσίου, Βιθυνίας ὡς πατρῴας ὑπὸ Ῥωμαίων ἀπο-
δειχθέντι βασιλεύειν, Σωκράτη τὸν ἀδελφὸν αὐτοῦ
Νικομήδους, ὅτῳ Χρηστὸς ἐπώνυμον ἦν, μετὰ στρατιᾶς ἐπέπεμψε· καὶ τὴν Βιθυνῶν ἀρχὴν ὁ Σωκράτης ἐς
33 αὐτὸν περιέσπασεν. τοῦ δ᾽ αὐτοῦ χρόνου Μισθράως[2]
καὶ Βαγώας Ἀριοβαρζάνη τόνδε τὸν ὑπὸ Ῥωμαίων
κατηγμένον ἐς τὴν Καππαδοκίαν ἐκβαλόντες, Ἀριαράθην κατήγαγον ἐς αὐτήν.

34   11. Ῥωμαῖοι δὲ Νικομήδην ὁμοῦ καὶ Ἀριοβαρζάνην
ἐπανῆγον ἐς τὴν οἰκείαν ἑκάτερον, πρέσβεις τέ τινας
αὐτοῖς ἐς τοῦτο συνέπεμψαν, ὧν Μάνιος Ἀκύλιος
ἡγεῖτο· καὶ συλλαβεῖν ἐς τὴν κάθοδον ἐπέστειλαν
Λουκίῳ τε Κασσίῳ, τῆς περὶ τὸ Πέργαμον Ἀσίας
ἡγουμένῳ, στρατιὰν ἔχοντι ὀλίγην, καὶ τῷδε τῷ Εὐ-
πάτορι Μιθριδάτῃ. ἀλλ᾽ ὁ μὲν αὐτῆς τε Καππαδοκίας
οὕνεκα Ῥωμαίοις ἐπιμεμφόμενος, καὶ Φρυγίαν ἔναγχος ὑπ᾽ αὐτῶν ἀφῃρημένος, ὡς διὰ τῆς Ἑλληνικῆς

---

[2] Μισθράως LP: Μισθράος BJ: Μιθράος edd.

14 By this stage (ca. 92) Nicomedes IV, Prusias' great-grandson,
was ruling.

15 The exact form of this man's name is uncertain.

seemed to have a more legitimate claim to the kingdom of Cappadocia than Mithridates; or else they were suspicious of the size of Mithridates' kingdom, which was large, and were surreptitiously seeking to partition it into several parts. Mithridates put up with this, but he gave an army 32 to Socrates Chrestus, and sent him against his brother Nicomedes, the son of Nicomedes and grandson of Prusias, who had been appointed by the Romans as king of Bithynia, on the grounds that it was his by hereditary right.[14] Socrates annexed the kingdom of Bithynia for himself. At the same time, Misthraos[15] and Bagoas expelled 33 Ariobarzanes, who had been installed in Cappadocia by the Romans, and restored Ariarathes to the throne.[16]

11. The Romans set about simultaneously restoring 34 Nicomedes and Ariobarzanes to their respective kingdoms, and for this purpose sent an embassy with them, led by Manius Aquillius.[17] They also ordered both Lucius Cassius[18]—who was governor of the Asiatic territory around Pergamum and had a small army—and Mithridates Eupator himself, to assist in this restoration. But Mithridates did not cooperate, as he had a grievance against the Romans both on account of Cappadocia itself, and because he had recently been deprived of Phrygia by them (as

---

[16] Ariarathes IX Eusebes Philopator, son of Mithridates Eupator and installed by his father as king of Cappadocia. Appian's chronology of the first thirty years of Eupator's reign is extremely compressed: he races straight down to the outbreak of the First Mithridatic War.

[17] Consul in 101. The embassy dates to 90/89.

[18] His *praenomen* was Gaius, not Lucius.

APPIAN

35 γραφῆς δεδήλωται, οὐ συνέπραττε· Κάσσιος δὲ καὶ
Μάνιος τῷ τε Κασσίου στρατῷ, καὶ πολὺν ἄλλον
ἀγείραντες Γαλατῶν καὶ Φρυγῶν, Νικομήδη τε κατήγαγον ἐς Βιθυνίαν καὶ Ἀριοβαρζάνην ἐς Καππαδοκίαν. εὐθύς τε ἀνέπειθον ἄμφω, γείτονας ὄντας Μιθριδάτου, τὴν γῆν τὴν Μιθριδάτου κατατρέχειν καὶ ἐς
πόλεμον ἐρεθίζειν, ὡς Ῥωμαίων αὐτοῖς πολεμοῦσι
36 συμμαχησόντων. οἱ δὲ ὤκνουν μὲν ὁμοίως ἑκάτερος
γείτονος πολέμου τοσοῦδε κατάρξαι, τὴν Μιθριδάτου
δύναμιν δεδιότες· ἐγκειμένων δὲ τῶν πρέσβεων, ὁ Νικομήδης πολλὰ μὲν ὑπὲρ τῆς ἐπικουρίας τοῖς στρατηγοῖς καὶ τοῖς πρέσβεσιν ὡμολογηκὼς χρήματα
δώσειν καὶ ἔτι ὀφείλων, πολλὰ δ' ἄλλα παρὰ τῶν
ἑπομένων Ῥωμαίων δεδανεισμένος καὶ ὀχλούμενος,
37 ἄκων ἐσέβαλεν ἐς τὴν Μιθριδάτου γῆν καὶ ἐλεηλάτη-
σεν ἕως ἐπὶ πόλιν Ἄμαστριν, οὐδενὸς οὔτε κωλύοντος
αὐτὸν οὔτε ἀπαντῶντος. ὁ γάρ τοι Μιθριδάτης ἑτοίμην
ἔχων δύναμιν ὅμως ὑπεχώρει, πολλὰ καὶ δίκαια διδοὺς ἐγκλήματα τῷ πολέμῳ γενέσθαι.
38   12. Ἀναζεύξαντος δὲ τοῦ Νικομήδους μετὰ πολλῶν
λαφύρων, Πελοπίδαν ὁ Μιθριδάτης ἔπεμπεν ἐς τοὺς
Ῥωμαίων στρατηγούς τε καὶ πρέσβεις, οὐκ ἀγνοῶν
μὲν αὐτοὺς πολεμησείοντας αὐτῷ καὶ τῆσδε τῆς

19 Phrygia had been given to Eupator's father, Mithridates V
Eurgetes, for his assistance in the war against Aristonicus (130–
129). It was taken from Pontic control, probably on Euergetes'
death in 120 or shortly after (Just. *Epit.* 38.5.3). Appian's use of

demonstrated in my book of Hellenic history).[19] Cassius 35
and Manius, with Cassius' army and another large force
they had collected of Galatians and Phrygians, restored
Nicomedes to Bithynia and Ariobarzanes to Cappadocia.
They immediately tried to persuade both of them, as they
were neighbors of Mithridates, to overrun his territory
and provoke him into war, assuring them of Roman military assistance once they were at war. They were both 36
equally hesitant to begin a conflict against such a strong
neighbor, since they were afraid of Mithridates' power. So,
when the ambassadors pressed him, Nicomedes, who had
agreed to pay the generals and ambassadors a large sum
of money, which he still owed, in return for their help, and
had borrowed other large amounts from Roman agents,
who were harassing him for payment, he reluctantly in- 37
vaded the territory of Mithridates and plundered it as far
as the town of Amastris. No one resisted or confronted
him. For although he was ready with his army, Mithridates
nevertheless retired, in order to have many and genuine
grievances to offer for the war.

12. When Nicomedes struck camp with a large amount 38
of plunder, Mithridates sent Pelopidas to the Roman
generals and ambassadors. He was well aware that they
wanted war with him, and were behind this attack on him.

the adverb "recently" in relation to the Pontic loss of Phrygia
thirty years earlier indicates that he has gotten something wrong:
here and elsewhere, he seems to believe Phrygia was taken from
Eupator not long before the outbreak of the first war with Rome
in 89. Scholarly explanations vary considerably. Appian's Hellenic
and Ionian Book was the tenth in his *Roman History*, but nothing
of it survives.

ἐσβολῆς αἰτίους γεγονότας, ὑποκρινόμενος δέ ἔτι, καὶ
πλείονας ὁμοῦ καὶ εὐπρεπεστέρας αἰτίας τοῦ γενησο-
μένου πολέμου πορίζων, ἀνεμίμνησκε φιλίας καὶ
39 συμμαχίας ἰδίας τε καὶ πατρῴας. ἀνθ᾽ ὧν αὐτὸν ὁ
Πελοπίδας ἔφη Φρυγίαν ἀφῃρῆσθαι καὶ Καππαδοκίαν, τὴν μὲν ἀεὶ τῶν προγόνων αὐτοῦ γενομένην καὶ
ὑπὸ τοῦ πατρὸς ἀναληφθεῖσαν, "Φρυγίαν δὲ ἐπινίκιον
ἐπὶ Ἀριστονίκῳ παρὰ τοῦ ὑμετέρου στρατηγοῦ δοθεῖ-
σάν τε καὶ οὐχ ἧσσον παρὰ τοῦ αὐτοῦ στρατηγοῦ
40 πολλῶν χρημάτων ἐωνημένην. νῦν δ᾽," ἔφη, "Καὶ Νικομήδη τὸ στόμα τοῦ Πόντου διακλείοντα περιορᾶτε,
καὶ τὴν γῆν μέχρι Ἀμάστριδος ἐπιτρέχοντα, καὶ
λείαν ἄγοντα ὅσην ἴστε ἀκριβῶς, οὐκ ἀσθενῶς οὐδὲ
ἀνετοίμως ἔχοντος πρὸς ἄμυναν τοῦ ἐμοῦ βασιλέως,
ἀλλ᾽ ἀναμένοντος ὑμᾶς ἐν ὄψει μάρτυρας τῶν γιγνο-
41 μένων γενέσθαι. ἐπειδὴ δὲ ἐγένεσθέ τε καὶ εἴδετε,
παρακαλεῖ Μιθριδάτης, φίλος ὢν ὑμῖν καὶ σύμμαχος,
φίλους ὄντας ὑμᾶς καὶ συμμάχους (ὧδε γὰρ αἱ συνθῆκαι λέγουσιν), ἐπικουρεῖν ἡμῖν ἀδικουμένοις ὑπὸ
Νικομήδους, ἢ κωλύειν αὐτὸν ἀδικοῦντα."

42   13. Ὁ μὲν τοιαῦτα εἶπε, Νικομήδους δὲ πρέσβεις
ἐς ἀντιλογίαν αὐτῷ παρόντες ἔφασαν· "Νικομήδει μὲν
ἐκ πολλοῦ Μιθριδάτης ἐπιβουλεύων Σωκράτη μετὰ
στρατιᾶς ἐπὶ τὴν βασιλείαν ἐπῆγεν, ἡσυχάζοντα καὶ
43 δικαιοῦντα τὸν πρεσβύτερον ἄρχειν. καὶ ὧδε Μιθριδάτης ἐς Νικομήδην ἐξέπραξεν, ὃν ὑμεῖς, ὦ Ῥωμαῖοι,
Βιθυνῶν ἐστήσασθε βασιλεύειν· ὃ καὶ δῆλόν ἐστιν
οὐκ ἐς ἡμᾶς μᾶλλον ἢ ἐς ὑμᾶς γεγονέναι. τῷ δ᾽ αὐτῷ

But still keeping up his pretense, and in order to acquire more—and at the same time, more convincing—reasons for the coming war, Mithridates reminded them both of his own and his ancestral friendship and alliance with them. In return for this, Pelopidas said, Phrygia and Cap- 39 padocia had been taken away from him. Cappadocia had always belonged to his ancestors and had been recovered by his father. "And Phrygia was given to him by your general as a reward for his help in the victory over Aristoni- cus—indeed, it was no less a purchase, and a very expen- sive one, from that same general. Now," he said, "you even 40 allow Nicomedes to block the entrance of the Pontus, to overrun the land as far as Amastris and to carry off plun- der—and you know exactly how much. My king was not weak or unprepared to defend himself, but he waited for you to witness for yourselves what was happening. Since 41 you are now eyewitnesses and know the truth, Mithri- dates, who is your friend and ally, invites you, who are his friends and allies (for this is the wording of the treaty), to assist us, the victims of wrongs perpetrated by Nicomedes, or to prevent him from doing us wrong."

13. Such was his speech, but the ambassadors of Nico- 42 medes who were there to argue against him, replied as follows. "Mithridates has been plotting against Nicomedes for a long time, and installed Socrates on the throne with armed force, even though Socrates himself espoused peace and thought it right that his elder brother should rule. This is what Mithridates forced on Nicomedes, 43 whom you, men of Rome, set up as king of Bithynia: it is clear that he was targeting this action more against you

λόγῳ κεκελευκότων ὑμῶν τοῖς ἐν Ἀσίᾳ βασιλεῦσι τῆς
Εὐρώπης μηδὲ ἐπιβαίνειν, τὰ πολλὰ Χερρονήσου
περιέσπασεν. καὶ τάδε μὲν ἔστω τῆς ἐς ὑμᾶς ὕβρεώς
44 τε καὶ δυσμενείας αὐτοῦ καὶ ἀπειθείας ἔργα· ἡ παρασκευὴ δὲ ὅση, καὶ πᾶσα ἑτοίμως ὡς ἐπὶ μέγαν δὴ καὶ
ἐγνωσμένον πόλεμον ἤδη, τοῦ τε ἰδίου στρατοῦ καὶ
συμμάχων Θρᾳκῶν καὶ Σκυθῶν, ὅσα τε ἄλλα πλησίον ἔθνη. ἐς δὲ τὸν Ἀρμένιον αὐτῷ καὶ ἐπιγαμία
γέγονε, καὶ ἐς Αἴγυπτον καὶ Συρίαν περιπέμπει προσ-
εταιριζόμενος τοὺς βασιλέας. νῆές τε εἰσὶν αὐτῷ
κατάφρακτοι τριακόσιαι, καὶ ἑτέρας προσαπεργάζε-
ται ἐπί τε πρῳρέας καὶ κυβερνήτας ἐς Φοινίκην καὶ
45 ἐς Αἴγυπτον περιέπεμψεν. ἅπερ οὐκ ἐπὶ Νικομήδει
που, τοσάδε ὄντα, ἀλλ᾽ ἐφ᾽ ὑμῖν, ὦ Ῥωμαῖοι, Μιθριδάτης, ἐργάζεται, δυσμεναίνων μὲν ἐξ οὗ Φρυγίαν
αὐτὸν πανούργως πριάμενον, καὶ δεκάσαντα τῶν ὑμετέρων τινὰ στρατηγῶν, ἀποθέσθαι προσετάξατε, τῆς
οὐ δικαίας κτήσεως καταγνόντες, χαλεπαίνων δ᾽ ἐπὶ
Καππαδοκίᾳ, δεδομένῃ καὶ τῇδε πρὸς ὑμῶν Ἀριοβαρζάνῃ, δεδιὼς δ᾽ αὐξομένους ὑμᾶς, καὶ παρασκευαζό-
μενος ἐν τῇ καθ᾽ ἡμᾶς προφάσει καὶ ὑμῖν, εἰ δύναιτο,
46 ἐπιθέσθαι. σωφρόνων δ᾽ ἐστὶ μὴ περιμένειν ὅτε πολεμεῖν ὑμῖν ὁμολογήσει, ἀλλ᾽ ἐς τὰ ἔργα αὐτοῦ μᾶλλον
ἢ τοὺς λόγους ἀφορᾶν μηδὲ φιλίας ὄνομα ἐπίπλα-
στον ὑποκρινομένῳ τοὺς ἀληθεῖς καὶ βεβαίους ἐκδοῦ-
ναι φίλους, μηδὲ τὴν σφετέραν περὶ τῆς ἡμετέρας
βασιλείας κρίσιν ὑπεριδεῖν ἀκυρουμένην ὑπ᾽ ἀνδρὸς
ὁμοίως ἡμῖν τε καὶ ὑμῖν ἐχθροῦ.” ·

than against us. With the same rationale, although you had ordered the kings in Asia not even to set foot in Europe, he annexed most of Chersonesus. Let these deeds be an illustration of his arrogance toward you, his ill will, his disobedience. But observe the size of his armament—and 44 how it is fully prepared for a major war, which he has already decided on—observe the size, not just of his own army, but also of his Thracian and Scythian allies, and how powerful the other neighboring peoples are. He has made a marriage connection with Armenia, and sends embassies to Egypt and Syria, in an attempt to make friends with their kings. He has three hundred decked warships and is completing others in addition; and he has sent to Phoenicia and Egypt to recruit lookouts and helmsmen. It is not 45 against Nicomedes, we believe, that Mithridates is making such extensive preparations, but against you, the Romans. For he has been angry with you since the time you ordered him to give up Phrygia, which he had fraudulently bought after corrupting one of your generals, an illegal acquisition which you condemned. He is angry about Cappadocia, although this too was given by you to Ariobarzanes. And fearing your expanding power, he is using the pretext of preparing against us to attack you too, if he can. It would 46 be wise not to wait until he openly declares that he is at war with you, but to observe his deeds rather than his words; nor should you surrender true and firm friends to someone acting falsely in the name of friendship, or allow your decision concerning our kingdom to be set aside by a man who is equally your enemy as well as ours."

47   14. Ὧδε μὲν καὶ οἱ Νικομήδους ἔλεξαν· ἐπελθὼν δὲ
αὖθις ὁ Πελοπίδας ἐς τὸ τῶν Ῥωμαίων συνέδριον
περὶ μὲν τῶν πάλαι γεγονότων, εἴ τι Νικομήδης ἐπι-
μέμφοιτο, δικάσαι Ῥωμαίους ἠξίου, τὰ δὲ νῦν "(Ἐν
ὄψει γὰρ ὑμῶν γέγονε, τῆς τε γῆς τῆς Μιθριδάτου
δῃουμένης³ καὶ τῆς θαλάττης ἀποκεκλεισμένης καὶ
λείας τοσῆσδε ἐλαυνομένης) οὐ λόγων" ἔφη "χρῄζειν
48   οὐδὲ κρίσεως, Ἀλλ' αὖθις ὑμᾶς παρακαλοῦμεν ἢ κωλύειν τὰ γιγνόμενα ἢ Μιθριδάτῃ συμμαχεῖν ἀδι-
κουμένῳ, ἢ τελευταῖον, ὦ ἄνδρες Ῥωμαῖοι, μηδὲ κωλύειν ἀμυνόμενον, ἀλλ' ἀμφοῖν ἐκστῆναι τοῦ πόνου."
τοσαῦτα τοῦ Πελοπίδου παλιλλογήσαντος, ἔγνωστο
μὲν ἐκ πολλοῦ τοῖς Ῥωμαίων στρατηγοῖς ἐπικουρεῖν
Νικομήδει, καὶ ἐς ὑπόκρισιν τῆς ἀντιλογίας ἠκρο-
49   ῶντο· τὰ δὲ εἰρημένα ὅμως ὑπὸ τοῦ Πελοπίδου, καὶ
τὴν τοῦ Μιθριδάτου φιλίαν ἐνσύνθηκον ἔτι οὖσαν,
αἰδούμενοι ἠπόρουν ἀποκρίσεως ἐπὶ πολύ, μέχρι ἐπι-
στήσαντες μετὰ σοφίας ὧδε ἀπεκρίναντο· "Οὔτε Μιθριδάτην ἄν τι βουλοίμεθα πάσχειν ἄχαρι πρὸς Νικομήδους, οὔτε Νικομήδους ἀνεξόμεθα πολεμουμένου·
οὐ γὰρ ἡγούμεθα Ῥωμαίοις συμφέρειν βλάπτεσθαι
Νικομήδη." ταῦτα δ' εἰπόντες τὸν Πελοπίδαν, βουλό-
μενον διελέγχειν τῆς ἀποκρίσεως τὴν ἀπορίαν, ἀπέ-
πεμψαν ἐκ τοῦ συνεδρίου.

50   15. Μιθριδάτης μὲν οὖν, ὡς ἐμφανῶς ἤδη πρὸς
Ῥωμαίων ἀδικούμενος, ἔπεμπε σὺν πολλῇ χειρὶ τὸν

---

³ δῃουμένης BJ: μειουμένης LP

14. Such was the speech of Nicomedes' representa- 47
tives. When Pelopidas again went before the council of the
Romans, he requested that, if Nicomedes had a charge to
make about past events, the Romans should give judgment; but the present situation, he said, needed neither
speeches nor judicial decision. "For it was under your very
eyes that the territory of Mithridates was raided, the sea
shut off to him and such large quantities of plunder carried
off. But again we invite you, either to prevent such occur- 48
rences, or to come to the assistance of Mithridates who is
the aggrieved party; or finally, men of Rome, not to prevent him from defending himself, but to help neither side
in their struggle." With such words Pelopidas repeated his
case, but the Roman generals had long since decided to
come to the aid of Nicomedes, and only pretended to
listen to Pelopidas' side of the argument. Nevertheless, 49
they were shamed by Pelopidas' words and the treaty of
friendship with Mithridates, which was still in force, and
for a long time were at a loss how to answer, until, after
concentrating on the matter, they replied with the following sophistry. "We would not want Mithridates to suffer
any unpleasantness at the hands of Nicomedes, nor will
we allow war to be waged against Nicomedes. For we do
not believe it is in Rome's best interests for Nicomedes to
be harmed." With these words they dismissed Pelopidas
from the council chamber, although he wanted to prove
the inadequacy of their answer.

15. So Mithridates, presenting himself as now mani- 50
festly the victim of injustice inflicted by the Romans, sent

υἱὸν Ἀριαράθην βασιλεύειν Καππαδοκίας. καὶ εὐθὺς
ἦρχεν αὐτῆς ὁ Ἀριαράθης, Ἀριοβαρζάνην ἐκβαλών.
Πελοπίδας δὲ ἐς τοὺς Ῥωμαίων στρατηγοὺς αὖθις
51 ἐλθὼν ἔλεγεν ὧδε. "Ἃ μὲν ἠδικημένος πρὸς ὑμῶν, ὦ
Ῥωμαῖοι, βασιλεὺς Μιθριδάτης ἔφερε, Φρυγίαν τε
καὶ Καππαδοκίαν ἀφηρημένος ἔναγχος, ἠκούσατε· ἃ
δὲ Νικομήδης αὐτὸν ἔβλαπτεν, ὁρῶντες ὑπερείδετε.
φιλίαν τε καὶ συμμαχίαν ἡμῖν προφέρουσιν, ὥσπερ
οὐκ ἐγκαλοῦσιν ἀλλ' ἐγκαλουμένοις ἀπεκρίνασθε μὴ
νομίζειν συμφέρειν τοῖς Ῥωμαίων πράγμασι βλάπτε-
52 σθαι Νικομήδη οἷά περ αὐτὸν ἀδικούμενον. ὑμεῖς οὖν
αἴτιοι τῷ κοινῷ Ῥωμαίων τοῦδε τοῦ περὶ Καππαδοκίαν γεγονότος· διὰ γὰρ ὑμᾶς, ὧδε μὲν ἡμᾶς ὑπερ-
ορῶντας ὧδε δὲ σοφίζοντας ἐν ταῖς ἀποκρίσεσιν,
οὕτως ἔπραξεν ὁ Μιθριδάτης. καὶ πρεσβεύσεται καθ'
ὑμῶν ἐς τὴν ὑμετέραν βουλήν, ἐφ' ἣν ὑμῖν ἀπολογη-
σομένοις ἐπαγγέλλει παρεῖναι, φθάνειν δὲ μηδέν,
μηδ' ἐξάρχειν ἄνευ τοῦ κοινοῦ τῶν Ῥωμαίων τοσοῦδε
53 πολέμου, ἐνθυμουμένους ὅτι Μιθριδάτης βασιλεύει
μὲν τῆς πατρῴας ἀρχῆς, ἣ δισμυρίων ἐστὶ σταδίων
τὸ μῆκος, προσκέκτηται δὲ πολλὰ περίχωρα, καὶ
Κόλχους, ἔθνος ἀρειμανές, Ἑλλήνων τε τοὺς ἐπὶ τοῦ
Πόντου κατῳκισμένους, καὶ βαρβάρων τοὺς ὄντας
ὑπὲρ αὐτούς. φίλοις δ' ἐς πᾶν τὸ κελευόμενον ἑτοίμοις
χρῆται Σκύθαις τε καὶ Ταύροις καὶ Βαστέρναις καὶ
Θρᾳξὶ καὶ Σαρμάταις καὶ πᾶσι τοῖς ἀμφὶ Τάναΐν τε
54 καὶ Ἴστρον καὶ τὴν λίμνην ἔτι τὴν Μαιώτιδα. Τι-

his son Ariarathes with a large force to take the throne of Cappadocia. Ariarathes expelled Ariobarzanes and immediately took control of the government. Pelopidas again went to the Roman generals and addressed them in this manner: "You have heard, men of Rome, how King Mithridates bore the wrongs he suffered at your hands, when deprived recently of Phrygia and Cappadocia; and the harm Nicomedes did him, you saw, but ignored. And when we invoked your friendship and alliance, in your reply you treated us as the accused rather than the accusers, saying that you did not think it was in Rome's interests for Nicomedes to be harmed, as if he was the one who was being wronged. So it is you who bear the responsibility to the Roman Commonwealth for what has happened in Cappadocia: it is because of the way you disdained us, and the way you resorted to sophistry in your replies to us, that Mithridates acted as he did. He will be sending an embassy to your senate with charges against you, and invites you to attend to defend yourselves, but to do nothing before that, and certainly not to begin such a great war without the approval of the Roman Commonwealth. You should bear in mind that Mithridates is king of his ancestral domain, which is twenty thousand stades long; and that he has acquired many neighboring states in addition, among them the Colchians, a furiously warlike people, the Greeks who live on the Pontus, and the barbarians beyond them. As friends ready to obey his every command, he has both Scythians and Taurians, and Bastarnae and Thracians and Sarmatians and all those who dwell in the region of the Tanais and Ister and even the Maeotid lake.[20] Tigranes

51

52

53

54

[20] The Don, the Danube, and the Sea of Azov.

γράνης δ' ὁ Ἀρμένιος αὐτῷ κηδεστής ἐστι, καὶ Ἀρσάκης ὁ Παρθυαῖος φίλος. νεῶν τε πλῆθος ἔχει, τὸ μὲν ἕτοιμον τὸ δὲ γιγνόμενον ἔτι, καὶ παρασκευὴν ἐς πάντα ἀξιόλογον.

55   16. "Οὐκ ἐψεύσαντο δ' ὑμῖν ἔναγχος οἱ Βιθυνοὶ καὶ περὶ τῶν ἐν Αἰγύπτῳ καὶ Συρίᾳ βασιλέων· οὓς οὐ μόνον εἰκός ἐστιν ἡμῖν, εἰ πόλεμος γένοιτο, προσθήσεσθαι, ἀλλὰ καὶ τὴν νεόκτητον ὑμῖν Ἀσίαν καὶ Ἑλλάδα καὶ Λιβύην καὶ πολλὰ καὶ αὐτῆς Ἰταλίας, ὅσα τὴν ὑμετέραν πλεονεξίαν οὐ φέροντα πολεμεῖ νῦν ὑμῖν
56   πόλεμον ἄσπειστον. ὃν οὔπω διαθέσθαι δυνηθέντες ἐπιχειρεῖτε Μιθριδάτῃ, Νικομήδην αὐτῷ καὶ Ἀριοβαρζάνην παρὰ μέρος ἐπιπέμποντες· καὶ φατὲ μὲν εἶναι φίλοι καὶ σύμμαχοι, καὶ ὑποκρίνεσθε οὕτω,
57   χρῆσθε δὲ ὡς πολεμίῳ. φέρετε οὖν, καὶ νῦν, εἴ τι πρὸς τῶν γεγονότων ἐς μετάνοιαν ἠρέθισθε, ἢ Νικομήδη κωλύσατε τοὺς ὑμετέρους ἀδικεῖν φίλους (καὶ τάδε πράξασιν ὑμῖν ὑπίσχομαι συμμαχήσειν ἐπὶ τοὺς Ἰταλοὺς βασιλέα Μιθριδάτην), ἢ τὴν δοκοῦσαν ἐς ἡμᾶς φιλίαν λύσατε, ἢ ἐς Ῥώμην ἐπὶ κρίσιν ἴωμεν."
58   ὁ μὲν δὴ Πελοπίδας ὧδε ἔλεξεν, οἱ δὲ φορτικώτερον αὐτὸν εἰπεῖν ἡγούμενοι, Μιθριδάτην μὲν ἐκέλευον ἀπέχεσθαι Νικομήδους καὶ Καππαδοκίας (αὐτοὶ γὰρ αὖθις Ἀριοβαρζάνην ἐς αὐτὴν κατάξειν), Πελοπίδαν δ' εὐθὺς ἐξιέναι τοῦ στρατοπέδου, καὶ μηκέτι πρεσβεύειν ἐς αὐτούς, εἰ μὴ τοῖς κελευομένοις ὁ βασιλεὺς ἐμμένοι.

of Armenia is his son-in-law and Arsaces the Parthian his friend;[21] and he has a large number of ships, some ready, others under construction, and military equipment remarkable in every respect.

16. "The Bithynians were not lying to you in what they 55 just said about the kings of Egypt and Syria, and it is likely that these are not the only ones who will take our side if war breaks out, but we will be joined by your new acquisitions in Asia and Greece and Africa, and even much of Italy itself, which at this very moment wages implacable war against you, as it cannot endure your greed.[22] Al- 56 though you have not yet been able to settle that war, you attack Mithridates, sending Nicomedes and Ariobarzanes against him in turn; you say you are his friends and allies, and pretend to be, but you treat him as an enemy. So I 57 urge you, if, even now, you are in any way affected by what has happened to change your mind, either prevent Nicomedes from wronging your friends—and if you do, I promise that king Mithridates will be your ally against the Italians—or stop pretending to be our friends and let us go for a decision to Rome." This is what Pelopidas said. 58 But they thought he spoke in rather impertinent fashion, and issued orders, to Mithridates to keep his hands off Nicomedes and Cappadocia—for they said they themselves would again restore Ariobarzanes to the latter—and to Pelopidas to leave their camp immediately and not return to them as an ambassador again, unless Mithridates was going to obey their commands.

[21] Tigranes I of Armenia (95–ca. 56). Eupator may have sought the friendship of the Arsacid king Mithridates II, but he never received any concrete assistance from him.

[22] The Social War (91–87).

59   17. Οὕτω μὲν ἀπεκρίναντο, καὶ ἀπιόντι φυλακὴν
συνέπεμψαν, ἵνα μή τινας ἐπιτρίψειε παροδεύων.
ταῦτα δὲ εἰπόντες καὶ οὐκ ἀναμείναντες περὶ τοσοῦδε
πολέμου τὴν βουλὴν ἢ τὸν δῆμον ἐπιγνώμονα γενέσθαι, στρατιὰν ἤγειρον ἔκ τε Βιθυνίας καὶ Καππαδο-
60   κίας καὶ Παφλαγονίας καὶ Γαλατῶν τῶν ἐν Ἀσίᾳ. ὡς
δὲ αὐτοῖς ὅ τε ἴδιος στρατός, ὃν εἶχε Λούκιος Κάσσιος ὁ τῆς Ἀσίας ἡγούμενος, ἕτοιμος ἦν ἤδη, καὶ τὰ
συμμαχικὰ πάντα συνεληλύθει, διελόμενοι τὸ πλῆθος
ἐστρατοπέδευον, Κάσσιος μὲν ἐν μέσῳ Βιθυνίας τε
καὶ Γαλατίας, Μάνιος δὲ ᾗ διαβατὸν ἦν ἐς Βιθυνίαν
τῷ Μιθριδάτῃ, Ὄππιος δὲ ἕτερος στρατηγὸς ἐπὶ τῶν
ὀρῶν τῶν Καππαδοκίας, ἱππέας ἔχων ἕκαστος αὐτῶν
⟨τετρακισχιλίους⟩[4] καὶ πεζοὺς ἀμφὶ τοὺς τετρακισμυ-
61   ρίους. ἦν δὲ καὶ νεῶν στόλος αὐτοῖς, οὗ περὶ Βυζάντιον Μινούκιός τε Ῥοῦφος καὶ Γάιος Ποπίλιος
ἡγοῦντο, τὸ στόμα τοῦ Πόντου φυλάσσοντες. παρῆν
δὲ αὐτοῖς καὶ Νικομήδης, ἄρχων ἑτέρων πεντακισμυ-
ρίων πεζῶν καὶ ἱππέων ἑξακισχιλίων. τοσόσδε μὲν
62   αὐτοῖς ἀθρόως στρατὸς ἀγήγερτο· Μιθριδάτῃ δὲ τὸ
μὲν οἰκεῖον ἦν μυριάδες πεζῶν πέντε καὶ εἴκοσι καὶ
ἱππεῖς τετρακισμύριοι, καὶ νῆες κατάφρακτοι τριακόσιαι, δίκροτα δὲ ἑκατόν, καὶ ἡ ἄλλη παρασκευὴ τούτων κατὰ λόγον, στρατηγοὶ δὲ Νεοπτόλεμός τε καὶ
Ἀρχέλαος, ἀλλήλων ἀδελφώ, καὶ τοῖς πλείστοις αὐ-
63   τὸς παρεγίνετο. συμμαχικὰ δὲ ἦγον αὐτῷ Ἀρκαθίας
μέν, αὐτοῦ Μιθριδάτου παῖς, ἐκ τῆς βραχυτέρας
Ἀρμενίας μυρίους ἱππέας, καὶ Δορύλαος ⟨. . .⟩ ἐν

17. This was their answer, and on Pelopidas' departure   59
they sent a guard with him, so that he would not incite
anyone on the road. After issuing their statement they did
not wait for the senate or people to make a decision about
such a great war, but raised an army from Bithynia and
Cappadocia and Paphlagonia and the Galatians of Asia.
When their own army under the command of Lucius Cas-   60
sius, governor of Asia, was ready, and all the allied forces
had assembled, they divided their whole force and established their camps, Cassius midway between Bithynia and
Galatia, Manius where Mithridates would have to cross
into Bithynia, and Oppius, another general, in the mountains of Cappadocia; each of them had four thousand cavalry and about forty thousand infantry. They also had a   61
naval force commanded by Minucius Rufus and Gaius
Popilius at Byzantium, guarding the mouth of the Pontus.
Nicomedes too was with them, commanding another fifty
thousand infantry and six thousand cavalry. Such was the
total combined strength of the army they had collected. In   62
his own forces Mithridates had two hundred and fifty
thousand infantry and forty thousand cavalry; three hundred decked ships of war, one hundred biremes; and the
remainder of the armament was in the same proportion.
His generals were Neoptolemus and Archelaus, two
brothers, but the king himself commanded the largest
part. Of the allied forces, Arcathias, a son of Mithridates   63
himself, brought him ten thousand cavalry from Armenia

---

4 τετρακισχιλίους add. Schweig.

φάλαγγι ταττομένους, Κρατερὸς δ' ἑκατὸν καὶ τριάκοντα ἄρματα.

64   18. Τοσαύτη μὲν ἦν ἑκατέροις ἡ παρασκευή, ὅτε
πρῶτον ἦεσαν ἐς ἀλλήλους Ῥωμαῖοί τε καὶ Μιθριδάτης, ἀμφὶ τὰς ἑκατὸν καὶ ἑβδομήκοντα ⟨τρεῖς⟩[5]
ὀλυμπιάδας. ἐν δὲ πεδίῳ πλατεῖ παρὰ τὸν Ἀμνειον
ποταμὸν κατιδόντες ἀλλήλους ὅ τε Νικομήδης καὶ οἱ
τοῦ Μιθριδάτου στρατηγοὶ παρέταττον ἐς μάχην, Νικομήδης μὲν ἅπαντας τοὺς ἑαυτοῦ, Νεοπτόλεμος δὲ
καὶ Ἀρχέλαος τοὺς εὐζώνους μόνους, καὶ οὓς Ἀρκαθίας εἶχεν ἱππέας καί τινα τῶν ἀρμάτων· ἡ γὰρ
65   φάλαγξ ἔτι προσῄει. ἐς δέ τινα γήλοφον τοῦ πεδίου
πετρώδη προλαβόντες ἀνέπεμψαν ὀλίγους, ἵνα μὴ κυκλωθεῖεν ὑπὸ τῶν Βιθυνῶν πολὺ πλειόνων ὄντων. ὡς
δὲ ἐξωθουμένους εἶδον αὐτοὺς ἐκ τοῦ γηλόφου, δείσας
ὁ Νεοπτόλεμος περὶ τῇ κυκλώσει προσεβοήθει μετὰ
66   σπουδῆς, καλῶν ἅμα καὶ τὸν Ἀρκαθίαν. Νικομήδης
δ' ὁρῶν ἀντιπαρῄει· καὶ γίγνεται πολὺς ἐνταῦθα ἀγὼν
καὶ φόνος. βιασαμένου δὲ τοῦ Νικομήδους ἔφευγον οἱ
Μιθριδάτειοι, ἕως ὁ Ἀρχέλαος ἀπὸ τοῦ δεξιοῦ μετελ-
θὼν ἐνέβαλεν ἐς τοὺς διώκοντας. οἱ δ' ἐς αὐτὸν ἐπ-
εστράφησαν. ὁ δ' ὑπεχώρει κατ' ὀλίγον, ἵν' ἔχοιεν ἐκ
τῆς φυγῆς ἐπανελθεῖν οἱ περὶ Νεοπτόλεμον. ὡς δὲ

[5] ἑβδομήκοντα codd: τρεῖς add. edd.

Minor, Dorylaus ‹. . . ,›[23] arrayed in phalanx, and Craterus one hundred and thirty chariots.

18. Such were the huge armed forces on each side 64 when the Romans and Mithridates first confronted each other, in about the 173rd (?) Olympiad.[24] It was in a wide plain beside the river Amnias that Nicomedes and the generals of Mithridates came into view of each other and drew up for battle. Nicomedes had all his troops, Neoptolemus and Arcathias only their light infantry, the cavalry Arcathias had at his disposal, and a few chariots: for the phalanx was still on its way. They sent a small force up a 65 rocky hill in the plain ahead of the enemy, to avoid being surrounded by the Bithynians, who were much more numerous. When they saw them being driven off the hill, Neoptolemus, fearing encirclement, hurried to their assistance, and at the same time called on Arcathias for help. Nicomedes saw this and took countermeasures; and 66 a large and bloody struggle develops there. Overpowered by Nicomedes, the Mithridatic forces began to flee, until Archelaus, coming across from the right, attacked the pursuers, who turned to face him. He fell back little by little to give Neoptolemus' troops the chance to check their flight and return to the battle. When he thought they had done so sufficiently, he wheeled about; and his scythed

[23] The number of infantry brought by Dorylaus has dropped out of the text.

[24] The manuscripts say the 170th Olympiad. This ran from 100 to 96, obviously too early for the actual outbreak of the first war in 89, or even the maneuvering that led up to it. Editors usually emend the text to read Olympiad 173. There is no manuscript support for this, but it may be the best solution to the problem.

179

εἴκασεν αὐτάρκως ἔχειν, ἐπέστρεφε, καὶ τοῖς Βιθυνοῖς
τὰ δρεπανηφόρα ἅρματα ἐμπίπτοντα μετὰ ῥύμης δι-
έκοπτε καὶ διέτεμνε τοὺς μὲν ἀθρόως ἐς δύο τοὺς δ' ἐς
67 μέρη πολλά. τό τε γιγνόμενον ἐξέπληττε τὴν στρατιὰν τοῦ Νικομήδους, ὅτε ἴδοιεν ἡμιτόμους ἄνδρας ἔτι
ἔμπνους, ἢ ἐς πολλὰ διερριμμένους, ἢ τῶν δρεπάνων
ἀπηρτημένους. ἀηδίᾳ τε μᾶλλον ὄψεως ἢ μάχης ἥσσῃ
68 τὴν τάξιν ὑπὸ φόβου συνέχεαν. ταραχθεῖσι δ' αὐτοῖς
ὁ μὲν Ἀρχέλαος ἐκ τοῦ μετώπου, Νεοπτόλεμος δὲ καὶ
Ἀρκαθίας ἐκ τῆς φυγῆς ἀναστρέφοντες ἐπέκειντο ὄπισθεν. οἱ δ' ἐπὶ πολὺ μὲν ἠμύνοντο, ἐς ἑκατέρους ἐπι-
στρεφόμενοι· ὡς δὲ τὸ πλεῖστον ἐπεπτώκει, Νικομήδης μὲν ἔφευγε μετὰ τῶν ὑπολοίπων ἐς Παφλαγονίαν,
οὐδ' ἐς χεῖρας ἐλθούσης πω τῆς Μιθριδατείου φάλαγγος, ἑάλω δ' αὐτοῦ τὸ χαράκωμα καὶ τὰ χρήματα
69 πολλὰ ὄντα καὶ πλῆθος αἰχμαλώτων. οὓς πάντας ὁ
Μιθριδάτης φιλανθρωπευσάμενός τε καὶ ἐφόδια δοὺς
ἀπέλυσεν ἐς τὰ οἰκεῖα ἀπιέναι, δόξαν ἐμποιῶν τοῖς
πολεμίοις φιλανθρωπίας.

70 19. Ἔργον δ' ἦν⁶ τόδε πρῶτον τοῦ Μιθριδατείου
πολέμου καὶ οἱ στρατηγοὶ τῶν Ῥωμαίων κατεπεπλήγεσαν, ὡς οὐκ εὐβουλίᾳ μᾶλλον ἢ προπετῶς, ἄνευ τοῦ
κοινοῦ, τοσόνδε πόλεμον ἅψαντες. ὀλίγοι τε γὰρ πολὺ
πλειόνων ἐκεκρατήκεσαν, καὶ οὐδεμιᾷ συντυχίᾳ χω-
ρίων ἢ πολεμίου σφάλματος, ἀλλ' ἀρετῇ στρατηγῶν
71 καὶ ἀνδρείᾳ στρατοῦ. Νικομήδης μὲν οὖν Μανίῳ παρεστρατοπέδευε, Μιθριδάτης δ' ἐπὶ τὸ Σκόροβαν ὄρος
ἀνῄει, ὃ τέλος ἐστὶ Βιθυνῶν καὶ τῆς Ποντικῆς χώρας.

chariots, falling on the Bithynians with a rush, broke
through, at a stroke cutting some men in half, others into
many pieces. These events terrified Nicomedes' army: in- 67
asmuch as they saw men cut in half still breathing, or torn
into many pieces, or hanging off the scythes, it was more
the nauseating sight than military defeat that disordered
their ranks with fear. Thrown into confusion as they were, 68
Archelaus attacked them in the front, while Neoptolemus
and Arcathias, turning from flight, pressed on them from
the rear. Facing in both directions they defended themselves for a long time; but when most had fallen, Nicomedes fled with the survivors into Paphlagonia, although
Mithridates' phalanx had not even entered the battle.
Nicomedes' camp was captured along with his money, a
large amount of it, and many prisoners. All of these Mith- 69
ridates treated with kindness: he freed them and gave
them supplies for their journey home, thus gaining among
his enemies a reputation for clemency.

19. This was the first engagement of the Mithridatic 70
War, and the Roman generals were in shock, as it was more
in haste than as a result of sound judgment that they had
ignited such a great war without a decision of the Repub-
lic; and a small force had overcome a much larger one, not
because they had been favored by the terrain or a mistake
of the enemy, but by the excellence of their commanders
and bravery of their soldiers. Nicomedes now encamped 71
opposite Manius, while Mithridates climbed mount Scoro-
bas, which lies on the frontier between Bithynia and Pon-

---

6 δ' ἦν Goukowsky: δὴ codd.

πρόδρομοί τε αὐτοῦ, Σαυρομάτων ἑκατὸν ἱππεῖς,
ὀκτακοσίοις ἱππεῦσι τοῦ Νικομήδους ἐντυχόντες αἱ-
ροῦσι καὶ τούτων τινάς· οὓς πάλιν ὁ Μιθριδάτης σὺν
72 ἐφοδίοις μεθῆκεν ἐς τὰς πατρίδας ἀπιέναι. Μάνιον δ᾽
ὑποφεύγοντα Νεοπτόλεμός τε καὶ Νεμάνης ὁ Ἀρμένιος ἀμφὶ τὸ Πρῶτον Πάχιον χωρίον ἑβδόμης ὥρας
καταλαβόντες, οἰχομένου πρὸς Κάσσιον Νικομήδους,
ἠνάγκασαν ἐς μάχην ἱππέας ἔχοντα τετρακισχιλίους
καὶ πεζοὺς ἔτι τούτων δεκαπλασίονας, κτείναντες δ᾽
73 αὐτοῦ περὶ μυρίους, ἐζώγρησαν ἐς τριακοσίους· οὓς
ὁμοίως ὁ Μιθριδάτης ἐς αὐτὸν ἀναχθέντας ἀπέλυσε,
καταδημοκοπῶν τοὺς πολεμίους. Μανίου δ᾽ ἐλήφθη
ἐπὶ τὸ στρατόπεδον, καὶ φεύγων αὐτὸς ἐπὶ τὸν Σαγ-
γάριον ποταμὸν νυκτὸς γενομένης ἐπέρασέ τε καὶ ἐς
74 Πέργαμον ἐσώθη. Κάσσιος δὲ καὶ Νικομήδης, καὶ
ὅσοι ἄλλοι Ῥωμαίων πρέσβεις παρῆσαν, ἐς Λεόντων
Κεφαλήν, ὃ τῆς Φρυγίας ἐστὶν ὀχυρώτατον χωρίον,
μετεστρατοπέδευον· καὶ τὸ πλῆθος ὅσον εἶχον, οὐ
πάλαι συνειλεγμένον, χειροτεχνῶν ἢ γεωργῶν ἢ ἰδι-
ωτῶν, ἐγύμναζον, καὶ τοὺς Φρύγας αὐτοῖς προσκα-
75 τέλεγον. ὀκνούντων δὲ ἑκατέρων ἀπέγνωσαν πολεμεῖν
ἀνδράσιν ἀπολέμοις, καὶ διαλύσαντες αὐτοὺς ἀνεχώρουν, Κάσσιος μὲν ἐς Ἀπάμειαν σὺν τῷ ἑαυτοῦ
στρατῷ, Νικομήδης δὲ ἐς Πέργαμον, Μαγκῖνος δὲ ἐπὶ
Ῥόδου. ὧν, ὅσοι τὸ στόμα τοῦ Πόντου κατεῖχον, πυθόμενοι διελύθησαν, καὶ τάς τε κλεῖς τοῦ Πόντου, καὶ
ναῦς ὅσας εἶχον, τῷ Μιθριδάτῃ παρέδοσαν.

tic territory. Scouts of his, one hundred Sarmatian cavalry, encounter eight hundred of Nicomedes' horse, and capture some of them too; once again Mithridates gave them supplies and sent them off to their homelands. Manius 72 withdrew, but Neoptolemus and Nemanes the Armenian overtook him at the seventh hour near Proton Pachion; and, with Nicomedes having gone off to join Cassius, they forced him into battle. Manius had four thousand cavalry and ten times as many infantry, but the enemy killed about ten thousand of his men and captured almost three hundred. When these were brought to Mithridates he re- 73 leased them in similar fashion as before, seeking to get the better of his enemies by popular appeal. Manius' camp was also captured, and he himself fled to the river Sangarius, crossed it when night fell, and found refuge in Pergamum. Cassius, Nicomedes, and the other Roman 74 ambassadors present moved camp to Leonton Cephale, a very strongly fortified town in Phrygia, and began to train their newly collected force, such as it was, of artisans, farmers, and raw recruits; and they enrolled the Phrygians with them. When both groups proved hesitant, they de- 75 cided not to go to war with unwarlike men, but dismissed them and retreated—Cassius to Apamea with his own army, Nicomedes to Pergamum, and Mancinus[25] to Rhodes. When they heard this news, those guarding the mouth of the Pontus dispersed, and surrendered to Mithridates both the keys to the Pontus and the ships in their possession.

[25] Possibly T. Manlius Mancinus, tribune in 108/7. He has not been mentioned before, but there is no justification for emending the text to Manius, as Gelzer suggested.

76　20. Ὁ δὲ ὁρμῇ τῇδε μιᾷ τὴν ἀρχὴν ὅλην τοῦ Νικομήδους ὑπολαβὼν ἐπῄει, καὶ καθίστατο τὰς πόλεις. ἐμβαλὼν δὲ καὶ ἐς Φρυγίαν, ἐς τὸ τοῦ Ἀλεξάνδρου Πανδοκεῖον κατέλυσεν, αἰσιούμενος ἄρα, ἔνθαπερ Ἀλέξανδρος ἀνεπαύσατο, καὶ Μιθριδάτην σταθμεῦ-

77　σαι. ὁ μὲν δὴ καὶ Φρυγίας τὰ λοιπὰ καὶ Μυσίαν καὶ Ἀσίαν, ἃ Ῥωμαίοις νεόκτητα ἦν, ἐπέτρεχε, καὶ ἐς τὰ περίοικα περιπέμπων ὑπηγάγετο Λυκίαν τε καὶ

78　Παμφυλίαν καὶ τὰ μέχρι Ἰωνίας. Λαοδικεῦσι δὲ ἔτι ἀντέχουσι, τοῖς περὶ τὸν Λύκον ποταμόν (Ῥωμαίων γάρ τις στρατηγὸς Κόιντος Ὄππιος, ἱππέας ἔχων καὶ μισθοφόρους τινάς, ἐς τὴν πόλιν ἐσδραμὼν ἐφύλαττεν αὐτήν), κήρυκα ἐπιπέμψας ἐπὶ τὰ τείχη λέγειν ἐκέλευσεν ὅτι βασιλεὺς Μιθριδάτης ὑπέχεται Λαοδι-

79　κεῦσιν ἄδειαν, εἰ τὸν Ὄππιον αὐτῷ προσαγάγοιεν. οἱ δ᾽ ἐπὶ τῷ κηρύγματι τοὺς μὲν μισθοφόρους Ὀππίου μεθῆκαν ἀπαθεῖς ἀπιέναι, αὐτὸν δ᾽ ἤγαγον τῷ Μιθριδάτῃ τὸν Ὄππιον, ἡγουμένων αὐτῷ τῶν ῥαβδοφόρων ἐπὶ γέλωτι. καὶ αὐτὸν ὁ Μιθριδάτης οὐδὲν <δεινὸν>[7] διαθεὶς ἐπήγετο πανταχοῦ λελυμένον, ἐπιδεικνύμενος ἄρα Ῥωμαίων αἰχμάλωτον στρατηγόν.

80　21. Μετ᾽ οὐ πολὺ δὲ καὶ Μάνιον Ἀκύλιον, τὸν τῆσδε τῆς πρεσβείας καὶ τοῦδε τοῦ πολέμου μάλιστα αἴτιον, ἑλὼν δεδεμένον ἐπὶ ὄνου περιήγετο, κηρύσσων τοῖς ὁρῶσιν ὅτι Μάνιος ᾔει, μέχρι ἐν Περγάμῳ τοῦ στόματος αὐτοῦ κατεχώνευσε χρυσίον, δωροδοκίαν ἄρα

81　Ῥωμαίοις ὀνειδίζων. σατράπας δὲ τοῖς ἔθνεσιν ἐπιστήσας, ἐς Μαγνησίαν καὶ Ἔφεσον καὶ Μιτυλήνην

20. After taking possession of Nicomedes' whole king- 76
dom in this single offensive, Mithridates traveled around
it reorganizing the towns. He also invaded Phrygia and
lodged at the Inn of Alexander, no doubt regarding it as
a good omen that where Alexander had halted for rest,
Mithridates too should have his quarters. He overran the 77
rest of Phrygia, and Mysia and Asia, recently acquired by
Rome; and sending his men into the surrounding areas, he
brought under his control Lycia and Pamphylia and the
lands all the way up to Ionia. When the inhabitants of 78
Laodicea-on-the-Lycus continued to resist—for a Roman
praetor, Quintus Oppius, had gotten through to the town
with cavalry and some mercenaries and was defending
it—he sent a herald up to the walls and ordered him to say
that King Mithridates was offering immunity to the La-
odiceans, if they brought Oppius to him. At this procla- 79
mation they allowed Oppius' mercenaries to depart unharmed, but took Oppius himself to Mithridates, with his
lictors preceding him to make fun of him. Mithridates did
him no harm, and took him everywhere unchained, no
doubt to show off a Roman praetor as his prisoner.

21. Not long after, he captured Manius Aquillius too, 80
the person particularly responsible for the embassy and
the war; he led him around in chains on a donkey, announcing to onlookers that this was Manius passing by,
until at Pergamum he poured molten gold down his throat,
as a rebuke, I suppose, to the Romans for their venality.
Having put satraps in charge of his provinces, he made his 81
way to Magnesia, Ephesus, and Mytilene, where everyone

---

7 δεινὸν add. Schweig.

παρῆλθεν, ἀσμένως αὐτὸν ἁπάντων δεχομένων, Ἐφεσίων δὲ καὶ τὰς Ῥωμαίων εἰκόνας τὰς παρὰ σφίσι
καθαιρούντων, ἐφ' ᾧ δίκην ἔδοσαν οὐ πολὺ ὕστερον.

82 ἐπανιὼν δὲ ἐκ τῆς Ἰωνίας Στρατονίκειαν εἷλε καὶ ἐζη-
μίωσε χρήμασι, καὶ φρουρὰν ἐς τὴν πόλιν ἐσήγαγεν.
παρθένον τε εὔμορφον ἰδὼν ἐς τὰς γυναῖκας ἀνε-
δέξατο· καὶ εἴ τῳ σπουδὴ καὶ τὸ ὄνομα πυθέσθαι,
Μονίμη Φιλοποίμενος ἦν. Μάγνησι δὲ καὶ Παφλα-
γόσι καὶ Λυκίοις ἔτι ἀντέχουσι διὰ τῶν στρατηγῶν
ἐπολέμει.

83   22. Καὶ τάδε μὲν ἦν ἀμφὶ τὸν Μιθριδάτην· Ῥωμαῖοι
δ' ἐξ οὗ τῆς πρώτης αὐτοῦ ὁρμῆς τε καὶ ἐς τὴν Ἀσίαν
ἐσβολῆς ἐπύθοντο, στρατεύειν ἐπ' αὐτὸν ἐψηφίσαντο,
καίπερ ἀσχολούμενοι στάσεσιν ἀτρύτοις ἐν τῇ πόλει
καὶ οἰκείῳ πολέμῳ χαλεπῷ, τῆς Ἰταλίας ἀφισταμένης

84 σχεδὸν ἁπάσης ἀνὰ μέρος. κληρουμένων δὲ τῶν
ὑπάτων, ἔλαχε μὲν Κορνήλιος Σύλλας ἄρχειν τῆς
Ἀσίας καὶ πολεμεῖν τῷ Μιθριδάτῃ, χρήματα δ' οὐκ
ἔχοντες αὐτῷ ἐσενεγκεῖν, ἐψηφίσαντο πραθῆναι ὅσα
Νουμᾶς Πομπίλιος βασιλεὺς ἐς θυσίας θεῶν διετέτακτο. τοσήδε μὲν ἦν τότε πάντων ἀπορία καὶ ἐς
πάντα φιλοτιμία. καί τινα αὐτῶν ἔφθασε πραθῆναι
καὶ συνενεγκεῖν χρυσίου λίτρας ἐνακισχιλίας, ἃς μό-

85 νας ἐς τηλικοῦτον πόλεμον ἔδοσαν. Σύλλαν μὲν οὖν
ἐς πολὺ αἱ στάσεις κατέσχον, ὡς ἐν τοῖς ἐμφυλίοις
συγγέγραπται· ἐν τούτῳ δ' ὁ Μιθριδάτης ἐπί τε Ῥοδίους ναῦς πλείονας συνεπήγνυτο, καὶ σατράπαις
ἅπασι καὶ πόλεων ἄρχουσι δι' ἀπορρήτων ἔγραφε,

gladly received him; the Ephesians even destroyed the Roman statues set up in their city, for which they paid the penalty a short time later. On his return from Ionia he took 82 Stratonicea, imposed a monetary fine on it, and installed a garrison in the city. When he saw a beautiful young girl, he selected her as one of his wives: if anyone is eager to know her name, it was Monime, daughter of Philopoemen. And he made war through his generals on the Magnesians and Paphlagonians and Lycians who still held out against him.

22. This was the situation facing Mithridates. As for the 83 Romans, as soon as they learned of his attack and invasion of Asia, they voted to make war on him. This was in spite of the fact that they were preoccupied by continuous political unrest in Rome and by a troublesome civil war, almost the whole of Italy having risen in revolt, one place after the other. When the consuls drew lots for their prov- 84 inces, Cornelius Sulla got command of Asia and of the war against Mithridates.[26] As there were no funds available to assign to him, a motion was passed to sell what king Numa Pompilius had bequeathed to Rome to pay for sacrifices to the gods. Such was their complete lack of resources at the time, and the totality of their ambition. They quickly sold some of Numa's bequest, which yielded nine thousand pounds of gold. This was all they contributed to pay for such a major war. The political unrest delayed Sulla for 85 a long time, as I have explained in my civil war books. During this time, Mithridates constructed a large fleet for an assault on Rhodes. He also wrote a secret message to all his satraps and city governors ordering them to launch

[26] L. Cornelius Sulla (consul 88, 80), the famous dictator.

τριακοστὴν ἡμέραν φυλάξαντας ὁμοῦ πάντας ἐπιθέσθαι τοῖς παρὰ σφίσι Ῥωμαίοις καὶ Ἰταλοῖς, αὐτοῖς τε καὶ γυναιξὶν αὐτῶν καὶ παισὶ καὶ ἀπελευθέροις ὅσοι γένους Ἰταλικοῦ, κτείναντάς τε ἀτάφους ἀπορρῖψαι, καὶ τὰ ὄντα αὐτοῖς μερίσασθαι πρὸς βασιλέα
86 Μιθριδάτην. ἐπεκήρυξε δὲ καὶ ζημίαν τοῖς καταθάπτουσιν αὐτοὺς ἢ ἐπικρύπτουσι, καὶ μήνυτρα τοῖς ἐλέγχουσιν ἢ τοὺς κρυπτομένους ἀναιροῦσι, θεράπουσι μὲν ἐπὶ δεσπότας ἐλευθερίαν, χρήσταις δ' ἐπὶ
87 δανεισταῖς ἥμισυ τοῦ χρέους. τάδε μὲν δὴ δι' ἀπορρήτων ὁ Μιθριδάτης ἐπέστελλεν ἅπασιν ὁμοῦ, καὶ τῆς ἡμέρας ἐπελθούσης συμφορῶν ἰδέαι ποικίλαι κατὰ τὴν Ἀσίαν ἦσαν, ὧν ἔνια τοιάδε ἦν.

88   23. Ἐφέσιοι τοὺς ἐς τὸ Ἀρτεμίσιον καταφυγόντας, συμπλεκομένους τοῖς ἀγάλμασιν, ἐξέλκοντες ἔκτεινον. Περγαμηνοὶ τοὺς ἐς τὸ Ἀσκληπιεῖον συμφυγόντας, οὐκ ἀφισταμένους, ἐτόξευον τοῖς ξοάνοις συμπλεκομένους. Ἀδραμυττηνοὶ τοὺς ἐκνέοντας ἐσβαίνοντες ἐς τὴν θάλασσαν ἀνήρουν, καὶ τὰ βρέφη
89 κατεπόντουν. Καύνιοι Ῥοδίοις ὑποτελεῖς ἐπὶ τῷ Ἀντιόχου πολέμῳ γενόμενοι, καὶ ὑπὸ Ῥωμαίων ἀφεθέντες οὐ πρὸ πολλοῦ, τοὺς Ἰταλοὺς ἐς τὴν βουλαίαν Ἑστίαν καταφυγόντας ἕλκοντες ἀπὸ τῆς Ἑστίας, τὰ βρέφη σφῶν πρῶτα ἔκτεινον ἐν ὄψει τῶν μητέρων,
90 αὐτὰς δὲ καὶ τοὺς ἄνδρας ἐπ' ἐκείνοις. Τραλλιανοὶ δ' αὐθένται τοῦ κακοῦ φυλαξάμενοι γενέσθαι, Παφλαγόνα Θεόφιλον, ἄγριον ἄνδρα, ἐς τὸ ἔργον ἐμισθώσαντο, καὶ ὁ Θεόφιλος αὐτοὺς συναγαγὼν ἐπὶ τὸν τῆς

a simultaneous attack, thirty days later, on the Romans and Italians resident with them, including their wives and children, and any freedmen of Italian birth. They were to kill them and throw them out unburied, and share their property and belongings with king Mithridates. He also an- 86 nounced penalties for anyone burying the dead or hiding the living, and rewards for informers and those who killed people in hiding. Slaves who informed on their masters were to be freed, and debtors who informed on their creditors were to be relieved of half their debt. These were the 87 orders Mithridates sent secretly to everyone at the same time, and when the appointed day came around, a wide variety of disasters happened throughout Asia. Here are some examples.

23. The Ephesians dragged away and killed those who 88 had taken refuge in the temple of Artemis and were still clutching the sacred statues. At Pergamum, the people shot with arrows those who had gathered together for safety in the temple of Asclepius and refused to move, while they were clinging to the sacred images. At Adramyttium, they killed those who had run into the sea to escape by swimming, and they drowned their children. After the war against Antiochus, the city of Caunus was 89 made tributary to Rhodes and had been liberated by Rome a short time before. Here the Italians fled to the statue of Vesta in the senate chamber, but the people of Caunus dragged them away from it, and first killed the children as their mothers watched, then the mothers and after them the men. In an attempt to avoid responsibility 90 for carrying out the crime themselves, the people of Tralles hired a fierce Paphlagonian man called Theophilus to do the job. He led the victims off to the temple of Con-

189

Ὁμονοίας νεὼν ἥπτετο τοῦ φόνου, καὶ τινῶν τοῖς ἀγάλμασι συμπλεκομένων τὰς χεῖρας ἀπέκοπτεν.

91 τοιαύταις μὲν τύχαις οἱ περὶ τὴν Ἀσίαν ὄντες Ἰταλοὶ καὶ Ῥωμαῖοι συνεφέροντο, ἄνδρες τε ὁμοῦ καὶ βρέφη καὶ γυναῖκες, καὶ ἐξελεύθεροι καὶ θεράποντες αὐτῶν, ὅσοι γένους Ἰταλικοῦ. ᾧ καὶ μάλιστα δῆλον ἐγένετο τὴν Ἀσίαν οὐ φόβῳ Μιθριδάτου μᾶλλον ἢ μίσει Ῥω-

92 μαίων τοιάδε ἐς αὐτοὺς ἐργάσασθαι. ἀλλ' οὗτοι μὲν δίκην ἔδοσαν διπλῆν, αὐτοῦ τε Μιθριδάτου μετ' ὀλίγον ἀπίστως ἐξυβρίσαντος ἐς αὐτούς, καὶ ὕστερον

93 Κορνηλίῳ Σύλλᾳ· Μιθριδάτης δὲ ἐς μὲν Κῶ κατέπλευσε, Κῴων αὐτὸν ἀσμένως δεχομένων, καὶ τὸν Ἀλεξάνδρου παῖδα τοῦ βασιλεύοντος Αἰγύπτου, σὺν χρήμασι πολλοῖς ὑπὸ τῆς μάμμης Κλεοπάτρας ἐν Κῷ καταλελειμμένον, παραλαβὼν ἔτρεφε βασιλικῶς, ἔκ τε τῶν Κλεοπάτρας θησαυρῶν γάζαν πολλὴν καὶ τέχνην καὶ λίθους καὶ κόσμους γυναικείους καὶ χρήματα πολλὰ ἐς τὸν Πόντον ἔπεμψεν.

94 24. Ἐν δὲ τούτῳ Ῥόδιοι τά τε τείχη σφῶν καὶ τοὺς λιμένας ἐκρατύναντο, καὶ μηχανὰς ἅπασιν ἐφίστανον· καί τινες αὐτοῖς Τελμισέων τε καὶ Λυκίων συνέμαχουν. ὅσοι τε ἐξ Ἀσίας Ἰταλοὶ διεπεφεύγεσαν, ἐς Ῥόδον ἅπαντες ἐχώρουν, καὶ σὺν αὐτοῖς Λεύκιος

95 Κάσσιος ὁ τῆς Ἀσίας ἀνθύπατος. ἐπιπλέοντος δὲ τοῦ Μιθριδάτου τὰ προάστεια καθῄρουν, ἵνα μηδὲν εἴη χρήσιμα τοῖς πολεμίοις, καὶ ἐπὶ ναυμαχίαν ἀνήγοντο,

cord where he carried out their murder, even cutting off the hands of some of them, while they were holding on to the sacred statues. Such was the fate that befell the Italians and Romans in Asia—men, women and children, their freedman and slaves, anyone of Italian blood. These events made it very clear that it was just as much hatred of Rome as fear of Mithridates that drove the inhabitants of Asia to carry out such crimes against these people. But they were punished twice over, first by Mithridates himself when he treated them with treacherous violence shortly after, and then by Cornelius Sulla. For his part, Mithridates sailed over to Cos, where he was warmly received, and where he found and gave a royal upbringing to the son of Alexander, the reigning king of Egypt, who had been left there by his grandmother, Cleopatra, along with considerable sums of money.[27] From Cleopatra's storerooms Mithridates sent back to the Pontus a great deal of treasure and works of art and precious stone and women's jewelry and large sums of money.

24. Meanwhile the Rhodians were reinforcing their walls and harbor, and setting up artillery batteries everywhere. Offering military assistance were some Telmessians and Lycians, and all the Italians who had escaped from Asia also made their way to Rhodes, along with Lucius Cassius, the proconsul of Asia. When Mithridates approached with his fleet, the Rhodians destroyed the suburbs of the city to leave nothing of use to the enemy, and put to sea for battle, with some of their ships arrayed

91

92

93

94

95

---

[27] Ptolemy X Alexander sent his son, Ptolemy XI Alexander, for protection to the island of Cos while he was fighting the Seleucids.

96 ταῖς μὲν ἐκ μετώπου ταῖς δὲ πλαγίοις. ὁ δὲ βασιλεὺς
ἐπὶ πεντήρους περιπλέων ἐκέλευε τοὺς ἰδίους ἐς τὸ
πέλαγος ἀνάγειν ἐπὶ κέρως, καὶ τὴν εἰρεσίαν ἐπι-
ταχύναντας περικυκλοῦσθαι τοὺς πολεμίους ὀλιγω-
τέρους ὄντας, μέχρι δείσαντες οἱ Ῥόδιοι περὶ τῇ κυκλώσει ὑπεχώρουν κατ᾽ ὀλίγον· εἶτ᾽ ἐπιστρέψαντες ἐς
τὸν λιμένα κατέφυγον, καὶ κλείθροις αὐτὸν διαλαβόν-
97 τες ἀπὸ τῶν τειχῶν τὸν Μιθριδάτην ἀπεμάχοντο. ὁ
δὲ τῇ πόλει παραστρατοπεδεύων καὶ συνεχῶς τῶν
λιμένων πειρώμενος καὶ ἀποτυγχάνων, ἀνέμενε τὸ
98 πεζὸν ἐκ τῆς Ἀσίας οἱ παραγενέσθαι. κἀν τούτῳ βρα-
χεῖαι καὶ συνεχεῖς ἐγίγνοντο ἀψιμαχίαι τῶν ἐφεδρευ-
όντων τοῖς τείχεσιν, ἐν αἷς οἱ Ῥόδιοι πλεονεκτοῦντες
ἀνεθάρσουν κατ᾽ ὀλίγον, καὶ τὰς ναῦς διὰ χειρὸς εἶχον ὡς, εἴ πῃ καιρὸν εὕροιεν, ἐπιθησόμενοι τοῖς πολεμίοις.

99   25. Ὀλκάδος δὲ βασιλικῆς ἱστίῳ παραπλεούσης,
Ῥοδία δίκροτος ἐπ᾽ αὐτὴν ἀνήχθη· καὶ ταῖσδε κατὰ
σπουδὴν ἑκατέρων ἐπιβοηθούντων ναυμαχία γίγνεται
καρτερά, Μιθριδάτου μὲν ἐπιβαρύνοντος ὀργῇ καὶ
πλήθεσι νεῶν, Ῥοδίων δ᾽ αὐτοῦ τὰ σκάφη σὺν ἐμπει-
ρίᾳ περιπλεόντων τε καὶ ἀνατιτρώντων, ὥστε καὶ τρι-
ήρη αὐτοῖς ἀνδράσιν ἀναδησάμενοι καὶ ἀκροστόλια
πολλὰ καὶ σκῦλα ἐς τὸν λιμένα φέροντες ἐπανελθεῖν.
100 πεντήρους δὲ σφῶν εἰλημμένης ὑπὸ τῶν πολεμίων,
ἀγνοοῦντες οἱ Ῥόδιοι ἐπὶ ζήτησιν αὐτῆς ἐξ ταῖς μάλιστα ταχυναυτούσαις ἀνέπλεον, καὶ Δαμαγόρας ἐπ᾽
αὐτῶν ὁ ναύαρχος ἐνέπλει. πέντε δ᾽ αὐτῷ καὶ εἴκοσιν

for a frontal attack, others for flanking movements. The 96
king, who was sailing on a quinquereme, ordered his own
sailors to head out to the open sea in column, and by
quickening their rowing stroke, surround the numerically
inferior Rhodians. Fearing encirclement, the Rhodians
eventually began to withdraw slowly, and then wheeling
around, took cover in their harbor, closed it off with a
boom, and defended themselves against Mithridates from
the walls. He encamped beside the city, but failing in his 97
repeated attempts to break into their harbor, waited for
his army to arrive from Asia. Meanwhile, the Rhodians on 98
the walls were engaged in minor but continuous skirmishing, and as they mostly got the better of these encounters,
they gradually began to recover their confidence and kept
their ships in a state of readiness, to attack the enemy,
whenever they saw the opportunity.

25. When one of the royal merchantmen was passing 99
by under sail, a Rhodian bireme set out against it. With
both sides hurriedly sending assistance, a fierce sea battle
develops. Mithridates pressed heavily and angrily with his
bigger fleet, but, using their experience, the Rhodians
sailed around his ships and rammed them. They succeeded in towing away one trireme with its crew and returning to harbor with a number of figureheads and other
spoils. The Rhodians failed to notice when one of their 100
quinqueremes was captured by the enemy, and they set
sail with six of their very fastest vessels to look for it, Damagoras, their admiral, joining the flotilla at sea. Mithri-

ἐπιπέμψαντος τοῦ Μιθριδάτου, μέχρι μὲν ἐς δύσιν ὁ
Δαμαγόρας ὑπεχώρει, συσκοτάζοντος δ' ἤδη ταῖς βα-
σιλικαῖς ἐς ἀπόπλουν ἐπιστρεφομέναις ἐμβαλὼν δύο
κατεπόντωσε, δύο δ' ἄλλας ἐς Λυκίαν συνεδίωξε, καὶ
101 τὴν νύκτα πελαγίσας ἐπανῆλθεν. τοῦτο Ῥοδίοις καὶ
Μιθριδάτῃ τέλος ἦν τῆς ναυμαχίας, παρὰ δόξαν Ῥοδίοις τε διὰ τὴν ὀλιγότητα καὶ Μιθριδάτῃ διὰ τὸ
πλῆθος γενόμενον. ἐν δὲ τῷ ἔργῳ περιπλέοντι τῷ βασιλεῖ, καὶ τοὺς οἰκείους ἐπισπέρχοντι, Χία συμμαχὶς
ἐμβαλοῦσα ἐκ θορύβου κατέσεισε· καὶ ὁ βασιλεύς,
οὐδὲν ἀνακρινάμενος,[8] τὸν κυβερνήτην ὕστερον ἐκόλασε καὶ τὸν πρῳρέα, καὶ Χίοις ἐμήνισε πᾶσιν.

102 26. Τῶν δ' αὐτῶν ἡμερῶν τοῦ πεζοῦ τῷ Μιθριδάτῃ
παραπλέοντος ἐπὶ ὁλκάδων καὶ τριήρων, πνεῦμα
Καυνικὸν ἐμπεσὸν ἐς αὐτὰς ἐς Ῥόδον παρήνεγκε· καὶ
οἱ Ῥόδιοι τάχιστα ἐπαναχθέντες, ἐνοχλουμέναις ὑπὸ
τοῦ κλύδωνος ἔτι καὶ διεσπαρμέναις ἐμβαλόντες, ἀνε-
δήσαντό τινας καὶ διέτρησαν ἑτέρας καὶ ἐνέπρησαν
ἄλλας, καὶ ἄνδρας αἰχμαλώτους εἷλον ἐς τετρακοσί-
103 ους. ἐφ' οἷς ὁ Μιθριδάτης ἐς ἑτέραν ναυμαχίαν ὁμοῦ
καὶ πολιορκίαν ἡτοιμάζετο, σαμβύκην δέ τινα, μηχάνημα μέγιστον, ἐπὶ δύο νεῶν φερόμενον ἐποίει.
αὐτομόλων δ' αὐτῷ λόφον ὑποδειξάντων ἐπιβατόν, ᾗ
Ἀταβυρίου Διὸς ἱερὸν ἦν καὶ κολοβὸν τειχίον ἐπ'
αὐτοῦ, τὴν στρατιὰν ἐς τὰς ναῦς νυκτὸς ἐπέβησε, καὶ

---

[8] ἀνακρινάμενος Goukowsky: ὑποκρινάμενος codd: οὐδὲν
τότε φροντίζειν ὑποκρινάμενος edd. varii

dates sent twenty-five of his own ships after him. Damagoras withdrew a little before sunset, but just as it was getting dark, he managed to sink two of the king's ships as they were turning around to sail back, and he chased two others to Lycia. After spending the night at sea, he returned to Rhodes. This is how the naval engagement between Mithridates and the Rhodians turned out, a surprise both to the Rhodians because their fleet was so small, and to Mithridates because his was so big. During the battle, when the king was sailing around urging his men on, an allied ship from Chios rammed his in the confusion and shook it. Although Mithridates conducted no inquiry,[28] he later punished the helmsman and lookout, and developed an intense dislike for all Chians.

26. In that same period, when Mithridates' army was sailing along the coast in merchant ships and triremes, a wind hit them from the direction of Caunus and drove them toward Rhodes. The Rhodians quickly put to sea and attacked them while they were still scattered and shaken by the storm. They towed some away, rammed others, set fire to the rest, and took about four hundred prisoners. In response, Mithridates began to prepare for another sea battle and siege at the same time. He built an enormous device known as a sambuca, and mounted it on two ships. Deserters showed him a hill that was easy to climb, where there was a temple of Zeus Atabyrius surrounded by a low wall. During the night he embarked the army on the ships

---

[28] Some editors want to emend the text at this point to give a meaning, "At the time the king pretended not to care, but he later punished. . . ."

ἑτέροις ἀναδοὺς κλίμακας ἐκέλευσε χωρεῖν ἑκατέρους
μετὰ σιωπῆς, μέχρι τινὲς αὐτοῖς πυρσεύσειαν ἐκ τοῦ
Ἀταβυρίου, καὶ τότε ἀθρόως, μετὰ βοῆς ὅτι μάλιστα
μεγάλης, τοὺς μὲν τοῖς λιμέσιν ἐμπίπτειν, τοὺς δὲ τὰ
104 τείχη βιάζεσθαι. οἱ μὲν δὴ μετὰ σιγῆς βαθείας προσ-
επέλαζον, Ῥοδίων δ' οἱ προφύλακες αἰσθόμενοι τῶν
γιγνομένων ἐπύρσευσαν, καὶ ἡ στρατιὰ τοῦ Μιθριδάτου, νομίσασα τοῦτο εἶναι τὸν ἐκ τοῦ Ἀταβυρίου
πυρσόν, ἐκ βαθείας σιωπῆς ἠλάλαξαν ὁμοῦ πάντες,
οἵ τε κλιμακοφόροι καὶ ὁ στόλος ὁ νηΐτης. Ῥοδίων δ'
αὐτοῖς ἀκαταπλήκτως ἀντανακραγόντων, καὶ ἀθρόως
ἀναδραμόντων ἐς τὰ τείχη, οἱ βασιλικοὶ νυκτὸς μὲν
οὐδὲν ἐπεχείρουν, ἡμέρας δ' ἀπεκρούσθησαν.
105 27. Ἡ σαμβύκη δ' ἐπαχθεῖσα τοῦ τείχους ᾗ τὸ τῆς
Ἴσιδος ἱερόν ἐστιν, ἐφόβει μάλιστα, βέλη τε πολλὰ
ὁμοῦ καὶ κριοὺς καὶ ἀκόντια ἀφιεῖσα. στρατιῶταί τε
σκάφεσι πολλοῖς αὐτῇ μετὰ κλιμάκων παρέθεον ὡς
ἀναβησόμενοι δι' αὐτῆς ἐπὶ τὰ τείχη. οἱ δὲ Ῥόδιοι καὶ
τάδε εὐσταθῶς ὑπέμενον, ἕως τό τε μηχάνημα ὑπὸ
βάρους ἐνεδίδου, καὶ φάσμα τῆς Ἴσιδος ἔδοξε πῦρ
106 ἀφιέναι πολὺ κατ' αὐτοῦ. καὶ ὁ Μιθριδάτης ἀπογνοὺς
καὶ τῆσδε τῆς πείρας ἀνεζεύγνυεν ἐκ τῆς Ῥόδου, Πα-
τάροις δὲ τὴν στρατιὰν περιστήσας ἔκοπτε Λητοῦς
ἄλσος ἱερὸν ἐς μηχανάς. μέχρι φοβήσαντος αὐτὸν
ἐνυπνίου τῆς τε ὕλης ἐφείσατο, καὶ Πελοπίδαν Λυκίοις πολεμεῖν ἐπιστήσας, Ἀρχέλαον ἐς τὴν Ἑλλάδα
ἔπεμπε, προσεταιριούμενον ἢ βιασόμενον αὐτῆς ὅσα
107 δύναιτο. αὐτὸς δ' ἀπὸ τοῦδε τοῖς στρατηγοῖς τὰ

and gave scaling ladders to others, issuing orders for both groups to advance in silence until a fire signal was lit from the shrine of Atabyrius, at which point they were to attack en masse, with the loudest possible war cries, the fleet assaulting the harbor, the others forcing the walls. Al- 104 though they did indeed advance in complete silence, the Rhodian sentries realized what was happening and lit their own fire signal. Mithridates' men thought this was the signal from the Atabyrius shrine, and broke the deep silence with a great collective roar from both the ladder men and the naval section. This failed to unsettle the Rhodians, who let out their own war cry in response, and rushed to the walls together. The royal forces made no attempt to attack in the dark, and were driven off during the day.

27. The sambuca was brought up against the section of 105 the wall where the temple of Isis is located, and was particularly frightening, as it could employ many projectiles simultaneously, both rams and missiles. Accompanying it in a great many boats were soldiers with their scaling ladders who intended to use it to climb the walls. This danger too, however, the Rhodians calmly awaited, and in the end the sambuca collapsed under its own weight, and a vision of Isis appeared to bombard it with fire. Mithridates de- 106 spaired of this attempt too, and withdrew from Rhodes. He invested the town of Patara with his army, and began to cut down the sacred grove of Leto to construct artillery, until he was frightened by a dream into sparing the trees. After appointing Pelopidas to campaign against the Lycians, he sent Archelaus to Greece, to win over or reduce by force as much of it as he could. From now on, Mithri- 107

πολλὰ μεθεὶς ἐστρατολόγει καὶ ὡπλοποίει, καὶ τῇ
Στρατονικίδι γυναικὶ διετέρπετο, καὶ δίκας ἐδίκαζε
τοῖς ἐπιβουλεύειν ἐς τὸ σῶμα αὐτοῦ λεγομένοις ἢ
νεωτερίζουσιν ἢ ὅλως ῥωμαΐζουσιν.

108   28. Καὶ ὁ μὲν ἐπὶ τοῖσδε ἦν, κατὰ δὲ τὴν Ἑλλάδα
τοιάδε ἐγίγνετο. Ἀρχέλαος δ' ἐπιπλεύσας καὶ σίτῳ
καὶ στόλῳ πολλῷ, Δῆλόν τε ἀφισταμένην ἀπὸ Ἀθηναίων καὶ ἄλλα χωρία ἐχειρώσατο βίᾳ καὶ κράτει.
κτείνας δ' ἐν αὐτοῖς δισμυρίους ἄνδρας, ὧν οἱ πλέονες
ἦσαν Ἰταλοί, τὰ χωρία προσεποιεῖτο τοῖς Ἀθηναίοις·
καὶ ἀπὸ τοῦδε αὐτούς, καὶ τὰ ἄλλα κομπάζων περὶ
τοῦ Μιθριδάτου καὶ ἐς μέγα ἐπαίρων, ἐς φιλίαν ὑπη-
109   γάγετο· τά τε χρήματα αὐτοῖς τὰ ἱερὰ ἔπεμπεν ἐκ
Δήλου δι' Ἀριστίωνος ἀνδρὸς Ἀθηναίου, συμπέμψας
ἐς φυλακὴν τῶν χρημάτων ἐς δισχιλίους ἄνδρας, οἷς
ὁ Ἀριστίων συγχρώμενος ἐτυράννησε τῆς πατρίδος,
καὶ τῶν Ἀθηναίων τοὺς μὲν εὐθὺς ἔκτεινεν ὡς ῥωμαΐζοντας, τοὺς δ' ἀνέπεμψεν ἐς Μιθριδάτην, καὶ ταῦτα
110   μέντοι σοφίαν τὴν Ἐπικούρειον ἠσκηκώς. ἀλλὰ γὰρ
οὐχ ὅδε μόνος Ἀθήνησιν, οὐδὲ Κριτίας ἔτι πρὸ τούτου,
καὶ ὅσοι τῷ Κριτίᾳ συμφιλοσοφοῦντες ἐτυράννησαν,
ἀλλὰ καὶ ἐν Ἰταλίᾳ τῶν πυθαγορησάντων καὶ ἐν
τῇ ἄλλῃ Ἑλλάδι τῶν ἑπτὰ σοφῶν λεγομένων ὅσοι
πραγμάτων ἐλάβοντο, ἐδυνάστευσάν τε καὶ ἐτυράν-

---

29 Critias was one of the Thirty Tyrants who ruled Athens at
the end of the Peloponnesian War in 404. Pythagoras lived most
of his life in southern Italy, where he moved from his home in

dates delegated most of the work to his generals, while he himself took charge of recruitment and the production of armaments. He also enjoyed himself with his wife from Stratonicea, and put on trial those who had been accused of plotting against his person, or who were promoting insurrection, or in any way helping the Romans.

28. While Mithridates was occupied with these matters, the situation in Greece was as follows. Archelaus, having sailed with a large and well supplied expedition, subdued Delos by force—it had revolted from Athens—and a number of other places. He killed twenty thousand men in the process, mostly Italians, and handed over the strongholds to the Athenians. In this way, and by general boasting and extravagant praise of Mithridates, he won them over as allies. He sent them the sacred monies from Delos by means of Aristion, an Athenian citizen, accompanied by a guard of two thousand men, which Aristion used to make himself tyrant of his fatherland. In spite of the fact that he was a student of Epicurean philosophy, he immediately executed some Athenians for taking the Roman side, and sent others to Mithridates. But, of course, he was not the only Athenian to have done this. Take Critias, for example, some time before him, and Critias' fellow philosophers who ruled as tyrants, but also in Italy the Pythagoreans, and in the rest of Greece those of the so-called seven wise men who took up practical politics.[29] These all exercised power and conducted tyrannical rule

108

109

110

Samos in about 530, and founded a group that was influential in politics for more than a century. The seven sages included such politicians as Pittacus of Mytilene, Solon of Athens, and the tyrant Periander of Corinth.

νησαν ὠμότερον τῶν ἰδιωτικῶν τυράννων, ὥστε καὶ
περὶ τῶν ἄλλων φιλοσόφων ἄπορον ποιῆσαι καὶ ὕποπτον, εἴτε δι᾽ ἀρετήν, εἴτε πενίας καὶ ἀπραξίας τὴν
111 σοφίαν ἔθεντο παραμύθιον. ὧν γε καὶ νῦν πολλοὶ ἰδι-
ωτεύοντες καὶ πενόμενοι, καὶ τὴν ἀναγκαίαν ἐκ τῶνδε
σοφίαν περικείμενοι, τοῖς πλουτοῦσιν ἢ ἄρχουσι λοι-
δοροῦνται πικρῶς, οὐχ ὑπεροψίας πλούτου καὶ ἀρχῆς
δόξαν σφίσι μᾶλλον ἢ ζηλοτυπίας ἐς αὐτὰ προφέρον-
τες. ὑπερορῶσι δ᾽ αὐτῶν οἱ βλασφημούμενοι πολὺ
σοφώτερον.

112   29. Ταῦτα μὲν οὖν ἡγήσαιτο ἄν τις ἐς Ἀριστίωνα
τὸν φιλόσοφον εἰρημένα, αὐτὸν αἴτιον τῆς ἐκβολῆς
τῷ λόγῳ γενόμενον· Ἀρχελάῳ δ᾽ Ἀχαιοὶ καὶ Λάκωνες
προσετίθεντο, καὶ Βοιωτία πᾶσα χωρίς γε Θεσπιέων,
113 οὓς περικαθήμενος ἐπολιόρκει. τοῦ δ᾽ αὐτοῦ χρόνου
Μητροφάνης ἐπιπεμφθεὶς ὑπὸ Μιθριδάτου μεθ᾽ ἑτέρας στρατιᾶς Εὔβοιαν καὶ Δημητριάδα καὶ Μαγνησίαν, οὐκ ἐνδεχομένας τὰ Μιθριδάτεια, ἐλεηλάτει. καὶ
Βραίτιος[9] ἐκ Μακεδονίας ἐπελθὼν σὺν ὀλίγῳ στρατῷ
διεναυμάχησέ τε αὐτῷ, καὶ καταποντώσας τι πλοῖον
καὶ ἡμιολίαν ἔκτεινε πάντας τοὺς ἐν αὐτοῖς, ἐφορῶν-
114 τος τοῦ Μητροφάνους. ὁ δὲ καταπλαγεὶς ἔφευγεν. καὶ
αὐτὸν αἰσίῳ ἀνέμῳ χρώμενον ὁ Βραίτιος οὐ καταλαβὼν Σκίαθον ἐξεῖλεν, ἣ τῆς λείας τοῖς βαρβάροις
ταμιεῖον ἦν, καὶ δούλους τινὰς αὐτῶν ἐκρέμασε, καὶ
ἐλευθέρων ἀπέτεμε τὰς χεῖρας. ἐπί τε Βοιωτίαν τρα-

_____

[9] Βραίτιος Goukowsky: Βρύττιος LBJ: Βρύτιος P

more cruelly than ordinary tyrants, which makes one uncertain and suspicious of other philosophers, and wonder whether they adopted the pursuit of wisdom because of moral excellence or as a consolation for poverty and failure. There are certainly many men even today who, because they are poor and not engaged in politics, clothe themselves in wisdom out of necessity, and are always bitterly criticizing the rich and politically powerful, thus winning a reputation less for despising wealth and power, than for envying them. By ignoring these men, the targets of their criticism show themselves to be much wiser than their critics. 111

29. I would like the reader to know that what I have written is directed against the philosopher Aristion, who is the reason for this digression in my account. Achaea and Laconia both sided with Archelaus, and all of Boeotia except Thespis, which he invested and besieged. At the same time, Metrophanes was sent by Mithridates with another army to ravage Euboea and Demetrias and Magnesia, none of which would support the Mithridatic cause. Braetius now arrived from Macedonia with a small force and fought a naval engagement with Archelaus, sinking one boat and one skiff and killing all their crew, while Metrophanes watched on. He fled in alarm.[30] Metrophanes had a favorable wind and Braetius was unable to catch him, but he did capture Sciathos, where the barbarians had a storehouse for their plunder, and where he crucified some of their slaves and cut off the hands of the freemen. He then 112 113 114

---

[30] Q. Braetius Sura served as a legate in Macedonia from 93 to 87. The correct form of his name is known from an inscription from Thespiae.

πείς, ἑτέρων οἱ χιλίων ἱππέων καὶ πεζῶν ἐκ Μακεδονίας ἐπελθόντων, ἀμφὶ Χαιρώνειαν Ἀρχελάῳ καὶ
Ἀριστίωνι τρισὶν ἡμέραις συνεπλέκετο, ἴσου καὶ ἀγχωμάλου παρ' ὅλον τὸν ἀγῶνα τοῦ ἔργου γιγνομένου.

115 Λακώνων δὲ καὶ Ἀχαιῶν ἐς συμμαχίαν Ἀρχελάῳ καὶ
Ἀριστίωνι προσιόντων, ὁ Βραίτιος ἅπασιν ὁμοῦ γενομένοις οὐχ ἡγούμενος ἀξιόμαχος ἔτι ἔσεσθαι ἀνεζεύγνυεν ἐς τὸν Πειραιᾶ, μέχρι καὶ τοῦδε Ἀρχέλαος
ἐπιπλεύσας κατέσχεν.

116 30. Σύλλας δ' ὁ τοῦ Μιθριδατείου πολέμου στρατηγὸς ὑπὸ Ῥωμαίων αἱρεθεὶς εἶναι, τότε πρῶτον ἐξ
Ἰταλίας σὺν τέλεσι πέντε καὶ σπείραις τισὶ καὶ ἴλαις
ἐς τὴν Ἑλλάδα περαιωθεὶς χρήματα μὲν αὐτίκα καὶ
συμμάχους καὶ ἀγορὰν ἔκ τε Αἰτωλίας καὶ Θεσσαλίας συνέλεγεν, ὡς δ' ἀποχρώντως ἔχειν ἐδόκει,

117 διέβαινεν ἐς τὴν Ἀττικὴν ἐπὶ τὸν Ἀρχέλαον. παρο-
δεύοντι δ' αὐτῷ Βοιωτία τε ἀθρόως μετεχώρει, χωρὶς
ὀλίγων, καὶ τὸ μέγα ἄστυ αἱ Θῆβαι, μάλα κουφόνως
ἀντὶ Ῥωμαίων ἑλόμενοι τὰ Μιθριδάτεια, ὀξύτερον ἔτι,
πρὶν ἐς πεῖραν ἐλθεῖν, ἀπὸ Ἀρχελάου πρὸς Σύλλαν

118 μετετίθεντο. ὁ δ' ἐπὶ τὴν Ἀττικὴν ἐχώρει, καὶ μέρος τι
στρατοῦ ἐς τὸ ἄστυ περιπέμψας Ἀριστίωνα πολιορκεῖν, αὐτός, ἔνθαπερ ἦν Ἀρχέλαος, ἐπὶ τὸν Πειραιᾶ
κατῆλθε, κατακεκλεισμένων ἐς τὰ τείχη τῶν πο-

119 λεμίων. ὕψος δ' ἦν τὰ τείχη πήχεων τεσσαράκοντα
μάλιστα, καὶ εἴργαστο ἐκ λίθου μεγάλου τε καὶ τετραγώνου, Περίκλειον ἔργον, ὅτε τοῖς Ἀθηναίοις ἐπὶ
Πελοποννησίους στρατηγῶν, καὶ τὴν ἐλπίδα τῆς

turned against Boeotia, and when a further one thousand
cavalry and infantry arrived from Macedonia, he fought a
battle with Archelaus and Aristion at Chaeronea. The engagement lasted three days and the fight was evenly balanced throughout that time. But when the Spartans and   115
Achaeans arrived with assistance for Archelaus and Aristion, Braetius thought that he would no longer be a match
for their combined forces and withdrew to the Piraeus,
until Archelaus sailed in and took possession of it also.

30. Sulla, who had been appointed by the Romans to   116
take command of the war against Mithridates, now for the
first time crossed over from Italy to Greece bringing five
legions and some cohorts and troops of cavalry. He immediately began to collect money, allies, and supplies
from Aetolia and Thessaly. As soon as he thought he had
enough of everything, he made his way across to Attica to
face Archelaus. On his route, all the Boeotians, apart from   117
a small number, went over to him, including the great city
of Thebes, which had, very thoughtlessly, chosen the king's
side rather than the Romans'. They now changed allegiance from Archelaus to Sulla with even more agility,
before the issue came to the test. When Sulla arrived in   118
Attica, he sent part of his army to the city to besiege Aristion, while he himself went down to the Piraeus, where
Archelaus was stationed with the enemy troops shut inside
the walls. These walls, nearly forty cubits high, and made   119
of big square blocks of stone, were the work of Pericles
when he commanded the Athenians in their war against
the Peloponnesians. As it was on the Piraeus that he placed

νίκης ἐν τῷ Πειραιεῖ τιθέμενος, μᾶλλον αὐτὸν ἐκρα-
120 τύνατο. Σύλλας δὲ καὶ τοιοῖσδε οὖσι τοῖς τείχεσιν
εὐθὺς ἐπῆγε τὰς κλίμακας, καὶ πολλὰ μὲν ἔδρα πολλὰ
δ᾽ ἀντέπασχεν, ἰσχυρῶς τῶν Καππαδοκῶν αὐτὸν ἀμυνομένων, ἔστε κάμνων ἐς Ἐλευσῖνα καὶ Μέγαρα ἀνεχώρει, καὶ μηχανὰς ἐπὶ τὸν Πειραιᾶ συνεπήγνυτο,
121 καὶ χῶμα αὐτῷ προσχοῦν ἐπενόει. τέχναι μὲν δὴ καὶ
παρασκευὴ πᾶσα αὐτῷ καὶ σίδηρος καὶ καταπέλται,
καὶ εἴ τι τοιουτότροπον ἄλλο, ἐκ Θηβῶν ἐκομίζετο,
ὕλην δὲ τῆς Ἀκαδημείας ἔκοπτε, καὶ μηχανὰς εἰργάζετο μεγίστας. τά τε μακρὰ σκέλη καθήρει, λίθους
καὶ ξύλα καὶ γῆν ἐς τὸ χῶμα μεταβάλλων.

122 31. Δύο δ᾽ ἐκ τοῦ Πειραιῶς Ἀττικοὶ θεράποντες,
αἱρούμενοι τὰ Ῥωμαίων, ἢ σφίσιν αὐτοῖς καταφυγήν,
εἴ τι γίγνοιτο, προορώμενοι, πεσσοῖς ἐκ μολύβδου
πεποιημένοις ἐγγράφοντες ἀεὶ τὸ γιγνόμενον ἐς τοὺς
123 Ῥωμαίους ἠφίεσαν ἀπὸ σφενδόνης. καὶ τοῦδε γιγνομένου τε συνεχῶς καὶ ἐς γνῶσιν ἐλθόντος, Σύλλας
τοῖς ἐσφενδονημένοις προσέχων ηὗρε γεγραμμένον
ὅτι τῆς ἐπιούσης ἐκ μετώπου πεζοὶ κατὰ τοὺς ἐργα-
ζομένους ἐκδραμοῦνται καὶ ἱππεῖς ἑκατέρωθεν ἐς
τὰ πλάγια Ῥωμαίων ἐμβαλοῦσιν. κρύψας οὖν τινὰ
στρατιὰν ἀποχρῶσαν, ὡς ἐγένετο τῶν πολεμίων ἡ ἐκ-
δρομή, δόξασα δὴ μάλιστα αἰφνίδιος εἶναι, ὁ δὲ αἰφ-
νιδιώτερον αὐτοῖς τοὺς κεκρυμμένους ἐπαφεὶς ἔκτεινε
124 πολλοὺς καὶ ἐς τὴν θάλασσαν ἑτέρους περιέωσεν. καὶ
τοῦτο μὲν τῆς πείρας ἐκείνης τέλος ἦν· αἱρομένοις δὲ
ἐπὶ μέγα ἄνω τοῖς χώμασι πύργους ὁ Ἀρχέλαος ἀντε-

his hopes of victory, he made it particularly strong. In spite   120
of the size of the walls, Sulla immediately brought his ladders up against them, but after inflicting and suffering
much damage, for the Cappadocians fought him off cou-
rageously, he retired exhausted to Eleusis and Megara,
where he set about constructing siege engines for an attack on the Piraeus, and made plans to build a siege mound
to deal with it. Technical devices, equipment of every   121
kind, iron, catapults, and anything else of that sort were
brought for him from Thebes, and with the wood he
cut from the Academy, he built huge siege engines. He
knocked down the Long Walls, and used the stones, wood,
and earth for the construction of the siege mound.

31. Two Athenian slaves in the Piraeus, either because   122
they favored the Roman cause, or because they were looking to the future for a refuge for themselves, if trouble
arose, now began to write down everything that was happening there on lead balls, and fire them at the Romans
from slings. This was happening regularly and when it   123
came to Sulla's attention, he began to scrutinize the sling-
shots, and found one with a message written on it saying
that next day infantry would make a frontal sortie against
the construction workers, and cavalry would attack the
Romans from both sides on their flanks. So, he hid a suf-
ficient number of soldiers in an ambush. When the enemy
sortie took place, they thought it would be a complete
surprise, but Sulla was even more of a surprise to them,
when he let loose his hidden troops and killed many and
drove others into the sea. This was the end of that par-   124
ticular attempt. As the mounds rose to a great height,

μηχανᾶτο, καὶ πλεῖστα ἐπ' αὐτοῖς ὄργανα ἐτίθει, τάς τε δυνάμεις ἐκ Χαλκίδος καὶ τῶν ἄλλων νήσων μετεπέμπετο, καὶ τοὺς ἐρέτας καθώπλιζεν, ὡς ὄντος οἱ
125 τοῦ κινδύνου περὶ τῶν ὅλων. ἐγίγνετο μὲν δὴ πλείων οὖσα τῆς Σύλλα στρατιᾶς ἡ Ἀρχελάου καὶ ἐκ τῶνδε πολὺ πλείων, νυκτὸς δὲ μέσης ὁ μὲν Ἀρχέλαος ἐκθορὼν μετὰ λαμπτήρων ἐνέπρησε τὴν ἑτέραν τῶν χελωνῶν καὶ τὰ ἐπ' αὐτῇ μηχανήματα, ἡμέραις δὲ δέκα μάλιστα ἄλλα ὁ Σύλλας ἐργασάμενος ἐπέστησεν αὖθις ἔνθα καὶ τὰ πρότερα ἦν. καὶ τούτοις ὁ Ἀρχέλαος πύργον ἀνθίστη κατὰ τὸ τεῖχος.

126   32. Καταπλευσάσης δ' αὐτῷ παρὰ Μιθριδάτου στρατιᾶς ἑτέρας, ἧς ἡγεῖτο Δρομιχαίτης, ἐξῆγεν ἅπαντας ἐς μάχην. ἀναμίξας δ' αὐτοῖς σφενδονήτας καὶ τοξότας ὑπὸ τὸ τεῖχος αὐτὸ παρέταττεν, ἵνα καὶ οἱ τειχοφύλακες ἐφικνοῖντο τῶν πολεμίων· ἕτεροι δ' ὑπὸ ταῖς πύλαις αὐτῷ πυρφόροι καιρὸν ἐκδρομῆς ἐπε-
127 τήρουν. ἀγχωμάλου δ' ἐς πολὺ τῆς μάχης οὔσης ἐνέκλινον ἑκάτεροι παρὰ μέρος, πρῶτον μὲν οἱ βάρβαροι, μέχρι Ἀρχέλαος αὐτοὺς ἐπισχὼν ἐπανήγαγεν ἐς τὴν μάχην. ᾧ δὴ καὶ μάλιστα καταπλαγέντες οἱ Ῥωμαῖοι μετ' αὐτοὺς ἔφευγον, ἔστε καὶ τούσδε Μου-
128 ρήνας ὑπαντιάσας ἐπέστρεφεν. ἄλλο δ' ἀπὸ ξυλείας τέλος ἐπανιόν, καὶ σὺν αὐτοῖς οἱ ἄτιμοι, σπουδῇ τὸν ἀγῶνα εὑρόντες ἐπέπιπτον τοῖς Μιθριδατείοις πάνυ καρτερῶς, μέχρι κτεῖναι μὲν αὐτῶν ἐς δισχιλίους,
129 τοὺς δὲ λοιποὺς ἐς τὰ τείχη συνελάσαι. Ἀρχέλαος δ' αὐτοὺς ἐπιστρέφων αὖθις, καὶ τῷ ἀγῶνι διὰ τὴν προ-

Archelaus built towers to combat them, and placed a large number of machines on them. He also sent for contingents from Chalcis and the other islands, and he armed his rowers, knowing that his whole venture was at stake. Archelaus' army was already bigger than Sulla's, and with these reinforcements even more so. In the middle of the night he sortied from the city with torches and burned one of the two Roman sheds and its siege engines. Sulla built new ones, however, in about ten days and replaced them where they had been before. Archelaus raised a tower on the wall opposite them.

32. When another army arrived for him by sea from Mithridates, under the command of Dromichaetes, Archelaus led his entire force out for battle. He distributed slingers and archers among his troops and deployed the army close in under the wall, so that the guards stationed on the wall were also within range of the enemy. Others by the gates waited on his orders with torches for the right moment to make a sortie. For a long time the outcome of the battle remained in doubt, as both sides gave way in turn, first the barbarians, until Archelaus rallied them and led them back into battle. Then the Romans were so surprised by this that they took to flight, until Murena confronted them and faced them around.[31] Another Roman legion, which had been on a wood-gathering operation, now returned and, joined by the troops shamed by their flight, eagerly joined the struggle and fell on the Mithridatic forces with such violence that they killed about two thousand of them and drove the rest back inside the walls. While rallying his men again, Archelaus was led by his

---

[31] L. Licinius Murena held a command in Asia from 87 to 81.

θυμίαν ἐς πολὺ παραμένων, καὶ ἀποκλεισθεὶς ἀνιμήθη διὰ καλῳδίων. ὁ δὲ Σύλλας τοὺς μὲν ἀτίμους περιφανῶς ἀγωνισαμένους ἐξέλυσε τῆς ἀτιμίας, τοὺς δ᾽ ἄλλους ἐδωρήσατο πολλοῖς.

130   33. Καὶ χειμῶνος ἐπιόντος ἤδη στρατόπεδον ἐν Ἐλευσῖνι θέμενος, τάφρον ἄνωθεν ἐπὶ θάλατταν ἔτεμνε βαθεῖαν τοῦ μὴ τοὺς πολεμίους ἱππέας εὐμαρῶς ἐπιτρέχειν οἱ. καὶ τάδε αὐτῷ πονουμένῳ καθ᾽ ἑκάστην ἡμέραν ἐγίγνοντό τινες ἀγῶνες, οἱ μὲν ἀμφὶ τὴν τάφρον οἱ δὲ παρὰ τοῖς τείχεσιν, ἐπεξιόντων θαμινὰ τῶν πολεμίων, καὶ λίθοις καὶ βέλεσι καὶ μολυβδαίναις
131   χρωμένων. ὁ δὲ Σύλλας νεῶν δεόμενος μετεπέμψατο μὲν ἐκ Ῥόδου. καὶ Ῥοδίων οὐ δυνηθέντων διαπλεῦσαι θαλασσοκρατοῦντος τοῦ Μιθριδάτου, Λούκουλλον, ἄνδρα Ῥωμαῖον περιφανῆ καὶ τοῦδε τοῦ πολέμου στρατηγὸν ἐπὶ Σύλλᾳ γενόμενον, ἐκέλευεν ἐς Ἀλεξάνδρειαν καὶ Συρίαν λαθόντα διαπλεῦσαι, παρά τε τῶν βασιλέων καὶ πόλεων, ὅσαι ναυτικαί, στόλον τινὰ
132   ἀγείραντα τὸ Ῥοδίων ναυτικὸν παραπέμψαι. ὁ μὲν δὴ πολεμίας οὔσης τῆς θαλάσσης, οὐδὲν ἐνδοιάσας, ἐς κελήτιον ἐνέβη, καὶ ναῦν ἐκ νεώς, ἵνα λάθοι, διαμείβων ἐπ᾽ Ἀλεξανδρείας ἐφέρετο·

34. Οἱ δὲ προδιδόντες ἀπὸ τῶν τειχῶν, πεσσοῖς πάλιν ἐγγράψαντες ὅτι πέμψει τῆσδε τῆς νυκτὸς Ἀρχέλαος ἐς τὸ τῶν Ἀθηναίων ἄστυ λιμῷ πιεζόμενον πυροὺς ὑπὸ στρατιωτῶν φερομένους, ἐσφενδόνησαν, καὶ ὁ Σύλλας ἐνεδρεύσας ἐκράτησε τοῦ τε σίτου καὶ
133   τῶν φερόντων. τῆς δ᾽ αὐτῆς ἡμέρας αὐτῷ καὶ Μου-

eagerness into staying in the fight too long and got cut off, and had to be lifted up by ropes. Sulla restored their rights to those in disgrace who had fought with such distinction, and he generously rewarded the others.

33. Now, at the onset of winter, Sulla made camp at   130
Eleusis and set about digging a deep ditch from the high ground right down to the sea, to make it difficult for the enemy cavalry to attack him. As he labored away at this task, there were outbreaks of fighting every day, some at the ditch, others at the walls, from where the enemy emerged frequently to fire stones, missiles and lead shots at the Romans. Being short of ships, Sulla sent to Rhodes   131
for some, but the Rhodians could not make their way through by ship, as Mithridates controlled the seas. Sulla therefore ordered Lucullus, a very distinguished Roman who became commander of the Roman forces in this war after Sulla, to proceed in secret to Alexandria and Syria, to raise a naval force from the kings and seafaring towns, and use it to escort the Rhodian contingent of ships.[32] Undaunted by the enemy's mastery of the seas, Lucullus   132
embarked on a fast cutter, and by repeatedly changing boat to avoid detection, made his way to Alexandria.

34. Meanwhile, the traitors within the walls of the Piraeus used their slings to send another message written on lead balls, with information that Archelaus would that very night be sending a supply of wheat under military guard to the city of Athens, which was hard pressed by hunger. Sulla set an ambush and captured both the grain and those carrying it. The same day, in an engagement near Chalcis,   133

---

[32] L. Licinius Lucullus (consul 74) held the command against Mithridates from 74 until 67.

νάτιος περὶ Χαλκίδα Νεοπτόλεμον ἕτερον στρατηγὸν
κατατρώσας, ἔκτεινε μὲν ἐς χιλίους καὶ πεντακοσίους,
ἔλαβε δὲ αἰχμαλώτους ἔτι πλείονας. οὐ πολὺ δὲ ὕστερον τῷ Πειραιεῖ νυκτός, ἔτι κοιμωμένων τῶν φυλάκων,
Ῥωμαῖοι διὰ τῶν ἐγγὺς μηχανῶν κλίμακας ἐπενεγκόν-
τες ἐπὶ τὸ τεῖχος ἐπέβησαν, καὶ τοὺς φύλακας τοὺς
134 ἐγγὺς ἔκτειναν. ἐφ' ᾧ τῶν βαρβάρων οἱ μὲν εὐθὺς
ἀπεπήδων ἐς τὸν Πειραιᾶ, τὸ τεῖχος καταλιπόντες ὡς
εἰλημμένον ἅπαν, οἱ δ' ἐς ἀλκὴν τραπέντες ἔκτεινάν
τε τὸν ἡγεμόνα τῶν ἐπιβάντων καὶ τοὺς λοιποὺς ἔξω
κατεκρήμνισαν. οἱ δὲ καὶ διὰ τῶν πυλῶν ἐκδραμόντες
ὀλίγου τὸν ἕτερον τῶν Ῥωμαϊκῶν πύργων ἐνέπρησαν
ἄν, εἰ μὴ Σύλλας ἐπιδραμὼν ἀπὸ τοῦ στρατοπέδου,
νυκτός τε ὅλης καὶ δι' ἡμέρας ἐπιπόνως ἀγωνισάμε-
135 νος, περιέσωσεν. καὶ τότε μὲν ὑπεχώρουν οἱ βάρβαροι, τοῦ δ' Ἀρχελάου πύργον ἕτερον μέγαν ἐπὶ τὸ
τεῖχος ἄντικρυς τοῦ Ῥωμαϊκοῦ πύργου στήσαντος
ἐπυργομάχουν πρὸς ἀλλήλους, ἑκατέρωθεν πυκνὰ καὶ
θαμινὰ πάντα ἀφιέντες, ἕως ὁ Σύλλας ἐκ καταπελτῶν,
ἀνὰ εἴκοσιν ὁμοῦ μολυβδαίνας βαρυτάτας ἀφιέντων,
ἔκτεινέ τε πολλούς, καὶ τὸν πύργον Ἀρχελάου κατ-
έσεισε καὶ δυσάρμοστον ἐποίησεν, ὡς εὐθὺς αὐτὸν
ὑπὸ Ἀρχελάου διὰ δέος ὀπίσω κατὰ τάχος ὑπαχθῆ-
ναι.

136 35. Πιεζομένων δ' ἔτι μᾶλλον ὑπὸ τοῦ λιμοῦ τῶν ἐν
ἄστει, πεσσοὶ πάλιν ἐμήνυον ὅτι πέμψει νυκτὸς ἐς τὸ
ἄστυ τροφάς. καὶ ὁ Ἀρχέλαος ὑπονοῶν τι περὶ τὸν
σῖτον γίγνεσθαι μήνυμα καὶ προδοσίαν, ἅμα τὸν

Munatius wounded Neoptolemus, another of Mithridates' generals, killed about one thousand five hundred of his men, and took even more prisoners.[33] Shortly after, the Romans attacked the Piraeus at night, while the guards were still asleep, by using the machines nearby to bring up the ladders and climb the wall. They killed the guards in the vicinity, at which some of the barbarians abandoned 134 the wall in the belief that the whole of it had been captured, and immediately scrambled down to the port of the Piraeus. Others, however, taking the route of courage, killed the leader of the scaling party, and threw the rest down from the top of the wall. Others again ran out through the gates and nearly succeeded in burning one of the Roman towers, and would have, if Sulla had not saved it by rushing over from the camp and fighting hard all night and the following day. It was only then that the bar- 135 barians withdrew. When Archelaus built another big tower right opposite the Roman one, both sides fought a battle from their towers, repeatedly firing volleys of every sort of missile. Eventually, using catapults that could fire twenty very heavy lead balls at the same time, Sulla killed many of the enemy, and shook Archelaus' tower, destabilizing it, with the result that it was quickly withdrawn by Archelaus out of fear for its survival.

35. Those in the city were now increasingly hard 136 pressed by hunger, and the lead balls again reported that Archelaus was intending to send food into the city at night. Archelaus suspected that someone was treacherously giving information about his food supply, and at the same

[33] This is the only literary reference to L. Munatius Plancus. The name is also preserved on an inscription from Delos.

σῖτον ἔπεμπε, καί τινας ἐφίστη ταῖς πύλαις μετὰ πυ-
ρὸς ἐς τοὺς Ῥωμαίους ἐκδραμουμένους, εἰ Σύλλας
γίγνοιτο περὶ τὸν σῖτον. καὶ συνέπεσεν ἄμφω, Σύλλᾳ
μὲν ἑλεῖν τοὺς σιτηγοῦντας,[10] Ἀρχελάῳ δ' ἐμπρῆσαί

137 τινα τῶν μηχανημάτων. τοῦ δ' αὐτοῦ χρόνου καὶ Ἀρκαθίας ὁ Μιθριδάτου υἱός, μεθ' ἑτέρας στρατιᾶς ἐς
Μακεδονίαν ἐμβαλών, οὐ δυσχερῶς ὀλίγων ὄντων
τῶν ἐκεῖ Ῥωμαίων ἐκράτησε, καὶ Μακεδονίαν πᾶσαν
ὑπηγάγετο, καὶ σατράπαις ἐπιτρέψας αὐτὸς ἐπὶ τὸν
Σύλλαν ἐχώρει, μέχρι νοσήσας περὶ τὸ Τίσαιον ἐτελεύτησεν.

138 36. Ἐν δὲ τῇ Ἀττικῇ τῷ μὲν ἄστει πονουμένῳ σφόδρα ὑπὸ λιμοῦ πολλὰ ὁ Σύλλας ἐπετείχιζε φρούρια,
τοῦ μὴ διαδιδράσκειν ἀλλ' ἐμμένοντας ὑπὸ τοῦ πλήθους μᾶλλον ἐνοχλεῖσθαι· τῷ δὲ Πειραιεῖ, τὸ χῶμα ἐς
ὕψος ἐγείρας, τὰ μηχανήματα ἐπῆγεν. Ἀρχελάου δὲ
τὸ χῶμα ὑπορύττοντος καὶ τὴν γῆν ὑποφέροντός τε
καὶ ἐς πολὺ διαλανθάνοντος, τὸ χῶμα ὑφίζανεν ἄφνω·

139 καὶ ταχείας αἰσθήσεως γενομένης οἱ Ῥωμαῖοι τὰ μηχανήματα ὑφεῖλκον καὶ τὸ χῶμα ἀνεπλήρουν. τῷ δ'
αὐτῷ τρόπῳ καὶ αὐτοὶ τὴν γῆν ἐς τὰ τείχη τεκμαιρό-
μενοι διώρυττον· ἀλλήλοις τε συμπίπτοντες κάτω ξίφεσι καὶ δόρασιν ἐκ χειρός, ὡς δυνατὸν ἦν ἐν σκότῳ,

140 διεμάχοντο. ὁμοῦ δὲ ταῦτα ἐγίγνετο, καὶ ὁ Σύλλας
ἀπὸ τῶν χωμάτων μηχανήμασι πολλοῖς τὸ τεῖχος
ἐκριοκόπει, μέχρι μέρος αὐτοῦ καταβαλών, καὶ τὸν
πλησιάζοντα πύργον ἐπειγόμενος ἐμπρῆσαι, πολλὰ
μὲν ἠφίει πυρφόρα τοξεύματα ἐς αὐτόν, τοὺς δὲ

time as he sent the convoy, he also stationed some men at the gates with torches to rush out against the Romans, if Sulla attacked the convoy. Both things happened. Sulla captured those escorting the grain, and Archelaus burned some of the Roman siege machines. At the same time, Mithridates' son Arcathias invaded Macedonia with another army and easily overpowered the small Roman force there. He subjected the whole of Macedonia, appointed satraps to govern it and then advanced himself against Sulla, only to fall ill and die at Tisaeum.

36. In Attica, the city of Athens was suffering terribly from hunger, and Sulla built a large number of forts to prevent anyone escaping, and to make sure that those having to remain would be even more troubled by the weight of numbers. As for the Piraeus, having built the mound high enough, he brought up his siege engines. But Archelaus was undermining the mound and carrying the earth away for a long time without being detected, until the mound suddenly collapsed. The Romans quickly understood what was happening, pulled their siege engines back and filled up the mound. In the same manner as Archelaus, they too began to dig tunnels under the walls, where they estimated them to be. The two sides met underground and fought each other hand to hand with swords and spears, as best they could in the darkness. At the same time as this was going on, Sulla used the many siege engines on the mounds to ram the wall. When he knocked part of it, he urgently tried to burn the tower nearby, by firing volleys of burning arrows at it, and sending the brav-

---

10 σιτηγοῦντας Goukowsky: σιτολογοῦντας codd.

141 εὐτολμοτάτους ἀνέπεμπεν ἐπὶ κλιμάκων. σπουδῆς δὲ
πολλῆς γιγνομένης ἑκατέρωθεν ὅ τε πύργος ἐνεπίμ-
πρατο, καὶ μέρος τι τοῦ τείχους ὀλίγον ὁ Σύλλας
καταβαλὼν εὐθὺς ἐπέστησε φυλακεῖον· τά τε ὑπορω-
ρυγμένα τοῦ τείχους θεμέλια, ξύλοις ἀνηρτημένα καὶ
θείου καὶ στυππίου καὶ πίσσης γέμοντα, αὐτίκα
142 πάντα ἐνεπίμπρη. τῶν δ' ἄλλο παρ' ἄλλο κατέπιπτε
καὶ τοὺς ἐφεστῶτας αὐτοῖς συγκατέφερεν. ὅ τε θόρυβος οὗτος δὴ μάλιστα αἰφνίδιος καὶ πολὺς ὢν πάντῃ
τοὺς τειχοφύλακας ἐτάρασσεν, ὡς καὶ τὸ ὑπὸ σφίσιν
αὐτίκα πεσούμενον· ὅθεν ἐς πάντα συνεχῶς ἐπιστρεφόμενοι τήν τε γνώμην ὕποπτον εἶχον ὑπὸ τοῦ δέους
καὶ ἀσθενῶς τοὺς πολεμίους ἀπεμάχοντο.

143 37. Καὶ ὁ Σύλλας αὐτοῖς ὧδε ἔχουσιν ἐπικείμενος
ἀπαύστως, καὶ τῶν ἰδίων τὸ ἀεὶ πονοῦν ἐναλλάσσων,
ἑτέρους ἐφ' ἑτέροις ἀκμῆτας ἐπῆγε σὺν κλίμαξι καὶ
βοῇ καὶ παρακελεύσει, προτρέπων ἅμα καὶ ἀπειλῶν
καὶ παρακαλῶν ὡς ἐν τῷδε τῷ βραχεῖ τοῦ παντὸς
144 αὐτοῖς κριθησομένου. ἀντεπῆγε δὲ καὶ ὁ Ἀρχέλαος
ἑτέρους ἀντὶ τῶν τεθορυβημένων, ἀνακαινίζων καὶ ὅδε
τὸ ἔργον ἀεί, καὶ παρακαλῶν ἅμα καὶ ἐποτρύνων
ἅπαντας ὡς ἐν ὀλίγῳ σφίσιν ἔτι τῆς σωτηρίας οὔσης.
145 πολλῆς δὲ σπουδῆς καὶ προθυμίας ἑκατέρωθεν αὖθις
ἅπασιν ἐγγενομένης φερεπονώτατος ἦν ⟨ὁ ἀγὼν⟩[11]
καὶ ὁ φόνος ἴσος καὶ ὅμοιος ἐξ ἑκατέρων, ἕως ὁ Σύλλας ἔξωθεν ἐπιών, καὶ μᾶλλόν τι κάμνων, ἀνεκάλει τῇ
σάλπιγγι τὴν στρατιάν, καὶ τραυματίας[12] πολλοὺς

est men up the ladders. Although both sides fought with   141
great energy, the tower was burned, and Sulla demolished
a small section of the wall, where he immediately placed
a guard unit. With the foundations of the wall undermined
and supported only by wooden beams, Sulla filled the hole
with sulfur, tow, and pitch, and set fire to the whole lot at
once. One part of the wall after another now collapsed,   142
bringing down with it the men stationed on top. This
caused a tumult so sudden and substantial that the guards
on all parts of the wall were in dismay at the prospect that
the wall under their feet would suddenly collapse. Because of this they were continually turning in all directions, and they were too afraid to trust their own judgment, with the result that they offered only weak resistance
to the enemy.

37. Sulla pressed them relentlessly in their difficulty,   143
relieving his own men from the constant fighting by bringing up fresh troops with ladders one after another, shouting his encouragement and mixing entreaties, threats, and
reassurance, in the knowledge that the whole outcome for
them depended on this one brief moment. Archelaus too   144
relieved his demoralized men with fresh ones, constantly
renewing the struggle and at the same time issuing orders
and encouragement, and telling them that in a short time
they would all be safe. With every soldier on both sides   145
displaying great energy and purpose, the struggle was
extremely arduous, and casualties were similar in both
armies. Eventually Sulla, being the one attacking from
outside, and therefore more tired, sounded the trumpet
signal for his forces to retreat, and led back a large number

---

11 ὁ ἀγὼν add. Schweig.
12 τραυματίας Schweig: θαυμάσας codd.

146 ἀπῆγεν. ὁ δ' Ἀρχέλαος αὐτίκα νυκτὸς τὰ πεπτωκότα
τοῦ τείχους ᾠκοδόμει, μηνοειδῆ αὐτοῖς πολλὰ περιθεὶς ἔνδοθεν. οἷς ἔτι νεοδομήτοις ὁ Σύλλας αὖθις ἐπεχείρει παντὶ τῷ στρατῷ, νομίσας ἀσθενῆ καὶ ὑγρὰ ἔτι
ὄντα ῥαδίως κατερείψειν. κάμνων δὲ ὡς ἐν στενῷ, καὶ
βαλλόμενος ἄνωθεν ἔκ τε μετώπου καὶ τῶν κεραιῶν
ὡς ἐν μηνοειδέσι χωρίοις, τοῦ μὲν ἐπιχειρεῖν ἔτι τῷ
Πειραιεῖ πάμπαν ἀπεῖχε τῇ γνώμῃ, καὶ ἐς πολιορκίαν,
ὡς λιμῷ παραστησόμενος αὐτούς, καθίστατο.

147   38. Αἰσθόμενος δὲ τοὺς ἐν ἄστει μᾶλλόν τι πεπι-
εσμένους, καὶ κτήνη πάντα καταθύσαντας, δέρματά
τε καὶ βύρσας ἕψοντας καὶ λιχμωμένους τὸ γιγνόμενον ἐξ αὐτῶν, τινὰς δὲ καὶ τῶν ἀποθνησκόντων ἁπτο-
μένους, ἐκέλευσε τῷ στρατῷ τὴν πόλιν περιταφρεύειν,
148 ἵνα μηδὲ καθ' ἕνα τις ἐκφεύγοι λανθάνων. ὡς δὲ καὶ
τοῦτο ἐξείργαστο αὐτῷ, κλίμακας ἐπῆγεν ὁμοῦ καὶ τὸ
τεῖχος διώρυττεν. τροπῆς δ' ὡς ἐν ἀσθενέσιν ἀνδράσιν αὐτίκα γενομένης, ἐσέπεσεν ἐς τὴν πόλιν, καὶ
εὐθὺς ἐν Ἀθήναις σφαγὴ πολλὴ ἦν καὶ ἀνηλεής· οὔτε
γὰρ ὑποφεύγειν ἐδύναντο δι' ἀτροφίαν, οὔτε παιδίων
ἢ γυναικῶν ἔλεος ἦν, τοῦ Σύλλα τὸν ἐν ποσὶν ἀναι-
ρεῖν κελεύοντος ὑπ' ὀργῆς ὡς ἐπὶ ταχείᾳ δὴ καὶ ἐς
βαρβάρους ἀλόγῳ μεταβολῇ καὶ πρὸς αὐτὸν ἀκράτῳ
149 φιλονεικίᾳ. ὅθεν οἱ πλέονες, αἰσθανόμενοι τοῦ κη-
ρύγματος, ἑαυτοὺς τοῖς σφαγεῦσιν ὑπερρίπτουν ἐς
τὸ ἔργον. ὀλίγων δ' ἦν ἀσθενὴς ἐς τὴν ἀκρόπολιν

of wounded men. During the night Archelaus immedi-   146
ately repaired the wall where it had collapsed, and at many
points built crescent-shaped defenses inside. Sulla again
attacked these still newly repaired sections with his entire
army, thinking that they would be easy to tear down, when
they were weak and the mortar still wet. But he struggled
in the narrow space, taking fire from above, both to his
front and on his flanks—this is what happens in crescent-
shaped places—and he abandoned entirely any thoughts
of launching a new assault on the Piraeus, instead settling
down to a siege, and using famine to force them into surrender.

38. But when he learned that the people in the city of   147
Athens were even more hard pressed by hunger, had killed
all their animals, boiled skins and hides and licked what
they could get out of them, that some had even eaten the
flesh of the dying, he ordered his men to dig a ditch around
the city so that not even an individual on his own could
escape unnoticed. When this work had been completed,   148
he brought up scaling ladders and undermined the wall at
the same time. As was to be expected among such weak
men, a rout quickly followed, and the Romans poured into
the city, and a great and pitiless massacre took place in
Athens. For the inhabitants were too weakened by lack of
food to be able to flee, and no mercy was shown to women
or children, Sulla having given the order to kill everyone
they came across in his anger at what was indeed the quick
and unreasonable decision of the Athenians to go over to
the barbarian side, and at their intemperate pugnacity toward himself. Most Athenians, when they heard of the   149
order, threw themselves at their killers to get the job done.
A few ran feebly to the Acropolis, Aristion making his

APPIAN

δρόμος· καὶ Ἀριστίων αὐτοῖς συνέφυγεν, ἐμπρήσας
τὸ Ὠιδεῖον, ἵνα μὴ ἑτοίμοις ξύλοις αὐτίκα ὁ Σύλλας
150 ἔχοι τὴν ἀκρόπολιν ἐνοχλεῖν. ὁ δ' ἐμπιπράναι μὲν τὴν
πόλιν ἀπεῖπε, διαρπάσαι δὲ ἔδωκε τῷ στρατῷ· καὶ
ἕτοιμοι σάρκες ἀνθρώπων ἐς τροφὴν ἐν πολλοῖς
οἰκήμασιν ηὑρέθησαν. τῇ δὲ ἑξῆς ὁ Σύλλας τοὺς μὲν
δούλους ἀπέδοτο, τοῖς δ' ἐλευθέροις, ὅσοι νυκτὸς ἐπι-
λαβούσης οὐκ ἔφθασαν ἀναιρεθῆναι, πάμπαν οὖσιν
ὀλίγοις, τὴν μὲν ἐλευθερίαν ἔφη διδόναι, ψῆφον δὲ
καὶ χειροτονίαν τῶνδε μὲν ὡς οἱ πεπολεμηκότων
ἀφαιρεῖσθαι, τοῖς δ' ἐκγόνοις καὶ ταῦτα διδόναι.

151   39. Ὧδε μὲν ἄδην εἶχον αἱ Ἀθῆναι κακῶν· ὁ δὲ
Σύλλας τῇ μὲν ἀκροπόλει φρουρὰν ἐπέστησεν, ᾗ τὸν
Ἀριστίωνα καὶ τοὺς συμπεφευγότας λιμῷ καὶ δίψει
πιεσθέντας ἐξεῖλεν οὐ μετὰ πολύ. καὶ αὐτῶν ὁ Σύλλας
Ἀριστίωνα μὲν καὶ τοὺς ἐκείνῳ δορυφορήσαντας ἢ
ἀρχήν τινα ἄρξαντας, ἢ ὁτιοῦν ἄλλο πράξαντας παρ'
ἃ πρότερον ἁλούσης τῆς Ἑλλάδος ὑπὸ Ῥωμαίων
152 αὐτοῖς διετέτακτο, ἐκόλασε θανάτῳ, τοῖς δὲ ἄλλοις
συνέγνω, καὶ νόμους ἔθηκεν ἅπασιν ἀγχοῦ τῶν πρό-
σθεν αὐτοῖς ὑπὸ Ῥωμαίων ὁρισθέντων. συνηνέχθη δ'
ἐκ τῆς ἀκροπόλεως χρυσίου μὲν ἐς τεσσαράκοντα
λίτρας μάλιστα, ἀργύρου δ' ἐς ἑξακοσίας.

153   40. Καὶ τάδε μὲν ἀμφὶ τὴν ἀκρόπολιν ὀλίγον ὕστερον ἐγίγνετο· ὁ δὲ Σύλλας αὐτίκα τοῦ ἄστεος ληφθέ-
ντος, οὐ περιμένων ἔτι τὸν Πειραιᾶ διὰ πολιορκίας
ἐξελεῖν, κριοὺς ὁμοῦ καὶ βέλη καὶ ἀκόντια ἐπῆγεν,
ἄνδρας τε πολλοὺς οἳ διώρυσσον ὑπὸ χελώναις τὰ

218

escape with them, after burning the Odeum, so that Sulla
would not have wood immediately to hand for an assault
on the Acropolis. Sulla gave orders that the city was not to   150
be burned, but he allowed the army to plunder it. Human
flesh ready to eat was found in many houses. The next day
Sulla sold the slaves, and to the very small number of free
men who had managed to stay alive before night inter-
rupted the killing, he said he was granting them their
freedom, but taking away their right to vote in assembly
and participate in elections, as they had opposed him in
war; he would, however, give even these rights to their
descendants.

39. So it was that Athens had her fill of misery. Sulla   151
stationed a guard on the Acropolis, and soon after captured Aristion and those who had escaped with him, as
they were forced to surrender for lack of food and water.
He punished with death Aristion and his bodyguard, and
all those who had held any office in Athens, or had contra-
vened any of the arrangements made for them at any earlier time when Greece had first been conquered by Rome.
The others he pardoned, and he instituted laws for every-   152
one that were nearly the same as those established earlier
for them by Rome. Approximately forty pounds of gold
and about six hundred pounds of silver were brought from
the Acropolis.

40. But these events at the Acropolis happened a little   153
later. As soon as he had captured the city, Sulla did not
wait any longer to take the Piraeus by siege, but attacked
it with rams at the same time as missiles and artillery bolts.
He had a large force of men undermining the walls under

τείχη, καὶ σπείρας αἳ τοὺς ἐπὶ τῶν τειχῶν ἀκοντίζου-
154 σαί τε καὶ τοξεύουσαι θαμινὰ ἀνέκοπτον. καὶ κατ-
ήρειψέ τι τοῦ μηνοειδοῦς, ὑγροτέρου καὶ ἀσθενε-
στέρου ἔτι ὄντος ἅτε νεοδομήτου. ὑπιδομένου δὲ τοῦτο
ἔτι πρότερον Ἀρχελάου, καὶ προοικοδομήσαντος ἔνδοθεν ὅμοια πολλά, τὸ μὲν ἔργον ἦν τῷ Σύλλᾳ διη-
νεκὲς ἐμπίπτοντι ἐς ἕτερον ὅμοιον ἐξ ἑτέρου, ὁρμῇ δ᾽
ἀπαύστῳ καὶ στρατοῦ μεταβολῇ πυκνῇ χρώμενος,
καὶ περιθέων αὐτούς, καὶ παρακαλῶν ἐπὶ τὸ ἔργον ὡς
ἐν τῷδε ἔτι λοιπῷ τῆς ὅλης ἐλπίδος καὶ κέρδους τῶν
155 προπεπονημένων ὄντος· οἱ δὲ καὶ αὐτοὶ τῷ ὄντι τοῦτο
σφίσιν ἡγούμενοι τέλος εἶναι πόνων, καὶ ἐς τὸ ἔργον
αὐτὸ ὡς μέγα δὴ καὶ λαμπρόν, τοιῶνδε τειχῶν κρατῆσαι, φιλοτιμούμενοι, προσέκειντο βιαίως, μέχρι
καταπλαγεὶς αὐτῶν τὴν ὁρμὴν ὁ Ἀρχέλαος ὡς μα-
νιώδη καὶ ἄλογον ἐξέλιπεν αὐτοῖς τὰ τείχη, ἐς δέ τι
τοῦ Πειραιῶς ἀνέδραμεν ὀχυρώτατόν τε καὶ θαλάσσῃ
περίκλυστον, ᾧ ναῦς οὐκ ἔχων ὁ Σύλλας οὐδ᾽ ἐπιχειρεῖν ἐδύνατο.

156　41. Ἐντεῦθεν ὁ μὲν Ἀρχέλαος ἐπὶ Θεσσαλίαν διὰ
Βοιωτῶν ἀνεζεύγνυ, καὶ συνῆγεν ἐς Θερμοπύλας τὰ
λοιπὰ τοῦ τε ἰδίου στρατοῦ παντός, ὃν ἔχων ἦλθε, καὶ
τοῦ σὺν Δρομιχαίτῃ παραγεγονότος. συνῆγε δὲ καὶ
τὸ σὺν Ἀρκαθίᾳ τῷ παιδὶ τοῦ βασιλέως ἐς Μακεδονίαν ἐμβαλόν, ἀκραιφνέστατον δὴ καὶ πλῆρες ὂν τόδε
μάλιστα, καὶ οὓς αὐτίκα ἄλλους ὁ Μιθριδάτης ἀπέ-
157 στειλεν· οὐ γὰρ διέλιπεν ἐπιπέμπων. ὁ μὲν δὴ ταῦτα
σὺν ἐπείξει συνῆγεν, ὁ δὲ Σύλλας τὸν Πειραιᾶ τοῦ

cover of sheds, and units pushing back the defenders on the wall by firing volleys of javelins and arrows at them. He succeeded in knocking down part of the crescent-shape defenses, which as it had only recently been built, was still somewhat moist and weak. Since Archelaus had suspected even beforehand that this would happen, and had previously built many similar ones inside, Sulla faced an endless task coming across one after another of these walls. But he showed inexhaustible energy, frequently relieved the men, and circulated among them, encouraging them to do the work, as their whole hope of reward for their previous labors rested on this last remaining task. The men themselves believed that this was in fact their final effort, and taking pride in the task itself, as it would be a great and brilliant achievement to take such mighty walls, they applied themselves vigorously. Eventually, Archelaus, astounded by what seemed to him their mad and unaccountable intensity, abandoned the walls to them, and ran back to the strongest part of the Piraeus, which was surrounded by the sea. As Sulla did not have any ships, he could not even attack it.

41. From here Archelaus withdrew to Thessaly through Boeotia, and assembled at Thermopylae what was left of his entire force, both what he himself had brought with him, and the army that had come with Dromichaetes. He included in the muster the army that had invaded Macedonia under the command of Arcathias, the son of King Mithridates, which was still very fresh and almost at full strength. Included too were the recent arrivals from Mithridates, who had not stopped sending reinforcements. While Archelaus was urgently putting together this army,

154

155

156

157

ἄστεος μᾶλλον ἐνοχλήσαντά οἱ κατεπίμπρη, φειδόμενος οὔτε τῆς ὁπλοθήκης οὔτε τῶν νεωσοίκων οὔτε τινὸς ἄλλου τῶν ἀοιδίμων. καὶ μετὰ τοῦτ᾽ ἐπὶ τὸν Ἀρ-
158 χέλαον ᾔει διὰ τῆς Βοιωτίας καὶ ὅδε. ὡς δ᾽ ἐπλησίασαν
ἀλλήλοις, οἱ μὲν ἐκ Θερμοπυλῶν ἄρτι μετεχώρουν ἐς
τὴν Φωκίδα, Θρᾷκές τε ὄντες καὶ ἀπὸ τοῦ Πόντου καὶ
Σκύθαι καὶ Καππαδόκαι Βιθυνοί τε καὶ Γαλάται καὶ
Φρύγες, καὶ ὅσα ἄλλα τῷ Μιθριδάτῃ νεόκτητα γέ-
159 νοιτο, πάντες ἐς δυώδεκα μυριάδας ἀνδρῶν· καὶ στρατηγοὶ αὐτῶν ἦσαν μὲν καὶ κατὰ μέρος ἑκάστῳ, αὐτοκράτωρ δ᾽ Ἀρχέλαος ἐπὶ πᾶσιν. Σύλλας δ᾽ ἦγεν
Ἰταλιώτας, καὶ Ἑλλήνων ἢ Μακεδόνων ὅσοι ἄρτι
πρὸς αὐτὸν ἀπὸ Ἀρχελάου μετετίθεντο, ἢ εἴ τι ἄλλο
περίοικον, οὐδ᾽ ἐς τριτημόριον τὰ πάντα τῶν πολεμίων.

160   42. Ἀντικαταστάντες δ᾽ ἀλλήλοις, ὁ μὲν Ἀρχέλαος
ἐξέταττεν ἐς μάχην ἀεὶ προκαλούμενος, ὁ δὲ Σύλλας
ἐβράδυνε, τὰ χωρία καὶ τὸ πλῆθος τῶν ἐχθρῶν περι-
σκοπούμενος. ἀναχωροῦντι δ᾽ ἐς Χαλκίδα τῷ Ἀρ-
161 χελάῳ παρακολουθῶν καιρὸν ἐπετήρει καὶ τόπον. ὡς
δὲ αὐτὸν εἶδε περὶ Χαιρώνειαν ἐν ἀποκρήμνοις στρα-
τοπεδευόμενον, ἔνθα μὴ κρατοῦσιν ἀποχώρησις οὐ-
δεμία ἦν, πεδίον αὐτὸς εὐρὺ πλησίον καταλαβὼν
εὐθὺς ἐπῆγεν ὡς καὶ ἄκοντα βιασόμενος ἐς μάχην
Ἀρχέλαον· ἐν ᾧ σφίσι μὲν ὕπτιον καὶ εὐπετὲς ἐς δίωξιν καὶ ἀναχώρησιν ἦν πεδίον, Ἀρχελάῳ δὲ κρημνοὶ
περιέκειντο, οἳ τὸ ἔργον οὐκ εἴων ἐν οὐδενὶ κοινὸν
ὅλου τοῦ στρατοῦ γενέσθαι, συστῆναι διὰ τὴν ἀνω-

Sulla was burning down the Piraeus, which had caused him more trouble than the city itself. He spared neither the arsenal nor the shipsheds, nor any of the other famous buildings. After this he set out against Archelaus, like him, also marching through Boeotia. And so the two armies 158 approached each other. The Mithridatic forces, which were just moving from Thermopylae into Phocis, were made up of Thracians from the Pontus and Scythians and Cappadocians and Bithynians and Galatians and Phrygians, and others from Mithridates' newly acquired territories. In total they numbered about one hundred and twenty thousand men. Each of the contingents had their 159 own generals, but Archelaus was in overall command. Sulla led an army of Italians, along with those Greeks and Macedonians who had recently deserted Archelaus and joined him, as well as some from the surrounding country. But his army was not even a third the size of the enemy's.

42. When the two armies had taken up position facing 160 each other, Archelaus repeatedly arrayed his forces for battle, challenging the enemy to respond, but Sulla held back in consideration of the terrain and the large number of his opponents. But when Archelaus withdrew to Chalcis, Sulla stayed close to him, keeping an eye out for the right time and place to fight. On seeing Archelaus pitch 161 camp in a location cut by ravines near Chaeronea, where there would be no escape for the defeated, Sulla himself immediately occupied a wide plain nearby with the intention of forcing Archelaus to fight, even if he did not want to. For the Romans, the plain had an even surface and was well suited to both pursuit and retreat, while Archelaus was surrounded by ravines, which completely prevented his whole army fighting as a single body, as he would not

μαλίαν οὐκ ἔχοντος· τραπεῖσί τε αὐτοῖς ἄπορος διὰ
162 τῶν κρημνῶν ἐγίγνετο ἡ φυγή. ὁ μὲν δὴ τοιόσδε λογισμοῖς τῇ δυσχωρίᾳ μάλιστα πιστεύων, ἐπῄει ὡς
οὐδὲν ἐσομένου χρησίμου τοῦ πλήθους Ἀρχελάῳ· ὁ δ᾽
οὐκ ἐγνώκει μὲν αὐτῷ τότε συμπλέκεσθαι, διὸ καὶ
ἀμελῶς ἐστρατοπέδευσεν, ἐπιόντος δὲ ἤδη τῆς δυσχωρίας ὀψὲ καὶ μόγις ᾐσθάνετο, καὶ προύπεμπέ τινας
163 ἱππέας ἐς κώλυσιν αὐτοῦ. τραπέντων δ᾽ ἐκείνων καὶ
ἐς τοὺς κρημνοὺς καταρριφθέντων, ἑξήκοντα αὖθις
ἔπεμψεν ἅρματα, εἰ δύναιτο μετὰ ῥύμης κόψαι καὶ
164 διαρρῆξαι τὴν φάλαγγα τῶν πολεμίων. διαστάντων
δὲ τῶν Ῥωμαίων, τὰ μὲν ἅρματα ὑπὸ τῆς φορᾶς ἐς
τοὺς ὀπίσω παρενεχθέντι τε καὶ δυσεπίστροφα ὄντα
πρὸς τῶν ὑστάτων περιστάντων αὐτὰ καὶ ἐσακοντιζόν-
των διεφθείρετο·

43. Ὁ δ᾽ Ἀρχέλαος δυνηθεὶς ἂν καὶ ὡς ἀπὸ τοῦ
χάρακος εὐσταθῶς ἀπομάχεσθαι, τάχα οἱ καὶ τῶν
κρημνῶν ἐς τοῦτο συλλαμβανόντων, ἐξῆγε σὺν ἐπείξει καὶ διέτασσε μετὰ σπουδῆς τοσόνδε πλῆθος οὐ
προεγνωκότων ἀνδρῶν, ἐν στενωτάτῳ μάλιστα γεγο-
165 νὼς διὰ τὸν Σύλλαν ἤδη πλησιάζοντα. τοὺς δ᾽ ἱππέας
πρώτους ἐπαγαγὼν μετὰ δρόμου πολλοῦ, διέτεμε τὴν
φάλαγγα Ῥωμαίων ἐς δύο, καὶ εὐμαρῶς ἑκατέρους
166 ἐκυκλοῦτο διὰ τὴν ὀλιγότητα. οἱ δ᾽ ἀπεμάχοντο μὲν
ἐγκρατῶς, ἐς πάντας ἐπιστρεφόμενοι, μάλιστα δ᾽
ἐπόνουν οἱ περὶ Γάλβαν τε καὶ Ὁρτήσιον, καθ᾽ οὓς
αὐτὸς ὁ Ἀρχέλαος ἐτέτακτο, τῶν βαρβάρων ὡς ἐν
ὄψει στρατηγοῦ σὺν προθυμίᾳ σφοδρᾷ ἐπικειμένων,

be able to unite it, because of the uneven ground; and if he was defeated, the ravines would make flight unmanageable. Such was Sulla's reasoning for putting particular trust 162 in the adverse terrain, and he advanced to the attack in the belief that the size of Archelaus' army would be of no advantage to him. Because he had not intended to join battle at that time, Archelaus had been careless about the location of his camp, but now that Sulla was advancing, he began to see the difficulty of the terrain, slowly and too late, and sent out some of his cavalry to hinder the Romans. When they were put to flight and thrown down the 163 ravines, Archelaus next sent forward sixty chariots, to see if they could break through the enemy phalanx by hitting it with a violent charge. But the Romans opened gaps in 164 the ranks and the chariots were carried through to the rear by their own momentum, and here, because they were difficult to turn, they were surrounded by the rearguard and destroyed by volleys of javelins.

43. Even with the situation as it was, Archelaus could have put up a solid resistance from his palisade, even the ravines perhaps assisting him in this, but instead he led his men out hastily, and rushed to array his huge force of men, who had not been told beforehand that they would be fighting, in a space that had become severely restricted by the already approaching Sulla. He first sent in his cavalry 165 with a powerful charge that split the Roman phalanx in two, and then easily surrounded both groups, as they were so small. The Romans turned to face all comers and de- 166 fended themselves stoutly. Those under the command of Galba and Hortensius were particularly hard pressed, as it was Archelaus himself opposing them, and, under the eye of their general, the barbarians attacked with excep-

225

167 μέχρι τοῦ Σύλλα μεταχωροῦντος ἐς αὐτοὺς σὺν ἱππεῦσι πολλοῖς, ὁ Ἀρχέλαος ἀπὸ τῶν σημείων στρα-
τηγικῶν ὄντων καὶ τοῦ κονιορτοῦ πλείονος αἰρομένου
τεκμηράμενος εἶναι Σύλλαν τὸν ἐπιόντα, λύσας τὴν
168 κύκλωσιν ἐς τάξιν ἀνεχώρει. ὁ δὲ τῶν τε ἱππέων τὸ
ἄριστον ἄγων, καὶ δύο νεαλεῖς σπείρας ἐν τῇ παρόδῳ
προσλαβών, αἱ ἐτετάχατο ἐφεδρεύειν, οὔπω τὸν κύκλον τοῖς πολεμίοις ἐξελίξασιν, οὐδ' ἐς μέτωπον
εὐσταθῶς διατεταγμένοις, ἐνέβαλε, καὶ θορυβήσας
169 ἔκοψέ τε καὶ ἐς φυγὴν τραπέντας ἐδίωκεν. ἀρξαμένης
δ' ἐνταῦθα τῆς νίκης, οὐδὲ Μουρήνας ἠλίννεν ἐπὶ τοῦ
λαιοῦ τεταγμένος, ἀλλ' ὀνειδίσας τοῖς ἀμφ' αὐτὸν καὶ
γενναίως ἐμπεσὼν ἐδίωκε κἀκεῖνος.

44. Τρεπομένων δ' ἤδη τῶν Ἀρχελάου κερῶν, οὐδ'
οἱ μέσοι τὴν τάξιν ἐφύλασσον, ἀλλ' ἀθρόα πάντων
170 ἐγίγνετο φυγή. ἔνθα δὴ πάντα ὅσα εἴκασεν ὁ Σύλλας,
ἐνέπιπτε τοῖς πολεμίοις· οὐ γὰρ ἔχοντες ἀναστροφὴν
εὐρύχωρον οὐδὲ πεδίον ἐς φυγήν, ἐπὶ τοὺς κρημνοὺς
ὑπὸ τῶν διωκόντων ἐωθοῦντο, καὶ αὐτῶν οἱ μὲν ἐξέπιπτον πρὸς αὐτόν, οἱ δ' εὐβουλότερον ἐς τὸ στρα-
171 τόπεδον ἐφέροντο. Ἀρχέλαος δ' αὐτοὺς προλαβών,
ἀπειρότατα δὴ τότε μάλιστα συμφορῶν πολεμικῶν,
ἀπέκλειε, καὶ ἐπιστρέφειν ἐς τοὺς πολεμίους ἐκέλευεν.
οἱ δ' ἀνέστρεφον μὲν ἐκ προθυμίας, οὔτε δὲ στρατηγῶν ἢ ἐπιστατῶν ἐς διάταξιν ἔτι σφίσι παρόντων,
οὔτε τὰ σημεῖα ἕκαστοι τὰ ἑαυτῶν ἐπιγιγνώσκοντες
ὡς ἐν ἀκόσμῳ τροπῇ διερριμμένοι, χωρίου τε καὶ ἐς
φυγὴν καὶ ἐς μάχην ἀποροῦντες, στενωτάτου τότε

tional intensity.[34] Eventually Sulla moved across to them   167
with a large force of cavalry, and Archelaus, guessing from
the insignia of the commander in chief and the great cloud
of dust being raised, that it was Sulla who was approaching, abandoned his encirclement of the enemy and began
to resume his battle line. Sulla was bringing his best cav-   168
alry, reinforced on the way by two fresh detachments that
had been placed in reserve, and he attacked Archelaus
before he had finished unrolling his encircling movement
and had not yet deployed his men in a solid line facing the
front. The impact threw them into confusion, and when
they turned to flight, Sulla set off in pursuit. While the   169
victory began here, Murena, in command on the left wing,
was also busy: admonishing his men and bravely charging
the enemy, he too joined the pursuit.

44. With both wings now in flight, Archelaus' center
also failed to hold the line, but fled en masse. Now every-   170
thing that Sulla had predicted happened to the enemy. For
without enough room to turn around or flat terrain for
flight, they were forced into the ravines by their pursuers.
Some of them fell straight into his hands, others took the
wiser course of rushing to the camp. Archelaus, however,   171
got there first, and now in particular showing his acute lack
of experience of the fortunes of war, he shut them out, and
ordered them to turn and face the enemy. They wheeled
around with enthusiasm, but there was an absence of generals or officers to organize them into line, the units could
not find their own standards scattered as they were in
chaotic flight, and they lacked the space either to flee or

[34] Ser. Sulpicius Galba and L. Hortensius were legates of
Sulla.

227

μάλιστα αὐτοῖς διὰ τὴν δίωξιν γενομένου, ἐκτείνοντο
172 μετ' ἀργίας, οἱ μὲν ὑπὸ τῶν πολεμίων, οὐδὲν ἀντιδρᾶ-
σαι φθάνοντες, οἱ δὲ ὑπὸ σφῶν αὐτῶν ὡς ἐν πλήθει
173 καὶ στενοχωρίᾳ θορυβούμενοι. πάλιν τε κατέφυγον
ἐπὶ τὰς πύλας, καὶ εἰλοῦντο περὶ αὐτὰς ἐπιμεμφόμε-
νοι τοῖς ἀποκλείουσιν θεούς τε πατρίους αὐτοῖς καὶ
τὴν ἄλλην οἰκειότητα σὺν ὀνείδει προύφερον, ὡς οὐχ
ὑπὸ τῶν ἐχθρῶν μᾶλλον ἢ τῶνδε ὑπερορώντων αὐτοὺς
ἀναιρούμενοι, ἔστε μόλις αὐτοῖς ὁ Ἀρχέλαος, ὀψὲ
τῆς χρείας, ἀνέῳγνυ τὰς πύλας καὶ ὑπεδέχετο μετ'
174 ἀταξίας ἐστρέχοντας. οἱ δὲ Ῥωμαῖοι ταῦτα συνιδόν-
τες, καὶ παρακαλέσαντες τότε μάλιστα ἀλλήλους,
δρόμῳ τοῖς φεύγουσι συνεσέπιπτον ἐς τὸ στρατόπεδον, καὶ τὴν νίκην ἐς τέλος ἐξειργάσαντο.

45. Ἀρχέλαος δὲ καὶ ὅσοι ἄλλοι κατὰ μέρος ἐξέφυ-
γον, ἐς Χαλκίδα συνελέγοντο, οὐ πολὺ πλείους μυρίων ἐκ δώδεκα μυριάδων γενόμενοι. Ῥωμαίων δὲ
ἔδοξαν μὲν ἀποθανεῖν πεντεκαίδεκα ἄνδρες, δύο δ'
175 αὐτῶν ἐπανῆλθον. τοῦτο μὲν δὴ Σύλλᾳ καὶ Ἀρχελάῳ
τῷ Μιθριδάτου στρατηγῷ τῆς περὶ Χαιρώνειαν μάχης τέλος ἦν, δι' εὐβουλίαν δὴ μάλιστα Σύλλα καὶ
δι' ἀφροσύνην Ἀρχελάου τοιόνδε ἑκατέρῳ γενόμενον.
176 Σύλλας δὲ πολλῶν μὲν αἰχμαλώτων πολλῶν δ' ὅπλων
καὶ λείας κρατῶν, τὰ μὲν ἀχρεῖα σωρευθέντα, διαζω-
σάμενος ὡς ἔθος ἐστὶ Ῥωμαίοις, αὐτὸς ἐνέπρησε τοῖς
ἐνναλίοις θεοῖς, ἀναπαύσας δὲ τὴν στρατιὰν ἐπ' ὀλίγον, ἐς τὸν Εὔριπον σὺν εὐζώνοις ἐπὶ τὸν Ἀρχέλαον

to fight, as it had become more constricted than ever for
them because of the enemy's pursuit. And so they were   172
killed without a struggle, some at the hands of the enemy,
against whom they had no time to take countermeasures,
while others were killed by their own side in the confusion
caused by the crowd and the confined space. Again they   173
fled to the gates, and milled around them denouncing
those who were keeping them out. They reproached them
with their ancestral gods and other kindred connections,
complaining that they were dying more because of their
indifference toward them than at the hands of the enemy.
In the end, Archelaus reluctantly opened the gates for
them, later than he should have, and received them as they
ran in chaotically. When the Romans saw this, now more   174
than ever they urged each other on and poured into the
camp, charging alongside the fugitives, and made their
victory complete.

45. Archelaus and any others who had escaped in
groups gathered at Chalcis, not more than ten thousand
men of the original one hundred and twenty thousand. On
the Roman side it was estimated that fifteen died, although two of these turned up later. This was how the   175
battle at Chaeronea between Sulla and Mithridates' general, Archelaus, turned out, Sulla's sound judgment in
particular and Archelaus' imprudence contributing to
such a momentous result for each. Sulla captured a great   176
many prisoners and weapons, and a large quantity of
booty. What could not be used he piled up, and after ar-
ranging his tunic in the Roman manner, personally burned
the booty as a sacrifice to the gods of war. He gave the
army a short rest, and then hurried to the Euripus against
Archelaus with some light-armed troops. But the Romans

ἠπείγετο. Ῥωμαίων δὲ ναῦς οὐκ ἐχόντων, ἀδεῶς τὰς
νήσους περιέπλει τὰ παράλια πορθῶν. Ζακύνθῳ δ'
ἐκβὰς παρεστρατοπέδευσεν. καὶ τινῶν Ῥωμαίων, οἳ
ἐπεδήμουν, νυκτὸς ἐπιθεμένων αὐτῷ, κατὰ τάχος
ἐσβὰς αὖθις ἀνήγετο ἐς Χαλκίδα, λῃστεύοντι μᾶλλον
ἢ πολεμοῦντι ἐοικώς.

177   46. Μιθριδάτης δ' ἐπεὶ τοσῆσδε ἥττης ἐπύθετο,
κατεπλάγη μὲν αὐτίκα καὶ ἔδεισεν ὡς ἐπὶ ἔργῳ τοσ-
ούτῳ, στρατιὰν δ' ὅμως ἄλλην ἀπὸ τῶν ὑπ' αὐτὸν
ἐθνῶν ἁπάντων κατὰ σπουδὴν συνέλεγεν. νομίσας δ'
ἄν τινας αὐτῷ διὰ τὴν ἧτταν ἢ νῦν, ἢ εἴ τινα καιρὸν
ἄλλον εὕροιεν, ἐπιθήσεσθαι, τοὺς ὑπόπτους οἱ πάντας
178   πρὶν ὀξύτερον γενέσθαι τὸν πόλεμον, ἀνελέγετο. καὶ
πρῶτα μὲν τοὺς Γαλατῶν τετράρχας, ὅσοι τε αὐτῷ
συνῆσαν ὡς φίλοι καὶ ὅσοι μὴ κατήκουον αὐτοῦ,
πάντας ἔκτεινε μετὰ παίδων καὶ γυναικῶν χωρὶς
τριῶν τῶν διαφυγόντων, τοῖς μὲν ἐνέδρας ἐπιπέμψας,
τοὺς δ' ἐπὶ διαίτῃ μιᾶς νυκτός, οὐχ ἡγούμενος αὐτῶν
οὐδένα οἱ βέβαιον, εἰ πλησιάσει Σύλλας, ἔσεσθαι.
179   σφετερισάμενος δ' αὐτῶν τὰς περιουσίας, φρουρὰς
ἐσῆγεν ἐς τὰς πόλεις, καὶ σατράπην ἐς τὸ ἔθνος
Εὔμαχον ἔπεμπεν· ὃν αὐτίκα τῶν τετραρχῶν οἱ δια-
φυγόντες, στρατιὰν ἀγείραντες ἀπὸ τῶν ἀγρῶν, ἐξ-
έβαλον αὐταῖς φρουραῖς διώκοντες ἐκ Γαλατίας. καὶ
Μιθριδάτῃ περιῆν Γαλατῶν ἔχειν τὰ χρήματα μόνα.
180   Χίοις δὲ μηνίων ἐξ οὗ τις αὐτῶν ναῦς ἐς τὴν βασιλικὴν ἐν τῇ περὶ Ῥόδον ναυμαχίᾳ λαθοῦσα ἐνέβαλε,
πρῶτα μὲν ἐδήμευσε τὰ ὄντα Χίοις τοῖς ἐς Σύλλαν

had no ships, and Archelaus sailed around the islands with impunity, ravaging the coastal areas. He landed at Zacynthus and camped outside the town, but was attacked at night by some Romans who lived there, and hastily reembarking, set sail for Chalcis, more like a pirate than a warrior.

46. When Mithridates learned of this disastrous defeat, 177 although he was initially dazed and frightened, as was natural after such a momentous battle, nevertheless he quickly enlisted another army from all his subject peoples. Believing that some people would use his defeat to plot against him, either now or when they found another opportunity, he rounded up all suspects before the war became even more critical. First, with the exception of three 178 who escaped, he put to death all the Galatian tetrarchs, both those who attended him as courtiers and the ones not subject to him, along with their wives and children. He sent men to ambush some of them, others he murdered on a single night at a banquet, believing that none of them would remain loyal to him if Sulla came into the area. He confiscated their property, stationed garrisons in the 179 towns, and sent Eumachus to be satrap of the Galatian people. The tetrarchs who had escaped, however, soon raised an army from the countryside and expelled him and the garrisons, and chased them out of Galatia. So all that was left to Mithridates of Galatia was its money. With the 180 people of Chios he had been angry since the time that one of their ships had unintentionally run against his royal flagship during the sea battle at Rhodes. Now, he first confiscated the belongings of those Chians who had fled to

φυγοῦσιν, ἑξῆς δ' ἔπεμπε τοὺς τὰ Ῥωμαίων ἐρευνη-
181 σομένους ἐν Χίῳ. καὶ τρίτον Ζηνόβιος στρατιὰν ἄγων
ὡς ἐς τὴν Ἑλλάδα διαβαλών, τὰ τείχη τῶν Χίων, καὶ
ὅσα ἄλλα ἐρυμνὰ χωρία, τῆς νυκτὸς κατέλαβε, καὶ
ταῖς πύλαις φρουρὰν ἐπιστήσας ἐκήρυσσε τοὺς μὲν
ξένους ἀτρεμεῖν, Χίους δὲ ἐς ἐκκλησίαν συνελθεῖν, ὡς
182 διαλεξόμενος αὐτοῖς τι παρὰ τοῦ βασιλέως. ἐπεὶ δὲ
συνῆλθον, ἔλεξεν ὅτι "Βασιλεὺς ὕποπτον ἔχει τὴν
πόλιν διὰ τοὺς ῥωμαΐζοντας, παύσεται δὲ ἐὰν τά τε
ὅπλα παραδῶτε καὶ ὅμηρα τῶν παίδων τοὺς ἀρίστους." οἱ μὲν δὴ κατειλημμένην σφῶν τὴν πόλιν
ὁρῶντες ἔδοσαν ἄμφω, καὶ Ζηνόβιος αὐτὰ ἐς Ἐρυ-
θρὰς ἐξέπεμψεν ὡς αὐτίκα τοῖς Χίοις γράψοντος τοῦ
βασιλέως.

183   47. Ἐπιστολὴ δὲ ἧκε Μιθριδάτου τάδε λέγουσα·
"Εὖνοι καὶ νῦν ἐστε Ῥωμαίοις, ὧν ἔτι πολλοὶ παρ'
ἐκείνοις εἰσί, καὶ τὰ ἐγκτήματα Ῥωμαίων καρποῦσθε,
ἡμῖν οὐκ ἀναφέροντες. ἔς τε τὴν ἐμὴν ναῦν ἐν τῇ περὶ
Ῥόδον ναυμαχίᾳ τριήρης ὑμετέρα ἐνέβαλέ τε καὶ
κατέσεισεν. ὃ δ' ἐγὼ περιέφερον ἑκὼν ἐς μόνους τοὺς
κυβερνήτας, εἰ δυνήσεσθε σώζεσθαι καὶ ἀγαπᾶν.
184 λανθάνοντες δὲ καὶ νῦν τοὺς ἀρίστους ὑμῶν ἐς Σύλλαν διεπέμψατε, καὶ οὐδένα αὐτῶν ὡς οὐκ ἀπὸ τοῦ
κοινοῦ ταῦτα πράττοντα ἐνεδείξατε οὐδ' ἐμηνύσατε, ὃ
τῶν οὐ συμπεπραχότων ἔργον ἦν. τοὺς οὖν ἐπιβου-
λεύοντας μὲν τῇ ἐμῇ ἀρχῇ, ἐπιβουλεύσαντας δὲ καὶ
τῷ σώματι, οἱ μὲν ἐμοὶ φίλοι ἐδικαίουν ἀποθανεῖν,

Sulla; he then sent a mission to investigate the extent of
Roman property on Chios; and thirdly, Zenobius, who was 181
leading an army with the intention of taking it across to
Greece, seized the walls of Chios and all other fortified
places at night, stationed guards at the gates, and issued a
proclamation that resident aliens should stay at home,
while the Chians were to assemble in the public meeting
place so that he could communicate a message to them
from the king. When they had gathered, Zenobius told 182
them, "The king is suspicious of the city because of the
pro-Roman faction in it, but will cease to be suspicious if
you surrender your weapons and give children from the
best families as hostages." Seeing that their city was, of
course, already in his possession, they agreed to both
terms. Zenobius sent the arms and hostages to Erythrae,
and told the Chians that the king would soon write to
them.

47. And a letter did arrive from the king, which said the 183
following. "Even now, you are well disposed to the Romans, many of your citizens still live with them, and you
harvest the estates of the Romans without paying us anything. A trireme of yours ran against my ship and shook it
in the sea battle at Rhodes. For my own part I was happy
to attribute this just to the steersmen, as long as you were
capable of preserving your own safety and were content
with that. But even now you have secretly sent your lead- 184
ing men off to Sulla, and you have given no evidence or
statement that any of them are working without the authority of the state, which you should have done if you are
not cooperating with them. My courtiers were of the opinion that anyone plotting against my rule, or anyone who
has plotted against my person, should be executed, but

185 ἐγὼ δ' ὑμῖν τιμῶμαι δισχιλίων ταλάντων." τοσαῦτα
μὲν ἡ ἐπιστολὴ περιεῖχεν, οἱ δ' ἐβούλοντο μὲν ἐς
αὐτὸν πρεσβεῦσαι, Ζηνοβίου δὲ κατακωλύοντος,
ὅπλων τε ἀφῃρημένοι, καὶ παίδων σφίσι τῶν ἀρίστων
ἐχομένων, στρατιᾶς τε βαρβαρικῆς τοσαύτης ἐφεστώ-
σης, οἰμώζοντες ἔκ τε ἱερῶν κόσμους καὶ τὰ τῶν
γυναικῶν πάντα ἐς τὸ πλήρωμα τῶν δισχιλίων ταλάν-
186 των συνέφερον. ὡς δὲ καὶ ταῦτ' ἐπεπλήρωτο, αἰτιασά-
μενος τὸν σταθμὸν ἐνδεῖν ὁ Ζηνόβιος ἐς τὸ θέατρον
αὐτοὺς συνεκάλει, καὶ τὴν στρατιὰν περιστήσας μετὰ
γυμνῶν ξιφῶν ἀμφί τε τὸ θέατρον αὐτὸ καὶ τὰς ἀπ'
αὐτοῦ μέχρι τῆς θαλάσσης ὁδοὺς ἦγε τοὺς Χίους,
ἀνιστὰς ἕκαστον ἐκ τοῦ θεάτρου, καὶ ἐνετίθετο ἐς τὰς
ναῦς, ἑτέρωθι μὲν τοὺς ἄνδρας, ἑτέρωθι δ' αὐτῶν τὰ
γύναια καὶ τὰ παιδία, βαρβαρικῶς ὑπὸ τῶν ἀγόντων
ὑρβιζόμενα. ἀνάσπαστοι δ' ἐντεῦθεν ἐς Μιθριδάτην
γενόμενοι διεπέμφθησαν ἐς τὸν Πόντον τὸν Εὔξεινον.
187   48. Καὶ Χίοι μὲν ὧδε ἐπεπράγεσαν, Ζηνόβιον δὲ
Ἐφέσιοι μετὰ στρατιωτῶν προσιόντα ἐκέλευον ἐξ-
οπλίσασθαί τε παρὰ ταῖς πύλαις καὶ σὺν ὀλίγοις
ἐσελθεῖν. ὁ δ' ὑπέστη μὲν ταῦτα, καὶ ἐσῆλθε πρὸς
Φιλοποίμενα τὸν πατέρα Μονίμης τῆς ἐρωμένης Μιθριδάτου, ἐπίσκοπον Ἐφεσίων ἐκ Μιθριδάτου καθε-
στηκότα, καὶ συνελθεῖν οἱ τοὺς Ἐφεσίους ἐς ἐκκλη-
188 σίαν ἐκήρυττεν. οἱ δὲ οὐδὲν χρηστὸν ἔσεσθαι παρ'
αὐτοῦ προσδοκῶντες ἐς τὴν ἐπιοῦσαν ἀνέθεντο, καὶ
νυκτὸς ἀλλήλους ἀγείραντές τε καὶ παρακαλέσαντες,
Ζηνόβιον μὲν ἐς τὸ δεσμωτήριον ἐμβαλόντες ἔκτει-

instead I fine you two thousand talents." Such was the 185
drastic content of the letter. The Chians wanted to send
an embassy to the king, but Zenobius would not let them.
Seeing that they had been deprived of their weapons, the
children of their leading families were being held as hostages, and a large army of barbarians was threatening
them, they sorrowfully collected temple ornaments and all
the precious belongings of the women, to put together the
full sum of two thousand talents. But when the total had 186
been reached in full, Zenobius accused them of giving
short weight, and he summoned them to the theater. He
then stationed soldiers with drawn swords around the
theater itself and along the streets leading from it down
to the sea, and taking each one individually out of the
theater, he brought the Chians down to the ships, and
loaded them on, the men separately from the women and
children, who were treated in a barbarically degrading
manner by their escort. From here they were dragged off
to Mithridates, and then deported into the Euxine Sea.

48. This was how the Chians had fared. When Zenobius 187
approached Ephesus with his army, however, the Ephesians instructed him to leave his weapons at the gates and
enter with just a few men. He agreed to this, and went to
the house of Philopoemen, who was the father of Mithridates' favorite, Monime, and had been appointed overseer
of Ephesus by Mithridates. Zenobius then issued a proclamation that the Ephesians should gather in the public
meeting place. They did not expect anything good from 188
him, and postponed the meeting until the following day.
During the night, after inciting and encouraging each
other, they threw Zenobius into prison and killed him.

ναν, καὶ τὰ τείχη κατεῖχον, καὶ τὸ πλῆθος συνελόχι-
ζον, καὶ τὰ ἐκ τῶν ἀγρῶν συνέλεγον, καὶ τὴν πόλιν
189 ὅλως διὰ χειρὸς εἶχον. ὧν πυνθανόμενοι Τραλλιανοὶ
καὶ Ὑπαιπηνοὶ καὶ Μεσοπολῖται καί τινες ἄλλοι,
τὰ Χίων πάθη δεδιότες, ὅμοια τοῖς Ἐφεσίοις ἔδρων.
Μιθριδάτης δ' ἐπὶ μὲν τὰ ἀφεστηκότα στρατιὰν ἐξ-
έπεμπε, καὶ πολλὰ καὶ δεινὰ τοὺς λαμβανομένους
190 ἔδρα, δείσας δὲ περὶ τοῖς λοιποῖς τὰς πόλεις τὰς Ἑλ-
ληνίδας ἠλευθέρου, καὶ χρεῶν ἀποκοπὰς αὐτοῖς ἐκήρυσσε, καὶ τοὺς ἐν ἑκάστῃ μετοίκους πολίτας αὐτῶν
ἐποίει καὶ τοὺς θεράποντας ἐλευθέρους, ἐλπίσας, ὅπερ
δὴ καὶ συνηνέχθη, τοὺς κατάχρεως καὶ μετοίκους καὶ
θεράποντας, ἡγουμένους ἐν τῇ Μιθριδάτου ἀρχῇ βεβαίως τὰ δοθέντα αὐτοῖς ἕξειν, εὔνους αὐτῷ γενήσε-
191 σθαι. Μυννίων δὲ καὶ Φιλότιμος οἱ Σμυρναῖοι καὶ
Κλεισθένης καὶ Ἀσκληπιόδοτος οἱ Λέσβιοι, βασιλεῖ
γνώριμοι πάντες, ὁ δὲ Ἀσκληπιόδοτος αὐτῷ καὶ ξενα-
γήσας ποτέ, ἐπιβουλὴν ἐπὶ τὸν Μιθριδάτην συνετίθε-
σαν· ἧς αὐτὸς ὁ Ἀσκληπιόδοτος μηνυτὴς ἐγένετο, καὶ
ἐς πίστιν ὑπὸ κλίνῃ τινὶ παρεσκεύασεν ἀκοῦσαι τοῦ
192 Μυννίωνος. ἁλούσης δὲ τῆς ἐπιβουλῆς οἱ μὲν αἰκι-
σθέντες ἐκολάσθησαν, ὑποψίᾳ δ' ἐς τὰ ὅμοια πολλοὺς
κατεῖχεν. ὡς δὲ καὶ Περγαμηνῶν τὰ αὐτὰ βουλεύ-
οντες ὀγδοήκοντα ἄνδρες ἑάλωσαν, καὶ ἐν ἄλλαις
πόλεσιν ἕτεροι, ζητητὰς ὁ Μιθριδάτης πανταχοῦ
περιέπεμπεν, οἳ, τοὺς ἐχθροὺς ἐνδεικνύντων ἑκάστων,
ἔκτειναν ἀμφὶ τοὺς χιλίους καὶ ἑξακοσίους ἄνδρας.
193 ὧν οἱ κατηγορήσαντες οὐ πολὺ ὕστερον οἱ μὲν ὑπὸ

They then manned the walls, divided the population into companies, collected supplies from the fields, and kept complete control of the city. When Tralles and Hypaepa 189 and Mesopolis and some other towns learned of this, they followed the example of the Ephesians, fearing the fate of Chios. Mithridates sent an army against the insurgents, and did many terrible things to those he captured, but as 190 he was afraid about the loyalty of the rest, he gave freedom to the Greek towns, announced a cancellation of debts for them, gave citizenship to the resident aliens in each city, and freed the slaves. He did this in the hope, and it proved correct, that debtors, resident aliens, and slaves would believe that their best hope of retaining secure possession of these gifts lay in the rule of Mithridates, and that they would, therefore, be loyal to him. But a conspiracy was 191 formed against Mithridates by Mynnio and Philotimus from Smyrna, and Cleisthenes and Asclepiodotus from Lesbos, all of whom were acquaintances of the king, and Asclepiodotus had even once recruited mercenaries for him. It was Asclepiodotus himself who now gave information against the conspiracy, and to provide proof, he arranged for Mithridates to be hidden behind a couch so that he could hear what Mynnio said. With the uncovering 192 of the plot, the conspirators were tortured and killed, but the king was suspicious that there were many others similarly disposed. When eighty men from Pergamum were also caught making the same plans, and others in other towns, Mithridates sent spies everywhere, who, when everyone informed against their personal enemies, killed about one thousand six hundred people. Not long after, 193 some of the informers were captured and executed by

237

Σύλλα ληφθέντες διεφθάρησαν, οἱ δὲ προανεῖλον ἑαυ-
τούς, οἱ δ' ἐς τὸν Πόντον αὐτῷ Μιθριδάτῃ συνέφευ-
γον.

194   49. Γιγνομένων δὲ τῶνδε περὶ τὴν Ἀσίαν, ὀκτὼ
μυριάδων στρατὸς ἤθροιστο τῷ Μιθριδάτῃ, καὶ αὐτὸν
Δορύλαος πρὸς Ἀρχέλαον ἦγεν ἐς τὴν Ἑλλάδα,
ἔχοντα τῶν προτέρων ἔτι μυρίους. ὁ δὲ Σύλλας ἀντ-
εστρατοπέδευε μὲν Ἀρχελάῳ περὶ Ὀρχομενόν, ὡς δὲ
εἶδε τῆς ἐπελθούσης ἵππου τὸ πλῆθος, ὤρυσσε τά-
φρους πολλὰς ἀνὰ τὸ πεδίον, εὖρος δέκα πόδας, καὶ
195   ἐπιόντος αὐτῷ τοῦ Ἀρχελάου ἀντιπαρέταξεν. ἀσθενῶς
δὲ τῶν Ῥωμαίων διὰ δέος τῆς ἵππου μαχομένων, ἐς
πολὺ μὲν αὐτοὺς παριππεύων παρεκάλει καὶ ἐπ-
έσπερχε σὺν ἀπειλῇ, οὐκ ἐπιστρέφων δ' αὐτοὺς ἐς τὸ
ἔργον οὐδ' ὥς, ἐξήλατο τοῦ ἵππου, καὶ σημεῖον ἁρπά-
σας ἀνὰ τὸ μεταίχμιον ἔθει μετὰ τῶν ὑπασπιστῶν,
κεκραγώς· "Εἴ τις ὑμῶν, ὦ Ῥωμαῖοι, πύθοιτο, ποῦ
Σύλλαν τὸν στρατηγὸν ὑμῶν αὐτῶν προυδώκατε, λέ-
196   γειν, ἐν Ὀρχομενῷ μαχόμενον." οἱ δ' ἡγεμόνες αὐτῷ
κινδυνεύοντι συνεξέθεον ἐκ τῶν ἰδίων τάξεων, συνεξέθεον δὲ καὶ ἡ ἄλλη πληθὺς αἰδουμένη, παλίωξίν τε
εἰργάσαντο. καὶ τῆς νίκης ἀρχομένης, ἀναθορὼν
αὖθις ἐπὶ τὸν ἵππον ἐπῄνει τὸν στρατὸν περιιὼν καὶ
ἐπέσπερχεν, ἕως τέλεον αὐτοῖς τὸ ἔργον ἐξετελέσθη.
197   καὶ τῶν πολεμίων ἀπώλοντο μὲν ἀμφὶ τοὺς μυρίους
καὶ πεντακισχιλίους, καὶ τούτων ἦσαν οἱ μύριοι ἱππεῖς μάλιστα, καὶ σὺν αὐτοῖς ὁ παῖς Ἀρχελάου Διο-
γένης· οἱ πεζοὶ δ' ἐς τὸ στρατόπεδον συνέφυγον.

Sulla, others took their own lives first, and yet others fled to the Pontus and found refuge with Mithridates himself.

49. While this was happening in Asia, Mithridates collected another army of eighty thousand men, which Dorylaus brought over to Archelaus in Greece. Archelaus still had ten thousand troops left from his former army. Sulla pitched camp opposite him near Orchomenus, but when he saw the size of Archelaus' cavalry force as it advanced, he dug a large number of ditches in the plain ten feet wide, and arrayed his forces to meet Archelaus' attack. The Romans put up a weak fight out of fear of the enemy cavalry, even though Sulla rode along their lines for a long time, urging them on and pressing them with threats. But even this failed to bring them back into the battle, and so he jumped down from his horse, grabbed hold of a standard, and ran out into the middle of the battle field with his bodyguard, shouting, "If anyone ever asks you, men of Rome, where you betrayed your own general, Sulla, say that it was when he was fighting at Orchomenus." With Sulla in danger, the officers ran forward from their lines to help him and, driven by a sense of shame, the rank and file followed and succeeded in driving the enemy back. This started the victory, and leaping back on his horse, Sulla roused and cheered the troops on until they had brought the battle to a successful close. About fifteen thousand of the enemy died, some ten thousand of them cavalrymen, including Diogenes, the son of Archelaus. The infantry escaped to the camp.

194

195

196

197

198   50. Καὶ δείσας ὁ Σύλλας μὴ πάλιν αὐτὸν ὁ Ἀρχέλαος, οὐκ ἔχοντα ναῦς, ἐς Χαλκίδα ὡς πρότερον
διαφύγοι, τὸ πεδίον ὅλον ἐκ διαστηματων ἐνυκτοφυ-
λάκει. καὶ μεθ᾽ ἡμέραν, στάδιον οὐχ ὅλον ἀποσχὼν
τοῦ Ἀρχελάου, τάφρον αὐτῷ περιώρυσσεν οὐκ ἐπεξι-
199 όντι. καὶ παρεκάλει τότε μάλιστα τὴν ἑαυτοῦ στρατιὰν ἐκπονῆσαι τοῦ παντὸς πολέμου τὸ ἔτι λείψανον
ὡς τῶν πολεμίων αὐτὸν οὐδ᾽ ὑφισταμένων, καὶ ἐπῆγεν
αὐτὴν ἐπὶ τὸ χαράκωμα τοῦ Ἀρχελάου. ὅμοια δ᾽ ἐκ
μεταβολῆς ἐγίγνετο καὶ παρὰ τοῖς πολεμίοις ὑπ᾽
ἀνάγκης, τῶν ἡγεμόνων αὐτοὺς περιθεόντων, καὶ τὸν
παρόντα κίνδυνον προφερόντων τε, καὶ ὀνειδιζόντων
εἰ μηδ᾽ ἀπὸ χάρακος ἀπομαχοῦνται τοὺς ἐχθροὺς ὀλι-
200 γωτέρους ὄντας. ὁρμῆς δὲ καὶ βοῆς ἑκατέρωθεν γενομένης, πολλὰ μὲν ἐγίγνετο ἐπ᾽ ἀμφοῖν ἔργα πολέμου,
γωνίαν δέ τινα τοῦ χαρακώματος οἱ Ῥωμαῖοι, τὰς
ἀσπίδας σφῶν ὑπερσχόντες, ἤδη διέσπων, καὶ οἱ
βάρβαροι καταθορόντες ἀπὸ τοῦ χαρακώματος ἔσω
τῆς γωνίας περιέστησαν αὐτὴν ὡς τοῖς ξίφεσιν ἀμυ-
201 νούμενοι τοὺς ἐστρέχοντας. οὐδέ τις ἐτόλμα, μέχρι
Βάσιλλος ὁ τοῦ τέλους ταξίαρχος ἐσήλατο πρῶτος
καὶ τὸν ὑπαντήσαντα ἔκτεινεν. τότε δ᾽ αὐτῷ συνεισέ-
πιπτεν ὁ στρατὸς ἅπας, καὶ φυγὴ τῶν βαρβάρων
ἐγίγνετο καὶ φόνος, τῶν μὲν καταλαμβανομένων, τῶν
δ᾽ ἐς τὴν ἐγγὺς λίμνην ὠθουμένων τε καὶ νεῖν οὐκ
ἐπισταμένων, ἀξύνετα βαρβαριστὶ τοὺς κτενοῦντας
202 παρακαλούντων. Ἀρχέλαος δ᾽ ἐν ἕλει τινὶ ἐκρύφθη,
καὶ σκάφους ἐπιτυχὼν ἐς Χαλκίδα διέπλευσεν. καὶ εἴ

240

50. Without ships, Sulla was afraid that Archelaus 198
would again evade him and escape to Chalcis, as before.
So he stationed night watchmen at intervals over the
whole plain, and at daybreak, keeping not even a whole
stade away from Archelaus, he dug a ditch around his
position. Archelaus did not come out. Sulla now more than 199
ever exhorted his men to complete the last remaining task
of the whole war, as the enemy were not even resisting,
and he led them against the palisade of Archelaus. Similar
things were also happening among the enemy, over whom
a change had come out of necessity. Their officers moved
around the soldiers, emphasizing the danger they faced,
and rebuking them if they could not even manage to fight
off inferior numbers of the enemy from a palisade. There 200
was impetus and shouting from both sides, and both
armies carried out many brave deeds in the fighting. With
shields held above their heads the Romans were already
beginning to tear down one corner of the palisade, when
the barbarians jumped down from the parapet into that
corner, and stood guard around it with their swords drawn
to fight off anyone trying to rush in. No one dared to, 201
until the legion's military tribune Basillus was the first to
leap forward and kill the man facing him. It was then that
the whole army rushed in behind him, and there followed
a rout and slaughter of the barbarians. Some were over-
taken by their pursuers, others were pushed into the
nearby lake, and not knowing how to swim, begged their
killers for mercy in a foreign tongue they did not understand. Archelaus hid in a marsh, found a boat, and made 202
his way by sea to Chalcis, where he issued an urgent sum-

τις ἦν ἄλλη Μιθριδάτου στρατιὰ κατὰ μέρος ποι δια-
τεταγμένη, πάντας αὐτοὺς ἐκάλει κατὰ σπουδήν.

203   51. Ὁ δὲ Σύλλας τῆς ἐπιούσης τόν τε ταξίαρχον
ἐστεφάνου καὶ τοῖς ἄλλοις ἀριστεῖα ἐδίδου. καὶ τὴν
Βοιωτίαν συνεχῶς μετατιθεμένην διήρπαζε, καὶ ἐς
Θεσσαλίαν ἐλθὼν ἐχείμαζε, τὰς ναῦς τὰς μετὰ Λου-
204 κούλλου περιμένων. ἀγνοῶν δ᾽ ὅπη ὁ Λεύκολλος εἴη,
ἐναυπηγεῖτο ἑτέρας, καὶ ταῦτα μέντοι Κορνηλίου τε
Κίννα καὶ Γαΐου Μαρίου, τῶν ἐχθρῶν αὐτὸν ἐν Ῥώμῃ
ψηφισμένων εἶναι Ῥωμαίων πολέμιον, καὶ τὴν οἰκίαν
αὐτοῦ καὶ τὰς ἐπαύλεις καθῃρηκότων, καὶ τοὺς φίλους
ἀνελόντων. ὁ δὲ οὐδὲν οὐδ᾽ ὡς καθῄρει τῆς ἐξουσίας,
205 τὸν στρατὸν ἔχων εὐπειθῆ καὶ πρόθυμον. Κίννας δὲ
Φλάκκον ἑλόμενός οἱ συνάρχειν τὴν ὕπατον ἀρχήν,
ἔπεμπεν ἐς τὴν Ἀσίαν μετὰ δύο τελῶν, ἀντὶ τοῦ
Σύλλα, ὡς ἤδη πολεμίου γεγονότος, τῆς τε Ἀσίας
ἄρχειν καὶ πολεμεῖν τῷ Μιθριδάτῃ. ἀπειροπολέμῳ δ᾽
ὄντι τῷ Φλάκκῳ συνεξῆλθεν ἑκὼν ἀπὸ τῆς βουλῆς
206 ἀνὴρ πιθανὸς ἐς στρατηγίαν, ὄνομα Φιμβρίας. τούτοις ἐκ Βρεντεσίου διαπλέουσιν αἱ πολλαὶ τῶν νεῶν
ὑπὸ χειμῶνος διελύθησαν, καὶ τὰς πρόπλους αὐτῶν
ἐνέπρησε στρατὸς ἄλλος ἐπιπεμφθεὶς ἐκ Μιθριδάτου.
μοχθηρὸν δ᾽ ὄντα τὸν Φλάκκον καὶ σκαιὸν ἐν ταῖς
κολάσεσι καὶ φιλοκερδῆ ὁ στρατὸς ἅπας ἀπεστρέ-

---

35 L. Cornelius Cinna (consul 87–84) shared the consulship of
85 with the famous C. Marius (consul 107, 104–100, 85). When

mons for all remaining detachments of Mithridatic forces, wherever they were stationed.

51. The next day Sulla conferred a garland on the military tribune, and presented others with the prizes awarded for valor. He then pillaged Boeotia for continually changing sides, and went into winter quarters in Thessaly, where he waited for the fleet Lucullus was bringing. As he did not know where Lucullus was, he began to build new ships, in spite of the fact that his political opponents in Rome, Cornelius Cinna and Gaius Marius, had had him voted a public enemy of the Roman people, and had destroyed his house and his country villas, and had executed his associates.[35] Even so, he did not give up any of his power, as he still enjoyed the obedience and loyalty of his army. Cinna chose Flaccus to join him in holding the consulship, and sent him to Asia with two legions, to replace Sulla, who had already been declared a public enemy, both as governor of Asia and as commander in chief of the war against Mithridates. Flaccus, however, had limited military experience, and a senator by the name of Fimbria, whose credentials in command were plausible, volunteered to accompany him.[36] When Flaccus and Fimbria set sail from Brundisium, most of their fleet was scattered by a storm, and another army dispatched by Mithridates set fire to the advance flotilla. Flaccus was a bad man, avaricious and with poor judgment in dispensing punishments, and the whole army turned its back on him. One

203

204

205

206

Marius died, on January 13, he was replaced as suffect consul by L. Valerius Flaccus.

[36] C. Flavius Fimbria is known only from the events in Asia of 86 and 85.

φετο, καὶ μέρος αὐτῶν τι, προπεμφθὲν ἐς Θεσσαλίαν,
207 ἐς τὸν Σύλλαν μετεστρατεύσαντο. τοὺς δὲ ὑπολοίπους
ὁ Φιμβρίας, στρατηγικώτερος τοῦ Φλάκκου φαινόμε-
νος αὐτοῖς καὶ φιλανθρωπότερος κατεῖχε μὴ μεταθέ-
σθαι.

52. Ὡς δ᾽ ἔν τινι καταγωγῇ περὶ ξενίας ἔριδος αὐτῷ
καὶ τῷ ταμίᾳ γενομένης ὁ Φλάκκος διαιτῶν οὐδὲν ἐς
τιμὴν ἐπεσήμηνε τοῦ Φιμβρίου, χαλεπήνας ὁ Φιμ-
208 βρίας ἠπείλησεν ἐς Ῥώμην ἐπανελεύσεσθαι. καὶ τοῦ
Φλάκκου δόντος αὐτῷ διάδοχον ἐς ἃ τότε διῴκει, φυλάξας αὐτὸν ὁ Φιμβρίας ἐς Χαλκηδόνα διαπλέοντα,
πρῶτα μὲν Θέρμον τὰς ῥάβδους ἀφείλετο, τὸν ἀντι-
στράτηγον ὑπὸ τοῦ Φλάκκου καταλελειμμένον, ὡς οἱ
τοῦ στρατοῦ τὴν στρατηγίαν περιθέντος, εἶτα Φλάκκον αὐτὸν σὺν ὀργῇ μετ᾽ ὀλίγον ἐπανιόντα ἐδίωκεν,
209 ἕως ὁ μὲν Φλάκκος ἔς τινα οἰκίαν καταφυγὼν καὶ
νυκτὸς τὸ τεῖχος ὑπερελθὼν ἐς Χαλκηδόνα πρῶτον
καὶ ἀπ᾽ αὐτῆς ἐς Νικομήδειαν ἔφυγε καὶ τὰς πύλας
ἀπέκλεισεν, ὁ δὲ Φιμβρίας αὐτὸν ἐπελθὼν ἔκτεινεν ἐν
φρέατι κρυπτόμενον, ὕπατόν τε ὄντα Ῥωμαίων καὶ
στρατηγὸν τοῦδε τοῦ πολέμου ἰδιώτης αὐτὸς ὢν καὶ
210 ὡς φίλῳ κελεύοντι συνεληλυθώς. ἐκτεμών τε τὴν κεφαλὴν αὐτοῦ μεθῆκεν ἐς θάλασσαν, καὶ τὸ λοιπὸν
ἄταφον ἐκρίψας, αὑτὸν αὐτοκράτορα ἀπέφηνε τοῦ
στρατοῦ. καὶ μάχας τινὰς οὐκ ἀγεννῶς ἠγωνίσατο τῷ
παιδὶ τῷ Μιθριδάτου αὐτόν τε τὸν βασιλέα συνεδί-
ωξεν ἐς τὸ Πέργαμον, καὶ ἐς Πιτάνην ἐκ τοῦ Περ-

244

contingent that had been sent ahead to Thessaly went over to Sulla, but Fimbria, who appeared to the men as a better general and more humane than Flaccus, prevented the rest from deserting.   207

52. On one occasion in some inn, a dispute arose between Fimbria and the quaestor about their accommodation, and when Flaccus, acting as arbitrator, failed to show Fimbria due respect, the latter was annoyed and threatened to return to Rome. So Flaccus appointed a successor   208 to carry out his current administrative duties, but waiting until Flaccus sailed to Calchedon, Fimbria first took the *fasces* from Thermus, who had been left as propraetor by Flaccus, on the grounds that the army had granted the command to himself. Then when Flaccus himself returned soon afterward in a rage, Fimbria chased him off, until Flaccus took refuge in a house. During the night he   209 climbed over the wall and fled first to Calchedon, and from there to Nicomedea, where he closed the gates. But Fimbria went after him, and killed him while he was hiding in a well, even though he was a Roman consul and commander in chief of the Roman forces in this war, and Fimbria himself was a private person, who had accompanied him as a friend and at his invitation. Fimbria cut   210 Flaccus' head off and threw it in the sea, leaving the rest of the body cast out unburied. He then appointed himself commander in chief of the army, and fought a number of successful battles with Mithridates' son. The king himself he chased to Pergamum, but from there Mithridates es-

γάμου διαφυγόντα ἐπελθὼν ἀπετάφρευεν, ἕως ὁ μὲν
βασιλεὺς ἐπὶ νεῶν ἔφυγεν ἐς Μιτυλήνην.

211   53. Ὁ δὲ Φιμβρίας, ἐπιὼν τὴν Ἀσίαν, ἐκόλαζε τοὺς
καππαδοκίσαντας, καὶ τῶν οὐ δεχομένων αὐτὸν τὴν
χώραν ἐλεηλάτει. Ἰλιεῖς δὲ πολιορκούμενοι πρὸς
αὑτοῦ κατέφυγον μὲν ἐπὶ Σύλλαν, Σύλλα δὲ φήσαν-
τος αὐτοῖς ἥξειν, καὶ κελεύσαντος ἐν τοσῷδε Φιμβρίᾳ
φράζειν ὅτι σφᾶς ἐπιτετρόφασι τῷ Σύλλᾳ, πυθόμενος
ὁ Φιμβρίας ἐπῄνεσε μὲν ὡς ἤδη Ῥωμαίων φίλους,
ἐκέλευσε δὲ καὶ αὐτὸν ὄντα Ῥωμαίων ἔσω δέχεσθαι,
κατειρωνευσάμενός τι καὶ τῆς συγγενείας τῆς οὔσης
212   ἐς Ῥωμαίους Ἰλιεῦσιν. ἐσελθὼν δὲ τοὺς ἐν ποσὶ πάντας ἔκτεινε καὶ πάντα ἐνεπίμπρη, καὶ τοὺς πρεσβεύ-
σαντας ἐς τὸν Σύλλαν ἐλυμαίνετο ποικίλως, οὔτε τῶν
ἱερῶν φειδόμενος οὔτε τῶν ἐς τὸν νεὼν τῆς Ἀθηνᾶς
καταφυγόντων, οὓς αὐτῷ νεῷ κατέπρησεν. κατέσκα-
πτε δὲ καὶ τὰ τείχη, καὶ τῆς ἐπιούσης ἠρεύνα περιιὼν
213   μή τι συνέστηκε τῆς πόλεως ἔτι. ἡ μὲν δὴ χείρονα
τῶν ἐπὶ Ἀγαμέμνονος παθοῦσα ὑπὸ συγγενοῦς διω-
λώλει, καὶ οἰκόπεδον οὐδὲν αὐτῆς οὐδ' ἱερὸν οὐδ'
ἄγαλμα ἔτι ἦν· τὸ δὲ τῆς Ἀθηνᾶς ἕδος, ὃ Παλλάδιον
καλοῦσι καὶ διοπετὲς ἡγοῦνται, νομίζουσί τινες εὑρε-
θῆναι τότε ἄθραυστον, τῶν ἐπιπεσόντων τειχῶν αὐτὸ
περικαλυψάντων, εἰ μὴ Διομήδης αὐτὸ καὶ Ὀδυσσεὺς
214   ἐν τῷ Τρωικῷ ἔργῳ μετήνεγκαν ἐξ Ἰλίου. τάδε μὲν δὴ
Φιμβρίας ἐς Ἴλιον εἰργάζετο, ληγούσης ἄρτι τῆς
τρίτης ⟨καὶ ἑβδομηκοστῆς⟩[13] καὶ ἑκατοστῆς ὀλυμπιά-

caped to Pitane where Fimbria came up and tried to cut
him off with a ditch, until the king fled by ship to Mytilene.

53. Fimbria now traveled around Asia punishing the   211
Cappadocian partisans, and pillaging the territory of any
cities that refused to give him entry. When he besieged
Ilium, its people looked to Sulla for help. He told them he
would come, but instructed them in the meantime to say
to Fimbria that they had put themselves under Sulla's protection. When he heard this, Fimbria congratulated them
for being friends of Rome already, and ordered them to
grant him entry, as he was himself a Roman citizen, adding
an ironical reference to the ties of kinship between Ilium
and Rome. As soon as he got in, he killed everyone he met   212
and burned the whole place. Those who had taken part in
the embassy to Sulla, he tortured in a variety of ways. He
spared neither the temples nor those who had fled for
safety to the temple of Athena, whom he burned alive with
the temple itself. He demolished the walls, and the next
day went around checking that nothing of the city was still
standing. The destruction now by a kinsman was worse   213
than what the city had suffered in the time of Agamemnon, since not a house was left, not a temple, not a statue.
Some believe that the seated statue of Athena called the
Palladium, which is supposed to have fallen from heaven,
was found undamaged on this occasion, the walls protect-
ing it as they fell. An alternative is that Diomedes and
Odysseus took it from Ilium during the Trojan War. Such   214
was Fimbria's treatment of Ilium just as the 173rd (?)

---

13 καὶ ἑβδομηκοστῆς add. Palmer

δος. καί τινες ἡγοῦνται τὸ πάθος αὐτῇ τόδε μετ᾽
Ἀγαμέμνονα χιλίοις καὶ πεντήκοντα ἔτεσι γενέσθαι
μάλιστα.

215   54. Ὁ δὲ Μιθριδάτης ἐπεὶ καὶ τῆς περὶ Ὀρχομενὸν
ἥττης ἐπύθετο, διαλογιζόμενος τὸ πλῆθος ὅσον ἐξ
ἀρχῆς ἐς τὴν Ἑλλάδα ἐπεπόμφει, καὶ τὴν συνεχῆ καὶ
ταχεῖαν αὐτοῦ φθορὰν, ἐπέστελλεν Ἀρχελάῳ διαλύ-
216 σεις ὡς δύναιτο εὐπρεπῶς ἐργάσασθαι. ὁ δὲ Σύλλᾳ
συνελθὼν ἐς λόγους εἶπε· "Φίλος ὢν ὑμῖν πατρῷος, ὦ
Σύλλα, Μιθριδάτης ὁ βασιλεὺς ἐπολέμησε μὲν διὰ
στρατηγῶν ἑτέρων πλεονεξίαν, διαλύσεται δὲ διὰ τὴν
217 σὴν ἀρετήν, ἢν τὰ δίκαια προστάσσῃς." καὶ ὁ Σύλλας ἀπορίᾳ τε νεῶν, καὶ χρήματα οὐκ ἐπιπεμπόντων
οὐδ᾽ ἄλλο οὐδὲν οἴκοθεν αὐτῷ τῶν ἐχθρῶν ὡς πολεμίῳ, ἁψάμενος ἤδη τῶν ἐν Πυθοῖ καὶ Ὀλυμπίᾳ καὶ
Ἐπιδαύρῳ χρημάτων, καὶ ἀντιδοὺς πρὸς λόγον τοῖς
ἱεροῖς τὸ ἥμισυ τῆς Θηβαίων γῆς πολλάκις ἀποστάντων, ἔς τε τὴν στάσιν αὐτὴν τῶν ἐχθρῶν ἐπειγόμενος
ἀκραιφνῆ καὶ ἀπαθῆ τὸν στρατὸν μεταγαγεῖν, ἐνεδί-
218 δου πρὸς τὰς διαλύσεις, καὶ εἶπεν· "Ἀδικουμένου μὲν
ἦν, ὦ Ἀρχέλαε, Μιθριδάτου, περὶ ὧν ἠδικεῖτο πρεσβεύειν, ἀδικοῦντος δὲ γῆν τοσήνδε ἀλλοτρίαν ἐπιδραμεῖν, καὶ κτεῖναι πολὺ πλῆθος ἀνδρῶν, τά τε κοινὰ
καὶ ἱερὰ τῶν πόλεων καὶ τὰ ἴδια τῶν ἀνῃρημένων
σφετερίσασθαι. τῷ δ᾽ αὐτῷ λόγῳ καὶ ἐς τοὺς ἰδίους

---

[37] The manuscripts actually say the 103rd Olympiad, but that

Olympiad was ending.[37] Some estimate that this disaster happened to the town about one thousand and fifty years after Agamemnon.

54. When Mithridates learned of his defeat at Orcho- 215
menus, in consideration of the huge number of men he had sent to Greece right from the beginning and of their repeated and swift defeat, he ordered Archelaus to negotiate a peace on the best terms he could achieve. Entering 216
discussions with Sulla, Archelaus spoke as follows: "Al-
though, Sulla, he was a hereditary friend of you Romans, King Mithridates went to war because of the greed of generals other than you, but now, in deference to your integrity, he will come to terms, if you propose fair conditions." Sulla did not have any ships; his political opponents 217
at Rome refused to send him money or anything else, but treated him as an enemy of the state; he had already laid hands on the treasures of Pytho, Olympia, and Epidaurus, promising the sanctuaries as a proportional return half the territory of Thebes, on account of the latter's frequent defections; and he was in a hurry to lead his army fresh and intact against the hostile faction itself at home. He therefore agreed to peace negotiations, and spoke as follows. "Archelaus, if Mithridates was the aggrieved party, 218
it would have been fitting for him to send an embassy to discuss his grievances. But it was, rather, the act of a man causing the grievances to overrun so much territory that did not belong to him, to kill a large number of people, and to seize for himself both the public and sacred monies of the towns, and the private property of the people he

would put the date in 365 BC. Correcting the text to the 173rd Olympiad gives us the correct date of 85.

φίλους, ᾧ περὶ ἡμᾶς, ἄπιστος γενόμενος, ἔκτεινε καὶ
τῶνδε πολλούς, καὶ τῶν τετραρχῶν οὓς ὁμοδιαίτους
εἶχε, νυκτὸς μιᾶς, μετὰ γυναικῶν καὶ παίδων τῶν οὐ
219 πεπολεμηκότων. ἐπὶ δὲ ἡμῖν καὶ φύσεως ἔχθραν μᾶλλον ἢ πολέμου χρείαν ἐπεδείξατο, παντοίαις ἰδέαις
κακῶν τοὺς περὶ τὴν Ἀσίαν Ἰταλιώτας, σὺν γυναιξὶ
καὶ παισὶ καὶ θεράπουσι τοῖς οὖσι γένους Ἰταλικοῦ,
λυμηνάμενός τε καὶ κτείνας. τοσοῦτον ἐξήνεγκεν ἐς
τὴν Ἰταλίαν μῖσος ὁ νῦν ἡμῖν ὑποκρινόμενος φιλίαν
πατρῴαν, ἧς οὐ πρὶν ἑκκαίδεκα μυριάδας ὑμῶν ὑπ᾽
ἐμοῦ συγκοπῆναι ἐμνημονεύετε.

220   55. Ἀνθ᾽ ὧν δίκαιον μὲν ἦν ἄσπειστα αὐτῷ τὰ παρ᾽
ἡμῶν γενέσθαι, τοῦ δὲ χάριν ὑποδέχομαι συγγνώμης
αὐτὸν τεύξεσθαι παρὰ Ῥωμαίων, ἂν τῷ ὄντι μετα-
γιγνώσκῃ. εἰ δὲ ὑποκρίνοιτο καὶ νῦν, ὥρα σοι τὸ σαυ-
τοῦ σκοπεῖν, ὦ Ἀρχέλαε, ἐνθυμουμένῳ μὲν ὅπως ἔχει
τὰ παρόντα σοί τε κἀκείνῳ, σκοποῦντι δ᾽ ὅν τινα
τρόπον ἐκεῖνός τε ἑτέροις κέχρηται φίλοις καὶ ἡμεῖς
221 Εὐμένει καὶ Μασσανάσσῃ." ὁ δ᾽ ἔτι λέγοντος αὐτοῦ
τὴν πεῖραν ἀπεσείετο, καὶ δυσχεράνας ἔφη τὸν ἐγ-
χειρίσαντά οἱ τὴν στρατηγίαν οὔ ποτε προδώσειν·
"Ἐλπίζω δέ σοι διαλλάξειν, ἢν μέτρια προστάσσῃς."
222 διαλιπὼν οὖν ὁ Σύλλας ὀλίγον, εἶπεν· "Ἐὰν τὸν
στόλον ἡμῖν, ὃν ἔχεις, ὦ Ἀρχέλαε, παραδιδῷ πάντα
Μιθριδάτης, ἀποδῷ δὲ καὶ στρατηγοὺς ἡμῖν ἢ πρέσβεις ἢ αἰχμαλώτους ἢ αὐτομόλους ἢ ἀνδράποδα
ἀποδράντα, καὶ Χίους ἐπὶ τοῖσδε, καὶ ὅσους ἄλλους
ἀνασπάστους ἐς τὸν Πόντον ἐποιήσατο, μεθῇ,

had murdered. He even treated his own friends with the same measure of treachery as he treated us, killing many of them too, including the tetrarchs, on a single evening when he was entertaining them to dinner, along with their wives and children, who had committed no act of war against him. It was an innate animosity he displayed 219 against us rather than anything necessitated by the demands of war, when he inflicted every conceivable misery on the Italians in Asia, torturing and killing them, along with their wives, children and those slaves of Italian blood. Such was the hate he bore against Italy, this man who now pretends he is our ancestral friend, a friendship you made no mention of before one hundred and sixty thousand of your soldiers had been cut to pieces by me.

55. "In response to this behavior, it would be justifiable 220 for us to remain uncompromising toward Mithridates, but for your sake I promise to win pardon for him at Rome, if he is genuinely repentant. But if, even still, he is only pretending, it is time, Archelaus, for you to examine your own position, and take into account your and his relative situations. Observe, for example, how he has treated his other friends, and how we have treated Eumenes and Massinissa." Even while Sulla was still speaking, Archelaus 221 rejected the attempt to turn him, indignantly stating that he would never betray anyone who entrusted him with an army: "But I hope to agree terms with you," he continued, "if your demands are reasonable." Sulla was silent for a 222 time, but then said, "If Mithridates surrenders the entire fleet currently in your possession, Archelaus; if he returns to us all generals, ambassadors, prisoners of war, deserters, and runaway slaves; if, in addition to these, he restores to their homes the Chians and any others he dragged off

223 ἐξαγάγῃ δὲ καὶ τὰς φρουρὰς ἐκ πάντων φρουρίων,
χωρὶς ὧν ἐκράτει πρὸ τῆσδε τῆς παρασπονδήσεως,
ἐσενέγκῃ δὲ καὶ τὴν δαπάνην τοῦδε τοῦ πολέμου τὴν
δι᾽ αὐτὸν γενομένην, καὶ στέργῃ μόνης ἄρχων τῆς
πατρῴας δυναστείας, ἐλπίζω πείσειν Ῥωμαίους αὐτῷ
224 μηδὲν ἐπιμηνῖσαι τῶν γεγονότων." ὁ μὲν δὴ τοσάδε
εἶπεν, ὁ δὲ Ἀρχέλαος τὰς μὲν φρουρὰς αὐτίκα πανταχόθεν ἐξῆγε, περὶ δὲ τῶν ἄλλων ἐπέστελλε τῷ βασιλεῖ. καὶ Σύλλας τὴν ἐν τοσῷδε ἀργίαν διατιθέμενος,
Ἐνετοὺς καὶ Δαρδανέας καὶ Σιντούς, περίοικα Μακεδόνων ἔθνη, συνεχῶς ἐς Μακεδονίαν ἐμβάλλοντα,
ἐπιὼν ἐπόρθει, καὶ τὸν στρατὸν ἐγύμναζε, καὶ ἐχρη-
ματίζετο ὁμοῦ.

225 56. Ἐλθόντων δὲ τῶν Μιθριδάτου πρέσβεων, οἳ
τοῖς μὲν ἄλλοις συνετίθεντο, μόνην δ᾽ ἐξαιρούμενοι
Παφλαγονίαν ἐπεῖπον ὅτι "Πλεόνων ἂν ἔτυχε Μιθριδάτης, εἰ πρὸς τὸν ἕτερον ὑμῶν στρατηγὸν διελύετο
Φιμβρίαν," δυσχεράνας ὁ Σύλλας τῇ παραβολῇ, καὶ
Φιμβρίαν ἔφη δώσειν δίκην, καὶ αὐτὸς ἐν Ἀσίᾳ γενόμενος εἴσεσθαι πότερα συνθηκῶν ἢ πολέμου δεῖται
226 Μιθριδάτης. ὧδε δ᾽ εἰπὼν ἤλαυνεν ἐπὶ Κύψελα διὰ
Θρᾴκης, Λεύκολλον ἐς Ἄβυδον προπέμψας· ἤδη γὰρ
αὐτῷ καὶ ὅδε ἀφῖκτο, κινδυνεύσας μὲν ὑπὸ λῃστῶν
ἁλῶναι πολλάκις, στόλον δέ τινα νεῶν ἀγείρας ἀπό
τε Κύπρου καὶ Φοινίκης καὶ Ῥόδου καὶ Παμφυλίας,
καὶ πολλὰ δῃώσας τῆς πολεμίας, καὶ τῶν Μιθριδάτου
227 νεῶν ἀποπειράσας ἐν παράπλῳ. Σύλλας μὲν οὖν ἀπὸ
Κυψέλλων καὶ Μιθριδάτης ἐκ Περγάμου συνῄεσαν

to the Pontus; if he withdraws the garrisons from all his   223
strongholds, with the exception of those he held before his
breach of the treaty; if he pays for the cost of this war, of
which he was the cause; and if he is content to be ruler
solely of his ancestral principality—then I will hope to
persuade the Romans to drop their anger against him for
what he has done." This is the extent of what Sulla said.   224
Archelaus immediately withdrew his garrisons from all
locations, and referred everything else to the king. Meanwhile, Sulla used the lull to attack and pillage the lands of
the Eneti and Dardanians and Sinti, peoples who lived on
the border of Macedonia and continually launched raids
into it. This kept the army in training and was profitable
at the same time.

56. When Mithridates' envoys arrived, they were in   225
agreement on everything except Paphlagonia, but added,
"Mithridates would have gotten better terms if he had
negotiated with your other general, Fimbria." Sulla was
annoyed by the comparison, and said that Fimbria would
be punished, and that he himself would go to Asia and
establish whether Mithridates wanted a peace treaty or
war. With these words, he marched through Thrace to   226
Cypsella, having sent Lucullus ahead to Abydus. For
Lucullus too had now joined Sulla, having risked capture
by pirates on many occasions. He had collected a sizable
fleet from Cyprus and Phoenicia and Rhodes and Pamphylia, and raided much of the enemy's territory, as well
engaging with Mithridatic ships while in passage. Sulla,   227
therefore, coming from Cypsela and Mithridates from

αὖθις ἐς λόγους, καὶ κατέβαινον ἐς πεδίον ἄμφω σὺν
228 ὀλίγοις, ἐφορώντων τῶν στρατῶν ἑκατέρωθεν. ἦσαν
δ᾽ οἱ λόγοι Μιθριδάτου μὲν ὑπόμνησις φιλίας καὶ
συμμαχίας ἰδίας καὶ πατρῴας, καὶ ἐπὶ τοῖς Ῥωμαίων
πρέσβεσι καὶ προβούλοις καὶ στρατηγοῖς κατηγορία
ὧν ἐς αὐτὸν ἐπεπράχεσαν ἀδίκως, Ἀριοβαρζάνην τε
κατάγοντες ἐς Καππαδοκίαν, καὶ Φρυγίας αὐτὸν
ἀφαιρούμενοι, καὶ Νικομήδη περιορῶντες ἀδικοῦντα.
229 "Καὶ τάδε," ἔφη, "Πάντα ἔπραξαν ἐπὶ χρήμασι,
παραλλὰξ παρ᾽ ἐμοῦ τε καὶ παρ᾽ ἐκείνων λαμβάνον-
τες· ὃ γὰρ δὴ μάλιστ᾽ ἄν τις ὑμῶν, ὦ Ῥωμαῖοι, τοῖς
πλείοσιν ἐπικαλέσειεν, ἔστιν ἡ φιλοκερδία. ἀναρρα-
γέντος δὲ ὑπὸ τῶν ὑμετέρων στρατηγῶν τοῦ πολέμου,
πάντα ὅσα ἀμυνόμενος ἔπραττον, ἀνάγκῃ μᾶλλον ἢ
κατὰ γνώμην ἐγίγνετο."
230 57. Ὁ μὲν δὴ Μιθριδάτης ὧδε εἰπὼν ἐπαύσατο, ὁ
δὲ Σύλλας ὑπολαβὼν ἀπεκρίνατο· "Ἐφ᾽ ἕτερα μὲν
ἡμᾶς ἐκάλεις, ὡς τὰ προτεινόμενα ἀγαπήσων, οὐ μὴν
231 ὀκνήσω καὶ περὶ τῶνδε διὰ βραχέος εἰπεῖν. ἐς μὲν
Καππαδοκίαν ἐγὼ κατήγαγον Ἀριοβαρζάνην Κιλικίας ἄρχων, ὧδε Ῥωμαίων ψηφισαμένων· καὶ σὺ
κατήκουες ἡμῶν, δέον ἀντιλέγειν καὶ ἡμᾶς[14] μεταδιδά-
σκειν ἢ μηκέτι τοῖς ἐγνωσμένοις ἀντιτείναι. Φρυγίαν
δέ σοι Μάνιος ἔδωκεν ἐπὶ δωροδοκίᾳ, ὃ κοινόν ἐστιν
ἀμφοῖν ἀδίκημα. καὶ τῷδε μάλιστα αὐτὴν ὁμολογεῖς
οὐ δικαίως λαβεῖν, ἐκ δωροδοκίας. ὅ τε Μάνιος καὶ τὰ
ἄλλα ἠλέγχθη παρ᾽ ἡμῖν ἐπὶ χρήμασι πράξας, καὶ
232 πάντα ἀνέλυσεν ἡ βουλή. ᾧ λόγῳ καὶ Φρυγίαν

Pergamum, the two parties met again for discussions. Both went down into the plain with a small escort, while the armies watched on from their respective positions. Mithridates' words recalled the friendship and alliance 228 with Rome enjoyed both by himself and his ancestors, and accused the Roman ambassadors, advisers, and commanders of behaving unjustly toward him, by restoring Ariobarzanes to Cappadocia, taking Phrygia away from him, and allowing Nicomedes to mistreat him. "And all this they did 229 for money," he said, "taking it in turn from me and them. For, if there is one thing that most of you can rightly be accused of, men of Rome, it is avarice. After your generals caused the outbreak of war, everything I did was in self-defense, forced on me rather than the result of planning."

57. When he had finished this speech, Sulla took over 230 and replied: "You called this meeting for a different purpose, to approve the conditions offered, but I have no hesitation in speaking briefly about these matters too. When I was governor of Cilicia, I restored Ariobarzanes 231 to Cappadocia, in conformity with a decision of the Roman people. You complied with the order, but should have opposed it then and tried to change our mind, or stopped resisting what had been decided. As for Phrygia, Manius gave it to you in return for a bribe, which was an illegal act by both of you. But in admitting that you got it by bribery, you admit that it was not rightly yours to have. Manius was indicted in Rome on other financial charges, and the senate annulled all his actions. This was the reason they did 232

---

14 ἡμᾶς prop. Goukowsky: μὴ codd.

ἀδίκως σοι δοθεῖσαν οὐχ ἑαυτῇ συντελεῖν ἐπέταξεν ἐς
τοὺς φόρους, ἀλλ᾽ αὐτόνομον μεθῆκεν. ὧν δὲ ἡμεῖς οἱ
πολέμῳ λαβόντες οὐκ ἀξιοῦμεν ἄρχειν, τίνι λόγῳ σὺ
καθέξεις; Νικομήδης δὲ αἰτιᾶται μέν σε καὶ Ἀλέξανδρον αὐτῷ τὸν τὸ σῶμα τρώσοντα ἐπιπέμψαι, καὶ Σωκράτη τὸν Χρηστὸν ἐπὶ τὴν ἀρχήν, καὶ τάδε αὐτὸς
233 ἀμυνόμενος ἐς τὴν σὴν ἐμβαλεῖν. εἰ δέ τι ὅμως ἠδί-
κου, ἐς Ῥώμην πρεσβεύειν ἔδει καὶ τὰς ἀποκρίσεις
ἀναμένειν. εἰ δὲ καὶ θᾶσσον ἠμύνου Νικομήδη, πῶς
καὶ Ἀριοβαρζάνην ἀπήλαυνες οὐδὲν ἀδικοῦντα; ἐκβαλὼν δ᾽ ἀνάγκην ἐπέθηκας τοῖς παροῦσι Ῥωμαίων
κατάγειν αὐτόν, καὶ καταγόμενον κωλύων σὺ τὸν πό-
234 λεμον ἐξῆψας, ἐγνωκὼς μὲν οὕτω πρὸ πολλοῦ, καὶ ἐν
ἐλπίδι ἔχων γῆς ἄρξειν ἁπάσης εἰ Ῥωμαίων κρατή-
σειας, προφάσεις δ᾽ ἐπὶ τῇ γνώμῃ τάσδε ποιούμενος.
καὶ τούτου τεκμήριον, ὅτι καὶ Θρᾷκας καὶ Σκύθας καὶ
Σαυρομάτας, οὔπω τινὶ πολεμῶν, ἐς συμμαχίαν ἠπεί-
γου, καὶ ἐς τοὺς ἀγχοῦ βασιλέας περιέπεμπες, ναῦς
τε ἐποιοῦ, καὶ πρῳρέας καὶ κυβερνήτας συνεκάλεις.

235   58. "Μάλιστα δ᾽ ὁ καιρὸς ἐλέγχει σε τῆς ἐπιβουλῆς. ὅτε γὰρ τὴν Ἰταλίαν ἀφισταμένην ἡμῶν
ᾐσθάνου, τὴν ἀσχολίαν τήνδε ἡμῶν φυλάξας ἐπέθου
μὲν Ἀριοβαρζάνῃ καὶ Νικομήδει καὶ Γαλάταις καὶ
236 Παφλαγονίᾳ, ἐπέθου δὲ Ἀσίᾳ τῷ ἡμετέρῳ χωρίῳ. καὶ
λαβὼν οἷα δέδρακας ἢ τὰς πόλεις, αἷς τοὺς θεράποντας καὶ χρήστας ἐπέστησας ἐλευθερίας καὶ χρεῶν
ἀποκοπαῖς, ἢ τοὺς Ἕλληνας, ὧν μιᾷ προφάσει χιλίους καὶ ἑξακοσίους διέφθειρας, ἢ Γαλατῶν τοὺς

not make Phrygia, which had been given to you unjustly, tributary to themselves, but declared it independent. What justification is there for you to have it, when we decided not to govern it, even though we captured it in war? Nicomedes also accuses you of sending Alexander to assassinate him, and Socrates Chrestus to take his kingdom; he says it was to defend himself against these acts that he invaded your territory. Nevertheless, if you were 233 wronged, you should have sent ambassadors to Rome and waited for the response. But even if we allow that you were just defending yourself rather quickly against Nicomedes, why did you expel Ariobarzanes, who had done you no wrong at all? In driving him out, you forced the Roman authorities on the spot to restore him, and when you prevented his return, it was you who ignited the war. You had 234 decided this a long time before, hoping to rule the whole world if you could conquer Rome, and making these excuses in pursuit of your plan. The proof of this is that, although you were not yet at war with anyone, you pressed the Thracians and Scythians and Sarmatians into alliance with you, sent for help to the neighboring kings, and built a fleet for which you recruited lookouts and helmsmen.

58. "And it is particularly the timing that betrays your 235 plan. For when you saw that Italy had revolted from us, it was this preoccupation of ours that you took advantage of to launch an attack on Ariobarzanes and Nicomedes and Galatia and Paphlagonia, and to launch an attack on our bastion of Asia. And when you captured them how dis- 236 gracefully you behaved! Toward the towns, for instance, where you freed slaves and canceled debts, and put the slaves and debtors in charge; or toward the Greeks, of whom, on a single occasion, you murdered one thousand

τετράρχας, οὓς ὁμοδιαίτους ἔχων ἀπέκτεινας, ἢ τὸ
τῶν Ἰταλιωτῶν γένος, οὓς μιᾶς ἡμέρας σὺν βρέφεσι
καὶ μητράσιν ἔκτεινάς τε καὶ κατεπόντωσας, οὐκ ἀπο-
237   σχόμενος οὐδὲ τῶν ἐς τὰ ἱερὰ συμφυγόντων. ὢ πόσην
μὲν ὠμότητά σου, πόσην δὲ ἀσέβειαν καὶ ὑπερβολὴν
μίσους ἐς ἡμᾶς προενήνοχας. σφετερισάμενος δ᾽
ἁπάντων τὰ χρήματα, ἐς τὴν Εὐρώπην ἐπέρας μεγάλοις στρατοῖς, ἡμῶν ἀπειπόντων ἅπασι τοῖς Ἀσίας
βασιλεῦσι τῆς Εὐρώπης μηδὲ ἐπιβαίνειν. διαπλεύσας
δὲ Μακεδονίαν τε ἡμετέραν οὖσαν ἐπέτρεχες καὶ τοὺς
238   Ἕλληνας τὴν ἐλευθερίαν ἀφῃροῦ. οὐ πρίν τε ἤρξω
μετανοεῖν, οὐδ᾽ Ἀρχέλαος ὑπὲρ σοῦ παρακαλεῖν, ἢ
Μακεδονίαν μέν με ἀνασώσασθαι, τὴν δὲ Ἑλλάδα
τῆς σῆς ἐκλῦσαι βίας, ἑκκαίδεκα δὲ μυριάδας τοῦ
σοῦ στρατοῦ κατακόψαι, καὶ τὰ στρατόπεδά σου λα-
239   βεῖν αὐταῖς παρασκευαῖς. ὃ καὶ θαυμάζω σου δικαι-
ολογουμένου νῦν ἐφ᾽ οἷς δι᾽ Ἀρχελάου παρεκάλεις. ἢ
πόρρω μὲν ὄντα με ἐδεδοίκεις, ἀγχοῦ δὲ γενόμενον
ἐπὶ δίκην ἐληλυθέναι νομίζεις; ἧς ὁ καιρὸς ἀνάλωται,
σοῦ τε πολεμήσαντος ἡμῖν, καὶ ἡμῶν ἀμυναμένων
240   ἤδη καρτερῶς καὶ ἀμυνουμένων ἐς τέλος.ʺ τοσαῦτα
τοῦ Σύλλα μετ᾽ ὀργῆς ἔτι λέγοντος, μετέπιπτεν ὁ βασιλεὺς καὶ ἐδεδοίκει, καὶ ἐς τὰς δι᾽ Ἀρχελάου γενομένας συνθήκας ἐνεδίδου, τάς τε ναῦς καὶ τὰ ἄλλα
πάντα παραδοὺς ἐς τὸν Πόντον ἐπὶ τὴν πατρῴαν ἀρχὴν ἐπανῄει μόνην. ὧδε μὲν ὁ πρῶτος Μιθριδάτου καὶ
Ῥωμαίων πόλεμος κατεπαύετο.

241   59. Σύλλας δὲ Φιμβρίου δύο σταδίους ἀποσχὼν

six hundred; or toward the Galatian tetrarchs whom you invited to dinner and murdered; or toward those of Italian stock, whom you killed and drowned on a single day, mothers and children included, not even sparing those who had fled to the temples for refuge. What an extraordinary display of savagery, impiety, and excessive hatred toward us! After stealing everyone's money, you then crossed over to Europe with great armies, even though we had forbidden all the kings of Asia even to set foot in Europe. You sailed over to Macedon and overran it, even though it belonged to us, and you deprived the Greeks of their freedom. You did not begin to regret any of this, nor did Archelaus appeal for pardon on your behalf, until I had recovered Macedonia, delivered Greece from your violence, cut to pieces one hundred and sixty thousand of your men, and captured your camps with all their equipment. So I am astonished that you would now try to justify the actions for which you were asking for forgiveness through Archelaus. Or, were you afraid of me at a distance, but think that now I am here, I have come to listen to you make your case? The time for that ran out when you went to war with us and we defended ourselves vigorously then, and will continue to do so till the very end." While Sulla was still speaking angrily, the king suddenly changed his mind having been seized with fear, and yielded to the terms arranged by Archelaus. He surrendered his fleet and everything else required, and then returned to rule his ancestral domains in the Pontus, and nothing else. And so the first war between Mithridates and Rome came to an end.

59. Sulla now approached to within two stades of Fim-

237

238

239

240

241

ἐκέλευε παραδοῦναί οἱ τὸν στρατόν, οὗ παρανόμως
ἄρχοι. ὁ δ' ἀντεπέσκωπτε μὲν ὡς οὐδ' ἐκεῖνος ἐννόμως
ἔτι ἄρχοι, περιταφρεύοντος δ' αὐτὸν τοῦ Σύλλα, καὶ
πολλῶν οὐκ ἀφανῶς ἀποδιδρασκόντων, ἐς ἐκκλησίαν
τοὺς λοιποὺς ὁ Φιμβρίας συναγαγὼν παρεκάλει
242 παραμένειν. οὐ φαμένων δὲ πολεμήσειν πολίταις,
καταρρήξας τὸν χιτωνίσκον ἑκάστοις προσέπιπτεν.
ὡς δὲ καὶ τοῦτ' ἀπεστρέφοντο, καὶ πλείους ἐγίγνοντο
αἱ αὐτομολίαι, τὰς σκηνὰς τῶν ἡγεμόνων περιήει, καί
τινας αὐτῶν χρήμασι διαφθείρας ἐς ἐκκλησίαν αὖθις
243 συνεκάλει, καὶ συνόμνυσθαί οἱ προσέτασσεν. ἐκβοη-
σάντων δὲ τῶν ἐνετῶν ὅτι δέοι καλεῖν ἐπὶ τὸν ὅρκον
ἐξ ὀνόματος, ὁ μὲν ἐκήρυττε τοὺς εὖ τι παθόντας ὑφ'
ἑαυτοῦ, καὶ Νώνιον πρῶτον ἐκάλει, κοινωνόν οἱ πάντων γεγονότα. οὐκ ὀμνύοντος δ' οὐδ' ἐκείνου, τὸ ξίφος
ἐπισπάσας ἠπείλει κτενεῖν αὐτόν, μέχρι βοῆς ἐκ πάντων γενομένης καταπλαγεὶς καὶ τοῦδ' ἐπαύσατο.
244 θεράποντα δὲ χρήμασι καὶ ἐλπίσιν ἐλευθερίας ἀνα-
πείσας ἔπεμψεν ὡς αὐτόμολον ἐπιχειρεῖν τῷ Σύλλα
σώματι. ὁ δὲ τῷ ἔργῳ πλησιάζων καὶ ταρασσόμενος,
καὶ ἐκ τοῦδε ὕποπτος γενόμενος, συνελήφθη τε καὶ
245 ὡμολόγησεν. καὶ ὁ στρατὸς ὁ τοῦ Σύλλα, σὺν ὀργῇ
καὶ καταφρονήσει περιστάντες τὸ τοῦ Φιμβρίου χαράκωμα, κατελοιδόρουν αὐτὸν καὶ Ἀθηνίωνα ἐκάλουν,
ὃς δραπετῶν τῶν ἐν Σικελίᾳ ποτὲ ἀποστάντων ὀλιγή-
μερος γεγένητο βασιλεύς.

bria's position, and ordered him to transfer his army to him, the command of which he held illegally. Fimbria replied with derision that even Sulla himself no longer held his command legally. So Sulla surrounded him with a ditch, and many of Fimbria's men deserted openly. So he called the rest to a meeting at which he appealed to them to stay. But when they said they would not fight 242 against fellow citizens, he tore his tunic and implored each of them individually. But as they ignored this too, and the number of deserters increased, Fimbria went around the tents of his officers, and after bribing some of them with money, again called a meeting and ordered the assembly to swear an oath of loyalty to him collectively. But those 243 who had been bribed shouted out that he must invite individuals by name to swear the oath. So he called on those who owed him a favor, Nonius first, his partner in everything. But even he refused to swear the oath, and Fimbria drew his sword and threatened to kill him, until he was alarmed by the general outcry and desisted from the attempt. Next, he bribed a slave with money and the prom- 244 ise of freedom, and sent him supposedly as a deserter to make an attempt on Sulla's life. But the slave became nervous when he got close to the actual deed, aroused suspicion because of this, and confessed when he was arrested. Sulla's men stood around Fimbria's palisade with anger 245 and contempt, and insulted him by calling him Athenion, the name of a man who once for a few days became king of the slaves who had revolted in Sicily.[38]

[38] During the second Sicilian slave war (104–100), Diodorus (36.3–8) reports the actions of the two slave leaders who proclaimed themselves king, Salvius in the east of the island, Athenion in the west.

246   60. Ἐφ' οἷς ὁ Φιμβρίας πάντα ἀπογνοὺς ἐπὶ τὴν τάφρον προῆλθε, καὶ Σύλλαν αὐτῷ παρεκάλει συνελθεῖν ἐς λόγους. ὁ δὲ ἀνθ' αὑτοῦ Ῥουτίλιον ἔπεμπε· καὶ τόδε πρῶτον ἐλύπει τὸν Φιμβρίαν, οὐδὲ συνόδου, διδομένης καὶ τοῖς πολεμίοις, ἀξιωθέντα. δεομένῳ δ' αὐτῷ συγγνώμης τυχεῖν εἴ τι νέος ὢν ἐξήμαρτεν, ὁ Ῥουτίλιος ὑπέστη Σύλλαν ἀφήσειν ἐπὶ θάλασσαν ἀπαθῆ διελθεῖν, εἰ μέλλοι τῆς Ἀσίας, ἧς ἐστὶν ὁ Σύλ-
247 λας ἀνθύπατος, ἀποπλευσεῖσθαι. ὁ δὲ εἰπὼν ἑτέραν ὁδὸν ἔχειν κρείττονα, ἐπανῆλθεν ἐς Πέργαμον, καὶ ἐς τὸ τοῦ Ἀσκληπιοῦ ἱερὸν παρελθὼν ἐχρήσατο τῷ ξίφει. οὐ καιρίου δ' αὐτῷ τῆς πληγῆς γενομένης, ἐκέλευσε τὸν παῖδα ἐπερεῖσαι. ὁ δὲ καὶ τὸν δεσπότην
248 ἔκτεινε καὶ αὐτὸν ἐπὶ τῷ δεσπότῃ. οὕτω μὲν καὶ Φιμβρίας ἀπέθανε, πολλὰ τὴν Ἀσίαν ἐπὶ Μιθριδάτῃ λελυμασμένος. καὶ αὐτὸν ὁ Σύλλας ἐφῆκε τοῖς ἀπελευθέροις θάψαι, καὶ ἐπεῖπεν οὐ μιμεῖσθαι Κίνναν καὶ Μάριον ἐν Ῥώμῃ θάνατόν τε πολλῶν καὶ ἀταφίαν ἐπὶ
249 τῷ θανάτῳ καταγνόντας. τὸν δὲ στρατὸν τοῦ Φιμβρίου προσιόντα οἱ δεξιωσάμενός τε καὶ τῷ σφετέρῳ συναγαγών, Κουρίωνι προσέταξε Νικομήδην ἐς Βιθυνίαν καὶ Ἀριοβαρζάνην ἐς Καππαδοκίαν καταγαγεῖν, τῇ τε βουλῇ περὶ πάντων ἐπέστελλεν, οὐχ ὑποκρινόμενος ἐψηφίσθαι πολέμιος.

250   61. Αὐτὴν δὲ τὴν Ἀσίαν καθιστάμενος, Ἰλιέας μὲν καὶ Χίους καὶ Λυκίους καὶ Ῥοδίους καὶ Μαγνησίαν

60. At this, Fimbria despaired altogether and went up 246
to the ditch to invite Sulla to enter discussions with him.
Sulla did not go himself, but sent Rutilius instead.[39] This
annoyed Fimbria straight off, that he was not thought worthy of a meeting, while even the enemy had been granted
that much. When he asked to be pardoned for making a
youthful mistake, Rutilius assured him that Sulla would
allow him to go unharmed to the coast, if he would take
ship out of Asia, Sulla being the proconsul of the province.
Fimbria said that he had another and better way to go, and 247
he withdrew to Pergamum, where he entered the temple
of Asclepius and ran himself through with his sword. But
the wound was not fatal, and he ordered his slave to press
the sword home. The slave killed his master and then
himself. This was how Fimbria died, who like Mithridates 248
before him had done a great deal of damage to Asia. Sulla
released his body to his freedmen for burial, saying that
he would not copy Cinna and Marius at Rome, who had
condemned many to death and to a denial of burial after
death. He welcomed Fimbria's army when it came over to 249
him, and integrated it with his own, and ordered Curio to
restore Nicomedes to Bithynia and Ariobarzanes to Cappadocia.[40] He then sent a full report to the senate, pretending that he had not been declared a public enemy.

61. Having made arrangements for the province of Asia 250
itself, Sulla bestowed freedom on, and registered as
friends of Rome, Ilium and Chios and Lycia and Rhodes

[39] The famous P. Rutilius Rufus (consul 105) lived in Smyrna
after his conviction for extortion and may have been acting as a
legate for Sulla on this occasion.　　[40] C. Scribonius Curio
(consul 76) was one of Sulla's legates in Asia.

APPIAN

καί τινας ἄλλους, ἢ συμμαχίας ἀμειβόμενος, ἢ ὧν
διὰ προθυμίαν ἐπεπόνθεσαν οὗ ἕνεκα, ἐλευθέρους
ἠφίει καὶ Ῥωμαίων ἀνέγραφε φίλους, ἐς δὲ τὰ λοιπὰ
251 πάντα στρατιὰν περιέπεμπεν. καὶ τοὺς θεράποντας,
οἷς ἐλευθερίαν ἐδεδώκει Μιθριδάτης, ἐκήρυττεν αὐτίκα
ἐς τοὺς δεσπότας ἐπανιέναι. πολλῶν δὲ ἀπειθούντων,
καὶ πόλεων τινῶν ἀφισταμένων, ἐγίγνοντο σφαγαὶ
κατὰ πλῆθος ἐλευθέρων τε καὶ θεραπόντων ἐπὶ ποι-
κίλαις προφάσεσι, τείχη τε πολλῶν καθῃρεῖτο, καὶ
252 συχνὰ τῆς Ἀσίας ἠνδραποδίζετο καὶ διηρπάζετο. οἵ
τε καππαδοκίσαντες ἄνδρες ἢ πόλεις ἐκολάζοντο πικρῶς, καὶ μάλιστα αὐτῶν Ἐφέσιοι, σὺν αἰσχρᾷ κο-
λακείᾳ ἐς τὰ Ῥωμαίων ἀναθήματα ἐνυβρίσαντες. ἐπὶ
δὲ τοῖσδε καὶ κήρυγμα περιήει, τοὺς ἐν ἀξιώσει κατὰ
πόλιν ἐς ἡμέραν ῥητὴν πρὸς τὸν Σύλλαν ἀπαντᾶν ἐς
Ἔφεσον. καὶ συνελθοῦσιν αὐτοῖς ἐπὶ βήματος ἐδη-
μηγόρησεν οὕτως.

253   62. "Ἡμεῖς στρατῷ πρῶτον ἐς Ἀσίαν παρήλθομεν
Ἀντιόχου τοῦ Σύρων βασιλέως πορθοῦντος ὑμᾶς.
ἐξελάσαντες δ' αὐτόν, καὶ τὸν Ἅλυν καὶ Ταῦρον αὐτῷ
θέμενοι τῆς ἀρχῆς ὅρον, οὐ κατέσχομεν ὑμῶν ἡμε-
τέρων ἐξ ἐκείνου γενομένων, ἀλλὰ μεθήκαμεν αὐτονόμους, πλὴν εἴ τινας Εὐμένει καὶ Ῥοδίοις συμμαχή-
σασιν ἡμῖν ἔδομεν, οὐχ ὑποτελεῖς ἀλλ' ἐπὶ προστάταις
254 εἶναι. τεκμήριον δ' ὅτι Λυκίους αἰτιωμένους τι Ῥοδίων
ἀπεστήσαμεν. ἡμεῖς μὲν δὴ τοιοίδε περὶ ὑμᾶς γεγό-
ναμεν· ὑμεῖς δέ, Ἀττάλου τοῦ φιλομήτορος τὴν ἀρχὴν

264

and Magnesia, and a number of others, either as a reward for their military assistance, or as compensation for what they had suffered because of their enthusiastic support. He dispatched troops to all the other towns. The slaves to whom Mithridates had given their freedom he ordered to return to their masters immediately. Many of them refused, and with some towns rising in revolt, there was widespread slaughter both of free men and slaves on a variety of excuses, many town walls were torn down, and much of Asia was enslaved and plundered. Men and towns that had taken the Cappadocian side were cruelly punished, especially the Ephesians, who had demonstrated contemptible obsequiousness to Mithridates in doing violence to the Roman offerings in their temples. After this, a proclamation was circulated instructing those in positions of authority in the towns to meet Sulla at Ephesus on a specific day. When they had assembled, Sulla mounted the rostrum and delivered the following speech:

62. "We first came to Asia with an army when Antiochus king of Syria was ravaging your lands.[41] We drove him out and made the river Halys and Taurus mountains the boundary of his empire. When you came under our rule rather than his, we did not take ownership of you, but made you independent, apart from a few places we awarded to Eumenes and Rhodes, who had given us military assistance, and these were not to be tribute-paying subjects, but clients. This is proved by the case of the Lycians, who made a complaint against Rhodes, and we removed them from Rhodian authority. That is how we treated you. You, on the other hand, when Attalus Philome-

251

252

253

254

41 Antiochus III the Great was defeated by Rome in 189.

ἡμῖν ἐν διαθήκαις καταλιπόντος, Ἀριστονίκῳ καθ᾽
ἡμῶν τέτταρσιν ἔτεσι συνεμαχεῖτε, μέχρι καὶ Ἀρι-
στόνικος ἑάλω καὶ ὑμῶν οἱ πλείους ἐς ἀνάγκην καὶ
255 φόβον περιήλθετε. καὶ ὧδε πράσσοντες ὅμως ἐν ἔτεσιν εἴκοσι καὶ τέτταρσιν ἐς μέγα περιουσίας καὶ κάλλους κατασκευῆς ἰδιωτικῆς τε καὶ δημοσίας προελ-
θόντες, ὑπὸ εἰρήνης καὶ τρυφῆς ἐξυβρίσατε αὖθις,
καὶ τὴν ἀσχολίαν ἡμῶν τὴν ἀμφὶ τὴν Ἰταλίαν φυλά-
ξαντες οἱ μὲν ἐπηγάγεσθε Μιθριδάτην, οἱ δ᾽ ἐλθόντι
256 συνέθεσθε. ὃ δ᾽ ἐστὶ πάντων μιαρώτατον, ὑπέστητε
αὐτῷ μιᾶς ἡμέρας τοὺς Ἰταλιώτας ἅπαντας αὐτοῖς
παισὶ καὶ μητράσιν ἀναιρήσειν, καὶ οὐδὲ τῶν ἐς τὰ
ἱερὰ συμφυγόντων διὰ τοὺς ὑμετέρους θεοὺς ἐφεί-
257 σασθε. ἐφ᾽ οἷς ἔδοτε μέν τινα καὶ αὐτῷ Μιθριδάτῃ
δίκην, ἀπίστῳ τε ἐς ὑμᾶς γενομένῳ, καὶ φόνου καὶ
δημεύσεων ἐμπλήσαντι ὑμᾶς, καὶ γῆς ἀναδασμοὺς
ἐργασαμένῳ καὶ χρεῶν ἀποκοπὰς καὶ δούλων ἐλευ-
θερώσεις, καὶ τυράννους ἐπ᾽ ἐνίοις, καὶ λῃστήρια
πολλὰ ἀνά τε γῆν καὶ θάλασσαν, ὡς εὐθὺς ὑμᾶς
ἔχειν ἐν πείρᾳ καὶ παραβολῇ οἵους ἀνθ᾽ οἵων προ-
258 στάτας ἐπελέγεσθε. ἔδοσαν δέ τινα καὶ ἡμῖν δίκην οἱ
τῶνδε ἄρξαντες. ἀλλὰ δεῖ καὶ κοινὴν ὑμῖν ἐπιτεθῆναι
τοιάδε ἐργασαμένοις· ἢν εἰκὸς μὲν ἦν ὁμοίαν οἷς
ἐδράσατε γενέσθαι, μή ποτε δὲ Ῥωμαῖοι σφαγὰς
ἀσεβεῖς ἢ δημεύσεις ἀβούλους ἢ δούλων ἐπαναστάσεις, ἢ ὅσα ἄλλα βαρβαρικά, μηδ᾽ ἐπὶ νοῦν λάβοιεν.

tor left his kingdom to us in his will, fought alongside
Aristonicus for four years against us, until he was captured, and most of you came to your senses out of fear and
because there was no alternative.[42] In spite of this behav-   255
ior, after twenty-four years in which your resources advanced greatly and you attained a high level of both personal and public splendor in your buildings, under the
influence of peace and luxurious living you once again
turned to insolence, and using the distraction we faced
in Italy, some of you invited in Mithridates, others went
over to his side when he arrived. And most abominable of   256
all, you undertook on his behalf to kill on a single day all
the Italians in Asia, including mothers and children, and
you did not even spare those who fled to the temples to
seek refuge with your own gods. You paid a certain price   257
for this to Mithridates himself, when he turned treacherous toward you, and gave you your fill of murder and confiscations and redistributed your property and canceled
debts and freed slaves and appointed tyrants to govern
some of you, and did much raiding by land and sea. The
result was that you knew immediately by experience and
comparison what sort of champions you had chosen to
replace the previous ones. Those who started all this have   258
also paid a price to us, but there has to be a communal
penalty imposed on you all for the terrible things you
have done. While it should be one that fits the crime, may
Rome never even consider unholy slaughter or indiscrim-
inate confiscations or inciting slaves to revolt, or any other

[42] Attalus III Philometor ("Mother-loving") bequeathed Pergamum to Rome on his death in 133. Aristonicus made a bid for
the throne but was defeated in 130 and executed in Rome.

259 φειδοῖ δὲ γένους ἔτι καὶ ὀνόματος Ἑλληνικοῦ καὶ δόξης τῆς ἐπὶ τῇ Ἀσίᾳ, καὶ τῆς φιλτάτης Ῥωμαίοις
εὐφημίας οὕνεκα, μόνους ὑμῖν ἐπιγράφω πέντε ἐτῶν
φόρους ἐσενεγκεῖν αὐτίκα, καὶ τὴν τοῦ πολέμου δαπάνην, ὅση τε γέγονέ μοι καὶ ἔσται καθισταμένῳ τὰ
260 ὑπόλοιπα. διαιρήσω δὲ ταῦθ᾽ ἑκάστοις ἐγὼ κατὰ πόλεις, καὶ τάξω προθεσμίαν ταῖς ἐσφοραῖς, καὶ τοῖς οὐ
φυλάξασιν ἐπιθήσω δίκην ὡς πολεμίοις.᾽᾽

261   63. Τοσάδε εἰπὼν ἐπιδιήρει τοῖς πρέσβεσι τὴν ζημίαν, καὶ ἐπὶ τὰ χρήματα ἔπεμπεν. αἱ δὲ πόλεις ἀπο-
ροῦσαί τε καὶ δανειζόμεναι μεγάλων τόκων, αἱ μὲν τὰ
θέατρα τοῖς δανείζουσιν, αἱ δὲ τὰ γυμνάσια ἢ τεῖχος
ἢ λιμένας ἢ εἴ τι δημόσιον ἄλλο, σὺν ὕβρει στρατιωτῶν ἐπειγόντων, ὑπετίθεντο. τὰ μὲν δὴ χρήματα
ὧδε τῷ Σύλλᾳ συνεκομίζετο, καὶ κακῶν ἄδην εἶχεν ἡ
262 Ἀσία· ἐπέπλει δ᾽ αὐτὴν καὶ λῃστήρια πολύανδρα φανερῶς, στόλοις ἐοικότα μᾶλλον ἢ λῃσταῖς, Μιθριδάτου μὲν αὐτὰ πρῶτον καθέντος ἐς τὴν θάλασσαν,
ὅτε πάνθ᾽ ὡς οὐκ ἐς πολὺ καθέξων ἐλυμαίνετο, πλεο-
νάσαντα δ᾽ ἐς τότε μάλιστα, καὶ οὐ τοῖς πλέουσι
μόνοις ἀλλὰ καὶ λιμέσι καὶ χωρίοις καὶ πόλεσιν ἐπι-
263 χειροῦντα φανερῶς. Ἰασός γέ τοι καὶ Σάμος καὶ Κλα-
ζομεναὶ καὶ Σαμοθρᾴκη Σύλλα παρόντος ἐλήφθησαν,
καὶ τὸ ἱερὸν ἐσυλήθη τὸ Σαμοθρᾴκιον χιλίων ταλάντων κόσμον, ὡς ἐνομίζετο. ὁ δέ, εἴτε ἑκὼν ὡς ἁμαρ-
τόντας ἐνυβρίζεσθαι καταλιπών, εἴτ᾽ ἐπὶ τὴν ἐς

such barbarian measures. Wishing still to spare the Greek 259
people and their name and renown throughout Asia, and
for the sake of Rome's reputation, so treasured by its citizens, I impose on you as your sole penalty the immediate
payment of five years' tribute, along with the outlay of the
war, both what it has cost me and what it will cost in settling the remaining issues. I myself will divide the assess- 260
ment among everyone town by town, and I will fix a dead-
line for the payments. Those who do not keep it, I will
punish like enemies."

63. After making his speech, Sulla divided the indem- 261
nity up among the envoys, and sent out men to collect the
money. The towns lacked the resources to pay and borrowed money at high rates of interest, and some mort-
gaged their theaters, others their walls or harbors or any
other public properties, while the soldiers pressed them
brutally. In this way the money was collected for Sulla, and
Asia had its fill of misery. Large pirate groups that looked 262
more like regular fleets than squadrons of buccaneers
openly raided the coast. Mithridates first sent them to sea,
when he was despoiling the whole coast in the expectation
that he would not be able to hold it for long. It was then
in particular that their numbers grew substantially, and
their attacks were not just limited to ships, but included
open raids on harbors and forts and towns. They captured 263
Iassus and Samos and Clazomenae and Samothrace—in
spite of Sulla being there at the time—and robbed the
temple at Samothrace of what was estimated to be one
thousand talents worth of its sacred ornaments. Sulla himself, either intentionally leaving those who had done
wrong to their violent fate, or because he was in a hurry

Ῥώμην στάσιν ἐπειγόμενος, ἐς τὴν Ἑλλάδα καὶ ἀπ᾽ αὐτῆς ἐς τὴν Ἰταλίαν μετὰ τοῦ πλείονος στρατοῦ διέπλει.

264   64. Καὶ τὰ μὲν ἀμφὶ Σύλλαν ἐν τοῖς Ἐμφυλίοις ἀναγέγραπται, ἄρχεται δ᾽ ὁ δεύτερος Ῥωμαίων τε καὶ
265   Μιθριδάτου πόλεμος ἐνθένδε. Μουρήνας μὲν ὑπὸ Σύλλα σὺν δύο τέλεσι τοῖς Φιμβρίου καθίστασθαι τὰ λοιπὰ τῆς Ἀσίας ὑπελέλειπτο, καὶ πολέμων ἀφορμὰς ἠρεσχέλει δι᾽ ἐπιθυμίαν θριάμβου· Μιθριδάτης δ᾽ ἐς τὸν Πόντον ἐσπλεύσας Κόλχοις καὶ Βοσποριανοῖς
266   ἀφισταμένοις ἐπολέμει. ὧν Κόλχοι τὸν υἱὸν παρ᾽ αὐτοῦ, Μιθριδάτην, βασιλέα σφίσιν ἠτοῦντο δοθῆναι, καὶ λαβόντες αὐτίκα ὑπήκουσαν. ὑποπτεύσας δ᾽ ὁ βασιλεὺς τόδε πρὸς τοῦ παιδὸς αὐτοῦ βασιλείας ἐπιθυμοῦντος γενέσθαι, καλέσας αὐτὸν ἔδησεν ἐν πέδαις χρυσαῖς καὶ μετ᾽ οὐ πολὺ ἀπέκτεινε, πολλὰ χρήσιμόν οἱ περὶ τὴν Ἀσίαν ἐν τοῖς πρὸς Φιμβρίαν
267   ἀγῶσι γενόμενον. ἐπὶ δὲ Βοσποριανοὺς ναῦς τε συνεπήγνυτο καὶ στρατὸν ἡτοιμάζετο πολύν, ὡς τὸ μέγεθος αὐτοῦ τῆς παρασκευῆς δόξαν ἐγεῖραι ταχεῖαν, οὐκ ἐπὶ Βοσποριανοὺς ἀλλ᾽ ἐπὶ Ῥωμαίους τάδε συλλέγεσθαι. οὐ γάρ πω οὐδ᾽ Ἀριοβαρζάνῃ πᾶσαν ἐβεβαίου Καππαδοκίαν, ἀλλ᾽ ἔστιν αὐτῆς ἃ καὶ τότε
268   κατεῖχεν. Ἀρχέλαόν τε ἐν ὑποψίαις ἐτίθετο ὡς πολλὰ πέρα τοῦ δέοντος κατὰ τὴν Ἑλλάδα ἐν ταῖς διαλύσεσιν ἐπιχωρήσαντα τῷ Σύλλᾳ. ὧν ὁ Ἀρχέλαος αἰσθανόμενός τε καὶ δείσας ἐς Μουρήναν ἔφυγε, καὶ παροξύνας αὐτὸν ἔπεισε Μιθριδάτῃ προεπιχειρεῖν.

to move against the political faction at Rome, took most of
his army and sailed off to Greece and from there to Italy.

64. As for what concerns Sulla, I have written about this   264
in my civil war books. The second war between Mithridates and Rome begins at this point. Murena, who had   265
been left by Sulla with Fimbria's two legions to settle the
rest of Asian affairs, was looking for any excuse to start a
war, as he was ambitious for a triumph. Having sailed back
to the Pontus, Mithridates now made war on the Colchians
and Bosporan peoples who had revolted against him. The   266
Colchians asked him to give them his son, also called
Mithridates, as their king, and when they got their wish,
they immediately submitted to Roman authority. The king
was suspicious that his son was responsible for this in his
ambition to be king himself, and summoned him, bound
him in gold chains and shortly after executed him, even
though he had been of great service to him in Asia, in the
battles with Fimbria. Against the Bosporan peoples he   267
built a fleet and made ready a large army, but the size of
his military preparations quickly gave rise to the impression that they were intended for use not against the peoples of the Bosporus but against Rome. For he had not
even given secure possession of all of Cappadocia to Ariobarzanes yet, but was still holding on to part of it. He also   268
harbored suspicions about Archelaus, that he had yielded
far more than was necessary in the negotiations with Sulla
in Greece. When Archelaus realized this, he was frightened and fled to Murena, whose resolve he sharpened and
whom he persuaded to launch a preemptive strike against

269 Μουρήνας μὲν δὴ διὰ Καππαδοκίας αὐτίκα ἐσβαλὼν
ἐς Κόμανα, κώμην ὑπὸ τῷ Μιθριδάτῃ μεγίστην, σε-
βάσμιον ἱερὸν καὶ πλούσιον ἔχουσαν, ἱππέας τινὰς
ἔκτεινε τοῦ Μιθριδάτου, καὶ πρέσβεσιν αὐτοῦ τὰς
συνθήκας προτείνουσιν οὐκ ἔφη συνθήκας ὁρᾶν· οὐ
γὰρ συνεγέγραπτο Σύλλας, ἀλλ' ἔργῳ τὰ λεχθέντα
270 βεβαιώσας ἀπήλλακτο. ταῦτα δ' εἰπὼν ὁ Μουρήνας
εὐθέως ἐλεηλάτει, καὶ οὐδὲ τῶν ἱερῶν χρημάτων ἀπο-
σχόμενος ἐχείμαζεν ἐν Καππαδοκίᾳ.

271 65. Μιθριδάτης δ' ἐς Ῥώμην ἔπεμπε πρός τε τὴν
βουλὴν καὶ πρὸς Σύλλαν, αἰτιώμενος ἃ ποιεῖ Μουρήνας. ὁ δ' ἐν τούτῳ τὸν Ἅλυν ποταμὸν περάσας, μέγαν
τε ὄντα καὶ δύσπορον τότε μάλιστα αὐτῷ γενόμενον
ὑπ' ὄμβρων, τετρακοσίας τοῦ Μιθριδάτου κώμας
ἐπέτρεχεν, οὐκ ἀπαντῶντος ἐς οὐδὲν αὐτῷ τοῦ βασι-
272 λέως, ἀλλὰ τὴν πρεσβείαν ἀναμένοντος. λείας δὲ
πολλῆς καταγέμων ἐς Φρυγίαν καὶ Γαλατίαν ἐπανῄει,
ἔνθα αὐτῷ Καλίδιος, ἐπὶ ταῖς Μιθριδάτου μέμψεσι
πεμφθεὶς ἀπὸ Ῥώμης, ψήφισμα μὲν οὐδὲν ἐπέδωκεν,
ἔφη δ' ἐς ἐπήκοον ἐν μέσῳ τὴν βουλὴν αὐτὸν κελεύειν
273 φείδεσθαι τοῦ βασιλέως ὄντος ἐνσπόνδου. ταῦτα δ'
εἰπὼν ὤφθη διαλεγόμενος αὐτῷ μόνῳ, καὶ ὁ Μουρήνας οὐδὲν ἀνεὶς τῆς ὁρμῆς καὶ τότε τὴν γῆν ἐπῄει τὴν
τοῦ Μιθριδάτου. ὁ δὲ σαφῶς ὑπὸ Ῥωμαίων ἡγούμε-

---

43 Rather than a literal counting of four hundred villages overrun by Murena, the reference may conceal a place-name, Tetra-
cosiocomum ("the place of four hundred villages"), on analogy

Mithridates. Murena immediately advanced through Cappadocia against Comana, a very large settlement subject to Mithridates, with a rich and revered temple, and killed some of the king's cavalry. When the Pontic ambassadors referred to the treaty, Murena replied that he could not see any treaty. And indeed, Sulla had not committed anything to writing, but had left as soon as he confirmed that what had been agreed verbally had in fact been carried out. With these words Murena immediately began to pillage, not even keeping his hands off the sacred monies. He then went into winter quarters in Cappadocia.

269

270

65. Mithridates sent a mission to the senate in Rome and to Sulla, to complain about Murena's actions. Meanwhile, Murena crossed the river Halys, which was a big river anyway and particularly difficult to cross at this time because of the rains. He overran four hundred villages belonging to Mithridates, who made no move whatever to confront him, but waited for the outcome of his mission.[43] Murena then returned to Phrygia and Galatia, laden with booty, where he was met by Calidius, who had been sent from Rome to deal with Mithridates' complaints.[44] Calidius had no senatorial decree to give him, but said in public that the senate was ordering Murena to leave the king alone, as he had a treaty with them. This is what he said, but he was also seen talking in private with Murena, who subsequently showed no less aggression, but again attacked the territory of Mithridates. The king, believing

271

272

273

with Chiliocomum ("the place of a thousand villages") referred to by Strabo (12.3.39 C561).

[44] Perhaps the Q. Calidius who had been a Tribune of the People in 98.

νος πολεμεῖσθαι, Γόρδιον ἐς τὰς κώμας ἐσβαλεῖν
274 ἐκέλευσεν. καὶ αὐτίκα ὁ Γόρδιος ὑποζύγιά τε πολλὰ
καὶ σκευοφόρα καὶ ἀνθρώπους, ἰδιώτας τε καὶ στρατιώτας, συνήρπαζε, καὶ αὐτῷ Μουρήνα, μέσον λαβὼν
ποταμόν, ἀντεκαθέζετο. μάχης δ᾽ οὐδέτερος ἦρχεν,
275 ἕως ἀφίκετο Μιθριδάτης σὺν τῷ πλείονι στρατῷ. καὶ
εὐθὺς ἀμφὶ τῷ ποταμῷ μάχη γίγνεται καρτερά. καὶ
βιασάμενος ὁ Μιθριδάτης ἐπέρα τὸν ποταμόν, καὶ
τἆλλα πολὺ κρείττων τοῦ Μουρήνα γενόμενος. ὁ δ᾽ ἐς
λόφον καρτερὸν ἀναφυγών, ἐπιχειροῦντος αὐτῷ τοῦ
βασιλέως πολλοὺς ἀποβαλὼν ἔφευγε διὰ τῶν ὀρεινῶν
ἐπὶ Φρυγίας, ὁδὸν ἀτριβῆ, βαλλόμενός τε καὶ χαλε-
πῶς <ἀμυνόμενος>.[15]

276   66. Ἥ τε νίκη λαμπρὰ καὶ ὀξεῖα ἐξ ἐφόδου γενομένη ταχὺ διέπτη καὶ πολλοὺς ἐς τὸν Μιθριδάτην
μετέβαλεν. ὁ δὲ καὶ τὰ ἐν Καππαδοκίᾳ φρούρια τοῦ
Μουρήνα πάντα ἐπιδραμών τε καὶ ἐξελάσας ἔθυε τῷ
στρατίῳ Διὶ πάτριον θυσίαν ἐπὶ ὄρους ὑψηλοῦ, κορυ-
277 φὴν μείζονα ἄλλην ἀπὸ ξύλων ἐπιτιθείς. πρῶτοι δ᾽ ἐς
αὐτὴν οἱ βασιλεῖς ξυλοφοροῦσι, καὶ περιθέντες ἑτέραν ἐν κύκλῳ βραχυτέραν τῇ μὲν ἄνω γάλα καὶ μέλι
καὶ οἶνον καὶ ἔλαιον καὶ θυμιάματα πάντα ἐπιφο-
ροῦσι, τῇ δ᾽ ἐπιπέδῳ σῖτόν τε καὶ ὄψον ἐς ἄριστον
τοῖς παροῦσιν ἐπιτιθέντες, οἷόν τι καὶ ἐν Πασαρ-
γάδαις ἐστὶ τοῖς Περσῶν βασιλεῦσι θυσίας γένος,
278 ἅπτουσι τὴν ὕλην. ἡ δ᾽ αἰθομένη διὰ τὸ μέγεθος τη-
λοῦ τε χιλίων σταδίων γίγνεται τοῖς πλέουσι κατα-
φανής, καὶ πελάσαι φασὶν ἐς πολλὰς ἡμέρας, αἰθο-

that Rome was clearly making war on him, ordered Gordius to attack the villages. Gordius quickly seized many 274 transport and pack animals, as well as men, both civilians and soldiers, and took up position opposite Murena himself, with a river between them. Neither of them initiated combat, until Mithridates arrived with a large army, and a 275 fierce battle takes place beside the river. Mithridates forced his way across the river and got much the better of Murena in all respects. Murena escaped to a strong defensive position on a hill, but when the king attacked and killed many of his men, he fled across the mountains into Phrygia, along a difficult route where he was under attack by missiles and defended himself with difficulty.

66. News of this brilliant victory, rapidly achieved at 276 the first assault, quickly spread and caused many to change sides to Mithridates. The king then attacked and expelled all Murena's garrisons from Cappadocia, before offering the traditional sacrifice of his ancestors to Zeus Stratius on a high mountain, having placed on it another higher summit made out of wood. The procedure begins with the 277 kings collecting wood for this, and then building a lower pile around it. On the higher one they put milk and honey and wine and oil and all sorts of incense, and on the lower they lay out bread and meat and wine as a meal for those present, like the type of sacrifice made by the kings of Persia at Pasargadae. They then light the wood. As it 278 burns, the flames rise so high that it can clearly be seen up to one thousand stades away at sea, and they say it is not

---

15 ἀμυνόμενος add. Goukowsky

279 μένου τοῦ ἀέρος, οὐ δυνατὸν εἶναι. ὁ μὲν δὴ τὴν
θυσίαν ἦγε πατρίῳ νόμῳ· Σύλλα δ' οὐκ ἀξιοῦντος
Μιθριδάτην ἔνσπονδον πολεμεῖσθαι, Αὖλος Γαβίνιος
ἐπέμφθη Μουρήνᾳ μὲν ἀληθῆ τήνδε προαγόρευσιν
ἐρῶν, μὴ πολεμεῖν Μιθριδάτῃ, Μιθριδάτην δὲ καὶ
280 Ἀριοβαρζάνην ἀλλήλοις συναλλάξων. ὁ δὲ Μιθριδάτης ἐν τῇδε τῇ συνόδῳ παιδίον τετραετὲς ἐγγυήσας
τῷ Ἀριοβαρζάνῃ, καὶ ἐπὶ τῇδε προφάσει λαβὼν ἔχειν
Καππαδοκίας ὅσα τε εἶχε καὶ ἕτερα ἐπ' ἐκείνοις,
εἰστία πάντας, καὶ χρυσίον ἐπί τε τῇ κύλικι καὶ τῇ
τροφῇ καὶ ἐπὶ σκώμμασι καὶ ἐπὶ ᾠδῇ πᾶσιν, ὥσπερ
εἰώθει, προυτίθει· οὗ μόνος Γαβίνιος οὐχ ἥψατο.

281 67. Ὁ μὲν δὴ δεύτερος Μιθριδάτῃ καὶ Ῥωμαίοις
πόλεμος τρίτῳ μάλιστα ἔτει ἐς τοῦτο διελύετο. καὶ
σχολὴν ἄγων ὁ Μιθριδάτης Βόσπορον ἐχειροῦτο, καὶ
βασιλέα αὐτοῖς τῶν υἱέων ἕνα ἀπεδείκνυε Μαχάρην.
282 ἐς δ' Ἀχαιοὺς τοὺς ὑπὲρ Κόλχους ἐσβαλών, οἳ δοκοῦ-
σιν εἶναι τῶν ἐκ Τροίας κατὰ τὴν ἐπάνοδον πλανηθέν-
των, δύο μέρη τοῦ στρατοῦ πολέμῳ τε καὶ κρύει καὶ
ἐνέδραις ἀποβαλὼν ἐπανῆλθε, καὶ ἐς Ῥώμην ἔπεμπε
283 τοὺς συγγραψομένους τὰ συγκείμενα. ἔπεμπε δὲ καὶ
Ἀριοβαρζάνης, εἴθ' ἑκὼν εἴτε πρὸς τινων ἐνοχλούμενος, οὐκ ἀπολαμβάνειν Καππαδοκίαν, ἀλλὰ τὸ πλέον
αὐτῆς ἔτι Μιθριδάτην ἀφαιρεῖσθαι. Μιθριδάτης μὲν
οὖν, Σύλλα κελεύοντος αὐτῷ μεθεῖναι Καππαδοκίαν,
μεθῆκε, καὶ ἑτέραν πρεσβείαν ἐπέπεμπεν ἐπὶ τὰς τῶν

possible to go near it for many days, as the air is so hot. So 279
it was, then, that Mithridates made sacrifice in the manner
of his ancestors. Meanwhile, Sulla thought it was not right
to make war on their treaty partner Mithridates, and Aulus
Gabinius was sent both to tell Murena to treat the ban on
attacking Mithridates seriously, and to reconcile Mithridates and Ariobarzanes.[45] At their meeting Mithridates 280
betrothed his four-year-old daughter to Ariobarzanes, and
used this as an excuse both to keep the Cappadocian territory he already held and to get some more in addition.
Then he gave a banquet for everyone, and, as was the
custom, set gold prizes for the whole company for drinking and eating and telling jokes and singing. Gabinius was
the only one not to take part.

67. And so the second war between Mithridates and 281
Rome came to an end in this way after about three years.
Having no distractions, Mithridates now subdued Bosporus and appointed Machares, one of his sons, as their king.
He also attacked the Achaeans north of Colchis, who are 282
supposed to be descended from the Greeks who got lost
on their way home from Troy, but when two divisions of
his army were destroyed in the fighting, by the cold, and
as a result of ambushes, he withdrew, and sent representatives to Rome to sign the agreement. Ariobarzanes also 283
sent a mission to Rome, either because he wanted to or
because he had been lobbied to do so, to complain that he
had not received back Cappadocia, but that most of it was
still in Mithridates' possession. When Sulla ordered him
to evacuate it, however, Mithridates complied, and sent

[45] A. Gabinius was a military tribune in 86, now operating as
a legate of Sulla.

APPIAN

284 συνθηκῶν συγγραφάς· ἤδη δὲ Σύλλα τεθνεῶτος, οὐκ
ἐπαγόντων αὐτὴν ὡς ἐν ἀσχολίᾳ τῶν προβούλων ἐπὶ
τὸ κοινόν, Τιγράνη τὸν γαμβρὸν Μιθριδάτης ἔπεισεν
285 ἐς Καππαδοκίαν ἐμβαλεῖν ὥσπερ ἀφ᾽ ἑαυτοῦ. καὶ τὸ
μὲν σόφισμα οὐκ ἔλαθε Ῥωμαίους, ὁ δ᾽ Ἀρμένιος
Καππαδοκίαν σαγηνεύσας ἐς τριάκοντα μυριάδας ἀνθρώπων ἀνασπάστους ἐς Ἀρμενίαν ἐποίησε, καὶ συνῴκιζεν αὐτοὺς μεθ᾽ ἑτέρων ἔς τι χωρίον ἔνθα πρῶτον
Ἀρμενίας τὸ διάδημα αὐτὸς περιεθήκατο, καὶ Τιγρανόκερτα ἀφ᾽ ἑαυτοῦ προσεῖπεν· δύναται δ᾽ εἶναι Τι-
γρανόπολις.

286   68. Καὶ τάδε μὲν ἦν ἐν Ἀσίᾳ· Σερτώριος δ᾽ Ἰβηρίας
ἡγούμενος αὐτήν τε Ἰβηρίαν καὶ τὰ περίοικα πάντα
ἐπὶ Ῥωμαίους ἀνίστη, καὶ βουλὴν ἐκ τῶν οἱ συν-
287 όντων, ἐς μίμημα τῆς συγκλήτου, κατέλεγεν. δύο δ᾽
αὐτοῦ τῶν στασιωτῶν, Λούκιοι, Μάγιός τε καὶ Φάν-
νιος, Μιθριδάτην ἔπειθον συμμαχῆσαι τῷ Σερτωρίῳ,
πολλὰ περὶ τῆς Ἀσίας αὐτὸν καὶ τῶν ἐγγὺς ἐθνῶν
288 ἐπελπίζοντες. ὁ μὲν δὴ πεισθεὶς ἐς τὸν Σερτώριον
ἔπεμψεν· ὁ δὲ τοὺς πρέσβεις ἐς τὴν ἑαυτοῦ σύγκλητον
παραγαγών τε, καὶ μεγαλοφρονησάμενος ὅτι τὸ κλέος
αὐτοῦ καὶ ἐς τὸν Πόντον διίκετο καὶ Ῥωμαίους ἔξοι
πολιορκεῖν ἀπό τε δύσεως καὶ ἐξ ἀνατολῆς, συνε-
τίθετο τῷ Μιθριδάτῃ δώσειν Ἀσίαν τε καὶ Βιθυνίαν
καὶ Παφλαγονίαν καὶ Καππαδοκίαν καὶ Γαλατίαν,
στρατηγόν τε αὐτῷ Μάρκον Οὐάριον καὶ συμβούλους

another embassy to sign the treaty. But Sulla had died in 284
the meantime, and the senators refused to admit the ambassadors to the meeting on the grounds that they were
too busy. At this, Mithridates persuaded his son-in-law,
Tigranes, to invade Cappadocia as if on his own initiative.
But although the Romans saw through the trick, the Ar- 285
menian king still netted about three hundred thousand
Cappadocians, dragged them off to Armenia, and settled
them, with others, in the place he had first put on the royal
diadem of Armenia, and which he had named Tigranocerta after himself. It means "City of Tigranes."

68. This was the situation in Asia. As for Sertorius, the 286
governor of Iberia, he led Iberia itself and all the surrounding lands in revolt against Rome.[46] In imitation of
the Roman senate, he chose a council from among his
associates, and sent two of his partisans, Lucius Magius 287
and Lucius Fannius, to persuade Mithridates to make an
alliance with him, stirring great hopes in the king about
Asia and the peoples in the vicinity. Mithridates was con- 288
vinced and sent a mission to Sertorius. Sertorius brought
the king's ambassadors into his senate and took great pride
in the fact that his fame had spread as far as the Pontus
and that he would now be able to lay siege to the Roman
empire from both west and east. He made an agreement
with Mithridates, conceding Asia and Bithynia and Paphlagonia and Cappadocia and Galatia to him, and sending
him Marcus Varius as a general, and Lucius Magius and

---

[46] Q. Sertorius, praetor in 83, was assigned the province of
Nearer Spain. He set up a countersenate and controlled much of
Spain for a number of years, resisting official attempts to get rid
of him, until he was finally assassinated in 72.

289 τοὺς Λουκίους, Μάγιόν τε καὶ Φάννιον, ἔπεμψεν. μεθ᾽
ὧν ὁ Μιθριδάτης ἐξέφαινε τὸν τρίτον καὶ τελευταῖόν
οἱ γενόμενον ἐς Ῥωμαίους πόλεμον, ἐν ᾧ πᾶσαν
ἀπώλεσε τὴν ἀρχὴν Σερτωρίου μὲν ἀποθανόντος, ἐν
290 Ἰβηρίᾳ, ἐπιπεμφθέντων δέ οἱ στρατηγῶν ἀπὸ Ῥώμης
προτέρου Λουκούλλου τοῦδε τοῦ νεναυαρχηκότος
Σύλλᾳ, ὑστέρου δὲ Πομπηΐου, ἐφ᾽ ὅτου πάντα ὅσα ἦν
Μιθριδάτου καὶ ὅσα αὐτοῖς γειτονεύοντα, μέχρι ἐπὶ
ποταμὸν Εὐφράτην, προφάσει καὶ ὁρμῇ τοῦ Μιθριδατείου πολέμου ἐς Ῥωμαίους ἅπαντα περιηνέχθη.

291 69. Μιθριδάτης μὲν οὖν, οἷα Ῥωμαίων πολλάκις ἐς
πεῖραν ἐλθών, καὶ τόνδε μάλιστα τὸν πόλεμον ἡγούμενος, ἀπροφασίστως δὴ καὶ ὀξέως γενόμενον, ἄσπειστον ἕξειν, πᾶσαν ἐπενόει παρασκευὴν ὡς ἄρτι δὴ
292 κριθησόμενος περὶ ἁπάντων. καὶ τὸ λοιπὸν τοῦ θέρους
καὶ τὸν χειμῶνα ὅλον ὑλοτομῶν ἐπήγνυτο ναῦς καὶ
ὅπλα, καὶ σίτου διακοσίας μεδίμνων μυριάδας ἐπὶ
θαλάσσῃ διετίθει. σύμμαχοί τε αὐτῷ προσεγίγνοντο,
χωρὶς τῆς προτέρας δυνάμεως, Χάλυβες Ἀρμένιοι
Σκύθαι Ταῦροι Ἀχαιοὶ Ἡνίοχοι Λευκόσυροι, καὶ ὅσοι
περὶ Θερμώδοντα ποταμὸν γῆν ἔχουσι τὴν Ἀμαζόνων
293 λεγομένην. τοσαῦτα μὲν ἐπὶ τοῖς προτέροις αὐτῷ περὶ
τὴν Ἀσίαν προσεγίγνετο, περάσαντι δ᾽ ἐς τὴν Εὐρώπην Σαυρομάτων οἵ τε Βασίλειοι καὶ Ἰάζυγες καὶ
Κόραλλοι, καὶ Θρᾳκῶν ὅσα γένη παρὰ τὸν Ἴστρον ἢ
Ῥοδόπην ἢ τὸν Αἷμον οἰκοῦσι, καὶ ἐπὶ τοῖσδε Βα-
294 στέρναι, τὸ ἀλκιμώτατον αὐτῶν γένος. τοσάδε μὲν δὴ

Lucius Fannius as political advisers. With the assistance   289
of these men, Mithridates declared war. It was the third
and last war he fought against Rome, and in the course of
it he lost his entire kingdom and Sertorius was killed in
Iberia. Generals were sent out from Rome against him,   290
first Lucullus, who had commanded the fleet under Sulla,
and later Pompey, under whose command the whole of
Mithridates' empire, and all the neighboring lands as far
as the river Euphrates, were brought under Roman rule
thanks to the excuse and stimulus provided by the war
against Mithridates.

69. With his frequent experience of fighting Rome,   291
Mithridates knew that this war in particular, begun so
quickly and without any excuses, would be remorseless.
And so he made all his preparations keeping in mind that
everything would soon be at stake. The rest of the summer   292
and the whole winter he spent cutting timber, building
ships, and making weapons. He deposited two million
measures of grain along the coast. He acquired as new
allies, in addition to his existing forces, Chalybes, Armenians, Scythians, Taurians, Achaeans, Heniochi, Leuco-
syrians and those who have the land along the river Thermodon called Amazonia.[47] These were the additions to his   293
army from Asia. Crossing into Europe, he had from the
Sauromatian peoples the Basileioi and the Iazyges and the
Coralli, and from Thrace those who lived along the Ister
and in the Rhodope and Haemus mountains, and as well
as these, the Bastarnae, the most fierce of them all. These   294

[47] The Thermodon (mod. Terme) flows into the Black Sea
from Turkey about thirty-one miles east of Samsun (ancient Amisus).

καὶ τῆς Εὐρώπης τότε προσελάμβανεν ὁ Μιθριδάτης. καὶ μυριάδες ἐκ πάντων ἐς τὸ μάχιμον αὐτῷ συνελέγοντο τεσσαρεσκαίδεκα μάλιστα πεζῶν, καὶ ἱππεῖς ἐπὶ μυρίοις ἑξακισχίλιοι. πολὺς δὲ καὶ ἄλλος ὅμιλος ὁδοποιῶν καὶ σκευοφόρων εἵπετο καὶ ἐμπόρων.

295   70. Ἀρχομένου δ᾽ ἦρος ἀπόπειραν τοῦ ναυτικοῦ ποιησάμενος, ἔθυε τῷ στρατίῳ Διὶ τὴν συνήθη θυσίαν, καὶ Ποσειδῶνι λευκῶν ἵππων ἅρμα καθεὶς ἐς τὸ πέλαγος ἐπὶ Παφλαγονίας ἠπείγετο, στρατηγούντων

296   αὐτῷ Ταξίλου τε καὶ Ἑρμοκράτους. ὡς δ᾽ ἀφίκετο, ἐδημηγόρησε τῷ στρατῷ περί τε τῶν προγόνων μάλα σεμνολόγως καὶ περὶ αὑτοῦ μεγαληγόρως, ὅτι τὴν ἀρχὴν ἐκ βραχέος ἐπὶ πλεῖστον προαγαγὼν οὔποτε Ῥωμαίων ἡττηθείη παρών. εἶτα κατηγόρησεν αὐτῶν ἐς πλεονεξίαν καὶ ἀμετρίαν, "Ὑφ᾽ ἧς," ἔφη, "Καὶ τὴν

297   Ἰταλίαν καὶ τὴν πατρίδα αὐτὴν δεδούλωνται." καὶ τὰς γενομένας οἱ τελευταίας συνθήκας ἐπέφερεν ὡς οὐκ ἐθέλουσιν ἀναγράψασθαι, καιροφυλακοῦντες αὖθις ἐπιθέσθαι. καὶ τοῦτο αἴτιον τοῦ πολέμου τιθέμενος, ἐπῆγε τὴν ἑαυτοῦ στρατιὰν ὅλην καὶ παρασκευήν, καὶ Ῥωμαίων ἀσχολίαν πολεμουμένων ὑπὸ Σερτωρίου κατὰ κράτος ἐν Ἰβηρίᾳ καὶ στασιαζόντων ἐς ἀλ-

298   λήλους ἀνὰ τὴν Ἰταλίαν. "Διὸ καὶ τῆς θαλάσσης," ἔφη, "Καταφρονοῦσι ληστευομένης πολὺν ἤδη χρόνον, καὶ σύμμαχος αὐτοῖς οὐδείς ἐστιν, οὐδ᾽ ὑπήκοος ἑκούσιος ἔτι. οὐχ ὁρᾶτε δ᾽ αὐτῶν," ἔφη, "Καὶ τοὺς ἀρίστους," ἐπιδεικνὺς Οὐάριόν τε καὶ τοὺς Λουκίους,

were the additional forces from Europe recruited by Mithridates. In total he collected some hundred and forty thousand fighting men in the infantry and about sixteen thousand cavalry. Another large body of engineers, porters, and traders followed along.

70. At the beginning of spring, he put his fleet through 295 sea trials, and sacrificed to Zeus Stratius in the customary manner, and to Poseidon by plunging a chariot and white horses into the open sea. He then marched against Paphlagonia, with Taxiles and Hermocrates in command of his army. When he arrived there, he made a speech to the 296 army in which he talked of his ancestors with great pride and boasted about himself, how he had turned a small kingdom into a huge one, and how his forces had never been defeated by the Romans when he himself was present. He then accused them of immoderate greed. "It is greed," he said, "that has led them to enslave even Italy and their own fatherland itself." He also charged them 297 with refusing to have the latest treaty with him officially recorded, because they were looking for an opportunity to attack again. Identifying this as the cause of the war, he emphasized that his own army and military preparations were complete, while pointing to the preoccupations of the Romans, who were being attacked by Sertorius with all his might in Iberia, and facing civil dissension throughout Italy. "This is why," he said, "they have been paying no 298 attention to the sea, which has for a long time now been ravaged by pirate attack, why they have not a single ally nor subject who is still willingly ruled by them. Do you not see that even their noblest citizens," he said, pointing to

"Πολεμίους μὲν ὄντας τῇ πατρίδι, συμμάχους δ᾿ ἡμῖν;"

299   71. Ταῦτ᾿ εἰπὼν καὶ τὸν στρατὸν ἐρεθίσας ἐνέβαλεν ἐς Βιθυνίαν, Νικομήδους ἄρτι τεθνεῶτος ἄπαιδος καὶ τὴν ἀρχὴν Ῥωμαίοις ἀπολιπόντος. Κόττας δ᾿ ἡγούμενος αὐτῆς, ἀσθενὴς τὰ πολέμια πάμπαν, ἔφυγεν ἐς

300 Χαλκηδόνα μεθ᾿ ἧς εἶχε δυνάμεως. καὶ Βιθυνία μὲν ἦν αὖθις ὑπὸ τῷ Μιθριδάτῃ, τῶν πανταχοῦ Ῥωμαίων ἐς Χαλκηδόνα πρὸς Κότταν συνθεόντων. ἐπιόντος δὲ καὶ τῇ Χαλκηδόνι τοῦ Μιθριδάτου, Κόττας μὲν ὑπ᾿ ἀπραξίας οὐ προῄει, Νοῦδος δὲ ὁ ναύαρχος αὐτοῦ, σὺν μέρει τινὶ στρατοῦ τὰ ὀχυρώτατα τοῦ πεδίου καταλαβὼν καὶ ἐξελαθείς, ἔφυγεν ἐπὶ τὰς πύλας τῆς Χαλκηδόνος διὰ θριγκίων πολλῶν πάνυ δυσχερῶς.

301 ἀμφί τε τὰς πύλας ὠθισμὸς ἦν ἐσπηδώντων ὁμοῦ· ὅθεν οὐδὲν τοῖς διώκουσιν αὐτοὺς βέλος ἠτύχει. ὡς δὲ καὶ περὶ τῶν πυλῶν δείσαντες οἱ φύλακες τὰ κλεῖθρα

302 καθῆκαν ἐς αὐτὰς ἀπὸ μηχανῆς, Νοῦδον μὲν καὶ τῶν ἄλλων ἡγεμόνων τινὰς καλῳδίοις ἀνιμήσαντο, οἱ δὲ λοιποὶ μεταξὺ τῶν τε φίλων καὶ τῶν πολεμίων ἀπώλ-

303 λυντο, τὰς χεῖρας ἐς ἑκατέρους ὀρέγοντες. ὅ τε Μιθριδάτης τῇ φορᾷ τῆς εὐτυχίας χρώμενος ἐπῆγεν αὐτῆς ἡμέρας ἐπὶ τὸν λιμένα τὰς ναῦς, καὶ τὸ κλεῖθρον ἀλύσει χαλκῇ δεδεμένον ἀπορρήξας τέσσαρας μὲν ἐνέπρησε τῶν πολεμίων, τὰς δὲ λοιπὰς ἑξήκοντα ἀνεδήσατο, οὐδὲν οὔτε Νούδου κωλύοντος ἔτι οὔτε Κόττα,

Varius and the two Lucii, "are enemies of their own father-land, but allies of ours?"

71. After rousing his men with this speech, Mithridates 299 invaded Bithynia, where Nicomedes had recently died childless and bequeathed his kingdom to Rome.[48] Cotta, the governor of the province, was completely feeble when it came to military matters, and fled to Chalcedon with the forces he had under his command. And so once again 300 Bithynia fell under Mithridatic control, the Romans everywhere rushing to join Cotta in Chalcedon. When Mithridates advanced against the city, Cotta, given his military inexperience, did not go out to confront him, but Nudus, his fleet commander, occupied the strongest position on the plain with part of the army.[49] He was driven off, however, and fled with considerable difficulty across a number of walls to the gates of the city. Here there was a melee as 301 everyone rushed to get into the city at the same time, a situation that resulted in all missiles fired by the pursuers hitting their target. Fearing that the gates might even be captured, the guards used the winch to let down the portcullis. Nudus and some of the other officers were lifted up 302 by ropes, but the rest died, caught between their friends and the enemy, and stretching out their hands to both for mercy. Mithridates used the impetus of his success to 303 bring his ships up against the harbor on the same day. After breaking the boom secured with a bronze chain, he burned four enemy ships, and towed the remaining sixty

[48] Although the chronology is disputed, Nicomedes IV probably died in 74, and the Third Mithridatic War began in 73.

[49] M. Aurelius Cotta was consul in 74. P. Rutilius Nudus is known only from this action.

304 ἀλλ' ἐς τὰ τείχη συγκεκλεισμένων. ἀπέθανον δὲ Ῥωμαίων μὲν ἐς τρισχιλίους, καὶ Λεύκιος Μάλλιος, ἀνὴρ
ἀπὸ βουλῆς, Μιθριδάτου δὲ Βαστερνῶν τῶν πρώτων
ἐσπεσόντων ἐς τὸν λιμένα εἴκοσιν.

305 72. Λεύκιος δὲ Λεύκολλος ὑπατεύειν καὶ στρατηγεῖν
αἱρεθεὶς τοῦδε τοῦ πολέμου τέλος μέν τι στρατιωτῶν
ἦγεν ἐκ Ῥώμης, δύο δ' ἄλλα τὰ Φιμβρίου καὶ ἐπ'
αὐτοῖς ἕτερα δύο προσλαβών, σύμπαντας ἔχων πεζοὺς τρισμυρίους καὶ ἱππέας ἐς χιλίους ἐπὶ ἑξακο-
σίοις, παρεστρατοπέδευε τῷ Μιθριδάτῃ περὶ Κύζικον.

306 καὶ δι' αὐτομόλων ἐπιγνοὺς εἶναι τῷ βασιλεῖ στρατιὰν μὲν ἀνδρῶν ἀμφὶ μυριάδας τριάκοντα, ἀγορὰν
δὲ εἴ τι σιτολογοῦντες ἢ ἐκ θαλάσσης λάβοιεν, ἔφη
πρὸς τοὺς ἀμφ' αὐτὸν ἁμαχὶ λήψεσθαι τοὺς πολεμίους αὐτίκα, καὶ τοῦ ἐπαγγέλματος αὐτοῖς ἐνεκε-

307 λεύετο μνημονεύειν. ὄρος δὲ ἰδὼν εὔκαιρον ἐς στρα-
τοπεδείαν, ὅθεν αὐτὸς μὲν εὐπορήσειν ἔμελλεν ἀγορᾶς,
τοὺς δὲ πολεμίους ἀποκλείσειν, ἐπεχείρει καταλαβεῖν
ὡς ἐν τῷδε τὴν νίκην ἀκίνδυνον ἕξων. μιᾶς δ' οὔσης
ἐς αὐτὸ διόδου στενῆς, ὁ Μιθριδάτης αὐτὴν ἐφύλαττεν ἐγκρατῶς, ὧδε καὶ Ταξίλου καὶ τῶν ἄλλων

308 ἡγεμόνων αὐτῷ παραινούντων. Λεύκιος δὲ Μάγιος ὁ
Σερτωρίῳ καὶ Μιθριδάτῃ τὰ ἐς ἀλλήλους διαιτήσας,
ἀνηρημένου τοῦ Σερτωρίου πρὸς Λεύκολλον ἐπεπόμφει κρύφα, καὶ πίστιν λαβὼν μετέπειθε τὸν Μιθριδάτην ὑπεριδεῖν Ῥωμαίων παροδευόντων τε καὶ στρα-

309 τοπεδευόντων ὅπη θελήσειαν. τὰ γὰρ ὑπὸ Φιμβρίᾳ
γενόμενα δύο τέλη βουλεύειν αὐτομολίαν, καὶ αὐτίκα

away, with neither Nudus nor Cotta offering resistance, 304
confined as they were within the walls. Roman casualties
were about three thousand, including the senator, Lucius
Mallius; Mithridates lost twenty Bastarnae, the first to
break into the harbor.

72. Lucius Lucullus, who had been elected consul and 305
appointed to the command of this war, brought one legion
of soldiers from Rome, and added to it the two legions of
Fimbria and two new ones, his total force coming to thirty
thousand infantry and one thousand six hundred cavalry.
He made camp near Cyzicus opposite Mithridates. When 306
he learned from deserters that the king had an army of
about three hundred thousand men and that he got his
supplies either by foraging or by sea, Lucullus said to his
immediate entourage that he would quickly reduce the
enemy without a battle, and he told them to remember
this promise. Noticing an elevated location ideal for a 307
camp, from which he could easily supply his own army but
cut off the enemy's supply route, he moved forward to
occupy it in the belief that it would provide him with a
risk-free victory. There was only a single, narrow route up
to it, which Mithridates guarded securely on the advice of
Taxiles and his other officers. Lucius Magius, who negoti- 308
ated the agreement between Sertorius and Mithridates,
now contacted Lucullus secretly, as Sertorius had been
killed. On receiving assurances from Lucullus, he persuaded Mithridates to let the Romans march past and
camp wherever they wanted. For, according to him, the 309
two legions that had been under the command of Fimbria

APPIAN

τῷ βασιλεῖ προσέσεσθαι· τί οὖν χρῄζειν αὐτὸν ἀγῶνος καὶ φόνου, δυνάμενον ἀμαχὶ κρατῆσαι τῶν πο-
310 λεμίων; οἷς ὁ Μιθριδάτης συνθέμενος ἀνοήτως μάλα
καὶ ἀνυπόπτως, περιεῖδε Ῥωμαίους διὰ στενοῦ παρο-
δεύοντας ἀδεῶς καὶ ἐπιτειχίζοντας αὐτῷ μέγα ὄρος,
οὗ κρατοῦντες αὐτοὶ μὲν ὄπισθεν ἔμελλον ἀγορὰν
311 ἀδεῶς ἐπάξεσθαι, Μιθριδάτην δὲ λίμνῃ καὶ ὄρεσι καὶ
ποταμοῖς ἀποκλείσειν τῶν κατὰ γῆν ἁπάντων, ὅ τι
μὴ γλίσχρως ποτὲ λάβοι, οὔτε ἐξόδους εὐρείας ἔτι
ἔχοντα, οὔτε βιάζεσθαι δυνάμενον ἔτι Λεύκολλον ὑπὸ
312 τῆς δυσχωρίας, ἧς κρατῶν κατεφρόνησεν. ὅ τε χειμὼν ἤδη πλησιάζων ἔμελλε καὶ τῶν ἀπὸ τῆς θαλάσσης αὐτὸν ἐν ἀπορίᾳ καταστήσειν. ἃ θεωρῶν ὁ Λεύκολλος τοὺς φίλους ἀνεμίμνησκε τῆς ὑποσχέσεως,
καὶ τὸ ἐπαγγελθὲν ὡς παρὸν ἐδείκνυ.

313   73. Ὁ δὲ Μιθριδάτης δυνηθεὶς ἂν ἴσως καὶ τότε διὰ
τὸ πλῆθος διὰ μέσων ὤσασθαι τῶν πολεμίων, τούτου
μὲν ὑπερεῖδε, Κυζίκῳ δὲ οἷς παρεσκεύασε πρὸς πολιορκίαν ἐπετίθετο, νομίσας ἐν τῷδε διορθώσειν τὴν
δυσχωρίαν ὁμοῦ καὶ τὴν ἀπορίαν. οἷα δὲ εὐπορῶν
στρατοῦ πολλοῦ, πᾶσιν ἔργοις ἐπεχείρει, τόν τε
σταθμὸν ἀποτειχίζων τείχει διπλῷ, καὶ τὰ λοιπὰ τῆς
314 πόλεως ἀποταφρεύων. χώματά τε ἤγειρε πολλά, καὶ
μηχανὰς ἐπήγνυτο, πύργους καὶ χελώνας κριοφόρους,
ἑλέπολίν τε ἑκατὸν πήχεων, ἐξ ἧς ἕτερος πύργος
ἐπῆρτο καταπέλταις καὶ λίθους καὶ βέλη ποικίλα

were planning to desert and would immediately join Mithridates: what was the point of a battle and bloodshed, when it was possible to get the better of the enemy without fighting? To this, very foolishly and unsuspectingly, Mithridates agreed, and allowed the Romans to march through the narrow approach road unchallenged and fortify the big hill against him. This gave them control of a position from which they themselves could bring in supplies from their rear without danger, while cutting off Mithridates, who was hemmed in by a lake, mountains, and rivers from all landward provisions, apart from what he might occasionally get with difficulty. He now no longer had a wide route for withdrawal, nor could he dislodge Lucullus from the impregnable position which Mithridates had underestimated when he held it. And winter was now approaching, which would also cause difficulties for him with regard to supplies brought by sea. When Lucullus saw this he reminded his staff of the promise he had made, and pointed out that what he said would happen was almost a reality.

73. Mithridates might even then have been able to force his way through the middle of the enemy lines because of his sheer numbers, but he neglected to do so, and used the resources he had prepared to press on with the siege of Cyzicus, in the belief that capturing it would provide the solution for both his weak position and supply problems. Having large numbers of troops at his disposal, he pressed the attack with all means available, blockading the port with a double wall, and digging a trench around the rest of the city. He raised numerous mounds, built machines, towers, and sheds for rams. He constructed one siege tower one hundred cubits high, on top of which he placed another tower for firing stones and a variety of

315 ἀφιείς. κατὰ δὲ τοὺς λιμένας δύο πεντήρεις ἐζευγμέ-
ναι πύργον ἕτερον ἔφερον, ἐξ οὗ γέφυρα, ὁπότε προσ-
πελάσειαν ἐς τὸ τεῖχος, ὑπὸ μηχανῆς ἐξήλλετο. ὡς δ᾽
ἕτοιμα αὐτῷ πάντα ἐγεγένητο, πρῶτα μὲν τρισχιλίους
αἰχμαλώτους Κυζικηνοὺς ἐπὶ νεῶν τῇ πόλει προσῆ-
316 γεν, οἳ χεῖρας ἐς τὸ τεῖχος ὀρέγοντες ἐδέοντο σφῶν
κινδυνευόντων φείσασθαι τοὺς πολίτας, μέχρι Πεισί-
στρατος αὐτοῖς, ὁ στρατηγὸς ὁ τῶν Κυζικηνῶν, ἀπὸ
τοῦ τείχους ἐκήρυξε φέρειν τὸ συμβαῖνον ἐγκρατῶς,
αἰχμαλώτους γεγονότας.

317   74. Ὁ δὲ Μιθριδάτης ὡς ἀπέγνω τῆσδε τῆς πείρας,
ἐπῆγε τὴν ἐπὶ τῶν νεῶν μηχανήν· καὶ ἥ τε γέφυρα
ἐς τὸ τεῖχος ἐξήλατο ἄφνω, καὶ τέσσαρες ἀπ᾽ αὐτῆς
318 ἄνδρες ἐξέδραμον. ᾧ δὴ καὶ μάλιστα καινοτρόπῳ
φανέντι καταπλαγέντες οἱ Κυζικηνοὶ ἐπὶ μέν τι ὑπε-
χώρησαν, οὐκ ὀξέως δὲ ἑτέρων ἐπιδραμόντων ἀνεθάρ-
ρησάν τε καὶ τοὺς τέσσαρας κατέωσαν ἐς τὸ ἔξω,
ταῖς τε ναυσὶ πῦρ καὶ πίσσαν ἐπιχέαντες ἠνάγκασαν
πρύμναν τε κρούσασθαι καὶ ὑποχωρεῖν ὀπίσω μετὰ
319 τοῦ μηχανήματος. ὧδε μὲν δὴ τῶν κατὰ θάλασσαν
ἐπενεχθέντων ἐκράτουν οἱ Κυζικηνοί· τρίτα δ᾽ αὐτοῖς
ἐπήγετο τῆς αὐτῆς ἡμέρας τὰ ἐν τῇ γῇ μηχανήματα
ὁμοῦ πάντα, πονουμένοις τε καὶ μεταθέουσιν ἐς τὸ ἀεὶ
320 βιαζόμενον. τοὺς μὲν οὖν κριοὺς λίθοις ἀπεκαύλιζον
ἢ βρόχοις ἀνέκλων ἢ φορμοῖς ἐρίων τῆς βίας ἐξέλυον,
τῶν δὲ βελῶν τοῖς μὲν πυρφόροις ὑπήντων ὕδατι καὶ
ὄξει, τὰ δ᾽ ἄλλα προβολαῖς ἱματίων ἢ ὀθόναις κεχα-
λασμέναις τῆς φορᾶς ἀνέλυον, ὅλως τε οὐδὲν προθυ-

other missiles from catapults. To use against the harbor,   315
two quinqueremes tied together carried yet another
tower: from this a bridge could be let down mechanically
when the ships approached close to the wall. Once he had
everything ready, Mithridates first embarked three thousand Cyzicene prisoners on ships and sailed up to the city.
These stretched out their hands toward the wall begging   316
the citizens to spare them in their danger, until Pisistratus,
commander of the Cyzicene forces, declared from the wall
that as they had been made prisoners of war, they must
bear their fate resolutely.

74. When he abandoned this attempt, Mithridates   317
brought up the machine on the two ships. The bridge was
suddenly let down on the wall, and four men ran out from
it. The Cyzicenes were very unsettled by the strange ap-   318
pearance of the machine and pulled back a little, but,
encouraged by the failure of any others to rush into the
attack, they threw the four men over the wall, poured
burning pitch onto the ships and forced them to backwater
and withdraw with the device. In this way the Cyzicenes   319
got the better of the attackers brought against them from
the sea. A third assault, however, was launched against
them the same day, when all the siege engines on the
landward side were brought to bear at the same time
against the hard pressed defenders, who were running
everywhere to deal with the constant pressure. They   320
broke the heads off the rams with stones, fended them off
with halters, or absorbed the shock they caused with bas-
kets of wool. The burning missiles that were fired at them
they met with water and vinegar, and the impact of the
others they reduced by holding up cloaks in front of them
or unrolled linen cloths. In short, they spared no effort in

321 μίας ἀνδρὶ δυνατῆς ἐξέλειπον. καὶ τάδε αὐτοῖς φερε-
πονώτατα δὴ κακοπαθοῦσιν ὅμως γε τοῦ τείχους
ἐκαύθη τι καὶ συνέπεσεν ἐς ἑσπέραν. οὐ μὴν ἔφθασέ
τις ἐσαλάμενος ἔτι θερμόν, ἀλλ᾽ αὐτὸ νυκτὸς αὐτίκα
322 περιῳκοδόμησαν οἱ Κυζικηνοί. τῶν δὲ αὐτῶν ἡμερῶν
πνεῦμα σφοδρὸν ἐπιγενόμενον περιέκλασε τὰ λοιπὰ
τῶν μηχανημάτων τοῦ βασιλέως.

323   75. Λέγεται δ᾽ ἡ πόλις ἐμπροίκιον ὑπὸ Διὸς τῇ κόρῃ
δοθῆναι, καὶ σέβουσιν αὐτὴν οἱ Κυζικηνοὶ μάλιστα
θεῶν. ἐπελθούσης δὲ τῆς ἑορτῆς, ἐν ᾗ θύουσι βοῦν
μέλαιναν, οἱ μὲν οὐκ ἔχοντες ἔπλαττον ἀπὸ σίτου,
μέλαινα δὲ βοῦς ἐκ πελάγους πρὸς αὐτοὺς διενήχετο,
καὶ τὸ κλεῖθρον τοῦ στόματος ὑποδῦσά τε καὶ ἐς τὴν
πόλιν ἐσδραμοῦσα ὥδευσεν ἀφ᾽ ἑαυτῆς ἐς τὸ ἱερὸν
324 καὶ τοῖς βωμοῖς παρέστη. ταύτην μὲν οὖν οἱ Κυζικηνοὶ μετὰ χρηστῆς ἐλπίδος ἔθυον, οἱ δὲ φίλοι τῷ
Μιθριδάτῃ συνεβούλευον ὡς ἱερᾶς τῆς πόλεως ἀπο-
πλεῦσαι. ὁ δ᾽ οὐ πεισθεὶς ἐπὶ τὸ Δίνδυμον ὄρος ὑπερ-
κείμενον ἀνῄει, καὶ χῶμα ἀπ᾽ αὐτοῦ ἐς τὴν πόλιν
ἔχου, πύργους τε ἐφίστη, καὶ ὑπονόμοις τὸ τεῖχος
325 ἀνεκρήμνη. τοὺς δ᾽ ἵππους ἀχρείους οἱ τότε ὄντας, καὶ
ἀσθενεῖς δι᾽ ἀτροφίαν καὶ χωλεύοντας ἐξ ὑποτριβῆς,
ἐς Βιθυνίαν περιέπεμπεν· οἷς ὁ Λεύκολλος περῶσι τὸν
Ῥύνδακον ἐπιπεσὼν ἔκτεινε πολλούς, καὶ αἰχμαλώτους ἔλαβεν ἄνδρας μὲν ἐς μυρίους καὶ πεντακισχιλίους, ἵππους δ᾽ ἐς ἑξακισχιλίους καὶ σκευοφόρα
326 πολλά. καὶ τάδε μὲν ἦν περὶ Κύζικον, τῷ δ᾽ αὐτῷ
χρόνῳ Φρυγίαν Εὔμαχος Μιθριδάτου στρατηγὸς ἐπι-

doing everything humanly possible. In spite of the fact   321
that they toiled away with exceptional perseverance, a part
of the wall was set on fire and it collapsed toward evening,
although the heat was so great that no one rushed in, and
the Cyzicenes immediately built a wall inside it during the
night. In the same period of days, a strong wind blew up   322
and reduced the rest of the king's machines to twisted
wrecks.

75. The city of Cyzicus is said to have been given by   323
Zeus to Persephone as a dowry, and the citizens certainly
honor her especially among the gods. When her festival
came round, at which they sacrifice a black heifer, they did
not have a heifer and so made one out of bread. A real
black heifer, however, swam across to them from the sea:
ducking under the boom at the mouth of the harbor, it ran
into the city, found its own way to the temple and stood
beside the altar. So, it was this one that the Cyzicenes sac-   324
rificed with high hopes. Mithridates' courtiers, on the
other hand, advised him to sail away as the city was sacro-
sanct. He refused, and going up Mount Dindymus, which
overlooked the city, he built a ramp stretching from there
to the city, and stationed towers on it, while undermining
the walls at the same time. As it was not possible to use his   325
cavalry at this time, and the horses were weak from hunger
and lame from sore hooves, he sent them off to Bithynia.
While they were crossing the river Rhyndacus Lucullus
fell on them and killed many. He also captured about fifteen thousand men, six thousand horses and a large number of pack animals. At the same time that this was hap-   326
pening in Cyzicus, Mithridates' general, Eumachus, was

τρέχων ἔκτεινε Ῥωμαίων πολλοὺς μετὰ παίδων καὶ
γυναικῶν, Πισίδας τε καὶ Ἰσαύρους ὑπήγετο καὶ Κιλικίαν, μέχρι τῶν τις Γαλατικῶν τετραρχῶν Δηιότα-
ρος ἐπιπολάζοντα αὐτὸν συνεδίωξε καὶ πολλοὺς διέφθειρεν.

327   76. Καὶ περὶ μὲν Φρυγίαν τοιάδε ἐγίγνετο, Μιθριδάτου δὲ χειμὼν ἐπιγενόμενος ἀφήρητο καὶ τὴν ἐκ
τῆς θαλάττης ἀγοράν, εἴ τις ἦν, ὥστε πάμπαν ὁ
στρατὸς ἐλίμωττε, καὶ πολλοὶ μὲν ἀπέθνησκον, εἰσὶ
328   δ' οἳ καὶ σπλάγχνων ἐγεύοντο βαρβαρικῶς· οἱ δ' ἄλλοι ποηφαγοῦντες ἐνόσουν. καὶ τὰ νεκρὰ σφῶν ἀγχοῦ
ἄταφα ῥιπτούμενα λοιμὸν ἐπῆγεν ἐπὶ τῷ λιμῷ. δι-
εκαρτέρει δ' ὅμως ὁ Μιθριδάτης, ἐλπίζων ἔτι τὴν Κύζικον αἱρήσειν τοῖς χώμασι τοῖς ἀπὸ τοῦ Δινδύμου.
ὡς δὲ καὶ ταῦθ' ὑπεσύροντο οἱ Κυζικηνοί, καὶ τὰς ἐπ'
αὐτῶν μηχανὰς ἐπίμπρασαν, καὶ αἰσθήσει τοῦ λιμοῦ
πολλάκις ἐπεκθέοντες τοῖς πολεμίοις ἀσθενεστάτοις
γεγονόσιν ἐπετίθεντο, δρασμὸν ὁ Μιθριδάτης ἐβού-
329   λευε. καὶ ἔφευγε νυκτὸς αὐτὸς μὲν ἐπὶ τῶν νεῶν ἐς
Πάριον, ὁ δὲ στρατὸς αὐτοῦ κατὰ γῆν ἐς Λάμψακον.
περῶντας δ' αὐτοὺς τὸν Αἴσηπον ὅ τε ποταμὸς τότε
μάλιστα ἀρθεὶς μέγας, καὶ ἐπὶ τῷ ποταμῷ Λεύκουλ-
330   λος ἐπιδραμὼν ἔφθειρεν. ὧδε μὲν οἱ Κυζικηνοὶ πολλὴν
βασιλέως παρασκευὴν διέφθειραν, αὐτοί τε γενναίως
ἀγωνισάμενοι, καὶ λιμῷ πιεσθέντος ὑπὸ Λουκούλλου.
ἀγῶνά τε αὐτῷ θέμενοι μέχρι νῦν τελοῦσι, τὰ Λου-
331   κούλλεια καλούμενα. Μιθριδάτης δὲ τοὺς ἐς Λάμψακον ἐσφυγόντας, ἔτι τοῦ Λουκούλλου παρακαθημένου,

overrunning Phrygia, where he killed a great many Romans with their wives and children. He also subdued Pisidia and Isauria and Cilicia, until one of the Galatian tetrarchs, Deiotarus, chased the insolent marauder off, killing many of his men.

76. This is what was happening in Phrygia. For Mithridates, the onset of winter deprived him even of the meager supplies he was getting by sea, with the result that his army was completely starved, and many of them died. There were even some who, in barbarian fashion, ate human entrails, while others became ill from eating grass. Moreover, as corpses were thrown out unburied among the living, plague was now added to famine. Nevertheless, Mithridates persevered, still hoping to capture Cyzicus by means of the ramps extending from Mount Dindymus. But when the Cyzicenes undermined these ramps, set fire to the machines on them, and, aware of the presence of famine, made frequent sorties on a greatly weakened enemy, Mithridates began to think of running away. And when it was dark he did take to flight, he himself reaching Parium with the fleet, his army making its way by land to Lampsacus. But the river Aesopus, which was in full flood at the time, destroyed them as they were crossing it, and Lucullus' attack added to the effects of the river. This is the story of how the people of Cyzicus destroyed the huge armament of Mithridates, by their own brave resistance and the starvation forced on Mithridates by Lucullus. The citizens established a festival in his honor, called the Lucullan Games, which they celebrate to this very day. While those who had escaped to Lampsacus were still under siege by Lucullus, Mithridates sent ships to bring

327

328

329

330

331

ναῦς ἐπιπέμψας ἐξεκόμισε σὺν αὐτοῖς Λαμψακηνοῖς.

332 μυρίους δ᾽ ἐπιλέκτους ἐπὶ νεῶν πεντήκοντα Οὐαρίῳ, πεμφθέντι οἱ στρατηγεῖν ὑπὸ Σερτωρίου, καὶ Ἀλεξάνδρῳ τῷ Παφλαγόνι καὶ Διονυσίῳ τῷ εὐνούχῳ καταλιπών, ταῖς πλέοσιν αὐτῶν ἐς Νικομήδειαν ἔπλει. καὶ χειμὼν ἐπιγενόμενος πολλὰς ἑκατέρων διέφθειρεν.

333   77. Λεύκολλος δ᾽ ἐπεὶ τὸ κατὰ γῆν εἴργαστο διὰ τοῦ λιμοῦ, ναῦς ἐκ τῆς Ἀσίας ἀγείρας διέδωκε τοῖς ἀμφ᾽ αὐτὸν στρατηγοῦσιν. καὶ Τριάριος μὲν Ἀπάμειαν εἷλεν ἐπιπλεύσας, καὶ πολλὴ τῶν Ἀπαμέων

334 συμφυγόντων ἐς τὰ ἱερὰ ἐγίγνετο σφαγή· Βάρβας δὲ Προυσιάδα <καὶ Προῦσαν>[16] εἷλε τὴν πρὸς τῷ ὄρει, καὶ Νίκαιαν ἔλαβε, τῶν Μιθριδάτου φρουρῶν ἐκφυγόντων. Λεύκολλος δὲ περὶ τὸν Ἀχαιῶν λιμένα τρισ-

335 καίδεκα ναῦς εἷλε τῶν πολεμίων. Οὐάριον δὲ καὶ Ἀλέξανδρον καὶ Διονύσιον περὶ Λῆμνον ἐν ἐρήμῃ νήσῳ καταλαβών, ἔνθα δείκνυται βωμὸς Φιλοκτήτου καὶ χαλκοῦς ὄφις καὶ τόξα καὶ θώραξ ταινίαις περί-

336 δετος, μνῆμα τῆς ἐκείνου πάθης, ἐπέπλει μὲν αὐτοῖς ῥοθίῳ τε πολλῷ καὶ μετὰ καταφρονήσεως, εὐσταθῶς δ᾽ ἐκείνων ὑπομενόντων ἔστησε τὴν εἰρεσίαν, καὶ κατὰ δύο ναῦς ἐπιπέμπων ἠρέθιζεν ἐς ἔκπλουν. οὐ σαλευόντων δ᾽ ἐκείνων ἀλλ᾽ ἀπὸ γῆς ἀμυνομένων,

___

[16] καὶ Προῦσαν add. Goukowsky

50 C. Valerius Triarius was praetor in 78. Barba is not otherwise known. Prusa lay at the foot of Mount Olympus in Mysia, Prusias on the Propontis, some nineteen miles north of it.

them and the inhabitants to safety. Leaving ten thousand 332
select troops and fifty ships under the command of Varius
(the general sent to him by Sertorius), Alexander the
Paphlagonian, and Dionysius the eunuch, he sailed off to
Nicomedia with most of his forces. But a storm blew up
and destroyed many of both groups.

77. Having used famine to achieve this result by land, 333
Lucullus now collected ships from Asia and assigned them
to the generals in his command. Triarius sailed against
Apamea and captured it, slaughtering many of the citizens
who had fled to the temples for refuge. Barba captured 334
Prusias and the town of Prusa situated near the mountain,
and occupied Nicaea when Mithridates' garrison abandoned it.[50] At Achaean Harbor Lucullus captured thirteen
enemy ships, and then caught up with Varius, Alexander, 335
and Dionysius on a deserted island near Lemnos. Here
one can see the altar of Philoctetes and a snake made of
gold and a bow and a breastplate with bands attached, a
memorial of what that hero had suffered.[51] Lucullus at- 336
tacked them by sea with a great surge and in disdain for
the enemy, but when they steadfastly stood their ground,
he held his rowers back and sent in ships two at a time, to
try to lure them into putting out to sea. But as they refused
to do so, preferring to defend themselves on land, Lucul-

---

[51] Appian is referring to the story (which has many variations)
of how Philoctetes was bitten by a snake on the island of Lemnos,
thus preventing him from going with the Greek expedition to
Troy. The Greeks needed him, however, and the weapons of Heracles in his possession, and ten years later Odysseus, among
others, was sent to fetch him.

περιέπλευσε τὴν νῆσον ἑτέραις ναυσί, καὶ πεζοὺς ἐς αὐτὴν ἐκβιβάσας συνήλασε τοὺς ἐχθροὺς ἐπὶ τὰς
337 ναῦς. οἱ δ' ἐς μὲν τὸ πέλαγος οὐκ ἠφίεσαν, τὸν Λουκούλλου στρατὸν δεδιότες, παρὰ δὲ τὴν γῆν πλέοντες, ἔκ τε τῆς γῆς καὶ τῆς θαλάσσης ἀμφίβολοι γιγνόμενοι κατετιτρώσκοντο, καὶ φόνος πολὺς ἦν αὐτῶν καὶ
338 φυγή. ἐλήφθησαν δ' ἐν σπηλαίῳ κρυπτόμενοι Οὐάριός τε καὶ Ἀλέξανδρος καὶ Διονύσιος ὁ εὐνοῦχος. καὶ αὐτῶν ὁ μὲν Διονύσιος, πιὼν ὅπερ ἤγετο φάρμακον, αὐτίκα ἀπέθανε, Οὐάριον δ' ἀναιρεθῆναι προσέταξε Λεύκολλος· οὐ γὰρ ἐδόκει Ῥωμαῖον ἄνδρα βουλευτὴν θριαμβεύειν. Ἀλέξανδρος δὲ ἐς τὴν πομπὴν ἐφυλάσ
339 σετο. καὶ Λεύκολλος περὶ τῶνδε Ῥωμαίοις ἐπέστελλε, τὰ γράμματα δάφνῃ περιβαλών, ὡς ἔθος ἐστὶν ἐπὶ νίκαις· αὐτὸς δὲ ἠπείγετο ἐς Βιθυνίαν.
340   78. Μιθριδάτῃ δ' ἐς τὸν Πόντον ἐσπλέοντι χειμὼν ἐς δὶς ἐπιγίγνεται, καὶ τῶν ἀνδρῶν ἀμφὶ τοὺς μυρίους καὶ νῆες ἀμφὶ τὰς ἑξήκοντα διεφθάρησαν· αἱ δὲ λοιπαὶ διερρίφησαν, ὡς ἑκάστην ὁ χειμὼν ἐξήνεγκεν.
341 αὐτὸς δὲ ῥηγνυμένης τῆς στρατηγίδος ἐς λῃστῶν σκάφος, ἀπαγορευόντων τῶν φίλων, ὅμως ἐνέβη. καὶ
342 ἐς Σινώπην αὐτὸν οἱ λῃσταὶ διέσωσαν. ὅθεν ὁ μὲν ἐς Ἀμισὸν ἀπὸ κάλω διαπλέων, πρός τε τὸν κηδεστὴν Τιγράνην τὸν Ἀρμένιον καὶ ἐς Μαχάρην τὸν υἱόν, ἄρχοντα Βοσπόρου, περιέπεμπεν, ἐπικουρεῖν ἐπείγων ἑκάτερον. ἔς τε Σκύθας τοὺς ὁμόρους χρυσὸν καὶ
343 δῶρα πολλὰ Διοκλέα φέρειν ἐκέλευεν. ἀλλ' ὁ μὲν αὐτοῖς τε δώροις καὶ αὐτῷ χρυσίῳ πρὸς Λεύκολλον

advanced confidently after his victory, subduing all in his
path and foraging for supplies. As it was rich land, and   344
untouched by war for a long time, a slave soon cost four
drachmas, an ox one, and goats, sheep, clothing, and everything else in the same ratio. Lucullus invested Amisus   345
and Eupatoria, which Mithridates had founded beside
Amisus, named after himself and regarded as his royal
capital. With another army Lucullus also laid siege to Themiscyra, which is located on the river Thermodon and was
named after one of the Amazons. At Themiscyra, the be-   346
sieging force brought up towers against the town, raised
siege mounds, and dug such large tunnels that crowds of
soldiers fought each other in subterranean battles. The
defenders dug openings in the tunnels from above and
threw down bears, other wild animals, and swarms of bees
on those working below. The besiegers faced a different   347
type of difficulty at Amisus, where the inhabitants defended themselves bravely, making frequent sorties, and
issuing challenges to personal combat. Mithridates sent   348
his force plentiful supplies and weapons and soldiers from
Cabira, where he spent the winter raising a new army. He
collected about forty thousand infantry and four thousand
cavalry.

79. At the beginning of spring, Lucullus advanced   349
through the mountains against Mithridates, who stationed

ἦσαν ἐκείνῳ κωλύειν τε Λούκολλον, καὶ διαπυρσεύ-
σειν οἱ συνεχῶς, εἴ τι γίγνοιτο. καὶ ἦρχε τῆσδε τῆς
φυλακῆς ἐκ Μιθριδάτου τις ἀνὴρ τοῦ βασιλείου γέ-
350 νους, ὄνομα Φοῖνιξ. ὅς, ἐπεὶ Λεύκολλος ἐπέλαζε, Μιθριδάτῃ μὲν διεπύρσευσεν, ἐς δὲ Λούκολλον ηὐτο-
μόλησε μετὰ τῆς δυνάμεως. καὶ ὁ Λούκολλος ἀδεῶς
351 ἤδη τὰ ὄρη διεξελθὼν ἐς Κάβειρα κατέβη. γενομένης
δ' αὐτῷ τε καὶ Μιθριδάτῃ τινὸς ἱππομαχίας, ἡττώμενος αὖθις ἐς τὸ ὄρος ἀνέθορεν. ὁ δὲ ἵππαρχος αὐτοῦ
Πομπώνιος ἐς Μιθριδάτην τετρωμένος ἀνήχθη· καὶ
πυθομένῳ βασιλεῖ τίνα χάριν οἱ περισωθεὶς δύναιτο
352 ἀποδοῦναι, "Εἰ μέν," ἔφη, "Σὺ φίλος γένοιο Λουκούλλῳ, πάνυ πολλοῦ ἀξίαν· εἰ δ' ἐχθρὸς εἴης, οὐδὲ
βουλεύσομαι." ὧδε μὲν ὁ Πομπώνιος ἀπεκρίνατο· καὶ
αὐτὸν τῶν βαρβάρων κτείνειν ἀξιούντων, ὁ βασιλεὺς
εἶπεν οὐκ ἐξυβρίζειν ἐς ἀτυχοῦσαν ἀρετήν. ἐκτάσσων
δὲ συνεχῶς, οὐ κατιόντος ἐς μάχην τοῦ Λουκούλλου,
353 περιὼν ἀνάβασιν ἐπ' αὐτὸν ἐζήτει. καί τις ἀνὴρ ἐν
τούτῳ Σκύθης, ὄνομα Ὀλκάβας, αὐτόμολος ὢν ἐς
Λούκουλλον ἐκ πολλοῦ, καὶ παρὰ τήνδε τὴν ἱππομα-
χίαν πολλοὺς περισώσας, καὶ δι' αὐτὸ παρὰ τοῦ Λουκούλλου τραπέζης τε καὶ γνώμης καὶ ἀπορρήτων ἀξιούμενος, ἧκεν ἐπὶ τὴν σκηνὴν αὐτοῦ περὶ μεσημβρίαν
ἀναπαυομένου, καὶ ἐσελθεῖν ἐβιάζετο, βραχὺ καὶ
σύνηθες ἐπὶ τοῦ ζωστῆρος ἐγχειρίδιον περικείμενος.
354 κωλυόμενος δ' ἠγανάκτει, καὶ χρείαν τινὰ ἐπείγειν
ἔλεγεν ἐξαναστῆσαι τὸν στρατηγόν. τῶν δὲ θεραπευ-
τήρων οὐδὲν εἰπόντων χρησιμώτερον εἶναι Λουκούλλῳ

forward guard posts to hinder Lucullus' progress and send
him continuous fire signals if anything happened. In command of this forward guard post was a member of the royal
family of Mithridates, named Phoenix. At the approach of   350
Lucullus, Phoenix sent a signal to Mithridates, but then
deserted to the Roman side with his men. Lucullus now
crossed the mountains with nothing to fear and made his
way down to Cabira. In a cavalry engagement with Mith-   351
ridates, however, he was beaten and withdrew again rapidly up into the mountains. His cavalry commander, Pomponius, was wounded in the battle and taken to Mithridates.
When the king asked him what thanks he could pay in
return if his life was spared, he replied, "If you make your   352
peace with Lucullus, a very valuable thanks. If, on the
other hand, you remain his enemy, I will not even consider
the matter." At this reply of Pomponius, the barbarians
advised executing him, but the king refused to do violence
to a brave man who had fallen into misfortune. He then
repeatedly arrayed his army in battle order, but as Lucullus would not come down and fight, he looked around for
a route to climb up to him. In the meantime, a Scythian   353
man named Olcabas, who had long since deserted to
Lucullus and had saved many lives in the recent cavalry
engagement, and because of this was regarded as worthy
to share Lucullus' table, plans, and secrets, now came to
his tent around midday when the general was resting. He
tried to force his way in, wearing his usual short dagger on
a belt, but was not admitted and grew angry, claiming that   354
there was a pressing need to wake the general. When his
servants said there was nothing more important than

τῆς σωτηρίας, ἐπέβη τὸν ἵππον αὐτίκα καὶ ἐς τὸν
Μιθριδάτην ἐξήλασεν, εἴτε ἐπιβουλεύων καὶ δόξας
ὑποπτεύεσθαι, εἴτε σὺν ὀργῇ, περιυβρίζεσθαι νομί-
355 ζων. ἕτερόν τε Σκύθην, ὄνομα Σοβάδακον, ἐνέφηνε τῷ
Μιθριδάτῃ βουλεύειν ἐς Λούκουλλον αὐτομολίαν.

356   80. Σοβάδακος μὲν δὴ συνελαμβάνετο, Λούκολλος
δὲ τὴν κάθοδον τὴν ἐς τὸ πεδίον ἱπποκρατούντων τῶν
πολεμίων ἐκτρεπόμενος, καὶ περίοδον ἑτέραν οὐχ
ὁρῶν, ηὗρεν ἐν σπηλαίῳ κυνηγὸν θηρείων[17] ἀτραπῶν
ἐπιστήμονα, ᾧ χρώμενος ἡγεμόνι κατὰ ὁδοὺς ἀτρι-
357 βεῖς περιῆλθεν ὑπὲρ κεφαλῆς τοῦ Μιθριδάτου, καὶ
κατῄει μὲν ἐκκλίνας καὶ τότε τὸ πεδίον διὰ τοὺς
ἵππους, χαράδραν δὲ ὕδατος ἐν προβολῇ θέμενος
ἐστρατοπέδευσεν. ἀπορῶν δ' ἀγορᾶς ἐς Καππαδοκίαν
ἔπεμπεν ἐπὶ σῖτον, καὶ ἐς τοὺς πολεμίους ἠκροβολί-
358 ζετο, μέχρι, φευγόντων ποτὲ τῶν βασιλικῶν, ὁ Μιθριδάτης ἀπὸ τοῦ χάρακος ἐκδραμὼν καὶ ἐπιπλήξας
ἐπέστρεφεν αὐτούς, καὶ Ῥωμαίους οὕτω κατεφόβησεν
ὡς ἄνω διὰ τῶν ὀρῶν φεύγοντας οὐδ' ἀποστάντων
αἰσθέσθαι τῶν πολεμίων ἐς πολύ, ἀλλ' ἕκαστον ἡγεῖσθαι τὸν συμφεύγοντά οἱ καὶ ἐπιόντα ὄπισθεν εἶναι
359 πολέμιον· οὕτω πάνυ κατεπεπλήγεσαν. καὶ ὁ Μιθριδάτης περὶ τῆσδε τῆς νίκης πανταχοῦ γράφων περιέπεμπεν. τῶν δ' ἱππέων πολὺ μέρος, καὶ μάλιστα δὴ
τὸ μαχιμώτατον, ἐφεδρεύειν ἔταξε τοῖς ἐκ τῆς Καππαδοκίας τὴν ἀγορὰν τῷ Λουκούλλῳ φέρουσιν, ἐλπίζων ἐν ἀπορίᾳ τροφῶν αὐτὸν γενόμενον πείσεσθαι
οἷον αὐτὸς ἔπαθε περὶ Κύζικον.

Lucullus' security, Olcabas immediately mounted his horse and galloped over to Mithridates, either because he had been plotting against Lucullus and thought that he was now suspected of this, or because he was angry, feeling that he had been insulted. He betrayed another Scythian to Mithridates, called Sobadacus, revealing that he was planning to desert to Lucullus. 355

80. Sobadacus was, of course, arrested. Lucullus was wary of going down onto the plain because of the dominance of the enemy cavalry, and he could not see any other way around. But he found a hunter in a cave who was familiar with the tracks used by wild animals, and, with him as a guide, succeeded in getting around Mithridates' army while staying high above it on rough paths. He descended, still avoiding the plain because of the cavalry, and made camp with a mountain stream in front it. As he was short of supplies, he sent to Cappadocia for grain and skirmished with the enemy. Eventually, on one occasion, when the king's troops were fleeing, Mithridates rushed out of the palisade, rebuked them and led a counterattack, which so terrified the Romans that they fled up into the mountains without realizing for a long time that the enemy had withdrawn, but each person believing that every comrade in flight coming up behind him was an enemy soldier. That is how panic-stricken they were. Mithridates circulated reports of this victory everywhere. He then sent a large force of particularly battle-hardened cavalry with orders to look for an opportunity to attack Lucullus' supply train coming from Cappadocia, hoping that in falling short of food, he would suffer what Mithridates himself had suffered at Cyzicus. 356 357 358 359

---

17 θηρείων Goukowsky: θηρίων codd: ὀρείων prop. Schweig.

360 81. Καὶ τὸ μὲν ἐνθύμημα μέγα ἦν, ἀποκλεῖσαι τροφῶν Λεύκολλον, ἐκ μόνης ἔχοντα Καππαδοκίας· οἱ δ' ἱππεῖς οἱ βασιλέως τοῖς προδρόμοις τῶν σιτοφόρων ἐν στενῷ περιτυχόντες, καὶ οὐκ ἀναμείναντες ἐς εὐρυχωρίαν προελθεῖν, ἀχρεῖον ὡς ἐν στενῷ σφίσι

361 τὴν ἵππον ἐποίησαν. ἐν ᾧ καὶ Ῥωμαῖοι φθάσαντες ἐξ ὁδοιπορίας ἐς μάχην παρασκευάσασθαι, τοὺς μὲν ἔκτειναν τῶν βασιλικῶν, βοηθούσης οἷα πεζοῖς τῆς δυσχωρίας, τοὺς δὲ ἐς τὰς πέτρας κατήραξαν, τοὺς δὲ

362 διέρριψαν ὑποφεύγοντας. ὀλίγοι δὲ νυκτὸς ἐς τὸ στρατόπεδον διαδραμόντες τε καὶ μόνοι περιγενέσθαι λέγοντες, μέγα ὂν φύσει τὸ συμβὰν μειζόνως διεθρόησαν. Μιθριδάτης δ' αὐτὸ πρὸ τοῦ Λουκούλλου πυθόμενός τε, καὶ Λεύκολλον ἐλπίσας ἐπὶ τοσῇδε ἱππέων ἀπωλείᾳ αὐτίκα οἱ προσπεσεῖσθαι, φυγὴν ὑπ' ἐκπλήξεως ἐπενόει, καὶ τόδε τοῖς φίλοις εὐθὺς ἐξέφερεν

363 ἐν τῇ σκηνῇ. οἱ δέ, πρίν τι γενέσθαι παράγγελμα, νυκτὸς ἔτι, σπουδῇ τὰ ἴδια ἕκαστος ἐξέπεμπεν ἐκ τοῦ στρατοπέδου· καὶ ὠθουμένων περὶ τὰς πύλας σκευο-

364 φόρων πολὺ πλῆθος ἦν. ὅπερ ἡ στρατιὰ θεωμένη καὶ τοὺς φέροντας ἐπιγιγνώσκουσα, καὶ τοπάζουσα πολλὰ ἀτοπώτερα, σὺν δέει, καὶ ἀγανακτήσει τοῦ μηδὲν αὐτοῖς ἐπηγγέλθαι, τὸν χάρακα σφῶν ἐπιδραμόντες ἔλυον, καὶ διέφευγον ὡς ἐκ πεδίου πάντοθεν ἀκόσμως, ὅπῃ δύναιτο ἕκαστος αὐτῶν, ἄνευ στρατηγοῦ

365 καὶ ἐπιστάτου παραγγέλματος. ὧν ὁ Μιθριδάτης ὀξύτερόν τε καὶ σὺν ἀταξίᾳ γιγνομένων αἰσθόμενος, ἐξέδραμεν ἐκ τῆς σκηνῆς ἐς αὐτοὺς καὶ λέγειν τι ἐπε-

81. The idea of cutting off Lucullus' supplies was an 360
excellent one, given that he was getting them from Cappadocia alone, but when the king's cavalry came into contact with the advance guard of the supply convoy in a
narrow ravine, they did not wait for it to advance into open
space, and thus rendered their horses ineffective in the
confined setting. Meanwhile, the Romans were too quick 361
for them in deploying their marching column into line of
battle. Some of the royal troops they killed, the rough terrain, as always, favoring infantry, the others they broke up
among the rocks or scattered in flight. During the night a 362
few made their escape back to camp, claiming to be the
only survivors, thus causing an exaggerated rumor of what
was already in itself a serious setback. Mithridates learned
of events before Lucullus, fully expecting him to attack
after such heavy losses among the royal cavalry. In panic,
his thoughts turned to flight, and he communicated this
directly to his courtiers in his tent. They did not wait for 363
any orders, but while it was still dark, hastily began to send
their own belongings out of the camp, which caused a
serious congestion of pack animals at the gates. When the 364
soldiers saw this and recognized those carrying the baggage, they began to have many increasingly absurd
thoughts. Afraid, and annoyed that the order had not been
given to them as well, they now rushed at their own palisade, broke it down and, as the terrain was flat, fled in
disorder in every direction, wherever each individual
could go, no order having come from the general or any
officers. When Mithridates realized that things were hap- 365
pening too fast and in an undisciplined manner, he ran out
of his tent to address the men, but no one was listening

χείρει, οὐδενὸς δ᾽ ἐσακούοντος ἔτι, συνθλιβεὶς ὡς ἐν
πλήθει κατέπεσε, καὶ ἐς τὸν ἵππον ἀναβληθεὶς ἐς τὰ
ὄρη σὺν ὀλίγοις ἐφέρετο.

366   82. Λούκουλλος δὲ τῆς περὶ τὴν ἀγορὰν εὐπραγίας
πυθόμενος, καὶ τὴν φυγὴν τῶν πολεμίων ἰδών, ἐπὶ μὲν
τοὺς ἐκφυγόντας ἔπεμπε διώκειν ἱππέας πολλούς, τοῖς
δὲ συσκευαζομένοις ἔτι κατὰ τὸ στρατόπεδον τοὺς
πεζοὺς περιστήσας ἐκέλευε μὴ διαρπάζειν ἐν τῷ τότε
367   μηδέν, ἀλλὰ κτείνειν ἀφειδῶς. οἱ δὲ σκεύη τε χρυσᾶ
καὶ ἀργυρᾶ πολλὰ καὶ ἐσθῆτας πολυτελεῖς θεώμενοι
ἐξέστησαν τοῦ παραγγέλματος. αὐτόν τε τὸν Μιθριδάτην οἱ καταλαμβάνοντες, ἡμίονόν τινα τῶν χρυσο-
φόρων ἐς τὸ σάγμα πατάξαντες, προπεσόντος τοῦ
χρυσίου περὶ τόδε γενόμενοι διαφυγεῖν ἐς Κόμανα
368   περιεῖδον· ὅθεν ἐς Τιγράνην ἔφυγε σὺν ἱππεῦσι δισχιλίοις. ὁ δὲ αὐτὸν ἐς ὄψιν οὐ προσέμενος, ἐν χωρίοις
ἐκέλευσε διαίτης βασιλικῆς ἀξιοῦσθαι, ὅτε δὴ καὶ
μάλιστα τῆς ἀρχῆς ἀπογνοὺς ὁ Μιθριδάτης Βάκχον
εὐνοῦχων ἔπεμπεν ἐς τὰ βασίλεια, τὰς ἀδελφὰς αὐτοῦ
καὶ τὰς γυναῖκας καὶ παλλακάς, ὅπῃ δύναιτο, ἀνε-
369   λοῦντα. αἱ μὲν δὴ διεφθείροντο ξίφεσι καὶ φαρμάκοις
καὶ βρόχοις, δεινὰ ποιοῦσαι· ταῦτα δ᾽ ὁρῶντες οἱ
φρούραρχοι τοῦ Μιθριδάτου ἀθρόως ἐς τὸν Λεύ-
κουλλον μετετίθεντο, χωρὶς ὀλίγων. καὶ ὁ Λούκολλος
αὐτοὺς ἐπιὼν καθίστατο < . . .>[18] καὶ τὰς ἐπὶ τοῦ Πόντου πόλεις περιπλέων ᾔρει, Ἄμαστρίν τε καὶ Ἡράκλειαν καὶ ἑτέρας.

[18] Post καθίστατο lac. indic. Goukowsky

any more, and, jostled by the crowd, he fell over. But he was put on his horse and rode into the mountains with a small number of attendants.

82. When he learned of the success of his supply expedition and saw that the enemy had been routed, Lucullus sent a large force of cavalry to pursue the fugitives. Those of the king's men who were still packing up the camp he surrounded with infantrymen, whom he ordered to refrain from looting for the time being, and concentrate on killing without mercy. But when they saw so many gold and silver vessels and expensive garments, they disobeyed Lucullus' order. And those who caught up with Mithridates himself, when they cut open the packsaddle of one of the mules carrying the king's gold, and the gold fell out, they were too busy picking it up to prevent Mithridates from escaping to Comana. This enabled Mithridates, along with two thousand of his cavalry, to find refuge with Tigranes. Tigranes did not admit him to his presence, but ordered that he be treated with royal hospitality on his estates. Mithridates now gave up all hope of his kingdom, and sent Bacchus, one of his eunuchs, to his palaces to kill his sisters and wives and concubines, however he could manage it. Bitterly lamenting their fate, they died by the sword, by poison or by hanging. Seeing this, all but a few of Mithridates' garrison commanders went over to Lucullus. He advanced against those not complying, and settled the situation <. . .> and sailing along by the towns on the coast of the Pontus, he captured Amastris and Heraclea among others.[52]

366

367

368

369

---

[52] There is probably a lacuna in this sentence, since it was Triarius, not Lucullus who captured Heraclea.

370   83. Σινώπη δ' ἀντεῖχεν ἔτι καρτερῶς, καὶ διεναυμά-
χησεν οὐ κακῶς. πολιορκούμενοι δὲ τὰς ναῦς τὰς βα-
ρυτέρας σφῶν διέπρησαν, καὶ ἐς τὰς κουφοτέρας ἐμ-
βάντες ἀπέδρασαν. Λούκουλλος δὲ τὴν πόλιν εὐθὺς
371   ἐλευθέραν ἠφίει δι' ἐνύπνιον, ὃ τοιόνδε ἦν. Αὐτόλυκόν
φασιν, ἐπὶ τὰς Ἀμαζόνας Ἡρακλεῖ συστρατεύοντα,
ὑπὸ χειμῶνος ἐς Σινώπην καταχθῆναι καὶ τῆς πόλεως
κρατῆσαι· ἀνδριάς τε σεβάσμιος τοῖς Σινωπεῦσιν
ἔχρα, ὃν οἱ μὲν Σινωπεῖς οὐ φθάσαντες ἐς φυγὴν ἐπ-
372   αγαγέσθαι, ὀθόναις καὶ καλῳδίοις περιέδησαν· οὐδὲν
δ' ὁ Λούκουλλος εἰδὼς οὐδὲ προμαθὼν ἔδοξεν ὑπ'
αὐτοῦ κληθεὶς ὁρᾶν αὐτόν, καὶ τῆς ἐπιούσης τὸν ἀν-
δριάντα τινῶν περιβεβλημένον παραφερόντων ἐκλῦ-
373   σαι κελεύσας, εἶδεν οἷον ἔδοξε νυκτὸς ἑωρακέναι. τὸ
μὲν δὴ ἐνύπνιον τοιόνδε ἦν, Λούκουλλος δὲ καὶ Ἀμισὸν ἐπὶ τῇ Σινώπῃ συνῴκιζεν, ἐκφυγόντων μὲν ὁμοίως
τῶν Ἀμισέων διὰ θαλάσσης, πυνθανόμενος δ' ὑπ'
Ἀθηναίων αὐτοὺς θαλασσοκρατούντων συνῳκίσθαι,
καὶ δημοκρατίᾳ χρησαμένους ἐπὶ πολὺ τοῖς Περσι-
374   κοῖς βασιλεῦσιν ὑπακοῦσαι, ἀναγαγόντος δ' αὐτοὺς
ἐς τὴν δημοκρατίαν ἐκ προστάγματος Ἀλεξάνδρου
πάλιν δουλεῦσαι τοῖς Ποντικοῖς, ἐφ' οἷς ἄρα συμπα-
θὴς ὁ Λούκουλλος γενόμενός τε, καὶ φιλοτιμούμενός
γε καὶ ὅδε ἐπὶ Ἀλεξάνδρῳ περὶ γένος Ἀττικόν, αὐτόνομον ἠφίει τὴν πόλιν καὶ τοὺς Σινωπέας[19] κατὰ τά-
375   χος συνεκάλει. ὧδε μὲν δὴ Σινώπην καὶ Ἀμισὸν

[19] Σινωπέας codd: Ἀμισέας prop. Schweig.

83. Sinope, however, held out against him stubbornly, 370
their fleet fighting with some success. But when he laid
siege to them, they burned their heavier ships, embarked
on the lighter ones, and slipped away. Lucullus immediately declared the city free. He did this because of a dream
he had, which was as follows. There is a story that Autoly- 371
cus, who accompanied Heracles on his expedition against
the Amazons, was driven by a storm to Sinope and took
control of it, and that a sacred statue of Autolycus used to
give oracular responses to the citizens of Sinope. When
they were fleeing, the Sinopeans did not have time to take
the statue with them, and so they wrapped it up with linen
cloths tied down with ropes. Lucullus did not know this 372
story and was told nothing about it before he saw Autolycus calling to him in a dream. The next day, when some
men went past carrying the wrapped statue and he ordered them to unwrap it, he saw the vision he thought he
had seen in the night. Such was the dream he had. After 373
Sinope, Lucullus went on to return to their homes the
inhabitants of Amisus, who had fled by sea like the Sinopeans. He discovered that Amisus had been settled by the
Athenians during the period of their naval supremacy.
They had a democratic government for a long time before
they fell under Persian royal rule. A decree of Alexander 374
then restored their democracy, but they were forced into
subjection again by the kings of Pontus. Lucullus sympa-
thized with them, and he too, like Alexander, being keen
to distinguish himself by kindness to the Attic race, declared Amisus independent, and quickly summoned home
the citizens of Sinope. And so Lucullus destroyed and then 375

Λούκουλλος ἐπόρθει τε καὶ συνῴκιζε, καὶ Μαχάρῃ τῷ
παιδὶ τῷ Μιθριδάτου, Βοσπόρου τε βασιλεύοντι καὶ
στέφανόν οἱ πέμψαντι ἀπὸ χρυσοῦ, φιλίαν συνέθετο,
376 Μιθριδάτην δ' ἐξῄει παρὰ Τιγράνους. καὶ ἐς τὴν
Ἀσίαν αὐτὸς ἐπανελθών, ὀφείλουσαν ἔτι τι τῶν Συλ-
λείων ἐπιβολῶν, τέταρτα μὲν ἐπὶ τοῖς καρποῖς, τέλη
δ' ἐπὶ τοῖς θεράπουσι καὶ ταῖς οἰκίαις ὥριζεν. καὶ ἐπι-
νίκια ἔθυεν ὡς δὴ τὸν πόλεμον κατωρθωκώς.

377 84. Ἐπὶ δὲ ταῖς θυσίαις ἐπὶ τὸν Τιγράνην, οὐκ
ἐκδιδόντα οἱ τὸν Μιθριδάτην, ἐστράτευε σὺν δύο
τέλεσιν ἐπιλέκτοις καὶ ἱππεῦσι πεντακοσίοις. καὶ τὸν
Εὐφράτην περάσας, μόνα τὰ χρήσιμα τοὺς βαρβάρους αἰτῶν διώδευεν· οἱ γὰρ ἄνδρες οὐκ ἐπολέμουν,
οὐδ' ἠξίουν τι πάσχειν, ἔστε Λούκουλλον καὶ Τι-
378 γράνην ἐπ' ἀλλήλοις διακριθῆναι. Τιγράνῃ δ' οὐδεὶς
ἐμήνυεν ἐπιόντα Λεύκολλον· ὁ γάρ τοι πρῶτος εἰπὼν
ἐκεκρέμαστο ὑπ' αὐτοῦ, συνταράσσειν αὐτὸν τὰς
πόλεις νομίσαντος. ὡς δέ ποτε ᾔσθετο, Μιθροβαρζάνην προύπεμπε μετὰ δισχιλίων ἱππέων, Λούκουλ-
379 λον ἐπισχεῖν τοῦ δρόμου. Μαγκαίῳ δὲ Τιγρανόκερτα
φυλάττειν ἐπέτρεψεν, ἥν τινα πόλιν, ὥς μοι προείρηται, ἐπὶ τιμῇ τῇ ἑαυτοῦ <διὰ τὸ>[20] βασιλεὺς ἐν ἐκείνῳ
γενέσθαι τῷ χωρίῳ συνῴκιζε, καὶ τοὺς ἀρίστους ἐς
αὐτὴν συνεκάλει, ζημίαν ἐπιτιθείς, ὅσα μὴ μετα-
380 φέροιεν, δεδημεῦσθαι. τείχη τε αὐτοῦ περιέβαλε πεν-
τηκονταπήχη τὸ ὕψος, ἱπποστασίων ἐν τῷ βάθει

[20] διὰ τὸ add. Roos

resettled both Sinope and Amisus. He then made a pact of friendship with Mithridates' son, Machares, king of Bosporus, who had sent him a golden crown; and he demanded that Tigranes hand over Mithridates. Returning   376
to Asia, which still owed some of the indemnity imposed by Sulla, he introduced a twenty-five percent tax on agricultural produce, and taxes on slaves and houses. And he offered sacrifice for victory to the gods, as if he had already won the war.

84. After the sacrifice, Lucullus marched against Ti-   377
granes, who refused to give Mithridates up, with two specially picked legions and five hundred cavalry. After crossing the Euphrates, he only asked for bare necessities from the barbarians whose lands he marched through. For they were not at war and had decided not to risk harm, but to let Lucullus and Tigranes decide matters themselves. No-   378
body told Tigranes of Lucullus' advance, as he had hanged the first person to talk about this, in the belief that he was disturbing the towns of the kingdom. But once he realized it was happening, he sent Mithrobarzanes forward with two thousand cavalry to halt Lucullus' march. He en-   379
trusted to Mancaeus the defense of Tigranocerta, which, as I have already said,[53] he founded in his own honor in that region, because that is where he became king, and where he summoned the leading men of the kingdom to settle, threatening them with the confiscation of everything they did not bring with them to the city. He built a   380
wall fifty cubits high around the site, packed with stables

53 Above, 67.285.

313

γέμοντα, καὶ βασίλεια καὶ παραδείσους κατὰ τὸ προάστειον ἐποίει μακρούς, καὶ κυνηγέσια πολλὰ καὶ λίμνας· ἀγχοῦ δὲ καὶ φρούριον ἀνίστη καρτερόν. καὶ πάντα τότε Μαγκαίῳ ταῦτ' ἐπιτρέψας, περιῄει στρα-

381 τιὰν ἀγείρων. Μιθροβαρζάνην μὲν οὖν ὁ Λούκουλλος εὐθὺς ἐκ τῆς πρώτης συμβολῆς τρεψάμενος ἐδίωκε, Μαγκαῖον δὲ Σεξτίλιος ἐς Τιγρανόκερτα κατακλείσας τὰ μὲν βασίλεια αὐτίκα, ἀτείχιστα ὄντα, διήρπασε, τὴν δὲ πόλιν καὶ τὸ φρούριον ἀπετάφρευε, καὶ μη- χανὰς ἐφίστη, καὶ ὑπονόμοις ἀνεκρήμνη τὸ τεῖχος.

382 85. Καὶ Σεξτίλιος μὲν ἀμφὶ ταῦτα ἐγίγνετο, Τι- γράνης δέ, πεζῶν ἐς πέντε καὶ εἴκοσι μυριάδας ἀγεί- ρας καὶ ἱππέας ἐς πεντακισμυρίους, προύπεμψεν αὐτῶν ἐς Τιγρανόκερτα περὶ ἑξακισχιλίους, οἳ διὰ μέσων Ῥωμαίων ἐς τὸ φρούριον ὠσάμενοί τε καὶ τὰς παλλακὰς τοῦ βασιλέως ἐξαρπάσαντες ἐπανῆλθον.

383 τῷ δὲ λοιπῷ στρατῷ Τιγράνης αὐτὸς ἤλαυνεν ἐπὶ Λεύκολλον. καὶ αὐτῷ τότε πρῶτον Μιθριδάτης ἐς ὄψιν ἐλθὼν συνεβούλευε μὴ συμπλέκεσθαι Ῥωμαίοις, ἀλλὰ τῷ ἱππικῷ μόνῳ περιτρέχοντα καὶ τὴν γῆν λυ- μαινόμενον ἐς λιμὸν αὐτούς, εἰ δύναιτο, περικλεῖσαι, ᾧ τρόπῳ καὶ αὐτὸς ὑπὸ Λουκούλλου περὶ Κύζικον

384 ἀμαχὶ κάμνων τὸν στρατὸν ἀπολέσαι. ὁ δὲ γελάσας αὐτοῦ τὴν στρατηγίαν, προῄει συνεσκευασμένος ἐς μάχην· καὶ τὴν Ῥωμαίων ὀλιγότητα ἰδὼν ἐπέσκωψεν οὕτως· "Εἰ μὲν πρέσβεις εἰσὶν οἵδε, πολλοί, εἰ δὲ πο-

in its basement, and constructed a palace and large gardens in the suburbs, as well as a number of hunting enclosures and ponds, and a strong fort nearby. He then put all of this in the hands of Mancaeus, while he himself traveled around the country to raise an army. Lucullus immediately routed Mithrobarzanes and put him to flight in the first attack, while Sextilius shut Mancaeus up in Tigranocerta, quickly plundered the palace as it did not have any defensive wall, surrounded the city and fort with a ditch, brought up siege engines, and began to dig tunnels under the walls.[54]

85. While Sextilius busied himself with these tasks, Tigranes raised an army of about one hundred and fifty thousand infantry and fifty thousand cavalry. He sent about six thousand cavalry ahead to Tigranocerta, who broke through the middle of the Roman lines to the fort, grabbed the king's concubines and returned to base. Tigranes himself marched with the rest of the army against Lucullus. Now gaining admittance to Tigranes' presence for the first time, Mithridates advised him not to engage at close quarters with the Romans, but to circle around them just with his cavalry, ravaging the land and bringing on them, if possible, starvation, in the same way as he himself had been exhausted by Lucullus at Cyzicus without a fight, and had lost his army. Tigranes dismissed his strategy with derision, and advanced ready for battle. When he saw how small the Roman force was, he jokingly observed, "If these men are ambassadors, there are too many of them; and if

381

382

383

384

[54] This Sextilius may be the same person called Secilius by Dio (36.3.2–3), who was sent by Lucullus in 69/8 to negotiate with the Parthians.

385 λέμιοι, πάμπαν ὀλίγοι." Λεύκολλος δὲ λόφον εὔκαιρον ἰδὼν ὄπισθεν τοῦ Τιγράνους, τοὺς μὲν ἱππέας ἐκ
μετώπου προσέτασσεν ἐνοχλεῖν αὐτῷ καὶ περισπᾶν
ἐφ᾽ ἑαυτοὺς καὶ ὑποχωρεῖν ἑκόντας, ἵνα τῶν βαρβάρων διωκόντων ἡ τάξις παραλυθείη· τοῖς δὲ πεζοῖς
386 αὐτὸς ἐς τὸν λόφον περιοδεύσας ἀνῄει λαθών. καὶ ὡς
εἶδε τοὺς πολεμίους ὑπὸ τῆς διώξεως οἷα νικῶντας
ἐς πολλὰ διεσκεδασμένους, τὰ δὲ σκευοφόρα αὐτῶν
πάντα ὑποκείμενα, ἀνεβόησε· "Νικῶμεν, ὦ ἄνδρες,"
καὶ ἐπὶ τὰ σκευοφόρα πρῶτος ἵετο δρόμῳ. τὰ δὲ
αὐτίκα σὺν θορύβῳ φεύγοντα τοῖς πεζοῖς ἐνέπιπτε,
387 καὶ τοῖς ἱππεῦσιν οἱ πεζοί. τροπή τε ἦν εὐθὺς ὁλοσχε-
ρής· οἵ τε γὰρ ἐν τῇ διώξει μακρὰν ἀπεσπασμένοι
τῶν Ῥωμαϊκῶν ἱππέων ἐπιστρεψάντων ἐς αὐτοὺς
ἀπώλλυντο, καὶ τὰ σκευοφόρα τοῖς ἄλλοις ἐνέπιπτεν
388 ὡς ἐνοχλούμενα. πάντων τε ὡς ἐν τοσῷδε πλήθει θλι-
βομένων, καὶ τὸ ἀκριβὲς οὐκ εἰδότων, ὁπόθεν ἡ ἧσσα
αὐτοῖς ἄρχοιτο, πολὺς ἦν φόνος, οὐδενὸς σκυλεύοντος
οὐδέν· ἀπηγόρευτο γὰρ ἐκ Λουκούλλου μετ᾽ ἀπειλῆς,
ὥστε καὶ ψέλλια καὶ περιαυχένια παροδεύοντες ἔκτεινον ἐπὶ σταδίους ἑκατὸν καὶ εἴκοσιν, ἔστε νὺξ ἐπ-
έλαβε. τότε δ᾽ ἀναστρέφοντες ἐσκύλευον· ἐδίδου γὰρ
ὁ Λούκουλλος ἤδη.

389 86. Γιγνομένην δὲ τὴν ἧτταν ὁ Μαγκαῖος ἐφορῶν
ἀπὸ Τιγρανοκέρτων, τοὺς Ἕλληνας, οἳ ἐμισθοφόρουν
αὐτῷ, πάντας ἐξώπλισεν ὑποπτεύων· οἳ σύλληψιν

they are enemy soldiers, there are altogether too few of
them." Lucullus, observing that there was a strategically   385
located hill behind Tigranes, ordered his cavalry to make
a frontal attack to distract him and draw him forward
against themselves, but to withdraw readily so that the
barbarians would break rank in their pursuit. He himself
went around the back with the infantry and climbed the
hill without being noticed. As soon as he saw the enemy   386
scattered everywhere in what they assumed was a victorious pursuit, while their entire baggage train lay below him,
he shouted out, "Victory is ours, men," and was the first to
charge the baggage train. They immediately fled in confusion, crashing into the infantry, and then the infantry
crashed into the cavalry. In no time at all the rout was   387
complete. For in their pursuit they had been drawn far
away, and were then destroyed when the Romans wheeled
around against them, while the baggage train in their difficulties collided with the others. With everyone crammed   388
together in such a big crowd, and not knowing exactly
from which direction their problems were originating,
there was large-scale slaughter. But the Romans completely refrained from all looting, as they had been forbidden from doing so by Lucullus under threat of punishment. The result was that they did not stop for bracelets
and necklaces as they advanced some hundred and twenty
stades, killing all the way, until night overtook them. It was
only then that they turned back and started looting, Lucullus having now given his permission for this.

86. Witnessing this defeat unfold from Tigranocerta,   389
Mancaeus became suspicious of his Greek mercenaries
and disarmed them all. They were afraid they would be
arrested, and so they stayed close together, with clubs in

δεδιότες, ἀθρόοι σκυτάλας ἔχοντες ἐβάδιζόν τε καὶ
390 ηὐλίζοντο. Μαγκαίου δὲ τοὺς βαρβάρους ἐπάγοντος
αὐτοῖς ὡπλισμένους, διαδησάμενοι τὰ ἱμάτια ταῖς
λαιαῖς ἀντὶ ἀσπίδων, μετὰ τόλμης ἐσέδραμον ἐς αὐ-
τούς· καὶ ὅσους ἀνέλοιεν, εὐθὺς ἐμερίζοντο τὰ ὅπλα.
391 ὡς δὲ ἐκ τῶν δυνατῶν εἶχον αὐτάρκως, μεσοπύργιά
τινα κατέλαβον, καὶ Ῥωμαίους ἔξωθεν ἐκάλουν τε καὶ
ἀναβαίνοντας ἐδέχοντο. οὕτω μὲν ἑάλω Τιγρανόκερτα,
καὶ πλοῦτος διηρπάζετο πολύς, οἷα πόλεως νεοκατα-
σκευάστου, φιλοτίμως συνῳκισμένης.

392 87. Τιγράνης δὲ καὶ Μιθριδάτης στρατὸν ἄλλον
ἤθροιζον περιόντες, οὗ τὴν στρατηγίαν ἐπετέτραπτο
Μιθριδάτης, ἡγουμένου Τιγράνους αὐτῷ γεγονέναι τὰ
393 παθήματα διδάγματα. ἔπεμπον δὲ καὶ ἐς τὸν Παρ-
θυαῖον, ἐπικουρεῖν σφίσι παρακαλοῦντες. ἀντιπρε-
σβεύοντος δὲ Λουκούλλου, καὶ ἀξιοῦντος ἢ οἷ συμμαχῆσαι ἢ ἀμφοτέροις ἐκστῆναι τοῦ ἀγῶνος, ὁ μὲν
κρύφα συντιθέμενος ἑκατέροις, οὐκ ἔφθασεν οὐδε-
394 τέροις ἀμῦναι, ὁ δὲ Μιθριδάτης ὅπλα τε εἰργάζετο
κατὰ πόλιν ἑκάστην, καὶ ἐστρατολόγει σχεδὸν ἅπαντας Ἀρμενίους. ἐπιλεξάμενος δ᾽ αὐτῶν τοὺς ἀρίστους,
ἐς ἑπτακισμυρίους πεζοὺς καὶ ἱππέας ἡμίσεας, τοὺς
μὲν ἄλλους ἀπέλυσε, τοὺς δ᾽ ἐς ἴλας τε καὶ σπείρας
ἀγχοτάτω τῆς Ἰταλικῆς συντάξεως καταλέγων Πο-
395 ντικοῖς ἀνδράσι γυμνάζειν παρεδίδου. προσιόντος δ᾽
αὐτοῖς τοῦ Λουκούλλου, ὁ μὲν Μιθριδάτης τὸ πεζὸν
ἅπαν καὶ μέρος τι τῶν ἱππέων ἐπὶ λόφου συνεῖχε, τῇ
λοιπῇ δ᾽ ἵππῳ Τιγράνης τοῖς σιτολογοῦσι Ῥωμαίοις

their hands, as they moved around and bivouacked. Man- 390
caeus brought up his armed barbarians against them, but
the Greeks tied their cloaks around their left arms in place
of shields, bravely attacked them, and immediately shared
out the weapons of those they killed. When they had 391
armed themselves as far as possible, they occupied some
sections of the wall between the towers, invited the Romans in from outside, and welcomed them when they
climbed up. Such was the fall of Tigranocerta, where
much plunder was seized, as was to be expected in a newly
built city and ambitious foundation.

87. Mithridates and Tigranes now traveled around col- 392
lecting a new army, command of which Tigranes assigned
to Mithridates, in the belief that he must have learned
something from his experiences. They also sent word to 393
the Parthian king, asking for his help.[55] Lucullus sent a
counterembassy to require that either he give military assistance to him, or remain neutral in the struggle. The king
secretly made an agreement with both sides, but was in no
hurry to help either of them. Mithridates manufactured 394
arms in every town, and called up for military service vir-
tually the whole male population of Armenia. Out of these
he chose the best, about seventy thousand infantry and
half that number of cavalry, and released the others. He
organized the army into squadrons and cohorts, as near as
possible on the Italian model, and handed them over for
training to Pontic officers. When Lucullus advanced 395
against them, Mithridates kept all his infantry and a part
of the cavalry on a hill, while Tigranes took the rest of the

55 Phraates III ruled Parthia from 70 to 57.

περιπεσὼν ἡσσᾶτο. καὶ μᾶλλον ἀδεῶς ἀπὸ τοῦδε οἱ
Ῥωμαῖοι πλησίον αὐτοῦ Μιθριδάτου ἐσιτολόγουν τε
396 καὶ ἐστρατοπέδευον. κονιορτὸς δ' αὖθις ἠγείρετο πολὺς ὡς ἐπιόντος τοῦ Τιγράνους· καὶ τὸ ἐνθύμημα ἦν
ἐν μέσῳ Λούκουλλον ἀμφοῖν γενέσθαι. ὁ δ' αἰσθόμενος τοὺς μὲν ἀρίστους τῶν ἱππέων προύπεμψε πορρωτάτω συμπλέκεσθαι τῷ Τιγράνῃ καὶ κωλύειν αὐτὸν ἐξ
397 ὁδοιπορίας ἐς τάξιν καθίστασθαι, αὐτὸς δὲ τὸν Μιθριδάτην προκαλούμενος ἐς μάχην <. . .>[21] καὶ περι-
ταφρεύων οὐκ ἠρέθιζεν, ἕως χειμὼν ἐπιπεσὼν διέλυσε
τὸ ἔργον ἅπασιν.

88. Καὶ Τιγράνης μὲν ἐξώλης[22] Ἀρμενίας ἐς τὰ
ἐντὸς ἀνεζεύγνυεν, ὁ δὲ Μιθριδάτης ἐς τὸν Πόντον ἐπὶ
τὰ λοιπὰ τῆς ἰδίας ἀρχῆς ἠπείγετο, τετρακισχιλίους
οἰκείους ἔχων, καὶ τοσούσδε ἑτέρους παρὰ Τιγράνους
398 λαβών. ἐφείπετο δ' αὐτῷ καὶ ὁ Λούκουλλος, ἀναζευγ-
νὺς καὶ ὅδε διὰ τὴν ἀπορίαν. φθάσας δ' αὐτὸν ὁ
Μιθριδάτης ἐπέθετο Φαβίῳ τῷ δεῦρο ἐκ Λουκούλλου
στρατηγεῖν ὑπολελειμμένῳ, καὶ τρεψάμενος αὐτὸν
399 ἔκτεινε πεντακοσίους. ἐλευθερώσαντος δὲ τοῦ Φαβίου
θεράποντας ὅσοι ἦσαν ἐν τῷ στρατοπέδῳ, καὶ δι'
ὅλης ἡμέρας αὖθις ἀγωνιζομένου, παλίντροπος ἦν ὁ
ἀγών, μέχρι τὸν Μιθριδάτην, πληγέντα λίθῳ τε ἐς τὸ
γόνυ καὶ ὑπὸ τὸν ὀφθαλμὸν βέλει, κατὰ σπουδὴν
ἀποκομισθῆναι, καὶ πολλὰς ἡμέρας τοὺς μὲν φόβῳ

---

[21] Post μάχην lac. indic. Schweig.
[22] ἐξώλης Goukowsky: ἐξ ὅλης codd.

cavalry and attacked the Roman foragers. They were defeated, however, and from now on the Romans began to forage and pitch camp fearlessly near Mithridates himself. Again, a great cloud of dust was raised as Tigranes made 396 his attack. The plan was to surround Lucullus with the forces of both kings. But Lucullus understood the plan, and sent his best cavalry far in advance to engage Tigranes and prevent him from deploying his men from their marching column into line of battle. He himself chal- 397 lenged Mithridates to battle ⟨. . .⟩ and surrounding him with a ditch, stopped trying to provoke him.[56] Eventually winter intervened and put a stop to all operations.

88. With his forces destroyed, Tigranes now withdrew into the interior of Armenia, while Mithridates hurried off to what was left of his own kingdom in the Pontus, taking four thousand of his own men and as many again from Tigranes. Lucullus followed him, as lack of supplies forced 398 him to break camp also, but Mithridates got there first, attacked Fabius, who had been left there in command by Lucullus, defeated him and killed five hundred of his men.[57] Fabius then freed any slaves he had in camp, and 399 throughout a whole day again contested the issue, which was beginning to turn against him, until Mithridates was hit on the knee by a stone and by a missile under his eye, and quickly taken out of the battle. For many days, neither side took any further action, the Pontic army because they were afraid for Mithridates' welfare, the Romans because

[56] There seems to be something substantial missing from this sentence.

[57] M. Fabius Hadrianus, one of Lucullus' legates between 72 and 68.

τοῦ βασιλέως τῆς σωτηρίας, τοὺς δὲ ὑπὸ πλήθους
400 τραυματιῶν ἠρεμῆσαι. Μιθριδάτην μὲν οὖν ἐθερά-
πευον Ἄγαροι, Σκυθικὸν ἔθνος, ἰοῖς ὄφεων ἐς τὰς θε-
ραπείας χρώμενοι καὶ ἐπὶ τῷδε ἀεὶ βασιλεῖ συνόντες·
Φαβίῳ δὲ Τριάριος, ἕτερος Λουκούλλου στρατηγός,
ἐπελθὼν μετ' οἰκείου στρατοῦ, τήν τε ἀρχὴν παρὰ τοῦ
401 Φαβίου καὶ τὸ ἀξίωμα παρελάμβανεν. καὶ μετ' οὐ
πολὺ χωρούντων ἐς μάχην αὐτοῦ τε καὶ Μιθριδάτου,
πνεῦμα, οἷον οὐκ ἐμνημονεύετο γενέσθαι, τάς τε σκηνὰς ἀμφοτέρων διέρριψε καὶ τὰ ὑποζύγια παρέσυρε
καὶ τῶν ἀνδρῶν ἔστιν οὓς κατεκρήμνισεν.

402   89. Καὶ τότε μὲν ἀνεχώρουν ἑκάτεροι, ἀπαγγελλο-
μένου δὲ Λουκούλλου προσιέναι, προλαβεῖν τὸ ἔργον
ὁ Τριάριος ἐπειγόμενος ἔτι νυκτὸς ἐπεχείρει ταῖς Μι-
403 θριδάτου προφυλακαῖς. ἰσομάχου δ' ἐς πολὺ τοῦ ἀγῶνος ὄντος, ὁ βασιλεὺς ἐς τὸ καθ' αὑτὸν μέρος ἐπι-
βαρήσας ἔκρινε τὴν μάχην, καὶ διασπάσας τοὺς
πολεμίους τὸ πεζὸν αὐτῶν κατέκλεισεν ἐς διώρυχα
404 πηλοῦ, ἔνθα διεφθείροντο στῆναι μὴ δυνάμενοι. τοὺς
δ' ἱππέας ἀνὰ τὸ πεδίον ἐδίωκεν, ἐκθύμως τῇ φορᾷ
τῆς εὐτυχίας καταχρώμενος, ἔστε τις αὐτὸν Ῥωμαῖος
λοχαγός, οἷα θεράπων αὐτῷ συντροχάζων, ἐς τὸν μη-
ρὸν ἐπάταξε ξίφει πληγὴν βαθεῖαν, οὐκ ἐλπίσας ἐς
405 τὰ νῶτα διὰ τοῦ θώρακος ἐφίξεσθαι. καὶ τόνδε μὲν
εὐθὺς οἱ πλησίον συνέκοπτον, ὁ δὲ Μιθριδάτης ἀπε-
φέρετο ὀπίσω, καὶ οἱ φίλοι τὴν στρατιὰν ἀπὸ νίκης
406 λαμπρᾶς ἀνεκάλουν σὺν ἐπείξει βαρείᾳ. ἐνέπιπτε δὲ
τοῖς μαχομένοις ἐπὶ τῷ παραλόγῳ τῆς ἀνακλήσεως

so many of their men had been wounded. The Agari, a 400
Scythian people, treated Mithridates: they use snake poison as a cure and always accompanied the king for that
reason. Triarius, another of Lucullus' generals, now approached Fabius with his own force, and took over the
command and powers of Fabius.[58] Shortly after, he and 401
Mithridates fought a battle in which a wind blew up that
was greater than any in living memory: it ripped the tents
of both armies, carried off the pack animals and even blew
some men over the cliffs.

89. Both sides withdrew for the moment, until it was 402
reported that Lucullus was coming. In his eagerness to
fight before Lucullus actually arrived, Triarius attacked
Mithridates' pickets while it was still dark. The contest was 403
evenly fought for a long time, but Mithridates' heavy pressure on the section of the enemy line facing him decided
the battle, as he scattered the enemy before him. Their
infantry he forced into a muddy trench where they were
killed, unable even to stand. Their cavalry he pursued 404
across the plain, vigorously using the impetus of his success, until a Roman centurion, running alongside him like
one of his attendants, stabbed him with his sword, inflicting a deep wound in his thigh, as he did not think he
could penetrate his cuirass and wound him in the back.
Those nearby immediately cut the centurion down, but 405
Mithridates was carried to the rear, while his staff, urgently and with heavy heart, recalled the army from their
brilliant victory. The unexpectedness of the recall caused 406

[58] C. Valerius Triarius, praetor in 78, was another of Lucullus'
legates in the war against Mithridates.

APPIAN

θόρυβός τε καὶ ἀπορία, μή τι δεινὸν ἑτέρωθεν εἴη,
μέχρι μαθόντες εὐθὺς ἐν τῷ πεδίῳ τὸ σῶμα περι-
407 ίσταντο καὶ ἐθορύβουν, ἕως Τιμόθεος αὐτοῖς ὁ ἰατρός,
ἐπισχὼν τὸ αἷμα, ἐπέδειξεν αὐτὸν ἐκ μετεώρου, οἷόν
τι καὶ Μακεδόσιν ἐν Ἰνδοῖς, ὑπὲρ Ἀλεξάνδρου δεδιό-
σιν, ὁ Ἀλέξανδρος αὐτὸν ἐπὶ νεὼς θεραπευόμενον ἐπέδειξεν. ὁ δὲ Μιθριδάτης ὡς ἀνήνεγκεν, αὐτίκα τοῖς
ἀνακαλέσασιν ἐκ τῆς μάχης κατεμέμφετο, καὶ τὸν
στρατὸν αὐτῆς ἡμέρας ἦγεν αὖθις ἐπὶ τὸ Ῥωμαίων
στρατόπεδον. οἱ δὲ καὶ ἐκ τοῦδε ἐπεφεύγεσαν ἤδη σὺν
408 δέει. σκυλευομένων δὲ τῶν νεκρῶν ἐφαίνοντο χιλίαρ-
χοι μὲν εἴκοσι καὶ τέσσαρες, ἑκατόνταρχοι δὲ πεντήκοντα καὶ ἑκατόν, ὅσον ἡγεμόνων πλῆθος οὐ ῥᾳδίως
συνέπεσε Ῥωμαίοις ἐν ἥττῃ μιᾷ.

409   90. Ὁ δὲ Μιθριδάτης ἐς Ἀρμενίαν, ἣν δὴ νῦν Ῥωμαῖοι βραχυτέραν Ἀρμενίαν καλοῦσιν, ἀνεζεύγνυ, τὰ
μὲν εὐκόμιστα πάντα σιτολογῶν, τὰ δὲ δυσχερῆ δια-
φθείρων τε καὶ Λούκουλλον ἐπιόντα προαφαιρούμε-
410 νος. καί τις ἀνὴρ Ῥωμαῖος, ἀπὸ βουλῆς, Ἀττίδιος
ὄνομα, διὰ δίκην φυγὼν ἐκ τῆς πατρίδος ἐς Μιθριδάτην πρὸ πολλοῦ φιλίας ἀξιούμενος, ἑάλω τότε
ἐπιβουλεύων αὐτῷ. καὶ τόνδε μὲν ὁ βασιλεὺς οὐ δι-
καιῶν βασανίσαι, Ῥωμαίων ποτὲ βουλευτὴν γενόμενον, ἔκτεινε, τοὺς δὲ συναμαρτόντας ἠκίσατο δεινῶς.
411 ἀπελεύθεροι δ' ὅσοι τῷ Ἀττιδίῳ συνεγνώκεσαν, ἀπαθεῖς ἀφῆκεν ὡς δεσπότῃ διακονησαμένους. Λουκούλλου δ' ἤδη τῷ Μιθριδάτῃ παραστρατοπεδεύοντος, ὁ
τῆς Ἀσίας στρατηγὸς περιπέμπων ἐκήρυσσε Ῥω-

324

confusion among the troops, who did not know what to do, as they were afraid that something bad may have happened elsewhere. As soon as they learned the truth, they gathered around the king's person in the plain in a state of commotion until Timotheus, the king's physician, 407 staunched the bleeding and held the king up on high for them to see, just as in India Alexander, while he was being treated, showed himself on a ship to his Macedonians when they were afraid for his life. As soon as he recovered, Mithridates reprimanded those who had issued the recall order, and on the very same day again led his army against the Roman camp. But the Romans had already fled in fear. When they stripped the armor from the dead, they found 408 twenty-four military tribunes and one hundred and fifty centurions: so many officers had rarely fallen in a single Roman defeat.

90. Mithridates withdrew to Armenia, or what the Ro- 409 mans now call Armenia Minor, foraging for all supplies that could easily be carried, but destroying anything too heavy to carry, to deprive Lucullus of it on his march. A 410 certain Roman senator, called Attidius, who had long ago fled to Mithridates from his homeland because of a charge against him, and was thought worthy of his friendship, was now discovered in a conspiracy against him. The king did not think it was right to torture him, as he had once been a Roman senator, and he had him executed, but he subjected his coconspirators to appalling torments. The 411 freedmen of Attidius who were involved in the plot he released unharmed on the grounds that they had been serving their master. With Lucullus now encamped opposite Mithridates, the governor of Asia circulated a com-

μαίους ἐπικαλεῖν Λουκούλλῳ πέρα τοῦ δέοντος πολεμοῦντι, καὶ τοὺς ὑπ' αὐτῷ τῆς στρατείας ἀφιέναι, καὶ
412 τῶν οὐ πειθομένων τὰ ὄντα δημεύσειν. ὧν ἐξαγγελ-
θέντων ὁ στρατὸς αὐτίκα διελύετο, χωρὶς ὀλίγων,
ὅσοι πάνυ πένητες ὄντες καὶ τὴν ζημίαν οὐ δεδιότες
τῷ Λουκούλλῳ παρέμενον.

413   91. Ὧδε μὲν δὴ καὶ ὁ Λουκούλλου πρὸς Μιθριδάτην πόλεμος ἐς οὐδὲν βέβαιον οὐδὲ κεκριμένον
τέλος ἔληξεν· ἀφισταμένης γὰρ τῆς Ἰταλίας ἐνοχλού-
μενοι, καὶ λῃστευομένης τῆς θαλάσσης λιμῷ πιεζό-
μενοι, οὐκ ἐν καιρῷ σφίσιν ἡγοῦντο πολεμεῖν ἄλλον
414 τοσόνδε πόλεμον, πρὶν τὰ ἐνοχλοῦντα διαθέσθαι. ὧν
καὶ ὁ Μιθριδάτης αἰσθανόμενος ἐς Καππαδοκίαν ἐσέ-
βαλε καὶ τὴν ἰδίαν ἀρχὴν ὠχύρου. καὶ τάδε αὐτὸν
πράσσοντα οἱ Ῥωμαῖοι περιεώρων ἐφ' ὅσον αὐτοῖς ἡ
θάλασσα ἐκαθαίρετο. ὡς δ' ἐκεκάθαρτο καὶ ὁ καθήρας Πομπήιος ἔτι ἦν ἐν Ἀσίᾳ, τὸν Μιθριδάτειον
πόλεμον ἀνελάμβανον αὐτίκα, καὶ ἐπέστελλον καὶ
415 τοῦδε τῷ Πομπηίῳ στρατηγῆσαι. διό μοι δοκεῖ μέρος
ὄντα τῆς Πομπηίου στρατείας τὰ περὶ τὴν θάλασσαν
αὐτῷ πρὸ Μιθριδάτου κατειργασμένα, καὶ ἐς οὐδε-

---

59 Lucullus was stripped of his powers gradually (by tribuni-
cian legislation: see below, n. 61), being replaced in 67 for a short
time by one of the consuls of that year, M' Acilius Glabrio, before
Pompey assumed the command in 66. Lucullus eventually celebrated a triumph in 63.

munication announcing that Lucullus was being charged at Rome with unnecessarily prolonging the war, and that those under his command were being demobilized: anyone disobeying the order would have their property confiscated.[59] After this proclamation, the army immediately   412 dispersed, apart from those few who stayed with Lucullus because they were very poor and were not afraid of the penalty.

91. In this way the war of Lucullus against Mithridates   413 petered out without any clear and decisive result. The Romans were troubled by insurrection in Italy[60] and pressed by famine because of piracy at sea, and they thought it was not the right time for them to be fighting another major war, before they had settled their problems. As he was aware of this situation, Mithridates invaded   414 Cappadocia and reinforced his own kingdom. The Romans allowed Mithridates a free hand in this activity until they cleared the sea of pirates. As soon as they had done that, and while Pompey, the victor in the campaign against the pirates, was still in Asia, they resumed the war against Mithridates, assigning the command to Pompey.[61] Since   415 his achievements at sea, which preceded the war against Mithridates, were part of the story of Pompey's command,

[60] Appian seems to be thinking of the situation at the beginning of the First Mithridatic War, when Rome was involved in war against the Italian allies. Italy was not in a state of revolt in 67.

[61] In 67 a famous law of the tribune A. Gabinius assigned a huge Mediterranean command to Pompey to combat piracy. The following year, the tribune C. Manilius passed a law giving Pompey command of Cilicia, Bithynia, and Pontus, and of the war against Mithridates.

APPIAN

μίαν συγγραφὴν οἰκείαν ἄλλην ἀπαντῶντα, ἐς τόδε
τὸ μέρος συναγαγεῖν τε καὶ ἐπιδραμεῖν, ὡς ἐγένετο.

416   92. Μιθριδάτης ὅτε πρῶτον Ῥωμαίοις ἐπολέμει καὶ
τῆς Ἀσίας ἐκράτει, Σύλλα περὶ τὴν Ἑλλάδα πονουμέ-
νου, ἡγούμενος οὐκ ἐς πολὺ καθέξειν τῆς Ἀσίας, τά
τε ἄλλα, ὥς μοι προείρηται, πάντα ἐλυμαίνετο, καὶ ἐς
τὴν θάλασσαν πειρατὰς καθῆκεν, οἳ τὸ μὲν πρῶτον
ὀλίγοις σκάφεσι καὶ μικροῖς οἷα λῃσταὶ περιπλέοντες
ἐλύπουν, ὡς δὲ ὁ πόλεμος ἐμηκύνετο, πλέονες ἐγί-
417   γνοντο καὶ ναυσὶ μεγάλαις ἐπέπλεον. γευσάμενοι δὲ
κερδῶν μεγάλων, οὐδ᾽ ἡττωμένου καὶ σπενδομένου
τοῦ Μιθριδάτου καὶ ἀναχωροῦντος ἔτι ἐπαύοντο· οἱ
γὰρ βίου καὶ πατρίδων διὰ τὸν πόλεμον ἀφῃρημένοι,
καὶ ἐς ἀπορίαν ἐμπεσόντες ἀθρόαν, ἀντὶ τῆς γῆς
ἐκαρποῦντο τὴν θάλασσαν, μυοπάρωσι πρῶτον καὶ
ἡμιολίαις, εἶτα δικρότοις καὶ τριήρεσι κατὰ μέρη
περιπλέοντες, ἡγουμένων λῃστάρχων οἷα πολέμου
418   στρατηγῶν. ἔς τε ἀτειχίστους πόλεις ἐμπίπτοντες, καὶ
ἑτέρων τὰ τείχη διορύττοντες ἢ κόπτοντες ἢ πολιορ-
κίᾳ λαμβάνοντες, ἐσύλων· καὶ τοὺς ἄνδρας, οἷς τι
πλέον εἴη, ἐς ναυλοχίαν ἐπὶ λύτροις ἀπῆγον. καὶ τάδε
τὰ λήμματα, ἀδοξοῦντες ἤδη τὸ τῶν λῃστῶν ὄνομα,
419   μισθοὺς ἐκάλουν στρατιωτικούς. χειροτέχνας τε εἶχον
ἐπ᾽ ἔργοις δεδεμένους, καὶ ὕλην ξύλου καὶ χαλκοῦ καὶ
σιδήρου συμφέροντες οὔποτε ἐπαύοντο· ἐπαιρόμενοι
γὰρ ὑπὸ τοῦ κέρδους, καὶ τὸ λῃστεύειν οὐκ ἐγνωκότες
ἔτι μεθεῖναι, βασιλεῦσι δ᾽ ἤδη καὶ τυράννοις ἢ στρα-

328

but do not fit properly any separate treatment of their own, I have decided to collect them and run over what happened in this part of my history.

92. When Mithridates first went to war with Rome 416 and was conquering Asia while Sulla was in difficulty in Greece, believing that he would not be able to hold Asia for long, the king plundered it in all sorts of other ways, as I have already described,[62] and also sent pirates out on the sea. At first they sailed around in a few small boats harassing neighborhoods like bandits, but when the war dragged on, they became more numerous and sailed to the attack in big ships. Once they had tasted the delights of large 417 profits, they did not stop their activities, even when Mithridates was defeated, made peace, and withdrew. For they had lost their living and home towns on account of the war, and had fallen into widespread poverty. So instead of harvesting the land, they now harvested the sea, using skiffs and hemiolii to start with, but then sailing in squadrons of biremes and triremes under the command of pirate leaders who were like generals fighting a war. In their plunder- 418 ing operations they attacked both unfortified towns and towns with walls, which they undermined, knocked down, or took by siege. The wealthier inhabitants they carried off to their anchorages to hold for ransom. They now objected to being called pirates, and described their gains as military wages. They kept workmen chained to their tasks, and 419 they continually collected the materials to make things in wood, bronze, and iron. Exhilarated by their profits and with no intention of giving up their raiding, they began to

[62] See above, 46.177–48.193.

τοπεδάρχοις[23] μεγάλοις ἑαυτοὺς ὁμοιοῦντες, καὶ νομίζοντες, ὅτε συνέλθοιεν ἐς τὸ αὐτὸ πάντες, ἄμαχοι
420 γενήσεσθαι, ναῦς τε καὶ ὅπλα πάντα ἐτεκταίνοντο,
μάλιστα περὶ τὴν τραχεῖαν λεγομένην Κιλικίαν, ἣν
κοινὸν σφῶν ὕφορμον ἢ στρατόπεδον ἐτίθεντο εἶναι,
φρούρια μὲν καὶ ἄκρας καὶ νήσους ἐρήμους καὶ ναυλοχίας ἔχοντες πολλαχοῦ, κυριωτάτας δὲ ἀφέσεις
ἡγούμενοι τὰς περὶ τήνδε τὴν Κιλικίαν, τραχεῖάν τε
καὶ ἀλίμενον οὖσαν καὶ κορυφαῖς μεγάλαις ἐξέχου-
421 σαν. ὅθεν δὴ καὶ πάντες ὀνόματι κοινῷ Κίλικες ἐκα-
λοῦντο, ἀρξαμένου μὲν ἴσως τοῦ κακοῦ παρὰ τῶν
Τραχεωτῶν Κιλίκων, συνεπιλαβόντων δὲ Σύρων τε
καὶ Κυπρίων καὶ Παμφύλων καὶ τῶν Ποντικῶν καὶ
422 σχεδὸν ἁπάντων τῶν ἑῴων ἐθνῶν, οἳ πολλοῦ καὶ χρο-
νίου σφίσιν ὄντος τοῦ Μιθριδατείου πολέμου δρᾶν τι
μᾶλλον ἢ πάσχειν αἱρούμενοι τὴν θάλασσαν ἀντὶ
τῆς γῆς ἐπελέγοντο, ὥστε πολλαὶ τάχιστα αὐτῶν μυριάδες ἦσαν, καὶ οὐ μόνης ἔτι τῆς ἑῴας θαλάσσης
ἐκράτουν, ἀλλὰ καὶ τῆς ἐντὸς Ἡρακλείων στηλῶν
ἁπάσης.

423   93. Καὶ γάρ τινας ἤδη Ῥωμαίων στρατηγοὺς ναυμαχίᾳ ἐνενικήκεσαν, ἄλλους τε καὶ τὸν τῆς Σικελίας
περὶ αὐτῇ Σικελίᾳ. ἅπλωτά τε ἤδη πάντα ἦν, καὶ ἡ
424 γῆ τῶν ἔργων ἐνδεὴς διὰ τὴν ἀνεπιμιξίαν. ἥ τε πόλις
ἡ Ῥωμαίων ᾔσθετο μάλιστα τοῦ κακοῦ, τῶν τε ὑπη-
κόων σφίσι καμνόντων, καὶ αὐτοὶ διὰ πλῆθος ἴδιον

---

[23] στρατοπεδάρχοις Goukowsky: στρατοπέδοις codd.

of them. It seemed to them a major and difficult undertak-   425
ing to destroy such large naval forces, scattered all around
the sea and land, so unhampered by possessions that flight
was easy, with no ancestral towns or known places as their
base of operations, and having nothing that was their own
or private, but always just what they happened upon. The   426
war was so strange—there was nothing lawful, definite, or
clear about it—that it caused feelings of helplessness and
fear. Murena attacked the pirates but achieved nothing of
significance, nor Servilius Isauricus after him.[64] Indeed,   427
now the pirates even attacked the shores of Italy itself with
impunity, in the region of Brundisium and Etruria, and
seized some women from noble families who were traveling on the coast road, and two praetors with their insignia
of office.[65]

94. When they could no longer stand the losses or the   428
disgrace, the Romans pass a law appointing Gnaeus Pompey, who enjoyed the highest reputation among them at
that time, as general for three years with unlimited authority over the whole Mediterranean as far as the Pillars of
Heracles, and over the coast for four hundred stades inland. They sent letters to kings, princes, peoples and all   429
the towns with orders to help Pompey in every way, and
they gave him authority to enlist troops and collect money.
They sent him off with a large army raised from their own   430

[64] L. Licinius Murena was left by Sulla in command of Asia in
84 and took action against the pirates. As governor of Cilicia from
78 to 74, P. Servilius Vatia Isauricus (consul 79) fought with some
success against the pirates.   [65] Plutarch (*Pomp.* 24.6) records the seizure of the daughter of the great orator M. Antonius
(consul 99) and of two praetors, Sextilius and Bellienus in 68.

ἐκ καταλόγου, καὶ ναῦς ὅσας εἶχον, καὶ χρημάτων ἐς
ἑξακισχίλια τάλαντα Ἀττικά. οὕτω μέγα καὶ δυσεργὲς ἡγοῦντο εἶναι τοσῶνδε κρατῆσαι στρατοπέδων, ἐν
τοσῇδε θαλάσσῃ καὶ μυχοῖς τοσοῖσδε διαλανθανόν-
των τε εὐμαρῶς καὶ ὑποχωρούντων ῥᾳδίως καὶ ἐμ-
431 πιπτόντων αὖθις ἀφανῶς. ἀνήρ τε οὐδείς πω πρὸ τοῦ
Πομπηίου ἐπὶ τοσήνδε ἀρχὴν αἱρεθεὶς ὑπὸ Ῥωμαίων
ἐξέπλευσεν, ᾧ στρατιὰ μὲν αὐτίκα ἦν ἐς δώδεκα μυριάδας πεζῶν καὶ ἱππεῖς τετρακισχίλιοι, νῆες δὲ σὺν
ἡμιολίαις ἑβδομήκοντα καὶ διακόσιαι, ὑπηρέται δ᾽
ἀπὸ τῆς βουλῆς, οὓς καλοῦσι πρεσβευτάς, πέντε καὶ
432 εἴκοσιν· οἷς ὁ Πομπήιος ἐπιδιῄρει τὴν θάλασσαν, καὶ
ναῦς ἐδίδου καὶ ἱππέας ἑκάστῳ καὶ στρατὸν πεζόν,
καὶ στρατηγίας σημεῖα περικεῖσθαι, ἵν᾽ αὐτοκράτωρ
433 ἐντελὴς οὗ πιστεύοιτο μέρους ἕκαστος ὑπάρχοι, αὐτὸς
δ᾽, οἷα δὴ βασιλεὺς βασιλέων, αὐτοὺς περιθέοι καὶ
ἐφορῴη μένοντας ἐφ᾽ ὧν ἐτάχθησαν, μηδὲ μεταδιώ-
κων τοὺς λῃστὰς περιφέροιτο ἐξ ἔργων ἀτελῶν ἔτι
ὄντων ἐς ἕτερα, ἀλλ᾽ εἶεν οἱ πανταχόθεν αὐτοῖς ἀπαν-
τῶντές τε καὶ τὰς ἐς ἀλλήλους διαδρομὰς ἀποκλείον-
τες.

434 95. Οὕτω διαθεὶς ὁ Πομπήιος ἅπαντα, ἐπέστησεν
Ἰβηρίᾳ μὲν καὶ ταῖς Ἡρακλείοις στήλαις Τιβέριον
Νέρωνα καὶ Μάλλιον Τορκουᾶτον, ἀμφὶ δὲ τὴν Λιγυ-
στινήν τε καὶ Κελτικὴν θάλασσαν Μᾶρκον Πομπώ-
νιον, Λιβύῃ δὲ καὶ Σαρδόνι καὶ Κύρνῳ, καὶ ὅσαι πλησίον νῆσοι, Λέντουλον τε Μαρκελλῖνον καὶ Πούπλιον
Ἀτίλιον, περὶ δὲ αὐτὴν Ἰταλίαν Λεύκιον Γέλλιον καὶ

service lists and any ships they had, and about six thousand
Attic talents. This is an indication of how great and difficult a task they thought it would be to overcome such
numerous forces, over such a wide area of sea, who could
hide easily in so many remote corners, and retire at will
and then attack again unnoticed. No one before Pompey   431
had ever sailed from Italy having been appointed by the
Romans to such a big command. He soon had an army of
one hundred and twenty thousand infantry, four thousand
cavalry, and two hundred and seventy ships, including
hemiolii, and twenty-five senatorial assistants, whom the
Romans call legates. He divided up the Mediterranean   432
between his legates, giving each of them ships, cavalry,
and an infantry force. He invested them with praetorian
insignia so that that they would each have absolute authority in the area entrusted to them, while he himself, like a   433
king of kings, would move around them all, making sure
they stayed on their allotted stations, and that while he was
in pursuit of pirates he would not be diverted from still
unfinished business to something else, but that there
would be Roman forces everywhere confronting the pirates and preventing them from joining up with each
other.

95. Pompey's overall arrangements were as follows. He   434
assigned Iberia and the Pillars of Heracles to Tiberius
Nero and Manlius Torquatus; the Ligurian and Celtic sea
to Marcus Pomponius; Africa, Sardinia, Corsica and all the
neighboring islands to Lentulus Marcellinus and Publius
Atilius; the coast of Italy itself to Lucius Gellius and

435 Γναῖον Λέντουλον. Σικελίαν δὲ καὶ τὸν Ἰόνιον
ἐφύλασσον αὐτῷ Πλώτιός τε Οὐᾶρος καὶ Τερέντιος
Οὐάρρων μέχρι Ἀκαρνανίας, Πελοπόννησον δὲ καὶ
τὴν Ἀττικήν, ἔτι δ' Εὔβοιαν καὶ Θεσσαλίαν καὶ Μα-
436 κεδονίαν καὶ Βοιωτίαν Λούκιος Σισιννᾶς, τὰς δὲ νήσους καὶ τὸ Αἰγαῖον ἅπαν καὶ τὸν Ἑλλήσποντον ἐπ'
ἐκείνῳ Λούκιος Λόλλιος, Βιθυνίαν δὲ καὶ Θρᾴκην καὶ
τὴν Προποντίδα καὶ τὸ τοῦ Πόντου στόμα Πούπλιος
Πείσων, Λυκίαν δὲ καὶ Παμφυλίαν καὶ Κύπρον καὶ
437 Φοινίκην Μέτελλος Νέπως. ὧδε μὲν αὐτῷ διετετάχατο
οἱ στρατηγοὶ ἐπιχειρεῖν τε καὶ ἀμύνεσθαι, καὶ φυ-
λάσσειν τὰ τεταγμένα, καὶ τοὺς παρ' ἀλλήλων ἐκφεύγοντας ὑπολαμβάνειν, ἵνα μὴ διώκοντες ἀφίσταιντο
μακράν, μηδὲ ὡς ἐν δρόμῳ περιφέροιντο, καὶ χρόνιον
438 εἴη τὸ ἔργον. αὐτὸς δ' ἅπαντας ἐπέπλει. καὶ τὰ ἐς
δύσιν πρῶτα ἡμέραις τεσσαράκοντα ἐπιδὼν ἐς Ῥώμην παρῆλθεν. ὅθεν ἐς Βρεντέσιον, καὶ ἐκ Βρεντεσίου
τοσῷδε διαστήματι τὴν ἕω περιπλεύσας, ἐξέπληξεν
ἅπαντας τάχει τε ἐπίπλου καὶ μεγέθει παρασκευῆς
439 καὶ φόβῳ δόξης, ὥστε τοὺς λῃστὰς ἐλπίσαντας αὐτῷ
προεπιχειρήσειν, ἢ οὐκ εὐμαρές γε τὸ κατὰ σφᾶς ἔργον ἀποδείξειν, δείσαντας εὐθὺς τῶν τε πόλεων ἃς
ἐπολιόρκουν ἐξαναχθῆναι, καὶ ἐς τὰς συνήθεις ἄκρας
440 καὶ ναυλοχίας ὑποφεύγειν, καὶ Πομπηίῳ τὴν μὲν
θάλασσαν αὐτίκα ἀμαχὶ κεκαθάρθαι, τοὺς δὲ λῃστὰς
ὑπὸ τῶν στρατηγῶν ἁλίσκεσθαι πανταχοῦ κατὰ
μέρη.

441   96. Αὐτὸς δὲ ἐς Κιλικίαν ἠπείγετο μετὰ ποικίλου

Gnaeus Lentulus. Plotius Varus and Terentius Varro   435
guarded Sicily and the Ionian sea for him as far as Acarnania, and Lucius Sisenna had the Peloponnese, Attica,
Euboea, Thessaly, Macedonia, and Boeotia; Lucius Lol-   436
lius watched over the islands, the whole Aegean, and also
the Hellespont; Publius Piso was assigned Bithynia,
Thrace, the Propontis and the mouth of the Pontus, and
Metellus Nepos got Lycia, Pamphylia, Cyprus, and Phoenicia. This was how Pompey deployed his commanders,   437
for them to go on the attack and defend, and to guard their
assigned zone. They were to intercept the fugitives from
each other's zones, so that they would not be drawn far
away from their own when chasing the enemy, or led
around in circles like in a race, thus making the task a long
one. Pompey sailed to each of the stations himself. First   438
he spent forty days inspecting arrangements in the west
and returned to Rome. From here he went to Brundisium,
and from there he spent an equal amount of time at sea in
the east. He astonished everyone with the speed of his
movement and the size of his armament, and he instilled
fear with his reputation. The result was that the pirates,   439
who had expected to attack him first, or at least make clear
that the campaign against them would not be easy, were
immediately cowed, sailed off from the towns they were
besieging, and took refuge in their usual citadels and anchorages. Pompey thus cleared the seas in a short time and   440
without a battle, while the pirates were caught everywhere,
one group after another, by his commanders.

96. He himself hurried to Cilicia with a variety of   441

στρατοῦ καὶ μηχανημάτων πολλῶν, ἐλπίσας παν-
τοίας μάχης καὶ πολιορκίας αὐτῷ δεήσειν ἐπὶ ἄκρας
ἀποκρήμνους. οὐδενὸς δὲ ἐδέησε· τὸ γὰρ κλέος αὐτοῦ
καὶ τὴν παρασκευὴν οἱ λῃσταὶ καταπλαγέντες, καὶ
ἐλπίσαντες, εἰ μὴ διὰ μάχης ἔλθοιεν, τεύξεσθαι φι-

442 λανθρώπου, πρῶτοι μὲν οἱ Κράγον καὶ Ἀντίκραγον
εἶχον, φρούρια μέγιστα, μετὰ δ᾽ ἐκείνους οἱ ὄρειοι
Κίλικες καὶ ἐφεξῆς ἅπαντες ἑαυτοὺς ἐνεχείρισαν,
ὅπλα τε ὁμοῦ πολλά, τὰ μὲν ἕτοιμα τὰ δὲ χαλκευό-
μενα, παρέδωκαν, καὶ ναῦς τὰς μὲν ἔτι πηγνυμένας
τὰς δ᾽ ἤδη πλεούσας, χαλκόν τε καὶ σίδηρον ἐς ταῦτα
συνενηνεγμένον καὶ ὀθόνας καὶ κάλως καὶ ὕλην ποι-
κίλην, αἰχμαλώτων τε πλῆθος, τῶν μὲν ἐπὶ λύτροις

443 τῶν δὲ ἐπὶ ἔργοις δεδεμένων. ὧν ὁ Πομπήιος τὴν μὲν
ὕλην ἐνέπρησε, τὰς δὲ ναῦς ἀπήγαγε, τοὺς δ᾽ αἰχμαλώτους ἐς τὰς πατρίδας ἀφῆκε· καὶ πολλοὶ κενοτάφια

444 σφῶν κατέλαβον ὡς ἐπὶ νεκροῖς γενόμενα. τοὺς δὲ
πειρατὰς οἳ μάλιστα ἐδόκουν οὐχ ὑπὸ μοχθηρίας
ἀλλ᾽ ἀπορίᾳ βίου διὰ τὸν πόλεμον ἐπὶ ταῦτα ἐλθεῖν,
ἐς Μαλλὸν καὶ Ἄδανα καὶ Ἐπιφάνειαν, ἢ εἴ τι ἄλλο
πόλισμα ἔρημον ἢ ὀλιγάνθρωπον ἦν τῆσδε τῆς τρα-
χείας Κιλικίας, συνῴκιζε· τοὺς δέ τινας αὐτῶν καὶ ἐς

445 Δύμην τῆς Ἀχαΐας ἐξέπεμπεν. ὧδε μὲν ὁ λῃστρικὸς
πόλεμος, χαλεπώτατος ἔσεσθαι νομισθείς, ὀλιγήμε-
ρος ἐγένετο τῷ Πομπηίῳ· καὶ ναῦς ἔλαβε τὰς μὲν
ἁλούσας μίαν καὶ ἑβδομήκοντα, τὰς δὲ ὑπ᾽ αὐτῶν
παραδοθείσας ἓξ καὶ τριακοσίας, πόλεις δὲ καὶ

troops and a large number of siege engines, expecting that he would need to engage in all sorts of fighting and siege warfare against their steep citadels. But he needed none of it. For the pirates were intimidated by his reputation and size of his armament, and, hoping to meet with a generous response if they did not resort to fighting, they surrendered. First to do so were the inhabitants of Cragus 442 and Anticragus, their most important forts, after them the mountain-dwelling men of Cilicia, and then everyone followed suit, one after the other. At the same time they handed over a great many weapons, some already finished products, others still in the process of being forged; and ships, some still under construction, others in the water, and the bronze and iron collected for their completion, as well as sails, ropes, and all sorts of wood; and a large number of prisoners, some kept for ransom, others chained to their tasks. Pompey burned the wood, took the ships 443 away, and sent the prisoners back to their hometowns, where many found memorials to themselves set up in the belief that they were dead. The pirates, whom he firmly 444 believed had turned to piracy not because they were naturally wicked, but because the war had deprived them of the means to make a living, he settled in Mallus, Adana, or Epiphanea and other deserted or thinly populated towns in Cilicia Trachea. There were also some he sent off to Dyme in Achaea. And so the pirate war, which it was 445 believed would prove extremely difficult, was brought to an end by Pompey in a matter of days. He captured seventy-one ships, while the pirates handed over three hundred and six to him, and he took possession of about

φρούρια καὶ ὁρμητήρια ἄλλα αὐτῶν ἐς εἴκοσι καὶ
ἑκατόν. λῃσταὶ δ' ἀνῃρέθησαν ἐν ταῖς μάχαις ἀμφὶ
τοὺς μυρίους.

446   97. Ἐπὶ δὴ τούτοις ὀξές τε οὕτω καὶ παραδόξως
γενομένοις οἱ Ῥωμαῖοι τὸν Πομπήιον μέγα ἐπαίρον-
τες, ἔτι ὄντα περὶ Κιλικίαν εἵλοντο τοῦ πρὸς Μιθριδάτην πολέμου στρατηγὸν ἐπὶ τῆς ὁμοίας ἐξουσίας,
αὐτοκράτορα ὄντα, ὅπῃ θέλοι, συντίθεσθαί τε καὶ
447   πολεμεῖν, καὶ φίλους ἢ πολεμίους Ῥωμαίοις οὓς δο-
κιμάσειε ποιεῖσθαι· στρατιᾶς τε πάσης, ὅση πέραν
ἐστὶ τῆς Ἰταλίας, ἄρχειν ἔδωκαν. ἅπερ οὐδενί πω
448   παντάπασι πρὸ τοῦδε ὁμοῦ πάντα ἐδόθη. καὶ ἴσως
αὐτὸν καὶ διὰ τάδε μέγαν ὀνομάζουσιν· ὁ γάρ τοι
πόλεμος ὁ τοῦ Μιθριδάτου καὶ ὑπὸ τῶν προτέρων
449   στρατηγῶν ἐξήνυστο ἤδη. Πομπήιος μὲν οὖν εὐθὺς ἐκ
τῆς Ἀσίας στρατὸν ἀγείρας μετεστρατοπέδευεν ἐπὶ
τοὺς ὅρους τοῦ Μιθριδάτου· Μιθριδάτῃ δὲ ἦν ἐπί-
λεκτος οἰκεῖος στρατός, τρισμύριοι πεζοὶ καὶ ἱππεῖς
450   τρισχίλιοι, καὶ προὐκάθητο τῆς χώρας. ἄρτι δ' αὐτὴν
Λουκούλλου διεφθαρκότος ἀπόρως εἶχεν ἀγορᾶς· ὅθεν
αὐτομολίαις ἐπετίθεντο πολλοί. καὶ τούσδε μὲν ὁ Μιθριδάτης ἐρευνώμενος ἐκρήμνη καὶ ὀφθαλμοὺς ἀνώ-
451   ρυττε καὶ ἔκαιεν. καὶ τὰ μὲν τῶν αὐτομολιῶν ἧσσον
ἠνώχλει διὰ φόβον τῶν κολάσεων, ἐπέτριβε δ' ἡ
ἀπορία.

452   98. Πρέσβεις οὖν ἐς Πομπήιον πέμψας ἠξίου μαθεῖν, τίς ἂν εἴη τοῦ πολέμου διάλυσις. ὁ δέ, "Ἂν τοὺς
αὐτομόλους ἡμῖν παραδῷς," ἔφη, "Καὶ σεαυτὸν ἡμῖν

one hundred and twenty of their towns, forts, and other bases. Some ten thousand pirates were killed in battle.

97. The Romans praised Pompey to the skies for such 446 rapid and unexpected success, and while he was still in Cilicia, appointed him to the command of the war against Mithridates with the same powers as he held already: that is, he had unlimited authority to wage war or make peace as he wished, to use his own judgment in declaring who was to be friends or enemies of Rome, and to have com- 447 mand of all Rome's armed forces outside Italy. All these powers had never been granted at the same time to one man before. This is perhaps the reason they call him "The 448 Great." For the Mithridatic War had already been brought to an end by his predecessors in command. Pompey now 449 quickly recruited an army in Asia and moved his camp to the borders of Mithridates' kingdom. The king had an elite force of his own men, thirty thousand infantry and three thousand cavalry, and he stationed them to protect his territory. But as Lucullus had lately ravaged the area, 450 Mithridates found himself short of supplies, causing many of his soldiers to desert. He tracked these down and cruci- fied, blinded, or burned them at the stake. Fear of such 451 punishment reduced the problem of desertion, but the shortage of food was wearing.

98. So Mithridates sent an embassy to Pompey to ask 452 what conditions would bring an end to hostilities. Pompey replied, "You would have to return our deserters to us, and

ἐπιτρέψῃς." ὧν ὁ Μιθριδάτης πυθόμενος τοῖς αὐτο-
μόλοις τὸ περὶ αὐτῶν ἔφρασε, καὶ δεδιότας ὁρῶν ὤμο-
σεν ὅτι οἱ τὰ πρὸς Ῥωμαίους ἐστὶν ἄσπονδα διὰ τὴν
πλεονεξίαν αὐτῶν, καὶ οὐκ ἐκδώσει τινά, οὐδὲ πράξει
453 ποτὲ ὃ μὴ κοινῇ πᾶσι συνοίσει. ὁ μὲν δὴ ὧδε εἶπεν,
ὁ δὲ Πομπήιος ἐνέδραν ποι καθεὶς ἱππέων, ἑτέρους
ἔπεμπεν ἐκ φανεροῦ τοῖς προφύλαξι τοῦ βασιλέως
ἐνοχλεῖν· καὶ εἴρητο αὐτοῖς ἐρεθίζειν καὶ ὑποφεύγειν
ὥσπερ ἡττωμένους <. . .>[24] ἔστε περ οἱ ἐκ τῆς ἐνέδρας
454 περιλαβόντες αὐτοὺς ἐτρέψαντο. καὶ φεύγουσι τάχ'
ἂν καὶ ἐς τὸ στρατόπεδον συνεισεπήδησαν, εἰ μὴ δείσας ὁ βασιλεὺς προήγαγε τὸ πεζόν. οἱ δ' ἀπεχώρουν.
καὶ τέλος ἦν τοῦτο τῇ πρώτῃ Πομπηίου καὶ Μιθριδάτου πείρᾳ ἐς ἀλλήλους καὶ ἱππομαχίᾳ.

455   99. Ἐνοχλούμενος δ' ὑπὸ τῆς ἀπορίας ὁ βασιλεὺς
ἄκων ὑπεχώρει, καὶ ἐσεδέχετο Πομπήιον ἐς τὴν ἑαυτοῦ, ἐλπίζων καθήμενον ἐν τῇδε τῇ διεφθαρμένῃ κα-
κοπαθήσειν. ὁ δὲ ἀγορὰν μὲν ἐπακτὸν ἐκ τῶν ὄπισθεν
εἶχε, περιελθὼν δὲ τὰ πρὸς ἕω τοῦ Μιθριδάτου, καὶ
φρούρια αὐτῷ καὶ στρατόπεδα πολλὰ ἐς ἑκατὸν καὶ
πεντήκοντα σταδίους περιθεὶς ἀπετάφρευε τοῦ μὴ σι-
456 τολογεῖν αὐτὸν ἔτι εὐμαρῶς. καὶ ὁ βασιλεὺς ἀποτα-
φρεύοντι μὲν οὐκ ἐπετίθετο, εἴθ' ὑπὸ δέους εἴθ' ὑπ'

---

[24] Lac. post ἡττωμένους indic. Schweig.

---

[66] Viereck and Roos argued that there is no need to suggest a
lacuna in the text in this sentence, Appian's negligence being suf-

hand yourself over." When he heard this, Mithridates told
the deserters about the terms, and seeing their consternation, swore that he was implacably hostile to the Romans
because they were so greedy, and would surrender no one
to them and never do anything that was not in the common
interest of everyone. That is what he said. Pompey now   453
laid an ambush at a particular location with his cavalry, and
sent others openly with orders to harass the king's pickets
and provoke them, but then withdraw as if defeated <. . .>
until those in the ambush intercepted the enemy and put
them to flight.[66] The Romans could have rushed into   454
Mithridates' camp along with the men in flight, if the king,
fearing this possibility, had not led his infantry forward.
The Romans withdrew. This was how the first engagement, a cavalry action, between Pompey and Mithridates
turned out.

99. Mithridates, distressed by lack of supplies, reluc-   455
tantly retreated, thus letting Pompey into his kingdom,
but fully expecting him to suffer badly from his position in
this region that had been so badly devastated. But Pompey
had his supplies brought in from the areas behind him,
and, circling around to the east of Mithridates, he established a series of forts and encampments around him at a
distance of about one hundred and fifty stades, and dug a
ditch around the area to prevent the king's foragers from
continuing to have easy access to supplies. Mithridates did 456
not attack Pompey while he was engaged in digging the

ficient to explain the incorrect grammar and elliptical expression.
But it seems easier to think that something is missing, even if the
sense is clear that Pompey's ambush worked as planned.

ἀνοίας, ἣ πᾶσιν ἐγγίγνεται πλησιαζόντων τῶν κακῶν, κάμνων δ' αὖθις ἐξ ἀπορίας τὰ ὑποζύγια ὅσα
εἶχε κατέκοπτε, τοὺς ἵππους μόνους περιποιούμενος,
457 ἔστε μόλις ἐς πεντήκοντα διαρκέσας ἡμέρας νυκτὸς
ἀπεδίδρασκε σὺν σιωπῇ βαθείᾳ δι' ὁδῶν δυσχερῶν.
ὡς δὲ αὐτὸν μόλις ἡμέρας ὁ Πομπήιος καταλαβὼν
εἴχετο τῶν ὑστάτων, ὁ μὲν καὶ τότε τῶν φίλων ἐκτά-
ξαι κελευόντων οὐκ ἐμάχετο, ἀλλὰ τοῖς ἱππεῦσι μόνοις τοὺς πλησιάζοντας ἀνακόπτων ἑσπέρας ἐν ὕλαις
458 ηὐλίσατο πυκναῖς. τῇ δ' ἐπιούσῃ χωρίον κατέλαβε
περίκρημνον, οὗ μία ἐς αὐτὸ ἄνοδος ἦν, καὶ τέσσαρες
αὐτὴν σπεῖραι προὐφύλασσον. ἀντεφύλασσον δὲ καὶ
Ῥωμαῖοι μὴ διαφυγεῖν Μιθριδάτην.

459   100. Ἅμα δ' ἡμέρᾳ τὸν μὲν στρατὸν αὐτῶν ὥπλιζεν
ἑκάτερος, οἱ προφύλακες δ' ἀλλήλων κατὰ τὸ πρανὲς
ἀπεπειρῶντο· καί τινες ἱππεῖς τοῦ Μιθριδάτου χωρίς
τε τῶν ἵππων καὶ χωρὶς ἐπαγγέλματος ἐβοήθουν τοῖς
σφετέροις προφύλαξιν. πλειόνων δέ σφισι Ῥωμαίων
ἱππέων ἐπιόντων, οἱ ἄνιπποι τῶν Μιθριδατείων οἵδε
ἀθρόως ἐς τὸ στρατόπεδον ἀνεπήδων, ἀναβησόμενοί
τε τοὺς ἵππους καὶ ἐξ ἴσου τοῖς ἐπιοῦσι Ῥωμαίοις
460 συνοισόμενοι. κατιδόντες δ' αὐτοὺς οἱ ἄνω ἔτι ὁπλι-
ζόμενοι σὺν δρόμῳ καὶ βοῇ προσθέοντας, καὶ τὸ
γιγνόμενον οὐκ εἰδότες ἀλλὰ φεύγειν αὐτοὺς ὑπολα-
βόντες, ὡς εἰλημμένου σφῶν ἤδη καθ' ἑκάτερα τοῦ
461 στρατοπέδου, τὰ ὅπλα μεθέντες ἔφευγον. ἀδιεξόδου δ'
ὄντος τοῦ χωρίου προσέπταιον ἀλλήλοις ἀναστρεφό-
μενοι, μέχρι καθήλαντο κατὰ τῶν κρημνῶν. οὕτω μὲν

ditch, either out of fear, or because he was suffering from
the sort of indecision that affects anyone facing the approach of disaster. Continuing to suffer from a lack of
food, he slaughtered all his pack animals, leaving just the
horses, until, with scarcely fifty days' provisions left, he   457
fled at night in deep silence along bad roads. Pompey
managed with difficulty to catch up with him during the
day, and engaged his rearguard. Although Mithridates'
advisers recommended that he deploy for battle, he refused to fight, and drove back the approaching enemy
forces using just his cavalry, and in the evening bivouacked
in thick woods. The next day he occupied a strong posi-   458
tion with steep approaches and only a single road up to
it, which he guarded with four cohorts. Pompey took
countermeasures to make sure that Mithridates could not
escape.

100. At dawn each commander put his soldiers under   459
arms, and the pickets began to skirmish with each other
on the slopes. Some of Mithridates' cavalrymen went to
help their sentries, but without horses and without orders.
When a larger body of Roman cavalry moved up to attack
them, these Mithridatic troops, not having their horses, all
ran together back to the camp to mount up and confront
the advancing Roman cavalry on equal terms. Those   460
higher up the slope were still arming, and when they
looked down and saw their own men running toward them
shouting, as they did not know what was happening, assumed they were fleeing. So they threw their weapons
down and ran, believing that both flanks of their camp had
been captured. But there was no way out of the place, and   461
when they turned around they kept bumping into each

ἡ στρατιὰ τῷ Μιθριδάτῃ διὰ προπέτειαν τῶν ἄνευ
προστάγματος τοῖς προμάχοις ἐπικουρεῖν ἑλομένων
462 θορυβηθεῖσα διέφθαρτο, καὶ τὸ λοιπὸν ἔργον εὔκολον
ἦν τῷ Πομπηίῳ, κτείνοντι καὶ συλλαμβάνοντι ἀνό-
πλους ἔτι καὶ ἐν περικρήμνῳ συγκεκλεισμένους. καὶ
ἀνῃρέθησαν ἐς μυρίους, καὶ τὸ στρατόπεδον ὅλῃ τῇ
παρασκευῇ κατελήφθη.

463   101. Μιθριδάτης δὲ μετὰ τῶν ὑπασπιστῶν μόνων
ὠσάμενος ἐς τὰ κατάκρημα καὶ διαφυγὼν ἐνέτυχέ
τισιν ἱππεῦσι μισθοφόροις καὶ πεζοῖς ὡς τρισχιλίοις,
οἳ εὐθὺς αὐτῷ συνείποντο ἐς Σινόρηγα φρούριον, ἔνθα
αὐτῷ χρήματα πολλὰ ἐσεσώρευτο· καὶ δωρεὰν καὶ
464 μισθὸν ἐνιαυτοῦ τοῖς συμφυγοῦσι διέδωκεν. φέρων δ᾽
ἐς ἑξακισχίλια τάλαντα ἐπὶ τὰς τοῦ Εὐφράτου πηγὰς
ἠπείγετο ὡς ἐκεῖθεν ἐς Κόλχους περάσων. δρόμῳ δ᾽
ἀπαύστῳ χρώμενος τὸν μὲν Εὐφράτην ὑπερῆλθεν
ἡμέρᾳ μάλιστα τετάρτῃ, τρισὶ δ᾽ ἄλλαις καθιστάμενος καὶ ὁπλίζων τοὺς συνόντας ἢ προσιόντας ἐς τὴν
465 Χωτηνὴν Ἀρμενίαν ἐνέβαλεν, ἔνθα Χωτηνοὺς μὲν καὶ
Ἴβηρας, κωλύοντας αὐτὸν βέλεσι καὶ σφενδόναις,
466 ἐλαύνων διῆλθεν ἐπὶ τὸν Ἄψαρον ποταμόν. Ἴβηρας
δὲ τοὺς ἐν Ἀσίᾳ οἱ μὲν προγόνους, οἱ δ᾽ ἀποίκους
ἡγοῦνται τῶν Εὐρωπαίων Ἰβήρων, οἱ δὲ μόνον ὁμω-
467 νύμους· ἔθος γὰρ οὐδὲν ἦν ὅμοιον ἢ γλῶσσα. Μιθριδάτης δ᾽ ἐν Διοσκούροις χειμάζων, ἥν τινα πόλιν οἱ
Κόλχοι σύμβολον ἡγοῦνται τῆς Διοσκούρων σὺν
Ἀργοναύταις ἐπιδημίας, οὐδὲν σμικρόν, οὐδ᾽ οἷον ἐν
φυγῇ, διενοεῖτο, ἀλλὰ τὸν Πόντον ὅλον ἐν κύκλῳ καὶ

other, until eventually they jumped down off the cliffs. And so it was through the rashness of those who went to help their sentries without orders that the army of Mithridates was thrown into confusion and destroyed. The 462 mopping-up operation was easy for Pompey, killing and capturing men who still did not have their weapons and were cut off in steep ravines. Some ten thousand were killed, and the camp and all its equipment were captured.

101. Mithridates, accompanied only by his bodyguard, 463 forced his way through to the cliffs and escaped, and met up with some mercenary cavalry and about three thousand infantry, who immediately accompanied him to the fort of Sinorex, where he had stored up a large amount of money. Here he distributed gifts and a year's pay to his fellow fugitives. Taking about six thousand talents with him, he 464 hurried to the source of the Euphrates, intending to cross from there into Colchis. After traveling without stopping for some four days, he crossed the Euphrates, and three days later, having organized and armed those who had accompanied him or joined him, he invaded the territory of Chotene in Armenia. Here, he drove off the Chotene- 465 ans and Iberians, who tried to hold him up with missiles and slings, and made his way through to the river Apsarus. Some people believe that the Iberians of Asia are ances- 466 tors of the European Iberians, others that they are emigrants from Europe. Others again think that they merely share the same name, since neither their customs nor language are at all similar. Mithridates wintered in Dioscu- 467 rias, a city whose name the Colchians believe recalls the visit of the Dioscuri and the Argonauts. Here he devised a grand plan, not the sort to be expected from a fugitive,

Σκύθας ἐπὶ τῷ Πόντῳ καὶ τὴν Μαιώτιδα λίμνην ὑπερ-
468 ελθὼν ἐς Βόσπορον ἐμβαλεῖν, τήν τε Μαχάρους τοῦ
παιδὸς ἀρχήν, ἀχαρίστου περὶ αὐτὸν γενομένου,
παραλαβὼν αὖθις ἐκ μετώπου Ῥωμαίοις γενέσθαι,
καὶ πολεμεῖν ἐκ τῆς Εὐρώπης οὖσιν ἐν τῇ Ἀσίᾳ, τὸν
πόρον ἐν μέσῳ θέμενος, ὃν κληθῆναι νομίζουσι Βόσπορον Ἰοῦς διανηξαμένης, ὅτε βοῦς γενομένη κατὰ
ζηλοτυπίαν Ἥρας ἔφευγεν.

469   102. Ἐς τοσοῦτον παραδοξολογίας ἐπειγόμενος ὁ
Μιθριδάτης ἐφικέσθαι ὅμως ἐπενόει, καὶ διώδευεν
ἔθνη Σκυθικὰ καὶ πολεμικὰ καὶ ἀλλότρια πείθων ἢ
470 βιαζόμενος· οὕτω καὶ φεύγων καὶ ἀτυχῶν αἰδέσιμος
ἔτι καὶ φοβερὸς ἦν. Ἡνιόχους μὲν οὖν δεχομένους
αὐτὸν παρώδευεν, Ἀχαιοὺς δ᾽ ἐτρέψατο διώκων· οὓς
ἀπὸ Τροίας ἐπανιόντας φασὶν ἐς τὸν Πόντον ὑπὸ χειμῶνος ἐκπεσεῖν, καὶ πολλὰ παθεῖν ὡς Ἕλληνας ὑπὸ
471 βαρβάρων, πέμψαντας δ᾽ ἐπὶ ναῦς ἐς τὰς πατρίδας
καὶ ὑπεροφθέντας μηνῖσαι τῷ Ἑλληνικῷ γένει, καὶ
Σκυθικῶς ὅσους ἕλοιεν Ἑλλήνων καταθύειν, πρῶτα
μὲν ἅπαντας ὑπ᾽ ὀργῆς, σὺν χρόνῳ δὲ τοὺς καλλί-
472 στους αὐτῶν μόνους, μετὰ δὲ τοὺς κληρουμένους. καὶ
τάδε μὲν περὶ Ἀχαιῶν τῶν Σκυθικῶν· ὁ δὲ Μιθριδάτης
ἐς τὴν Μαιῶτιν ἐμβαλών, ἧς εἰσι πολλοὶ δυνάσται,
πάντων αὐτὸν κατὰ κλέος ἔργων τε καὶ ἀρχῆς, καὶ
δυνάμεως ἔτι οἱ παρούσης ἀξιολόγου, δεχομένων τε
καὶ παραπεμπόντων, καὶ δῶρα πολλὰ φερόντων καὶ

to invade Bosporus, by going all the way around the Pontus, and then Scythia and the Maeotid lake. Taking back 468
the kingdom of his son, Machares, who had proved ungrateful to him, he intended to confront the Romans again head on, and make war on them from Europe while they were in Asia, putting between them the Bosporan strait, which is believed to have got its name from the time Io swam across it, after she had been changed into a cow and was trying to escape from the jealousy of Hera.[67]

102. This was the fantastic task Mithridates now 469
pressed ahead with, and, fully intending to complete it, he marched through the territory of alien and warlike Scythian peoples, using both force and persuasion. To them he 470
was still a formidable and respected figure, even if a fugitive who had fallen on hard times. He crossed the land of the Heniochi, who welcomed him, and the Achaeans, whom he defeated and pursued. They say that on their way back from Troy the Achaeans were driven by a storm into the Pontus where they suffered dreadfully at the hands of the barbarians because they were Greeks. When they sent 471
home for ships and were ignored, they developed a hatred for the Greek race, and used to sacrifice in the Scythian manner any Greek they caught. In the beginning they were so angry they did this to them all, but as time passed they targeted only the most handsome Greeks, and finally only some chosen by lot. So much for the Achaeans of 472
Scythia. Mithridates then made his way to the Maeotid lake, where the many princes welcomed him, gave him an escort, and exchanged gifts on a generous scale, because of the fame of his rule and achievements, and because his

---

[67] The word Bosporus means "strait of the cow."

473 κομιζομένων ἕτερα, ὁ δὲ καὶ συμμαχίαν αὐτοῖς ἐτίθετο, ἐπινοῶν ἕτερα καινότερα, διὰ Θράκης ἐς Μακεδονίαν καὶ διὰ Μακεδόνων ἐς Παίονας ἐμβαλὼν ὑπερ-
474 ελθεῖν ἐς τὴν Ἰταλίαν τὰ Ἄλπεια ὄρη· γάμους τε
θυγατέρων ἐπὶ τῇδε τῇ συμμαχίᾳ τοῖς δυνατωτέροις
αὐτῶν ἠγγύα. Μαχάρης δ' αὐτὸν ὁ παῖς πυνθανόμενος ὁδόν τε τοσαύτην ὀλίγῳ χρόνῳ καὶ ἄγρια ἔθνη
καὶ τὰ καλούμενα κλεῖθρα Σκυθῶν, οὐδενί πω γεγο-
475 νότα περατά, διοδεῦσαι, πρέσβεις μέν τινας ἐς αὐτὸν
ἔπεμπεν ἀπολογησομένους ὡς ἀνάγκη θεραπεύσειε
Ῥωμαίους, ὀργὴν δὲ ἄκρον εἰδὼς ἔφευγεν ἐς τὴν ἐν
τῷ Πόντῳ Χερρόνησον, τὰς ναῦς διαπρήσας, ἵνα μὴ
διώξειεν αὐτὸν ὁ πατήρ. ἑτέρας δ' ἐπιπέμψαντος ἐκεί-
476 νου, προλαβὼν ἑαυτὸν ἔκτεινεν. ὁ δὲ Μιθριδάτης
αὐτοῦ τῶν φίλων οὓς μὲν αὐτὸς ἐς τὴν ἀρχὴν ἀπιόντι
ἐδεδώκει, πάντας ἔκτεινε, τοὺς δὲ τοῦ παιδὸς ἀπαθεῖς
ὡς ὑπηρέτας ἰδίου φίλου γενομένους ἀφῆκεν.

477 103. Καὶ τάδε μὲν ἦν ἀμφὶ τὸν Μιθριδάτην, ὁ δὲ
Πομπήιος αὐτὸν εὐθὺς μὲν ἐπὶ τῇ φυγῇ μέχρι Κόλχων ἐδίωξε, μετὰ δέ, οὐδαμῇ δόξας αὐτὸν οὔτε τὸν
Πόντον οὔτε τὴν Μαιώτιδα λίμνην περιελεύσεσθαι,
οὐδὲ μεγάλοις ἔτι πράγμασιν ἐγχειρήσειν ἐκπεσόντα,
478 τοὺς Κόλχους ἐπήει καθ' ἱστορίαν τῆς Ἀργοναυτῶν
καὶ Διοσκούρων καὶ Ἡρακλέους ἐπιδημίας, τὸ πάθος
μάλιστα ἰδεῖν ἐθέλων ὃ Προμηθεῖ φασὶ γενέσθαι περὶ
479 τὸ Καύκασον ὄρος. χρυσοφοροῦσι δ' ἐκ τοῦ Καυκά-
σου πηγαὶ πολλαὶ ψῆγμα ἀφανές· καὶ οἱ περίοικοι
κώδια τιθέντες ἐς τὸ ῥεῦμα βαθύμαλλα, τὸ ψῆγμα

power was still worthy of respect. He even made an alli- 473
ance with them, with a view to his new and even more
remarkable plans to march through Thrace into Macedonia, through Macedonia into Paeonia and then cross the
Alps into Italy. To cement the alliance, he promised his 474
daughters in marriage to the more powerful princes.
When his son Machares learned that he had completed
such a long journey in such a short time, and had passed
through the land of fierce peoples, and through what were
known as the Scythian Gates, which no one had done before, he sent envoys to Mithridates to defend his actions, 475
on the grounds that it had been necessary to appease the
Romans. But knowing his father's fierce temper, he fled to
Pontic Chersonesus and burned his ships, so that the king
would not be able to follow him. But when Mithridates
sent for other ones, Machares stole a march on him by
taking his own life. Mithridates executed all of the court- 476
iers he had himself assigned to Machares when he was
leaving to take up his kingdom, but his son's courtiers he
released unharmed because they had been the assistants
of their personal friend.

103. That is how things stood for Mithridates. Pompey 477
had immediately pursued him in his flight as far as Colchis,
but no further, believing that he would not be able to make
his way around the Pontus and Maeotid lake, or embark
on any great ventures now that he was an exile from his
kingdom. He entered Colchis to investigate the visits 478
there of the Argonauts, the Dioscuri, and Heracles, and
was particularly keen to see where they say Prometheus
had been tortured on Mount Caucasus. There are many 479
streams that come down from the Caucasus which carry
invisible particles of gold. The people who live there put

351

ἐνισχόμενον αὐτοῖς ἐκλέγουσιν. καὶ τοιοῦτον ἦν ἴσως
480 καὶ τὸ χρυσόμαλλον Αἰήτου δέρος. τὸν οὖν Πομπήιον
ἐπὶ τῇ ἱστορίᾳ ἀνιόντα οἱ μὲν ἄλλοι παρέπεμπον, ὅσα
ἔθνη γείτονα· Ὀροίζης δ᾽ ὁ τῶν Ἀλβανῶν βασιλεὺς
καὶ Ἀρτώκης ὁ Ἰβήρων ἑπτὰ μυριάσιν ἐλόχων ἀμφὶ
τὸν Κῦρον ποταμόν, ὃς δυώδεκα στόμασι πλωτοῖς ἐς
τὴν Κασπίαν θάλασσαν ἐρεύγεται, πολλῶν ἐς αὐτὸν
ἐμβαλόντων ποταμῶν, καὶ μεγίστου πάντων Ἀράξου.
481 αἰσθόμενος δὲ τῆς ἐνέδρας ὁ Πομπήιος τὸν ποταμὸν
ἔζευγνυ, καὶ τοὺς βαρβάρους συνελάσας ἐς λόχμην
βαθεῖαν (ὑλομαχῆσαι δ᾽ εἰσὶ δεινοί, κρυπτόμενοί τε
καὶ ἐπιόντες ἀφανῶς) αὐτῇ λόχμῃ τὸν στρατὸν περιστήσας ἐνέπρησε, καὶ τοὺς ἐκφεύγοντας ἐδίωκεν, ἕως
482 ἅμα πάντες[25] ὅμηρά τε καὶ δῶρα ἤνεγκαν. καὶ ἐθριάμβευσεν ἐς Ῥώμην καὶ ἀπὸ τῶνδε. πολλαὶ δὲ ἔν τε
τοῖς ὁμήροις καὶ τοῖς αἰχμαλώτοις ηὑρέθησαν γυ-
483 ναῖκες, οὐ μείονα τῶν ἀνδρῶν τραύματα ἔχουσαι· καὶ
ἐδόκουν Ἀμαζόνες εἶναι, εἴτε τι ἔθνος ἐστὶν αὐτοῖς
γειτονεῦον αἱ Ἀμαζόνες, ἐπίκλητοι τότε ἐς συμμαχίαν
γενόμεναι, εἴτε τινὰς πολεμικὰς ὅλως γυναῖκας οἱ
τῇδε βάρβαροι καλοῦσιν Ἀμαζόνας.
484 104. Ἐπανιὼν δ᾽ ἐντεῦθεν ὁ Πομπήιος ἐστράτευεν
ἐς Ἀρμενίαν, ἔγκλημα ἐς Τιγράνη τιθέμενος ὅτι συνεμάχει Μιθριδάτῃ· καὶ ἦν ἤδη περὶ Ἀρτάξατα τὸ βα-
485 σίλειον. Τιγράνη δὲ οὐκ ἔγνωστο μὲν πολεμεῖν ἔτι,
παῖδες δ᾽ ἐκ τῆς Μιθριδάτου θυγατρὸς αὐτῷ τρεῖς

---

[25] ἅμα πάντες Goukowsky: ἂν πάντες codd.

thick fleeces in the flowing water, which catch the gold
dust and which they can then pick out. Perhaps the golden
fleece of Aeetes was something like this. All the other   480
neighboring peoples accompanied Pompey on his research
expedition, but not Oroezes, king of the Albanians, and
Artoces, king of the Iberians, who laid an ambush with
seventy thousand men at the river Cyrus. At its mouth this
river empties into the Caspian Sea through twelve navi-
gable channels, and has many rivers flowing into it, the
biggest of all being the river Araxes.[68] Pompey detected   481
the ambush, bridged the river, and drove the barbarians
into a deep wood (they are very good forest fighters, attacking from their hiding places without being seen). He
surrounded the wood itself with his own men and set fire
to it, pursuing those who escaped until they all brought
him hostages and gifts at the same time. Pompey later   482
celebrated a triumph at Rome over these too. Many
women were found among the hostages and prisoners,
wounded just as badly as the men. These were thought to   483
be Amazons, although it is not known whether the Amazons are neighbors of theirs, who were called on for military assistance at the time, or indeed whether the barbarians of that region call all warlike women Amazons.

104. On his return from Colchis Pompey marched   484
against Armenia—regarding it as a *casus belli* that Tigranes had been an ally of Mithridates—and was soon
near Artaxata, the royal capital. But Tigranes had decided   485
not to fight any longer. He had had three sons with Mith-

---

[68] The Araxes River (mod. Aras) joins the Cyrus (mod. Kura)
about seventy-five miles from its mouth on the Caspian.

γεγένηντο, ὧν δύο μὲν αὐτὸς ὁ Τιγράνης ἀνῃρήκει,
τὸν μὲν ἐν μάχῃ, πολεμοῦντά οἱ, τὸν δ' ἐν κυνηγεσίοις, αὐτοῦ πεσόντος ἀμελήσαντα καὶ τὸ διάδημα
486 περιθέμενον ἔτι κειμένου. ὁ δὲ τρίτος, Τιγράνης, ἐν
μὲν τοῖς κυνηγεσίοις ὑπεραλγήσας τοῦ πατρὸς ἐστε-
φάνωτο ὑπ' αὐτοῦ, μικρὸν δὲ διαλιπὼν ἀπέστη καὶ
ὅδε, καὶ πολεμῶν τῷ πατρὶ καὶ ἡττώμενος ἐς Φραάτην
ἐπεφεύγει τὸν Παρθυαίων βασιλέα, ἄρτι τὴν Σιν-
487 τρίκου τοῦ πατρὸς ἀρχὴν διαδεδεγμένον. πλησιάσαν-
τος δὲ τοῦ Πομπηίου κοινωσάμενος Φραάτῃ, συγχω-
ροῦντός τι κἀκείνου καὶ φιλίαν ἰδίαν ἐς τὸν Πομπήιον
μνωμένου, κατέφυγεν ὁ παῖς ἱκέτης ἐς τὸν Πομπήιον,
488 καὶ ταῦτα ὢν Μιθριδάτου θυγατριδοῦς. ἀλλὰ μέγα
δικαιοσύνης καὶ πίστεως κλέος ἦν τοῦ Πομπηίου
παρὰ τοῖς βαρβάροις, ᾧ δὴ πίσυνος καὶ ὁ πατὴρ
Τιγράνης οὐδ' ἐπικηρυκευσάμενος ᾔει, τά τε ἄλλα
πάντα ἑαυτὸν ἐπιτρέψων ἐς τὰ δίκαια Πομπηίῳ, καὶ
489 κατηγορήσων τοῦ παιδὸς ἐπὶ Πομπηίου. χιλιάρχους
δὲ αὐτῷ καὶ ἱππάρχους ἐπὶ τιμῇ κελεύσαντος ὑπαν-
τᾶν τοῦ Πομπηίου, οἱ μὲν ὄντες ἀμφὶ τὸν Τιγράνη τὸ
ἀκήρυκτον τῆς ὁδοῦ δεδιότες ἔφευγον ὀπίσω, ὁ δὲ Τιγράνης ἦλθε, καὶ τὸν Πομπήιον ὡς κρείττονα βαρβα-
490 ρικῶς προσεκύνησεν. εἰσὶ δ' οἳ λέγουσιν ὑπὸ ῥαβδού-
χοις αὐτὸν ἀχθῆναι, μετάπεμπτον ὑπὸ τοῦ Πομπηίου
γενόμενον. ὁποτέρως δ' ἦλθεν, ἐξελογεῖτο περὶ τῶν
γεγονότων, καὶ ἐδίδου Πομπηίῳ μὲν αὐτῷ τάλαντα

ridates' daughter, two of whom he had killed himself, one in battle when he was at war with his father, the other on a hunting expedition, when he himself had fallen and his son had failed to tend to him, but had put on the diadem while Tigranes was lying on the ground. The third son, also 486 called Tigranes, was very upset at what had happened to his father on the hunting expedition, and received a crown from him, but only a short time later he too deserted his father, went to war against him, but was defeated and fled for refuge to Phraates, king of Parthia, who had recently succeeded his father Sintricos as king.[69] At the approach 487 of Pompey the young Tigranes fled as a suppliant to him, having discussed this with Phraates, and agreed it with him, as he too wanted to win Pompey's friendship. Tigranes did this even though he was a grandson of Mithridates. But among the barbarians Pompey had a great 488 reputation for justice and good faith. It was his trust in these qualities that also brought Tigranes the father to Pompey without even being announced by heralds, in order to entrust himself entirely to Pompey's decisions, and complain to him about his son. Out of respect for him, 489 Pompey ordered military tribunes and cavalry officers to meet Tigranes, but the king's entourage were uneasy about approaching without official heralds, turned around, and fled. Tigranes himself, however, came and, in the barbarian manner, prostrated himself before Pompey as his superior. There are those who say that when Pompey sent 490 for him he was escorted by lictors. However that may be, he excused himself for what had happened, and gave Pompey himself a gift of six thousand talents, and fifty drach-

---

[69] Sinatruces was king of Parthia from about 77 to 70.

ἑξακισχίλια, τῇ στρατιᾷ δὲ δραχμὰς πεντήκοντα ἑκάστῳ, καὶ λοχαγῷ χιλίας, καὶ χιλιάρχῳ μυρίας.

491   105. Καὶ ὁ Πομπήιος αὐτῷ συνεγίγνωσκε τῶν γεγονότων καὶ συνήλασσε τῷ παιδί, καὶ διῄτησε τὸν μὲν υἱὸν ἄρχειν τῆς Σωφηνῆς καὶ Γορδυηνῆς, αἳ νῦν ἄρα εἰσὶν Ἀρμενία βραχυτέρα, τὸν δὲ πατέρα τῆς ἄλλης Ἀρμενίας ἐπὶ τῷδε τῷ παιδὶ κληρονόμῳ. τὴν

492   δὲ ἐπίκτητον αὐτὸν ἀρχὴν ἐκέλευεν ἤδη μεθεῖναι. καὶ μεθίει Συρίαν τὴν ἀπ' Εὐφράτου μέχρι τῆς θαλάσσης· εἶχε γὰρ δὴ καὶ τήνδε καὶ Κιλικίας τινὰ ὁ Τιγράνης, Ἀντίοχον ἐκβαλὼν τὸν εὐσεβῆ προσαγορευ-

493   θέντα. Ἀρμενίων δ' ὅσοι τὸν Τιγράνη πρὸς Πομπήιον ὁδεύοντα ἐγκατελελοίπεσαν, ἐν ὑποψίᾳ τοῦτ' ἔχοντες, τὸν παῖδα αὐτοῦ παρὰ τῷ Πομπηίῳ ἔτι ὄντα πείθου-

494   σιν ἐπιθέσθαι τῷ πατρί. καὶ ὁ μὲν ἐλήφθη καὶ ἐδέθη, καὶ μεταξὺ Παρθυαίους ἐρεθίζων ἐπὶ τὸν Πομπήιον ἐθριαμβεύθη καὶ ἀνῃρέθη· ὁ δὲ Πομπήιος ἐκτετελέσθαι οἱ τὸν πάντα πόλεμον ἡγούμενος, ᾤκιζε πόλιν ἔνθα τὴν μάχην ἐνίκα Μιθριδάτην, ἣ ἀπὸ τοῦ ἔργου Νικόπολις κλῄζεται, καὶ ἔστιν Ἀρμενίας τῆς βραχυ-

495   τέρας λεγομένης. Ἀριοβαρζάνῃ δ' ἀπεδίδου βασιλεύειν Καππαδοκίας, καὶ προσεπέδωκε Σωφηνὴν καὶ Γορδυηνήν, ἃ τῷ παιδὶ μεμέριστο τῷ Τιγράνους· καὶ στρατηγεῖται νῦν ἅμα τῇ Καππαδοκίᾳ καὶ τάδε.

496   ἔδωκε δὲ καὶ τῆς Κιλικίας πόλιν Καστάβαλα καὶ ἄλλας. Ἀριοβαρζάνης μὲν οὖν τὴν βασιλείαν ὅλην τῷ παιδὶ περιὼν ἐνεχείρισε. καὶ πολλαὶ μεταβολαὶ μέχρι

mas to every soldier in the army, one thousand to the
centurions and ten thousand to the military tribunes.

105. Pompey pardoned him for his past behavior and   491
reconciled him with his son. He decided that the younger
Tigranes should rule Sophene and Gordyene, which are
now called Armenia Minor, and his father the rest of Armenia, with this son as his heir. He also ordered that the
king should now give up the additional territory he had
acquired. And so Tigranes ceded Syria between the Eu-   492
phrates and the sea, which he held along with some of
Cilicia, having expelled Antiochus surnamed Eusebes.[70]
Those Armenians who had abandoned Tigranes when he   493
was approaching Pompey were suspicious of these arrangements and persuade the younger Tigranes, who was
still with Pompey, to make an attempt on his father's life.
He was arrested and put in prison, but when he later tried   494
to stir up the Parthians against Pompey, he was included
in Pompey's triumphal procession and then executed. Believing that he had now brought an end to the whole war,
Pompey founded a city on the site of his victory against
Mithridates, which is called Nicopolis after the event. It is
situated in what is called Armenia Minor. He returned   495
Cappadocia to the rule of Ariobarzanes, and added Sophene and Gordyene, which had been allocated to the
younger Tigranes, and which are now governed along with
Cappadocia. He also gave him Castabala and some other   496
towns in Cilicia. Ariobarzanes, however, abdicated and
gave his whole kingdom to his son. There were a great

[70] Antiochus X Eusebes ruled what was left of the Seleucid
kingdom from 95. It is not clear when his reign ended.

Καίσαρος ἐγένοντο τοῦ Σεβαστοῦ, ἐφ᾽ οὗ, καθάπερ τὰ
λοιπά, καὶ ἥδε ἡ βασιλεία περιῆλθεν ἐς στρατηγίαν.

497   106. Ὁ δὲ Πομπήιος καὶ τὸν Ταῦρον ὑπερελθὼν
ἐπολέμησε Ἀντιόχῳ τῷ Κομμαγηνῷ, ἕως ἐς φιλίαν ὁ
Ἀντίοχος αὐτῷ συνῆλθεν, ἐπολέμησε δὲ καὶ Δαρείῳ
τῷ Μήδῳ, μέχρι ἔφυγεν, εἴτε Ἀντιόχῳ συμμαχῶν εἴτε
498 Τιγράνῃ πρότερον. ἐπολέμησε δὲ καὶ Ἄραψι τοῖς Να-
βαταίοις, Ἀρέτα βασιλεύοντος αὐτῶν, καὶ Ἰουδαίοις,
Ἀριστοβούλου τοῦ βασιλέως ἀποστάντος, ἕως καθ-
499 εῖλεν Ἱεροσόλυμα τὴν ἁγιωτάτην αὐτοῖς πόλιν. καὶ
Κιλικίας δὲ ὅσα οὔπω Ῥωμαίοις ὑπήκουε, καὶ τὴν
ἄλλην Συρίαν, ὅση τε περὶ Εὐφράτην ἐστὶ καὶ κοίλη
καὶ Φοινίκη καὶ Παλαιστίνη λέγεται, καὶ τὴν Ἰδου-
μαίων καὶ Ἰτουραίων, καὶ ὅσα ἄλλα ὀνόματα Συρίας,
500 ἐπιὼν ἀμαχὶ Ῥωμαίοις καθίστατο, ἔγκλημα μὲν οὐδὲν ἔχων ἐς Ἀντίοχον τὸν εὐσεβοῦς, παρόντα καὶ δεό-
μενον ὑπὲρ ἀρχῆς πατρῴας, ἡγούμενος δέ, Τιγράνη
τὸν κρατήσαντα τοῦ Ἀντιόχου τῆς γῆς ἀπελάσας,
501 Ῥωμαίοις αὐτὴν κατὰ τόδε προσκεκτῆσθαι. ταῦτα δ᾽
αὐτῷ διοικουμένῳ πρέσβεις ἀφίκοντο Φραάτου καὶ
Τιγράνους ἐς πόλεμον ἀλλήλοις συμπεσόντων, οἱ μὲν
Τιγράνους ὡς φίλῳ συμμαχεῖν τὸν Πομπήιον ἀξιοῦν-
τες, οἱ δὲ τοῦ Παρθυαίου φιλίαν αὐτῷ πρὸς Ῥωμαίους
τιθέμενοι. καὶ ὁ Πομπήιος οὐκ ἀξιῶν Παρθυαίοις πολεμεῖν ἄνευ Ῥωμαίων ψηφίσματος, ἔπεμψεν ἀμφοτέροις διαλλακτάς.

502   107. Καὶ ὁ μὲν ἀμφὶ ταῦτα ἦν, Μιθριδάτῃ δὲ ἡ

number of changes up till the time of Caesar Augustus, in whose reign this kingdom too, along with the rest, became a Roman province.

106. Pompey now also crossed the Taurus mountains 497 and made war on Antiochus of Commagene, until the latter agreed to become his friend. He also waged war against Darius the Mede, who eventually took to flight, either because he had given assistance to Antiochus or earlier to Tigranes. He fought against the Nabataean Arabs too, and 498 their king, Aretas, and against the Jews, whose king, Aristobulus, had risen in revolt, until he captured Jerusalem, their most holy city. He marched against the following places and brought them under Roman rule without warfare: those parts of Cilicia that were not yet subject to 499 Rome; the rest of Syria around the Euphrates; the regions known as Coele Syria, Phoenicia, and Palestine; Idumea, Iturea, and all other parts of Syria, whatever name they bore. He had no accusation to make against Antiochus 500 Eusebes, who came and asked him for his ancestral kingdom, but his opinion was that as Tigranes had defeated Antiochus, and he himself had expelled Tigranes from the territory; on this basis it had been duly acquired by Rome. While he was in the process of making these arrange- 501 ments, representatives arrived from Phraates and Tigranes, who were at war with each other. Tigranes' envoys asked that Pompey provide military assistance to him since he was a friend of Rome, while the Parthian ambassadors were trying to establish friendly relations between Phraates and Rome. Pompey did not think it right to declare war on the Parthians without a senatorial decision, and sent arbitrators to both of them.

107. While Pompey was engaged in these matters, 502

περίοδος ἤνυστο τοῦ Πόντου· καὶ Παντικάπαιον, ἐμ-
πόριον Εὐρωπαῖον ἐπὶ τῆς ἐκβολῆς τοῦ Πόντου καταλαβὼν κτείνει τῶν υἱέων Ξιφάρην ἐπὶ τοῦ πόρου διὰ
503 μητρὸς ἁμάρτημα τοιόνδε. φρούριον ἦν τι Μιθριδάτῃ,
ἔνθα λανθάνοντες ὑπόγειοι θησαυροὶ πολλῶν σιδηρο-
δέτων χαλκέων πολλὰ χρήματα ἔκρυπτον. Στρατονίκη δέ, μία τῶν Μιθριδάτου παλλακῶν ἢ γυναικῶν,
ἢ τοῦδε τοῦ φρουρίου τὴν ἐπιστήμην καὶ φυλακὴν
504 ἐπετέτραπτο, περιόντος ἔτι τὸν Πόντον τοῦ Μιθριδάτου τὸ φρούριον ἐνεχείρισε τῷ Πομπηίῳ καὶ τοὺς
θησαυροὺς ἀγνοουμένους ἐμήνυσεν, ἐπὶ συνθήκῃ
μόνῃ τῇδε, ὅτι οἱ τὸν υἱὸν Ξιφάρην ὁ Πομπήιος, εἰ
505 λάβοι, περισώσει. καὶ ὁ μὲν τοῖς χρήμασιν ἐπιτυχὼν
ὑπέσχητο αὐτῇ τὸν Ξιφάρην καὶ ἐδεδώκει φέρεσθαι
καὶ τὰ ἴδια· αἰσθόμενος δὲ τῶν γεγονότων ὁ Μιθριδάτης κτείνει τὸν Ξιφάρην ἐπὶ τοῦ πόρου, ἐφορώσης
506 τῆς μητρὸς πέραθεν, καὶ ἐξέρριψεν ἄταφον. καὶ ὁ μὲν
υἱοῦ κατεφρόνησεν ἐς ἀνίαν τῆς ἁμαρτούσης, καὶ
πρέσβεις ἐς τὸν Πομπήιον, ἔτι περὶ Συρίαν ὄντα καὶ
οὐκ αἰσθανόμενον αὐτοῦ παρόντος, ἔπεμπεν, οἳ τῆς
πατρῴας ἀρχῆς αὐτὸν Ῥωμαίοις τελέσειν φόρους
507 ὑπισχνοῦντο· Πομπηίου δ᾽ αὐτὸν ἐλθόντα δεῖσθαι τὸν
Μιθριδάτην κελεύοντος, καθὰ καὶ Τιγράνης ἀφίκετο,
τοῦτο μὲν οὐκ ἔφη ποτὲ ὑποστήσεσθαι, Μιθριδάτης
γε ὤν, πέμψειν δὲ τῶν παίδων τινὰς καὶ φίλους.

snatched her out of danger. All the nearby forts that had   514
lately been taken over by Mithridates now revolted from
him, inspired by the quick thinking of Phanagoria: Chersonesus, Theodosia, Nymphaeum, and all the others
around the Pontus so strategically well located for war.
Observing these frequent defections, and suspicious that   515
the army would not remain loyal because service was com-
pulsory, taxes heavy, and like all soldiers, they did not trust
unlucky commanders, Mithridates had his daughters   516
brought by eunuchs to Scythia as wives for the princes,
with a request that they get an army to him now with all
speed. Five hundred men from his army provided an escort. Shortly after leaving Mithridates, however, the soldiers killed the escort of eunuchs, and delivered the young
women to Pompey. Eunuchs wielded great influence with
Mithridates, and the soldiers were always very hostile to
them.

109. In spite of losing so many children and forts, and   517
his entire kingdom, and although he was no longer at all
battle-ready and had no reason to think that he would get
assistance from the Scythians, nevertheless even now
there was nothing modest about Mithridates' plans, nothing that reflected the disasters he had suffered. For he   518
intended to make his way over to the Celts, longtime
friends of his for exactly this purpose, and launch an invasion of Italy with them. He expected that much of Italy
itself would join him out of hatred for Rome, having   519
learned that this is what Hannibal did when he was at war
with Rome in Iberia, and that this was how he instilled
such fear into the Romans. He also knew that almost the
whole of Italy had recently revolted from Rome in their
hatred, and had been at war with them for a very long

APPIAN

520 πλεῖστον αὐτοῖς πεπολεμηκυῖαν, Σπαρτάκῳ τε μονο-
μάχῳ συστᾶσαν ἐπ' αὐτούς, ἀνδρὶ ἐπ' οὐδεμιᾶς ἀξιώσεως ὄντι. ταῦτα ἐνθυμούμενος ἐς Κελτοὺς ἠπείγετο.
τοῦ δὲ τολμήματος ἂν αὐτῷ λαμπροτάτου γενομένου,
ὁ στρατὸς ὤκνει δι' αὐτὸ μάλιστα τῆς τόλμης τὸ μέγεθος, ἐπί τε χρόνιον στρατείαν καὶ ἐς ἀλλοτρίαν γῆν
ἀγόμενοι, καὶ ἐπὶ ἄνδρας ὧν οὐδ' ἐν τῇ σφετέρᾳ κρα-
521 τοῦσιν. αὐτόν τε τὸν Μιθριδάτην ἡγούμενοι, πάντων
ἀπογιγνώσκοντα, βούλεσθαί τι δρῶντα καὶ βασιλι-
ζόμενον μᾶλλον ἢ δι' ἀργίας ἀποθανεῖν, ὅμως ἐνεκαρ-
τέρουν καὶ ἡσύχαζον· οὐ γάρ τοι σμικρὸς οὐδ' εὐκα-
ταφρόνητος ἦν ὁ βασιλεὺς οὐδ' ἐν ταῖς συμφοραῖς.

522 110. Ὧδε δ' ἐχόντων ἁπάντων, Φαρνάκης ὁ τῶν
παίδων αὐτῷ τιμιώτατός τε καὶ πολλάκις ὑπ' αὐτοῦ
523 τῆς ἀρχῆς ἀποδεδειγμένος ἔσεσθαι διάδοχος, εἴτε
δείσας περὶ τοῦδε τοῦ στόλου καὶ τῆς ἀρχῆς, ὡς νῦν
μὲν ἔτι συγγνωσομένων τι Ῥωμαίων, ἀπολουμένης δὲ
πάμπαν ὁλοκλήρως εἰ ἐπὶ τὴν Ἰταλίαν ὁ πατὴρ στρα-
τεύσειεν, εἴθ' ἑτέραις αἰτίαις καὶ λογισμῶν ἐπιθυμίαις,
524 ἐπεβούλευε τῷ πατρί. ληφθέντων δὲ τῶν συνεγνωκότων αὐτῷ καὶ ἐς βασάνους ἀγομένων, Μηνοφάνης
μετέπεισε τὸν Μιθριδάτην ὡς οὐ δέον, ἀποπλέοντα
525 ἤδη, τὸν ἔτι οἱ τιμιώτατον υἱὸν ἀνελεῖν· εἶναι δ' ἔφη
τὰς τοιαύτας τροπὰς ἔργα πολέμων, ὧν παυσαμένων

---

[72] From 73 to 71 the Thracian gladiator Spartacus ravaged
Italy and defeated Roman forces sent against him, until he was
defeated and killed by Crassus. Appian seems to be running to-

time, and had joined forces against them with the gladiator 520
Spartacus, a man of no standing.[72] With these consider-
ations in mind, Mithridates was eager to reach the Celts.
Although such a daring expedition would have been a brilliant achievement for him, his army was hesitant because
of the very scale of the audacity, which would require a
long campaign in a foreign country, against men they
could not even overpower in their own land. They also 521
thought that Mithridates himself, in complete despair,
wanted to die in action leading as a king, rather than doing
nothing. But they put up with this state of affairs and held
their peace. For even in his misfortunes there was nothing
mean or contemptible about the king.

110. Such was the overall situation. As for Pharnaces, 522
the son most respected by Mithridates, and often desig-
nated by him as his successor to the throne, either because 523
he was afraid about this expedition and its effect on the
kingdom—for even now the Romans might be inclined to
forgive, but everything would be completely lost if his
father marched against Italy—or perhaps because of other
reasons and the desire to act rationally, now formed a
conspiracy against his father. Pharnaces' fellow conspira- 524
tors were arrested and tortured, but Menophanes persuaded Mithridates that it would not be fitting, just as he
was about to sail away, to execute the son whom he still
honored most highly. He said that wars were the cause of 525
such incongruities, but once the wars came to an end, the

gether the Social War (91–87) and the civil discord caused by M.
Aemilius Lepidus (consul 78), who made contact with Sertorius,
and whose followers, after his death in 77, eventually joined Sertorius.

καὶ τάδε καθίστασθαι. ὁ μὲν δὴ πεισθεὶς προὔτεινε
526 τῷ παιδὶ συγγνώμην. ὁ δὲ δείσας τι μήνιμα καὶ τὸν
στρατὸν εἰδὼς κατοκνοῦντα τὴν στρατείαν, νυκτὸς ἐς
πρώτους τοὺς Ῥωμαίων αὐτομόλους, ἀγχοτάτω τοῦ
527 Μιθριδάτου στρατοπεδεύοντας ἐσῆλθε, καὶ τὸν κίνδυνον αὐτοῖς ἰοῦσιν ἐπὶ τὴν Ἰταλίαν, ὅσος εἴη, σαφῶς
εἰδόσιν ὑπερεπαίρων, πολλὰ δὲ μένουσιν ἐπελπίσας
ἔσεσθαι παρ' ἑαυτοῦ, προήγαγεν ἐς ἀπόστασιν ἀπὸ
528 τοῦ πατρός. ὡς δ' ἐπείσθησαν οἵδε, τῆς αὐτῆς νυκτὸς
ἐς τὰ ἐγγὺς ἄλλα στρατόπεδα ἔπεμπεν ὁ Φαρνάκης.
συνθεμένων δὲ κἀκείνων, πρῶτοι μὲν ἅμα ἕῳ ἠλάλαξαν οἱ αὐτόμολοι, ἐπὶ δ' ἐκείνοις οἱ ἀεὶ πλησίον τὴν
529 βοὴν μετελάμβανον. καὶ τὸ ναυτικὸν αὐτοῖς ἐπήχη-
σεν, οὐ προειδότες μὲν ἅπαντες ἴσως, ὀξύρροποι δ'
ὄντες ἐς μεταβολὰς καὶ τὸ δυστυχοῦν ὑπερορῶντες,
ἐν δὲ τῷ καινῷ τὸ εὔελπι ἀεὶ τιθέμενοι. οἱ δὲ καὶ
ἀγνοίᾳ τῶν συνεγνωκότων, ἡγούμενοι πάντας δι-
εφθάρθαι καὶ μόνοι ἔτι ὄντες ἔσεσθαι τοῖς πλείοσιν
εὐκαταφρόνητοι, φόβῳ καὶ ἀνάγκῃ μᾶλλον ἢ ἑκουσίῳ
530 γνώμῃ συνεπήχουν. Μιθριδάτης δ' ἐγρόμενος ὑπὸ τῆς
βοῆς ἔπεμπέ τινας ἐρησομένους ὅ τι χρῄζοιεν οἱ
βοῶντες. οἱ δ' οὐκ ἐγκαλυψάμενοι, "Τὸν υἱόν," ἔφασαν, "Βασιλεύειν, νέον ἀντὶ γέροντος εὐνούχοις τε
ἐκδεδομένου καὶ κτείναντος ἤδη πολλοὺς υἱέας τε καὶ
ἡγεμόνας καὶ φίλους."

531   111. Ὧν ὁ Μιθριδάτης πυθόμενος, ἐξῄει διαλεξόμενος αὐτοῖς, καί τι πλῆθος ἐκ φρουρίου τοῖς αὐτο-
532 μόλοις συνέτρεχεν. οἱ δ' οὐκ ἔφασαν αὐτοὺς προσή-

incongruities too receded. The king was indeed persuaded and granted a pardon to his son. Pharnaces, however, fear- 526 ing there might be some resentment, and aware that the army was reluctant to embark on the expedition, first approached by night the Roman deserters who were encamped very close to Mithridates. By exaggerating the 527 dangers of marching to Italy, which they well knew, and by leading them to expect generous gifts from him if they refused to go, he induced them to abandon his father. Having persuaded this group, Pharnaces sent deputations 528 the same night to other encampments nearby and won their agreement too. At dawn, the deserters were the first to raise the battle cry, and then the groups near them took up the shout one after another. The sailors also joined in, 529 not perhaps because they were all privy to the conspiracy, but because they were volatile and quick to change allegiance, despised misfortune, and always placed their highest hopes in novelty. Others, who did not know the conspirators, but thought that everyone had been subverted, and that if they alone held out they would be easy for the majority to treat with disdain, took up the cry out of fear and necessity rather than of their own free will. Woken by 530 the shouting, Mithridates sent men to find out what those making the noise wanted. They replied without trying to hide anything, "We want your son to be king," they said, "a young man, not an old one dominated by his eunuchs, who has already murdered many of his sons and officers and courtiers."

111. When Mithridates heard this he went out to rea- 531 son with them, just as a contingent of men from a fort was running over to join the deserters. The latter refused to 532

369

σεσθαι πρίν τι ἀνήκεστον ἐς πίστιν ἐργάσασθαι,
δεικνύντες ὁμοῦ τὸν Μιθριδάτην. οἱ μὲν δὴ τὸν ἵππον
ἔφθασαν αὐτοῦ κτεῖναι φυγόντος, καὶ τὸν Φαρνάκην
533 ὡς ἤδη κρατοῦντες ἀνεῖπον βασιλέα· καὶ βύβλον τις
πλατεῖαν φέρων ἐξ ἱεροῦ ἐστεφάνωσεν αὐτὸν ἀντὶ
διαδήματος. ἅπερ ἄνωθεν ἐκ περιπάτου θεώμενος
ἔπεμπεν ἐς τὸν Φαρνάκην ἄλλον ἐπ᾽ ἄλλῳ, φυγὴν
534 αἰτῶν ἀσφαλῆ. οὐδενὸς δὲ τῶν πεμπομένων ἐπανιόντος, δείσας μὴ Ῥωμαίοις ἐκδοθείη, τοὺς μὲν σωματο-
φύλακας αὐτοῦ καὶ φίλους ἔτι παραμένοντας ἐπαινέ-
535 σας ἔπεμψεν ἐς τὸν νέον βασιλέα, καὶ αὐτῶν τινας
προσιόντας ἔκτεινεν ἡ στρατιὰ παραλόγως, αὐτὸς δὲ
παραλύσας ὃ περὶ τῷ ξίφει φάρμακον ἀεὶ περιέκειτο
536 ἐκίρνα. δύο δ᾽ αὐτῷ θυγατέρες ἔτι κόραι συντρεφό-
μεναι, Μιθριδατίς τε καὶ Νύσσα, τοῖς Αἰγύπτου καὶ
Κύπρου βασιλεῦσιν ἐνηγγυημέναι, προλαβεῖν τοῦ
φαρμάκου παρεκάλουν, καὶ σφόδρα εἴχοντο, καὶ πί-
537 νοντα κατεκώλυον ἕως ἔπιον λαβοῦσαι. καὶ τῶν μὲν
αὐτίκα τὸ φάρμακον ἥπτετο, τοῦ δὲ Μιθριδάτου, καίτοι συντόνως ἐξεπίτηδες βαδίζοντος, οὐκ ἐφικνεῖτο δι᾽
ἔθος καὶ συντροφίαν ἑτέρων φαρμάκων, οἷς ἐς ἄμυναν
δηλητηρίων ἐχρῆτο συνεχῶς· καὶ νῦν ἔτι φάρμακα
538 Μιθριδάτεια λέγεται. Βίτοιτον οὖν τινα ἰδών, ἡγεμόνα
Κελτῶν, "Πολλὰ μὲν ἐκ τῆς σῆς," ἔφη, "Δεξιᾶς ἐς
πολεμίους ὠνάμην, ὀνήσομαι δὲ μέγιστον εἰ νῦν με
κατεργάσαιο, κινδυνεύοντα ἐς πομπὴν ἀπαχθῆναι
θριάμβου τὸν μέχρι πολλοῦ τοσῆσδε ἀρχῆς αὐτοκράτορα καὶ βασιλέα, ἀδυνατοῦντα ἐκ φαρμάκων

take them in before they gave evidence of their good faith by doing some unforgivable deed, pointing at the same time to Mithridates. The king fled, but they killed his horse before he could get to it, and declared Pharnaces king as if they had already won. One of them took a broad 533 sheet of papyrus from the temple and used it instead of a diadem to crown him. While watching all this from a high portico, Mithridates sent one messenger after another to Pharnaces, asking for safe passage to flee. None of those 534 he sent returned, and, afraid of being handed over to the Romans, he praised those of his bodyguards and courtiers who had stayed with him, and sent them to the young king. Misunderstanding the situation, the soldiers killed some 535 of them as they approached. Mithridates himself now took out some poison he always kept near his sword, and mixed it. Two of his daughters who were still young girls growing 536 up at court, Mithridatis and Nyssa—they had been betrothed to the kings of Egypt and Cyprus—begged to take the poison first, and insisted on it, preventing him from doing so until they had taken some and drunk it. The 537 poison immediately worked its effect on them, but not on Mithridates, even though he walked around vigorously to help it work. The reason for this is that he had made a habit of getting used to other poisons which he took continually as a protection against poisoners. These are still called "Mithridatic drugs." So, seeing a certain Bituitus, one of 538 his Celtic officers, he said to him, "I have profited greatly from your right arm in the fight against our enemies, but I will now profit most of all if you would make an end of me, as I am in danger of being led in a triumphal procession, I who was the king and absolute ruler for a long time of such a great kingdom. I am unable to die of poison

ἀποθανεῖν δι᾽ εὐήθη προφυλακὴν ἑτέρων φαρμάκων·
539 τὸ γὰρ δὴ χαλεπώτατον καὶ σύνοικον ἀεὶ βασιλεῦσι
φάρμακον, ἀπιστίαν στρατοῦ καὶ παίδων καὶ φίλων,
οὐ προειδόμην ὁ τὰ ἐπὶ τῇ διαίτῃ πάντα προϊδὼν καὶ
φυλαξάμενος."

540   112. Ὁ μὲν δὴ Βίτοιτος ἐπικλασθεὶς ἐπεκούρησε
χρῄζοντι τῷ βασιλεῖ, καὶ ὁ Μιθριδάτης ἀπέθνησκεν,
ἑκκαιδέκατος ὢν ἐκ Δαρείου τοῦ Ὑστάσπου Περσῶν
βασιλέως, ὄγδοος δ᾽ ἀπὸ Μιθριδάτου τοῦ Μακεδόνων
ἀποστάντος τε καὶ κτησαμένου τὴν Ποντικὴν ἀρχήν.
541 ἐβίω δ᾽ ὀκτὼ ἢ ἐννέα ἐπὶ τοῖς ἑξήκοντα ἔτεσι, καὶ
τούτων ἑπτὰ καὶ πεντήκοντα ἔτεσιν ἐβασίλευσεν· ἐς
542 γὰρ ὀρφανὸν ὄντα περιῆλθεν ἡ ἀρχή. ἐχειρώσατο δὲ
τὰ περίοικα τῶν βαρβάρων, καὶ Σκυθῶν ὑπηγάγετο
πολλούς, Ῥωμαίοις τεσσαρακοντούτη πόλεμον ἐγκρατῶς ἐπολέμησεν, ἐν ᾧ Βιθυνίας ἐκράτησε πολλάκις
καὶ Καππαδοκίας, Ἀσίαν τε ἐπέδραμε καὶ Φρυγίαν
καὶ Παφλαγονίαν καὶ Γαλατίαν καὶ Μακεδόνας, ἔς τε
τὴν Ἑλλάδα ἐμβαλὼν πολλὰ καὶ μεγάλα ἔδρασε, καὶ
τῆς θαλάσσης ἀπὸ Κιλικίας ἐπὶ τὸν Ἰόνιον ἦρξε,
543 μέχρι Σύλλας αὐτὸν αὖθις ἐς τὴν πατρῴαν ἀρχὴν
συνέκλεισεν, ἑκκαίδεκα στρατοῦ μυριάδας ἀποβα-
λόντα. καὶ τοσῷδε πταίσματι συμπεσὼν ὅμως ἀνεκί-
544 νησε τὸν πόλεμον εὐμαρῶς. στρατηγοῖς τε συν-
ενεχθεὶς ἐς μάχας τοῖς ἀρίστοις, Σύλλα μὲν ἡττᾶτο
καὶ Λουκούλλου καὶ Πομπηίου, πολλὰ καὶ τῶνδε
πλεονεκτήσας πολλάκις, Λεύκιον δὲ Κάσσιον καὶ

because of my foolish practice of taking preventive measures against other poisons. For although I made provision 539 for, and took precautions against, all poisons at meal time, I failed to foresee the most troublesome poison of all, the one in the constant company of kings, the disloyalty of soldiers and sons and courtiers."

112. Moved by this plea, Bituitus obliged the king with 540 the service he desired. So died Mithridates, the sixteenth descendant of Darius son of Hystaspes, king of Persia, and the eighth after the Mithridates who revolted from the Macedonians and founded the kingdom of Pontus.[73] He 541 lived for sixty-eight or sixty-nine years, and was king for fifty-seven of them, having inherited the kingdom as an orphan. He conquered the neighboring barbarians and 542 reduced many of the Scythian peoples. He waged war resolutely for forty years against Rome. In that time he frequently conquered Bithynia and Cappadocia, and overran Asia and Phrygia and Paphlagonia and Galatia and Macedonia. He invaded Greece, where he did many great things. He was master of the sea from Cilicia to the Ionian Sea, until Sulla shut him up again in his ancestral kingdom, 543 Mithridates having lost one hundred and sixty thousand men. In spite of suffering such a disaster, he renewed the war without difficulty. He fought in battle against the best 544 generals, suffering defeat at the hands of Sulla, Lucullus, and Pompey, but often getting the better of them as well. He took prisoner and led around with him Lucius Cassius,

[73] Mithridates Eupator was the eighth king of Pontus since its foundation, but, as Appian says (at 9.29), the sixth named Mithridates: Ariobarzanes ruled in the third century, and Eupator's grandfather was called Pharnaces.

Ὄππιον Κόιντον καὶ Μάνιον Ἀκύλιον αἰχμαλώτους
ἑλὼν περιήγετο, μέχρι τὸν μὲν ἔκτεινεν, αἴτιον τοῦ
545 πολέμου γενόμενον, τοὺς δὲ ἀπέδωκε τῷ Σύλλᾳ. ἐνίκα
δὲ καὶ Φιμβρίαν καὶ Μουρήναν καὶ Κότταν ὕπατον
546 καὶ Φάβιον καὶ Τριάριον. τὸ φρόνημα δ᾽ ἦν ἀεί, κἂν
ταῖς συμφοραῖς, μέγας καὶ φερέπονος. οὐδεμίαν γέ
τοι κατὰ Ῥωμαίων ὁδὸν ἐς ἐπιχείρησιν, οὐδ᾽ ἡττώμενος, παρέλειπεν, ὃς καὶ Σαυνίταις καὶ Κελτοῖς συνε-
547 τίθετο, καὶ ἐς Σερτώριον ἔπεμπεν ἐς Ἰβηρίαν. τρωθείς
τε τὸ σῶμα πολλάκις ὑπὸ πολεμίων, καὶ ἑτέρων κατ᾽
ἐπιβουλάς, οὐκ ἀπέστη τινὸς οὐδ᾽ ὥς, καίπερ ὢν πρε-
548 σβύτης. οὐ μὴν οὐδὲ τῶν ἐπιβουλῶν τις αὐτὸν ἔλα-
θεν, οὐδ᾽ ἡ τελευταία, ἀλλ᾽ ἑκὼν ταύτην ὑπεριδὼν
ἀπώλετο δι᾽ αὐτήν· οὕτως ἀχάριστον ἡ πονηρία συγ-
549 γνώμης τυγχάνουσα. φονικὸς δὲ καὶ ὠμὸς ἐς πάντας
ἦν, καὶ τὴν μητέρα ἔκτεινε καὶ τὸν ἀδελφὸν καὶ τῶν
παίδων τρεῖς υἱοὺς καὶ τρεῖς θυγατέρας. τὸ σῶμα δ᾽
ἦν μέγας μέν, ὡς ὑποδεικνύουσιν ὅσα ὅπλα αὐτὸς
550 ἔπεμψεν ἐς Νεμέαν τε καὶ Δελφούς, εὔρωστος δέ, ὡς
μέχρι τέλους ἱππεῦσαί τε καὶ ἀκοντίσαι καὶ χίλια
στάδια τῆς ἡμέρας, περιμενόντων αὐτὸν ἐκ διαστήμα-
τος ἵππων, δραμεῖν. καὶ ἅρμα ἤλαυνεν ἑκκαίδεκα ἵππων ὁμοῦ. καὶ παιδείας ἐπεμέλετο Ἑλληνικῆς, διὸ καὶ
τῶν ἱερῶν ᾔσθετο τῶν Ἑλληνικῶν, καὶ μουσικὴν
ἠγάπα. καὶ σώφρων ἐς πολλὰ καὶ φερέπονος ὢν περὶ
μόνας ἡσσᾶτο τὰς τῶν γυναικῶν ἡδόνας.

551   113. Ὁ μὲν δὴ Εὐπάτωρ τε καὶ Διόνυσος ἐπικληθεὶς
Μιθριδάτης ὧδε ἐτελεύτα, καὶ Ῥωμαῖοι μαθόντες ἑώρ-

Quintus Oppius, and Manius Aquillius. Manius Aquillius
he executed, as he was the cause of the war, the others he
handed back to Sulla.[74] He defeated Fimbria and Murena   545
and the consul Cotta and Fabius and Triarius. He always   546
remained a man of great spirit and endurance, even when
affected by disaster. He left no avenue of attack against
Rome untried, not even when defeated. He made alliances with the Samnites and Celts and sent a mission to
Sertorius in Iberia. He was often wounded in battle by his   547
enemies, and also by others in plots against him, but he
did not back off anything, even when he was an old man.
Not a single one of the conspiracies escaped his attention,   548
not even the last one, which he chose to overlook and died
because of it: so ungrateful is the wickedness that has met
with forgiveness. He was murderous and cruel to all, kill-   549
ing his mother and brother and three of his sons and three
of his daughters. Physically he was a big man, as shown by
his armor, which he himself sent to Nemea and Delphi,
and he was strong too: he could ride a horse and throw a   550
javelin right up until the time of his death, and cover a
thousand stades in a day, with fresh horses waiting for him
at intervals. He could even ride a sixteen-horse chariot.
He had an interest in Greek culture, which is why he
learned about Greek cults, and he loved music. He had
great self-restraint and endurance, and yielded only to the
pleasures of women.

113. Such was the end of Mithridates, surnamed Eupa-   551
tor and Dionysus. When the Romans heard the news, they

---

[74] At *Mith.* 24.94 Appian says Cassius, whom he always calls
Lucius rather than the correct Gaius, escaped to Rhodes.

552 ταζον ὡς ἐχθροῦ δυσχεροῦς ἀπηλλαγμένοι· Φαρνάκης δὲ Πομπηίῳ τὸν νέκυν τοῦ πατρὸς ἐς Σινώπην
ἐπὶ τριήρους ἔπεμπε, καὶ τοὺς Μάνιον ἑλόντας, ὅμηρά
τε πολλὰ ὅσα ἦν Ἑλληνικά τε καὶ βαρβαρικά, δεόμενος ἢ τῆς πατρῴας ἀρχῆς ἢ Βοσπόρου γε βασιλεύειν μόνου, ἥν τινα καὶ Μαχάρης ὁ ἀδελφὸς αὐτοῦ
553 βασιλείαν παρὰ Μιθριδάτου παρειλήφει. Πομπήιος
δ᾽ ἐς μὲν τὸ σῶμα τοῦ Μιθριδάτου χορηγίαν ἔδωκε,
καὶ θάψαι βασιλείῳ ταφῇ τοῖς θεραπευτῆρσιν αὐτοῦ
προσέταξε, καὶ ἐν Σινώπῃ τοῖς βασιλείοις ἐνθέσθαι
554 τάφοις, ἀγάμενος αὐτὸν τῆς μεγαλουργίας ὡς τῶν
καθ᾽ αὑτὸν βασιλέων ἄριστον· Φαρνάκην δὲ ἀπαλλά-
ξαντα πόνου πολλοῦ τὴν Ἰταλίαν φίλον καὶ σύμμα-
555 χον Ῥωμαίοις ἐποιήσατο, καὶ βασιλεύειν ἔδωκεν
αὐτῷ Βοσπόρου, χωρὶς Φαναγορέων, οὓς ἐλευθέρους
καὶ αὐτονόμους ἀφῆκεν, ὅτι πρῶτοι μάλιστα οἴδε
ἀναρρωννυμένῳ τῷ Μιθριδάτῃ, καὶ ναῦς καὶ στρατὸν
ἄλλον καὶ ὁρμητήρια ἔχοντι, ἐπεχείρησαν, ἡγεμόνες
τε τοῖς ἄλλοις ἀποστάσεως ἐγένοντο, καὶ Μιθριδάτῃ
καταλύσεως αἴτιοι.

556   114. Αὐτὸς δὲ ἑνὶ τῷδε πολέμῳ τά τε ληστήρια
καθήρας καὶ βασιλέα καθελὼν μέγιστον, καὶ συν-
ενεχθεὶς ἐς μάχας, ἄνευ τοῦ Ποντικοῦ πόλεμον, Κόλχοις τε καὶ Ἀλβανοῖς καὶ Ἴβηρσι καὶ Ἀρμενίοις καὶ
Μήδοις καὶ Ἄραψι καὶ Ἰουδαίοις καὶ ἑτέροις ἔθνεσιν
ἑῴοις, τὴν ἀρχὴν ὡρίσατο Ῥωμαίοις μέχρι Αἰγύπτου.
557 ἐς δὲ Αἴγυπτον αὐτὴν οὐ παρῆλθε, καίτοι στασιάζου-
σαν ἐς τὸν βασιλέα, καὶ καλοῦντος αὐτὸν αὐτοῦ τοῦ

celebrated their release from an exasperating enemy. Pharnaces sent his father's body to Pompey at Sinope in a 552 trireme, along with the men who had captured Manius, and all the many Greek and barbarian hostages. He asked to rule either his ancestral kingdom or just Bosporus, which his brother, Machares, had received from Mithridates as his domain. Pompey paid the expenses for Mith- 553 ridates' corpse, and instructed his attendants to give him a royal funeral and bury him among the tombs of the kings at Sinope. For he admired him for his great deeds and 554 regarded him as the best of the kings of his time. He made Pharnaces a friend and ally of Rome as a reward for relieving Italy of great labor, and he gave him Bosporus to rule, 555 apart from Phanagoria, which he declared free and autonomous, because it was Phanagoria in particular which had been the first to stand against Mithridates when he was beginning to recover his strength with a fleet, new army, and bases; it was the people of Phanagoria who took the lead in revolt for the others to follow, and it was they who were responsible for the downfall of Mithridates.

114. As for Pompey himself, in this one war he had 556 cleared the seas of the pirate groups and destroyed the greatest king; and, quite apart from the Pontic conflict, having been brought to battle by Colchians and Albanians and Iberians and Armenians and Medes and Arabs and Jews and other eastern peoples, he extended the boundary of the Roman empire as far as Egypt. He did not enter 557 Egypt itself, although there was agitation against the king, who personally invited Pompey and sent him gifts and

βασιλέως, καὶ πέμψαντος αὐτῷ δῶρα καὶ χρήματα
καὶ ἐσθῆτας ἐς τὸν στρατὸν ἅπαντα, εἴτε δείσας
μέγεθος ἀρχῆς ἔτι εὐτυχούσης, εἴτε φυλαξάμενος
ἐχθρῶν φθόνον ἢ χρησμῶν ἀπαγόρευσιν, εἴτε ἑτέροις
558 λογισμοῖς, οὓς ἐξοίσω κατὰ τὰ Αἰγύπτια. τῶν δὲ
εἰλημμένων ἐθνῶν τὰ μὲν αὐτόνομα ἠφίει συμμαχίας
οὕνεκα, τὰ δὲ ὑπὸ Ῥωμαίοις εὐθὺς ἐγίγνετο, τὰ δ᾽ ἐς
βασίλεια διεδίδου, Τιγράνει μὲν Ἀρμενίαν καὶ Φαρ-
νάκῃ Βόσπορον καὶ Ἀριοβαρζάνῃ Καππαδοκίαν, καὶ
559 ὅσα προεῖπον ἕτερα. Ἀντιόχῳ δὲ τῷ Κομμαγηνῷ Σελεύκειαν ἐπέτρεψε, καὶ ὅσα τῆς Μεσοποταμίας ἄλλα
560 κατέδραμεν. ἐποίει δὲ καὶ τετράρχας, Γαλλογραικῶν
μέν, οἳ νῦν εἰσὶ Γαλάται Καππαδόκαις ὅμοροι,
Δηιόταρον καὶ ἑτέρους, Παφλαγονίας δὲ Ἄτταλον καὶ
Κόλχων Ἀρίσταρχον δυνάστην. ἀπέφηνε δὲ καὶ τῆς
ἐν Κομάνοις θεᾶς Ἀρχέλαον ἱερέα, ὅπερ ἐστὶ δυνα-
στεία βασιλική, καὶ τὸν Φαναγορέα Κάστορα Ῥωμαίων φίλον. πολλὴν δὲ καὶ ἑτέροις χώραν τε καὶ
χρήματα ἔδωκεν.
561   115. Καὶ πόλεις ᾤκισεν ἐν μὲν Ἀρμενίᾳ τῇ βραχυ-
τέρᾳ Νικόπολιν ἐπὶ τῇ νίκῃ, ἐν δὲ Πόντῳ Εὐπατορίαν,
ἣν αὐτὸς μὲν ὁ Εὐπάτωρ Μιθριδάτης ἔκτισε καὶ
Εὐπατορίαν ὠνόμασεν ἀφ᾽ ἑαυτοῦ, ὑποδεξαμένην
δὲ Ῥωμαίους καθῃρήκει, καὶ ὁ Πομπήιος ἐγείρας
562 Μαγνόπολιν ἐκάλει. ἐν δὲ Καππαδοκίᾳ Μάζακα, ὑπὸ
τοῦ πολέμου λελυμασμένην ἐς τέλος, ἤγειρεν αὖθις.
καὶ ἑτέρας πολλαχοῦ κατενεχθείσας ἢ βεβλαμμένας
διωρθοῦτο περί τε τὸν Πόντον καὶ Παλαιστίνην καὶ

money and clothing for the whole Roman army. It was still a flourishing kingdom, and either Pompey was afraid of its size, or he was taking precautions against the jealousy of his political enemies or against the response of oracles, or for other reasons which I will explain in my Egyptian history. Of the peoples he had conquered, Pompey declared 558 some independent, for the sake of making them allies, others came immediately under Roman rule, and others again he divided up among existing kingdoms. He gave Armenia to Tigranes, Bosporus to Pharnaces, Cappadocia and the other areas I have already mentioned to Ariobarzanes. To Antiochus of Cammagene he transferred Seleu- 559 cia and the other parts of Mesopotamia he had overrun. He made Deiotarus and others tetrarchs of the Gallo- 560 graeci, who are now the Galatians bordering on Cappadocia, and he made Attalus ruler of Paphlagonia, and Aristarchus ruler of Colchis. He also appointed Archelaus priest of the goddess at Comana, a royal fiefdom, and enrolled Castor of Phanagoria as a friend of Rome. To others he assigned large territories and a great deal of money.

115. He also founded towns. In Armenia Minor, Nicop- 561 olis, after his victory; in Pontus, Eupatoria, which Mithridates Eupator himself had founded and named Eupatoria after himself, but then destroyed because it had welcomed the Romans. Pompey rebuilt it and called it Magnopolis. Mazaca in Cappadocia had been totally destroyed in the 562 war, and he now rebuilt it. He restored other towns everywhere that had been destroyed or damaged, in Pontus

κοίλην Συρίαν καὶ Κιλικίαν, ἐν ᾗ δὴ καὶ μάλιστα
τοὺς λῃστὰς συνῴκιζε, καὶ ἡ πόλις ἡ πάλαι Σόλοι νῦν
563 Πομπηιόπολις ἐστίν. ἐν δὲ Ταλαύροις, ἥν τινα πόλιν
ὁ Μιθριδάτης εἶχε ταμιεῖον τῆς κατασκευῆς, δισχίλια
μὲν ἐκπώματα λίθου τῆς ὀνυχίτιδος λεγομένης ηὑρέθη
χρυσοκόλλητα, καὶ φιάλαι καὶ ψυκτῆρες πολλοὶ καὶ
ῥυτὰ καὶ κλῖναι καὶ θρόνοι κατάκοσμοι, καὶ ἵππων
χαλινοὶ καὶ προστερνίδια καὶ ἐπωμίδια, πάντα ὁμοίως
διάλιθα καὶ κατάχρυσα, ὧν ἡ παράδοσις διὰ τὸ
564 πλῆθος ἐς τριάκοντα ἡμέρας παρέτεινεν. καὶ ἦν τὰ
μὲν ἐκ Δαρείου τοῦ Ὑστάσπου, τὰ δὲ ἐκ τῆς Πτολε-
μαίων ἀρχῆς, ὅσα Κλεοπάτρα Κῴοις παρέθετο καὶ
Κῷοι Μιθριδάτῃ δεδώκεσαν· τὰ δὲ καὶ ὑπ᾽ αὐτοῦ Μιθριδάτου κατεσκεύαστο καὶ συνείλεκτο, φιλοκάλου
καὶ περὶ κατασκευὴν γενομένου.

565   116. Λήγοντος δὲ τοῦ χειμῶνος διέδωκεν ὁ Πομπήιος ἀριστεῖα τῷ στρατῷ, καθ᾽ ἕκαστον ἄνδρα χιλίας πεντακοσίας Ἀττικάς, καὶ τοῖς ἡγουμένοις αὐτῶν
ἀνάλογον· καί φασι γενέσθαι τάλαντα μύρια καὶ ἑξα-
566 κισχίλια. αὐτὸς δ᾽ ἐς Ἔφεσον καταβὰς διέπλευσεν ἐς
τὴν Ἰταλίαν καὶ ἐς Ῥώμην ἠπείγετο, διαφεὶς ἐν Βρεν-
τεσίῳ τὸν στρατὸν ἐς τὰ οἰκεῖα· ἐφ᾽ ὅτῳ μάλιστα ὡς
567 δημοτικῷ τοὺς Ῥωμαίους ἐξέπληξεν. καὶ αὐτῷ προσ-
ιόντι ἀπήντων κατὰ μέρος, πορρωτάτω μὲν οἱ νέοι,
ἑξῆς δὲ ὡς ἐδύναντο καθ᾽ ἡλικίαν ἕκαστοι, καὶ ἐπὶ
πᾶσιν ἡ βουλὴ θαυμάζουσα τῶν γεγονότων· οὐ γάρ
πώ τις ἐχθρὸν τηλικοῦτον ἑλὼν τοσάδε ὁμοῦ καὶ μέγιστα ἔθνη προσειλήφει, καὶ τὴν Ῥωμαίων ἀρχὴν ἐπὶ

and Palestine and Coele Syria, and in Cilicia where he had above all resettled the pirates, and where the town formerly called Soli is now Pompeiopolis. In the town of 563 Talaura, which Mithridates used as a storehouse for furnishings, were found two thousand drinking cups made out of the stone known as onyx and inlaid with gold, and a large number of bowls and wine coolers, and drinking horns and ornamental couches and chairs and horse bridles and ornaments for their chest and shoulders, all similarly set with precious stones and gold. There was so much 564 of this material that it took thirty days to remove it. Some of it came from Darius son of Hystaspes, some from the Ptolemaic kingdom, which Cleopatra had deposited on the island of Cos and the citizens had then handed on to Mithridates, and some of it had been made or collected by Mithridates himself, who was an admirer of beautiful things including furnishings.

116. At the end of winter Pompey distributed rewards 565 to his soldiers, one thousand five hundred Attic drachmas to each man, and a fittingly proportionate amount for their officers. They say the total paid out was sixteen thousand talents. Pompey himself went down to Ephesus and then 566 sailed for Italy, hurrying on to Rome after disbanding his army at Brundisium and sending the men to their homes. This was seen as a populist move that caused great surprise at Rome. As he approached the city he was met by differ- 567 ent groups of people, the young men at the greatest distance from Rome, then others in order according to what each could manage with respect to their age, and last of all the senate, who marveled at what he had done. For no one before had ever conquered such a great enemy and at the same time annexed so many mighty nations, extending

568 τὸν Εὐφράτην ὡρίκει. ὁ δὲ ἐθριάμβευσεν ἐπὶ λαμπρο-
τάτης καὶ ἧς οὔτις πρὸ τοῦ δόξης, ἔτη ἔχων πέντε καὶ
τριάκοντα, δύο ἐφεξῆς ἡμέραις, ἐπὶ πολλοῖς ἔθνεσιν,
ἀπό τε τοῦ Πόντου καὶ Ἀρμενίας καὶ Καππαδοκίας
καὶ Κιλικίας καὶ Συρίας ὅλης καὶ Ἀλβανῶν καὶ Ἡνιό-
χων καὶ Ἀχαίων τῶν ἐν Σκύθαις καὶ Ἰβηρίας τῆς
569 ἑῴας. καὶ παρῆγεν ἐς μὲν τοὺς λιμένας ἑπτακοσίας
ναῦς ἐντελεῖς, ἐς δὲ τὴν πομπὴν τοῦ θριάμβου ζεύγη
καὶ φορεῖα χρυσοφόρα καὶ ἕτερα κόσμου ποικίλου,
570 καὶ τὴν Δαρείου τοῦ Ὑστάσπου κλίνην, καὶ τὸν τοῦ
Εὐπάτορος αὐτοῦ θρόνον καὶ σκῆπτρον αὐτοῦ τε καὶ
εἰκόνα ὀκτάπηχυν ἀπὸ στερεοῦ χρυσίου παρῆγε, καὶ
ἐπισήμου ἀργυρίου μυριάδας ἑπτακισχιλίας καὶ πεντακοσίας καὶ δέκα, ἁμάξας δὲ ὅπλων ἀπείρους τὸ
πλῆθος, καὶ νεῶν ἔμβολα, καὶ πλῆθος αἰχμαλώτων τε
καὶ λῃστῶν, οὐδένα δεδεμένον ἀλλ' ἐς τὰ πάτρια
ἐσταλμένους.

571 117. Αὐτοῦ δὲ τοῦ Πομπηίου προῆγον ὅσοι τῶν
πεπολεμημένων βασιλέων ἡγεμόνες ἢ παῖδες ἢ στρατηγοὶ ἦσαν, οἱ μὲν αἰχμάλωτοι ὄντες οἱ δὲ ἐς ὁμη-
ρείαν δεδομένοι, τριακόσιοι μάλιστα καὶ εἴκοσι καὶ
572 τέσσαρες. ἔνθα δὴ καὶ ὁ Τιγράνους ἦν παῖς Τιγράνης,
καὶ πέντε Μιθριδάτου, Ἀρταφέρνης τε καὶ Κῦρος καὶ
Ὀξάθρης καὶ Δαρεῖος καὶ Ξέρξης, καὶ θυγατέρες Ὀρ-
573 σάβαρίς τε καὶ Εὐπάτρα. παρήγετο δὲ καὶ ὁ Κόλχων
σκηπτοῦχος Ὀλθάκης, καὶ Ἰουδαίων βασιλεὺς Ἀριστόβουλος, καὶ οἱ Κιλίκων τύραννοι, καὶ Σκυθῶν
βασίλειοι γυναῖκες, καὶ ἡγεμόνες τρεῖς Ἰβήρων καὶ

the frontier of the Roman empire to the Euphrates. At the   568
age of thirty-five, on two consecutive days, he celebrated
a triumph of previously unparalleled splendor and glory
over a multitude of nations from Pontus and Armenia and
Cappadocia and Cilicia and the whole of Syria, as well as
over the Albanians and Heniochii and the Achaeans of
Scythia, and the eastern Iberians. He had seven hundred   569
undamaged ships brought into the harbors, while in the
triumphal procession he had wagons and litters carrying
gold and other ones with various types of ornament, in-   570
cluding the couch of Darius and the throne and scepter of
Mithridates Eupator himself, as well as a statue of the king
eight cubits high and made of solid gold; there were
seventy five million one hundred thousand drachmas of
coined silver, countless wagons full of weapons, and ship
rams, and a host of prisoners of war and pirates, none of
them in chains, but dressed in native costume.

117. In front of Pompey himself leading the way were   571
the officers, children, or generals of all the kings against
whom he had fought. Some were prisoners, others given
as hostages, in total some three hundred and twenty four
of them. Tigranes, the son of Tigranes, was there, and five   572
sons of Mithridates, Artaphernes and Cyrus and Oxathres
and Darius and Xerxes, and two daughters, Orsabaris and
Eupatra. In the procession too were Olthaces, lord of the   573
Scythians, and Aristobulus king of the Jews, and the Cilician tyrants, and Scythian princesses, and three chiefs of

Ἀλβανῶν δύο, καὶ Μένανδρος ὁ Λαοδικεύς, ἵππαρχος
574 τοῦ Μιθριδάτου γενόμενος. τῶν δὲ οὐκ ἀφικομένων
εἰκόνες παρεφέροντο, Τιγράνους καὶ Μιθριδάτου, μαχομένων τε καὶ νικωμένων καὶ φευγόντων. Μιθριδάτου δὲ καὶ ἡ πολιορκία, καὶ ἡ νὺξ ὅτε ἔφευγεν,
575 εἴκαστο, καὶ ἡ σιωπή. ἐπὶ τέλει δὲ ἐδείχθη καὶ ὡς
ἀπέθανεν αἵ τε παρθένοι αἱ συναποθανεῖν αὐτῷ ἑλό-
μεναι παρεζωγράφηντο, καὶ τῶν προαποθανόντων
υἱέων καὶ θυγατέρων ἦσαν γραφαί, θεῶν τε βαρβα-
576 ρικῶν εἰκόνες καὶ κόσμοι πάτριοι. παρεφέρετο δὲ καὶ
πίναξ ἐγγεγραμμένων τῶνδε· "Νῆες ἑάλωσαν χαλκέμ-
βολοι ὀκτακόσιαι· πόλεις ἐκτίσθησαν Καππαδοκῶν
ὀκτώ, Κιλίκων δὲ καὶ κοίλης Συρίας εἴκοσι, Παλαιστίνης δὲ < . . .>[26] ἡ νῦν Σελευκίς· βασιλεῖς ἐνικήθη-
σαν Τιγράνης Ἀρμένιος, Ἀρτώκης Ἴβηρ, Ὀροίζης
Ἀλβανός, Δαρεῖος Μῆδος, Ἀρέτας Ναβαταῖος, Ἀντίο-
577 χος Κομμαγηνός." τοσαῦτα μὲν ἐδήλου τὸ διά-
γραμμα, αὐτὸς δὲ ὁ Πομπήιος ἐπὶ ἅρματος ἦν, καὶ
τοῦδε λιθοκολλήτου, χλαμύδα ἔχων, ὥς φασιν, Ἀλεξάνδρου τοῦ Μακεδόνος, εἴ τῳ πίστον ἐστιν· ἔοικε δ᾽
αὐτὴν εὑρεῖν ἐν Μιθριδάτου, Κώων παρὰ Κλεοπάτρας
578 λαβόντων. εἵποντο δὲ αὐτῷ μετὰ τὸ ἅρμα οἱ συστρα-
τευσάμενοι τῶν ἡγεμόνων, οἱ μὲν ἐπὶ ἵππων οἱ δὲ
πεζοί. παρελθὼν δ᾽ ἐς τὸ Καπιτώλιον οὐδένα τῶν
αἰχμαλώτων ἔκτεινεν ὡς ἕτεροι τῶν θριάμβους παρ-
αγαγόντων, ἀλλ᾽ ἐς τὰς πατρίδας ἔπεμψε δημοσίοις

26 Post δὲ lac. indic. Goukowsky

the Iberians, and two of the Albanians, and Menander of
Laodicea, who had commanded Mithridates' cavalry. Im-   574
ages were carried of those who had not come, Mithridates
and Tigranes, showing them fighting, being defeated and
fleeing. There were representations of Mithridates under
siege, and of the night he fled in silence. Finally, there was   575
a display of how he died and a picture of the daughters
who chose to die with him, as well as of the sons and
daughters who predeceased him, and images of the barbarian gods in native dress. Carried in the procession too   576
was a tablet with the following inscription: "Eight hundred
bronze-beaked ships were captured; eight towns were
founded in Cappadocia, twenty in Cilicia and Coele Syria,
and in Palestine <. . .>[75] the town now called Seleucis; the
Kings defeated were Tigranes of Armenia, Atoces of Iberia, Oroezes of Albania, Darius of Media, Aretas of Naba-
taea, Antiochus of Commagene." This is what the inscrip-   577
tion recorded. Pompey himself rode in a chariot inlaid
with precious stones. He was wearing, it is said, the cloak
of Alexander of Macedon—if anyone can believe that. Apparently it was found among the possessions of Mithridates that the people of Cos got from Cleopatra. Follow-   578
ing behind Pompey's chariot were the commanders who
campaigned with him, some riding, some on foot. When
he reached the Capitol, he executed none of the prisoners,
as others did when celebrating a triumph, but sent them
all back to their homelands at the public expense—with

[75] There should at least be the number of cities in Palestine,
as there is for Cappadocia and Cilicia. So there must be a short
lacuna in the text.

δαπανήμασι, χωρὶς τῶν βασιλικῶν. καὶ τούτων μόνος
Ἀριστόβουλος εὐθὺς ἀνῃρέθη, καὶ Τιγράνης ὕστερον.
ὁ μὲν δὴ θρίαμβος ἦν τοιόσδε.

579　　118. Ὧδε μὲν Ῥωμαῖοι Βιθυνοὺς καὶ Καππαδόκας
ὅσα τε αὐτοῖς ὅμορα ἔθνη ἐπὶ τὸν Πόντον κατοικεῖ
τὸν Εὔξεινον, βασιλέα Μιθριδάτην τεσσαράκοντα
δύο ἔτεσι μάλιστα καθελόντες, ὑπηγάγοντο σφίσιν
580　ὑπήκοα εἶναι. τῷ δὲ αὐτῷ πολέμῳ καὶ Κιλικίας τὰ
μήπω σφίσι κατήκοα καὶ Συρίας τήν τε Φοινίκην καὶ
κοίλην καὶ Παλαιστίνην καὶ τὴν ἐς τὸ μεσόγειον ἐπὶ
ποταμὸν Εὐφράτην, οὐδὲν ἔτι τῷ Μιθριδάτῃ προσ-
581　ήκοντα, ῥύμῃ τῆσδε τῆς νίκης προσέλαβον, καὶ
φόρους τοῖς μὲν αὐτίκα τοῖς δὲ ὕστερον ἔταξαν. Παφλαγονίαν τε καὶ Γαλατίαν καὶ Φρυγίαν καὶ τὴν ὅμο-
ρον τῇ Φρυγίᾳ Μυσίαν, καὶ ἐπὶ τοῖσδε Λυδίαν καὶ
Καρίαν καὶ Ἰωνίαν καὶ ὅσα ἄλλα Ἀσίας τῆς περὶ τὸ
Πέργαμόν ἐστι, καὶ τὴν ἀρχαίαν Ἑλλάδα καὶ Μακεδονίαν, Μιθριδάτου περισπάσαντος ὀξέως ἀνελά-
582　βοντο· καὶ τοῖς πολλοῖς αὐτῶν, οὔπω σφίσιν ὑποτελέ-
σιν οὖσιν, ἐπέθηκαν φόρους. δι’ ἅ μοι καὶ μάλιστα
δοκοῦσι τόνδε τὸν πόλεμον ἡγεῖσθαι μέγαν, καὶ τὴν
ἐπ’ αὐτῷ νίκην μεγάλην καλεῖν, καὶ τὸν στρατηγή-
σαντα Πομπήιον μέγαν τῇ ἰδίᾳ φωνῇ μέχρι νῦν ἐπο-
583　νομάζειν, ἐθνῶν τε πλήθους ἕνεκα ὧν ἀνέλαβον ἢ
προσέλαβον, καὶ χρόνου μήκους, τεσσαρακονταετοῦς
γενομένου, τόλμης τε αὐτοῦ Μιθριδάτου καὶ φερεπο-
νίας, δυνατοῦ σφίσιν ἐς ἅπαντα ὀφθέντος.

the exception of those of royal rank. Of these, only Aristobulus was executed immediately, Tigranes later. Such was Pompey's triumph.

118. This was how the Romans, after taking some forty-two years to destroy king Mithridates, brought under their rule Bithynia, Cappadocia, and all their Pontic neighbors living on the shore of the Euxine sea. In the same war they also annexed the parts of Cilicia not yet under their control, and in Syria, both Phoenicia and Coele Syria and Palestine, as well as the inland part of Syria up to the river Euphrates. These no longer had anything to do with Mithridates, but it was the impetus of their victory over him that enabled the Romans to seize and impose taxes on them, some of them immediately, others later. Mithridates had occupied Paphlagonia and Galatia and Phrygia and its neighbor Mysia, as well as Lydia and Caria and Ionia and the rest of Asia near Pergamum, and old Greece and Macedonia, but they were quickly recovered. The majority of these peoples had not yet been tributary to Rome, but were made so now. In my opinion this is the main reason the Romans considered this a "great" war, called their victory at the end of it "great," and named, and still call, their commanding general Pompey "the Great" in their own language,[76] on account of the large number of peoples they either recovered or annexed, the length of time it took to do so (some forty years), and the courage and endurance of Mithridates himself, whose capacity for all eventualities they had witnessed themselves.

579

580

581

582

583

[76] Plutarch (*Pomp.* 13.4) says that Sulla gave the title *Magnus* ("the Great") to Pompey in 81, in recognition of his achievements in Africa.

584   119. Ὧι νῆες μὲν ἦσαν οἰκεῖαι πολλάκις πλείους
τετρακοσίων, ἱππεῖς δ' ἔστιν ὅτε πεντακισμύριοι καὶ
πεζῶν μυριάδες πέντε καὶ εἴκοσι καὶ μηχαναὶ καὶ
βέλη κατὰ λόγον, συνεμάχουν δὲ βασιλεῖς καὶ δυνάσται ὅ τε Ἀρμένιος καὶ Σκυθῶν τῶν περὶ τὸν Πόντον,
ἐπί τε Μαιώτιδα λίμνην καὶ ἀπ' ἐκείνης ἐπὶ τὸν
585   Θρᾴκιον Βόσπορον περιπλέοντι. ἔς τε τοὺς Ῥωμαίων
δυνατούς, στασιάζοντας ἀλλήλοις τότε μάλιστα καὶ
Ἰβηρίαν ἀνιστάντας ἐπὶ Ῥωμαίους, περιέπεμπε, καὶ
Κελτοῖς φιλίαν ἐτίθετο ὡς καὶ τῇδε ἐσβαλὼν ἐς τὴν
586   Ἰταλίαν, λῃστῶν τε ἐνεπίμπλη τὴν θάλασσαν ἀπὸ
Κιλικίας ἐπὶ στήλας Ἡρακλείους, οἳ πάντα ἄμικτα
καὶ ἄπλωτα ταῖς πόλεσιν ἐς ἀλλήλους ἐποίουν, καὶ
587   λιμὸν ἐπίπονον ἐξειργάσαντο ἐπὶ πλεῖστον. ὅλως τε
οὐδὲν ἀνδρὶ δυνατὸν ἐξέλιπεν ἢ πράττων ἢ διανοού-
μενος, ὡς μέγιστον δὴ τόδε τὸ κίνημα ἐξ ἀνατολῆς
ἐπὶ δύσιν γενόμενον ἐνοχλῆσαι πᾶσιν ὡς ἔπος εἰπεῖν,
ἢ πολεμουμένοις ἢ συμμαχοῦσιν ἢ λῃστευομένοις ἢ
588   γειτονεύουσιν. τοσόσδε εἷς οὗτος πόλεμος καὶ ποι-
κίλος ἐγένετο. καὶ ἐς τὰ μέγιστα λήγων συνήνεγκε
Ῥωμαίοις· ὡρίσαντο γὰρ ἐπὶ τῷδε τὴν ἡγεμονίαν ἐκ
589   δύσεως ἐπὶ ποταμὸν Εὐφράτην. διελεῖν δ' αὐτὰ κατὰ
ἔθνος οὐκ ἦν, ὁμοῦ τε πραχθέντα καὶ ἀλλήλοις ἀνα-
πεπλεγμένα. ἃ δὲ καὶ ὡς ἐδύνατο αὐτῶν κεχωρίσθαι,
κατὰ μέρη τέτακται.

590   120. Φαρνάκης δ' ἐπολιόρκει Φαναγορέας καὶ τὰ
περίοικα τοῦ Βοσπόρου, μέχρι τῶν Φαναγορέων διὰ

119. He often had more than four hundred of his own   584
ships, sometimes as many as fifty thousand cavalry and two
hundred and fifty thousand infantry, with a proportionate
supply of machines and missiles. Kings and princes were
his allies, the king of Armenia, for instance, and the Scythian princes living near the Pontus, or on the Maeotid lake
and from there along the coast to the Thracian Cher-
sonese. He sent representatives to the leading Romans,   585
who were at that very moment involved in faction fighting
with each other, and to those who were stirring up revolt
against Rome in Iberia. He established friendly relations
with the Celts, with the intention of invading Italy from
their direction. He filled the sea with pirates from Cilicia   586
to the Pillars of Heracles, and they made it difficult for the
towns to have dealings with, or sail to each other, and they
caused dreadful famine for a very long time. In summary,   587
Mithridates planned and did everything humanly possible
to make this the greatest upheaval, from the rising of the
sun to its setting, and cause trouble for practically everyone in the world, whether by waging war against them, or
being allied to them, or setting the pirates on them, or just
being their neighbor. That is how extensive and varied this   588
war was. And in the end it was exceptionally advantageous
to Rome. For from now on, the boundaries of their empire
stretched from the setting of the sun to the river Euphrates. It was not possible for me to divide up this story   589
strictly nation by nation, as everything happened at the
same time and was interconnected. But, even so, where it
was possible to separate them out, they have been arranged in different sections.

120. Pharnaces now laid siege to Phanagoria and the   590
surrounding area of the Bosporus, until the inhabitants of

λιμὸν ἐς μάχην προελθόντων ἐκράτει τῇ μάχῃ, καὶ
βλάψας οὐδέν, ἀλλὰ φίλους ποιησάμενος καὶ λαβὼν
591 ὅμηρα, ἀνεχώρει. μετ᾽ οὐ πολὺ δὲ καὶ Σινώπην εἶλε
καὶ Ἀμισὸν ἐνθυμιζόμενος καὶ Καλουίνῳ στρατηγοῦντι ἐπολέμησεν, ᾧ χρόνῳ Πομπήιος καὶ Καῖσαρ
ἐς ἀλλήλους ἦσαν, ἕως αὐτὸν Ἄσανδρος ἐχθρὸς ἴδιος,
592 Ῥωμαίων οὐ σχολαζόντων, ἐξήλασε τῆς Ἀσίας. ἐπολέμησε δὲ καὶ αὐτῷ Καίσαρι καθελόντι Πομπήιον,
ἐπανιόντι ἀπ᾽ Αἰγύπτου, περὶ τὸ Σκότιον ὄρος, ἔνθα ὁ
πατὴρ αὐτοῦ Ῥωμαίων τῶν ἀμφὶ Τριάριον ἐκεκρα-
593 τήκει· καὶ ἡττηθεὶς ἔφευγε σὺν χιλίοις ἱππεῦσιν ἐς
Σινώπην. Καίσαρος δ᾽ αὐτὸν ὑπ᾽ ἀσχολίας οὐ διώξαν-
τος, ἀλλ᾽ ἐπιπέμψαντος αὐτῷ Δομίτιον, παραδοὺς τὴν
Σινώπην Δομιτίῳ ὑπόσπονδος ἀφείθη μετὰ τῶν ἱπ-
594 πέων. καὶ τοὺς ἵππους ἔκτεινε πολλὰ δυσχεραινόντων
τῶν ἱππέων, ναυσὶ δ᾽ ἐπιβὰς ἐς τὸν Πόντον ἔφυγε, καὶ
Σκυθῶν τινας καὶ Σαυρομάτων συναγαγὼν Θεοδο-
595 σίαν καὶ Παντικάπαιον κατέλαβεν. ἐπιθεμένου δ᾽
αὖθις αὐτῷ κατὰ τὸ ἔχθος Ἀσάνδρου, οἱ μὲν ἱππεῖς
ἀπορίᾳ τε ἵππων καὶ ἀμαθίᾳ πεζομαχίας ἐνικῶντο,
αὐτὸς δὲ ὁ Φαρνάκης μόνος ἠγωνίζετο καλῶς, μέχρι
κατατρωθεὶς ἀπέθανε, πεντηκοντούτης ὢν καὶ βασιλεύσας Βοσπόρου πεντεκαίδεκα ἔτεσιν.
596   121. Ὧδε μὲν δὴ καὶ Φαρνάκης ἐξέπεσε τῆς ἀρχῆς,
καὶ αὐτοῦ τὴν βασιλείαν Γάιος μὲν Καῖσαρ ἔδωκε

---

77 Cn. Domitius Calvinus (consul 53, 40) had a command in
Asia in 48 to 47. Appian does not mention here that he was de-

Phanagoria were forced by hunger to come out and fight. Pharnaces defeated them in battle, but inflicted no harm on them, and having established friendly relations with them and taken hostages, he withdrew. Shortly after, he 591 also captured Sinope, and with designs on Amisus too, he attacked the Roman commander Calvinus, just at the time when Caesar and Pompey were fighting each other. Eventually Asander, a personal enemy of Pharnaces, drove him out of Asia, the Romans being too busy to do so. Pharnaces 592 also fought a battle against Caesar himself, after Caesar had destroyed Pompey and was on his way back from Egypt, near Mount Scotius, where Pharnaces' father had overpowered the forces of Triarius. Pharnaces was de- 593 feated and fled to Sinope with a thousand cavalry. Caesar was too busy to pursue him, but sent Domitius.[77] Pharnaces surrendered Sinope to him, and was then allowed to leave under truce with his cavalry. Although his cavalry- 594 men objected strenuously, he killed their horses, embarked on ship, and fled into the Pontus, gathered a force of Scythians and Sarmatians and captured Theodosia and Panticapaeum. When Asander attacked him again out of 595 hatred, Pharnaces' army was defeated because his cavalrymen had no horses and did not know how to fight on foot. Pharnaces himself was the only one to fight bravely, until he was wounded and killed. He was fifty years old, and had been king of Bosporus for fifteen years.

121. This was how Pharnaces was deposed from his 596 rule. Gaius Caesar gave his kingdom to Mithridates of

feated by Pharnaces at Nicopolis in 48. Caesar's victory over Pharnaces at Zela in 47 was the occasion of his famous claim, *veni, vidi, vici.*

Μιθριδάτῃ τῷ Περγαμηνῷ συμμαχήσαντί οἱ προθύμως ἐν Αἰγύπτῳ· νῦν δ᾽ εἰσὶν οἰκεῖοι, Πόντου δὲ καὶ
Βιθυνίας πέμπεταί τις ἀπὸ τῆς βουλῆς στρατηγὸς

597 ἐτήσιος. τὰ δ᾽ ἑτέροις ὑπὸ τοῦ Πομπηίου δεδομένα ὁ
μὲν Γάιος, ἐπιμεμψάμενος τοῖς ἔχουσιν ὅτι Πομπηίῳ
καθ᾽ αὑτοῦ συνεμάχουν, ὅμως ἐφύλαξε, πλὴν τῆς ἐν
Κομάνοις ἱερωσύνης, ἣν ἐς Λυκομήδην μετήνεγκεν

598 ἀπὸ Ἀρχελάου· πάντα δὲ οὐ πολὺ ὕστερον, καὶ τάδε
καὶ ὅσα Γάιος Καῖσαρ ἢ Μᾶρκος Ἀντώνιος ἔχειν
ἑτέροις ἐδεδώκεσαν, ἐς στρατηγίας Ῥωμαίων περιῆλθεν, ἀπὸ τοῦ Σεβαστοῦ Καίσαρος ἑλόντος Αἴγυπτον,
ὀλίγης ἔτι Ῥωμαίων προφάσεως ἐς ἑκάστους δεο-

599 μένων. ὅθεν αὐτοῖς τῆς ἡγεμονίας ἐπὶ τῷδε τῷ Μιθρι-
δατείῳ πολέμῳ προελθούσης ἔς τε τὸν Πόντον τὸν
Εὔξεινον καὶ ἐπὶ ψάμμον τὴν πρὸ Αἰγύπτου καὶ ἐς
ποταμὸν Εὐφράτην ἀπὸ Ἰβήρων τῶν παρὰ στήλαις
Ἡρακλείοις, εἰκότως ἥ τε νίκη μεγάλη καὶ ὁ στρατη-

600 γήσας Πομπήιος Μέγας ἐκλήθη. ἔχουσι δ᾽ αὐτοῖς καὶ
Λιβύην, ὅση μέχρι Κυρήνης (Κυρήνην γὰρ αὐτὴν
Ἀπίων βασιλεὺς τοῦ Λαγιδῶν γένους νόθος ἐν διαθήκαις ἀπέλιπεν), Αἴγυπτος δὴ ἐς περίοδον τῆς ἐντὸς
θαλάσσης ἔτι ἔλειπεν.[27]

[27] Subscriptio: Μιθριδάτειος λόγος ΙΒ΄ P: Ῥωμαϊκῶν Μιθριδάτειος ΙΒ΄ B: Ἀππιανοῦ Μιθριδάτειος J

Pergamum, who had provided him with enthusiastic military assistance in Egypt. The people of the region now belong to us, and a senator is sent out each year to govern Pontus and Bithynia. As for the other recipients of Pompey's dispositions, Gaius Caesar, while blaming the beneficiaries because they had fought alongside Pompey against him, nevertheless kept them in place, except for the priesthood of Comana, which he transferred from Archelaus to Lycomedes. A short time later, all these areas, and those given by Gaius Caesar or Marc Antony to others, became Roman provinces, after Augustus Caesar had annexed Egypt: in each case Rome needed little excuse any more. Because this Mithridatic war extended the Roman empire into the Euxine Sea, and to the sands that border Egypt, stretching from the Pillars of Heracles in Iberia to the river Euphrates, it was only fitting that the victory was called great, and that the general in command, Pompey, was called "the Great."[78] Since Rome also possessed Africa up to and including Cyrene—for its king Apion, an illegitimate member of the family of the Lagids, had left Cyrene to Rome in his will[79]—all that was left to complete the full circuit of the Mediterranean sea, was, of course, Egypt.

597

598

599

600

[78] A repeat of the claim made in 118. 582.

[79] Ptolemy Apion, who died in 96, was a son of Ptolemy VIII Physcon ("Potbelly") and, according to Justin (*Epit.* 39.5), of an Egyptian concubine, who is often assumed to be Eirene (Diod. Sic. 33.13).